NEW FIRM FORMATION AND REGIONAL DEVELOPMENT

To   Stacy

New Firm Formation and Regional Development

MICHAEL CROSS
Small Business Centre,
Durham University
Business School

Gower

Published by
GOWER PUBLISHING COMPANY LIMITED,
Westmead, Farnborough, Hants., England.

 British Library Cataloguing in Publication Data

Cross, Michael
    New firm formation and regional development.
    1. Small business - Great Britain
    2. New business enterprises - Great Britain
    3. Regional planning - Great Britain
    I. Title
    338.6'42'0941   HD2346.G7

    ISBN 0-566-00372-4

Printed in Great Britain
by Biddles Limited, Guildford, Surrey

Contents

2219647

Preface

Interest in small and new firms has recently intensified with the publication of a number of major works. Foremost amongst these works are what has now become to be known as the 'Birch Report' (1979) and Graham Gudgin's (1978) exhaustive study of the East Midlands. Both works have highlighted the role of new firms in providing new employment opportunities, and have been seized by various groups to support policies to aid small and new firms. At the same time, with the worsening unemployment position, the inner city has come to be a major area of concern. Again, it has been suggested that small and new firms might help solve the problems of these areas. In fact, small and new firms are being frequently put forward as the solution for almost every economic ill. Is it fair to expect these firms to perform miracles? Will they create many new jobs? It would be too easy to answer these questions by saying, "No". However, the situation is too complex to be answered with such dismissive alacrity. It is the aim of this study to examine the potential role of new firms in providing jobs, their growth rates, where they have been established, who have set-up these firms, and many more topics.

Broad, wide ranging aims have therefore been set for the study. It represents an attempt to put new firms in perspective. However, it hopefully achieves slightly more than this by also providing a relatively up-to-date picture of the manufacturing industry in Scotland. Throughout the period of interest, 1968 - 77, Scotland received intensive regional assistance, and so the study can be seen as a partial evaluation of that programme of assistance. Are there any signs that a self-generating element is developing in the Scottish economy? It is hoped that the study goes some way to achieving its aims, and makes some contribution to the current small and new firms debate.

Apologies are made here to all those involved with sociology, with psychology and with all other subject areas into which the study often delves. These brief excursions into other fields of enquiry hopefully strengthen the overall study, and it is nowhere claimed as being comprehensive in these excursions. However, if the study achieves some of its main aims, and adds to our increasing knowledge of regional economics, it has served some useful purpose.

This study represents three and a half years of research. However, in research-man-years it probably represents something approaching seven to eight years, and that does not include the many helping hands that have been involved in some way. During my three year stay at Edinburgh University and the three previous years at University College, London, there have been many people who have made a lasting impression on my thinking. In London,

John Salt, Peter Wood and Gerald Manners sparked-off my initial interest
in this subject area. While in Edinburgh, Lyn Collins proved to be a
tolerant and stimulating supervisor. My research in Edinburgh was also
much the richer by the challenging and stimulating environment provided
by John McCalden and Charlie Piggott. I hope this work goes some way to
answering their many searching questions.

The study reported here draws on information provided by a number of public
bodies. A special thanks is due here to the Scottish Council (Development
and Industry) and the Department of Employment. And while too numerous to
mention, all of the District and Regional Councils provided much useful
data. Still further information was provided by many hundreds of
managing directors, chairmen (and women), and their colleagues of the
many firms and plants surveyed. Together they spent many hours with me,
and gave me a view of manufacturing industry as it actually operates, and
especially why, and how firms are formed and survive.

In preparing the manuscript for publication I have been lucky enough
to be able to call on the expert and professional hands of Glynnis Benison
and Eileen Wilkinson. Together they turned my notes and tables into this
book. This process was only made possible by a generous award made by
the Anglo-German Foundation for the Study of Industrial Society, and a
small loan made by the University of Durham. Of course, any errors
remain my responsibility.

Finally, the greatest debt is due to Stacy. No words can express how
important she was in seeing this work finished. Never complaining,
constantly smiling, and always understanding. While more often than
not apart, you distracted me in the nicest possible way, and I know it
is impossible to do justice to your kindness, but thank you Stacy.

Durham - August 1980   Michael Cross

1 New Firm Formation and Regional Development: An Introduction

This book is a detailed investigation of the process of new firm formation. Despite the large number of recent studies concerned with regional development, inner city decline, industrial dispersal, ownership and control, location theory etc., all of which implicitly relate to the development of new firms, there are still large gaps in our knowledge about some of the processes involved. The primary aim of this study is to contribute some understanding of the processes involved in the formation of new firms.

The purpose of this chapter is to outline why an understanding of new firm formation is considered to be important to industrial geography as a whole, to studies concerned with regional development, to studies concerned with inner city decline, to studies concerned with ownership and control, and to general theoretical studies. There are, then, several major issues with which the present study is concerned. First, it is concerned with the formation of new firms per se and forms part of the growing interest of research on this topic. Second, the study of new firms in a region that has received continual assistance prior to their founding is bound, in part, to be an evaluation of that assistance programme either directly, or indirectly. Third, the study is concerned with the methodological problems of combining two levels of analysis, the micro and macro levels. In the former approach, concern tends to lie with the individual firm and its actual behaviour. The latter approach relies upon the availability of large plant based data sets containing minimal information on every plant in an area or industry. As an approach it aims at making more general statements than is usually possible with the micro level approach. While these two categories for types of approach are not mutually exclusive, most studies can be broadly allocated to one or other of the two. This study attempts to combine both of these approaches in an assessment of the relative contributions made by new plants and firms to employment, and in the analyses of the new firm formation process (see Massey, 1977, 29).

1. NEW FIRM FORMATION AND INDUSTRIAL GEOGRAPHY

With the development of large plant based data sets for several of the major manufacturing areas of Great Britain (Liverpool and Manchester, LLOYD and DICKEN, 1978; Glasgow, FIRN, 1970; and East Midlands, FOTHERGILL and GUDGIN, 1979) an awareness has developed about the relative importance of new firms in providing employment.

These data bases to-date though have not been fully utilized in considering the new firm formation process as such, but a start has been made in this direction with the comparison of the fortunes of Birmingham (West Midlands Conurbation) and Glasgow (Clydeside Conurbation) in terms of the numbers of new firms and their associated employment (FIRN and SWALES, 1978). And further research has been undertaken by Fothergill and Gudgin at the Centre for Environmental Studies (FOTHERGILL and GUDGIN, 1978a, 1978b; GUDGIN and FOTHERGILL, 1978; GUDGIN et al, 1979) and is continuing on this topic. The present study represents an extension to these previous and on-going studies not only in that it adds to the analysis of new firms and assesses their relative importance in terms of employment provision, but also combines a large amount of establishment data with detailed 'behavioural' type information of individual new firms.

Furthermore, the present state of knowledge of the new firm formation process is uncertain, and in some respects is based upon supposition rather than 'fact'. The notion of 'seed-bed' growth that details the process of how a new firm comes into existance, for example, has not been the subject of any rigorous enquiry until recently (LEONE and STRUYK, 1976; FAGG, 1979). Until this time, the suppositions of Hill (1953) and Kerr and Spelt (1957, 1958) have been readily accepted. Still further, interest has grown with the study of high technology new firms in the United States (see Chapters Seven and Eight) and the subsequent realization that some regions of the UK might 'lack' new firms, let alone those operating in the high technology sectors. Thus, the bridge between the measurement of the numbers of new firms and the explanation of these numbers has only recently attracted a concerted research effort.

Concurrent with these recent studies of new firms and their associated employment, there has been the growing awareness that it is not just the size or number of plants in an area and the numbers employed in an industry that determines an area's industrial structure, but the organization and ownership of those plants as well. (1) While the growth of a new type of business enterprise during the 1920s had ushered in new conceptions of the firm (BERLE and MEANS, 1932; BEED, 1966; MACHLUP, 1967), they had not until recent times been connected with regional development. Yet these two aspects are related. The growth, but not the inexorable growth, of firms into larger and larger concerns has lead to marked concentrations of different parts of these firms in different regions e.g. Buswell and Lewis (1970) have described the large concentrations of research establishments in the South East of England, Evans (1973) has noted a similar distribution for the head-office of major companies as have other studies (FIRN, 1975; DICKEN and LLOYD, 1976; SMITH, I., 1978; GODDARD and SMITH, 1979). The question has thus arisen as to whether or not the regional variations in the number of new firms is in anyway related to the distribution of the various component parts of multi-plant companies?

During the last thirty-five years Scotland has witnessed the establishment of an increasing number of branch and subsidiary plants (SCOTTISH COUNCIL (Development and Industry), 1968; WELCH, 1970; FORSYTH, 1972; HOOD and YOUNG, 1976), and only a limited number of companies have completely transferred their operations to Scotland (HOWARD, 1968). The dispersal of industry to peripheral

and previously non-industrial regions is a phenomena common to most
other developed economies (EEC, 1975; SUMMERS et al, 1976; ERICKSON,
1978; LONSDALE and SEYLER, 1979; see Chapter Four) and would appear
to be an important part of the process of industrial change, and is
probably not solely a response to regional assistance. These
locational changes of industry are evident in Scotland not only by
the dispersion of industry to Scotland, but also by the dispersion
of industry within Scotland away from the major and traditional
manufacturing centres. It is into this changing environment that
the new firms studied have emerged. These changes have brought
about new industrial and institutional complexes from, and into
which new firms will also emerge. There may then be an interplay -
possibly a direct relationship - between these locational and
institutional complexes and the formation of new firms.

It is equally likely that the other features of industrial change,
for example, plant closures and contractions, also have an important
role in the new firm formation process. For example, while new
industrial areas are emerging and recently established centres
continue to grow, the areas of decline may possess a different
ownership and industrial structure than the growing areas, and may
therefore encourage the formation of new firms in different
industrial activities (FIRN and HUGHES, 1974; FIRN, 1975). But is
this in fact the case? And if so, why?

This study therefore attempts to combine many facets of
manufacturing industry at present being researched under a common
theme - the formation of new firms. The study also indicates the
possible benefits of combining some apparently disparate areas of
manufacturing industrial research for deriving an explanation. It
is only with reference to the whole of the manufacturing economy
that an attempt at a more complete explanation is possible. Of
course, the explanation offered is not complete, but it does give
some indication of the possibilities of such an approach.

2. NEW FIRM FORMATION AND REGIONAL ASSISTANCE

It is impossible to divorce the analysis of manufacturing industry
in the UK in any period since the 1930s without acknowledging the
existance and possible importance of the various regional
assistance policies. Many attempts have been made to evaluate the
impact of regional assistance upon the depressed regions (MOORE and
RHODES, 1973, 1974, 1975, 1976; with TYLER, 1977; MACKAY, 1973, 1974,
1978; ASHCROFT and TAYLOR, 1977, 1978), and while they are not
without their critics (CHISHOLM, 1970, 1976; MASSEY, 1978), they
have overall failed to move beyond the most limited aspects of
regional policy i.e. employment and plant movement (see MARQUAND,
1980, 44-5). For example, none of these studies have attempted to
assess the effect of 'migrant plants' upon the pool of local
entrepreneurs and hence the number of new firms formed (see THWAITES,
1978). Furthermore, they also tend to ignore the role of, say,
technology upon the regional distribution of industry (see BRIGHT,
1957; NELSON et al, 1967; DAVIES, 1979; REES, 1979). They also tend
to ignore the changes in the type of organisations concerned, and
the ability of many new multi-plant companies to product switch and
to cross-subsidise plants, all of which form important alternative

strategies open to the multi-plant company. The already completed studies of the direct impact of regional policies represent only a starting point for such analyses, and there remains much further work to be done in this area.

Another area in which further work is needed is into the indirect effects of regional policies. For example, McDermott (1977a) noted with necessary caution that:

> ... the dominance of external capital and lack of highly differentiated or developed firms in Scotland may be interpreted as the outcome of the increasing inter-regional integration of regional economies attendant upon policies orientated towards the achievement of spatial equilibrium. (ibid., 354)

Thus, the very policies implemented to promote regional equity, which under free-market conditions are unlikely (see WILLIAMSON, 1965; GILBERT and GOODMAN, 1972; and also FRANK, 1969; TAYLOR, 1970; BERNSTEIN, 1971; GALTUNG, 1971), have possibly imposed an industrial structure not conducive to self-generation. In fact, a regional economy is created which is even more dependent upon the impetus of another region. Though such a condemnation of regional assistance is unfair because it is more likely that it has encouraged the investment in new industrial plant in Scotland rather than having caused it. However, the basic premises of these policies rest upon the locational-structural explanation for the poor performance of the problem regions (the problems are due to some innate weakness of those regions) and not to the spatial outcome of the economic system itself. Consequently the bright future described by the Hudson Institute (1974, 99) for Scotland is unlikely to be long lived because of its dependence upon external investment.

The present analysis of the numbers and characteristics of new firms in Scotland is therefore an examination of a by-product of both regional policies and the economic system. It could be argued that a 'single region study' cannot by itself increase the understanding of the symptoms of either regional policy, or the economic system. However, by making comparisons with studies undertaken in other regions a degree of balance is given to the present study. One result of these analyses is to cast yet further doubt on the wisdom of continuing indiscriminant regional policies (see CAMERON, 1979; HUGHES, 1979).

3. THEORETICAL AND CONCEPTUAL CONSIDERATIONS

No one study could either attempt, or hope to achieve a unified theory of industrial location. Theoretical developments are generally the result of minor modifications and additions to existing theories rather than as a result of their complete overthrow (KOESTLER, 1959; KUHN, 1970). True to this history of theoretical development, this study modifies and adds minor refinements to previous theories of new firm formation. However, the study does present some new ideas and information which together helps to increase the present understanding of the new firm formation process.

4

Furthermore, the study neither aims, nor does it present a 'free-standing' theory of new firm formation. In fact a central theme of the study is that all of the changes occurring within manufacturing industry have some influence upon all other aspects of manufacturing industry to a greater or lesser degree. Several of these influences or inter-connections between changing elements of industry and their characteristics are highlighted. For example, Chapter Five considers the possible interplay between plant closure and contraction and the formation of new firms. And furthermore, explanation is sought at the spatial scale seen to be most appropriate, and depends upon the nature of the phenomena under examination. For example, the investment in new industrial plant by multi-plant firms in Scotland is seen to be a process best set within a UK, if not a European context. Whereas the actual sites of those investments are seen on a local basis. This use of several spatial scales is an implicit methodological feature of this study.

The model of new firm formation outlined in Chapter Seven relates the emergence of new firms to their local environment and the factors that affect that environment. It is structured so as to combine as many of the features of manufacturing industry as possible and it indicates the possible gains made by adopting this systems - or holistic - type approach.

4. STUDY ORGANISATION AND ITS CONTENTS

After describing the regional setting of the study (Chapter Two) and the sources and quality of the data used (Chapter Three), an assessment is made of the employment contribution made by the opening of new plants (Chapter Four). This employment contribution is analysed at various spatial scales and is compared to the findings of other studies. Two elements of employment change, plant closure and contraction, are further analysed in terms of their potential role in the new firm formation process (Chapter Five). In Chapter Six a detailed analysis is made of the characteristics of new plants and particular attention is paid to new firms. Several hypotheses concerning the number of new firms in each industry are formulated and tested. By using the evidence presented in the previous three chapters and the findings of previous studies, a descriptive aspatial model of new firm formation is outlined in Chapter Seven. This chapter is complemented by Chapter Eight which examines several aspects of new firm founders and further develops the model of new firm formation. The final analytical chapter extends the analysis of the individual new firm and of the aspatial analyses of the new firm founder in an attempt to develop a spatial model of new firm formation. In this model the functional form of the relationships between new firm formation and the local environment is thought to be the most important. However, due to the vagaries of the available data a full articulation of the model is not feasible in the present study. Finally, the implications of this study for both theory and research methodology are detailed in Chapter Ten.

NOTES

1. Throughout this book a plant's 'owernship' is referred to and rarely its 'control type'. Furthermore, this book could not do justice to the complex topic of control and the interested reader might find the following works useful as an introduction to the topic: Kamerschen (1968, 1969, 1973), Hindley (1970), Palmer (1972, 1973, 1974), Bond (1975), Holl (1975, 1977), Cledat and Crepeau (1976), Kania and McKean (1976), Pederson and Tabb (1976), and Round (1976).

2 The Origins and Structure of Manufacturing Industry in Scotland

INTRODUCTION

Just over a decade ago Robertson (1967, 272) observed that manufacturing activity had prospered in Scotland until the 1920s. Then:

> ... from about 1924 (up to 1945 approximately) onward much of this imposing edifice collapsed. Unknown and unseen, some of its main structural members had weakened to the point where they could no longer support a modern economy. (ibid., 272)

He continues:

> Now all that has been changed. Over the last 35 years (since 1945) a complete transformation has been effected. (ibid., 273)

Has the contemporary manufacturing industrial base of Scotland no legacy in the past? Is the present day (1977) structure a post-1945 creation? If the answer to both these questions is 'yes', then the processes that led to the formation, growth and finally, the decline of manufacturing industry in Scotland have little relevance to a present day analysis of manufacturing industry. However, it is most unlikely that the present industrial structure represents a complete break with the past. In fact, to divorce any period of history from any other may reduce, and possibly remove the likelihood of explanation. (1) For example, to argue that the major expansion of metal manufacture, shipbuilding and railway construction in the 1850-1875 period in Scotland (DUGDALE, 1962, 199) is not in some way related to the build up of externally owned establishments in Scotland after 1945 would be misleading. Surely they both represent major phases of development of the same economy less than a century apart and even if they are not related, which is unlikely, an explanation of the development of manufacturing industry in Scotland must be able to account for both events.

Accepting that an historic perspective might be useful, it still remains to be shown that Scotland either as a region or nation is a suitable area for analysis. The following discussion falls into three elements to satisfy this problem. First, it is shown that Scotland is perhaps not the ideal unit of analysis, but it offers distinct advantages and exhibits a regional economic identity.

Second, aspects of the industrial revolution as they relate to
Scotland are noted and it is argued that much of the present
economic structure is very much a part of the past industrial legacy.
Third, the present industrial structure is described and features of
its present form as they might influence new firm formation are
detailed. In fact, the discussions contained in both the second and
third sections are mainly concerned with those factors that might
play a role in the new firm formation process.

1. SCOTLAND: A REGION SUITABLE FOR ANALYSIS?

Even if one avoids the specific debate as to what actually
constitutes a region (BROWN, 1972; ALDEN and MORGAN, 1974), there is
still a question as to which spatial scale is the most appropriate
for the study. The spatial scale of analysis below that of Scotland
e.g. local office areas and the sub-regions is considered later
(Chapters Four and Nine) and the problem here revolves around the
suitability of Scotland as a region for study. Is Scotland
significantly different from the rest of the UK regions to warrant
special attention? Are these differences sufficient to make
Scotland a unique case, or is Scotland 'typical' of other peripheral
regions?

As regards Scotland representing a region, Brown (1972) considered
that:

> ... Scotland could make strong claims for planning
> region status within something like their present
> boundaries on the strength of economic geography
> alone ... Three-quarters of the Scottish
> population is in the compact industrial belt
> central Scotland, a hundred miles from the nearest
> major centre of English industry and population.
> This belt lies a good deal further from its
> nearest comparable neighbour than do any of the
> major English centres, and it is separated from
> England by a considerably emptier tract of country
> than lies between any pair of neighbouring centres
> south of the border. The border itself cuts
> across only small daily flows of commuting to
> Berwick and Carlisle, and the Scottish border
> counties are mainly served by their own cultural
> and distributive centres. (ibid., 31-2)

While Scotland may be regarded as a free-standing region, its
dependence upon other UK regions is great (MACKAY, 1973, 3; SCOTTISH
COUNCIL RESEARCH INSTITUTE LTD., 1977) although its industrial
development was not wholly independent of these regions (DUGDALE,
1962; HECHTER, 1972, 1975; SLAVEN, 1975). Despite the obvious
integration of the Scottish economy with the UK economy, there are
still differences between Scotland from other regions on the basis
of social indicators (BROWN, 1972, 44-51; SANT, 1974). Recent
commentaries have pointed towards the erosion of regional
inequalities (KEEBLE, 1977a; RANDALL, 1979a) though this is still
open to debate (WESTAWAY, 1974; FIRN, 1975; HUDSON, 1978; KEEBLE,
1978a; MASSEY, 1978a). What is clear, despite this debate, is that
Scotland has more in common with its peripheral neighbours of

Northern England (especially the North East), Wales and Northern Ireland than it has with, say, South East England or the West Midlands (BROWN, 1969).

Furthermore, beyond the indicators of unemployment or income, manufacturing industry in Scotland is largely externally owned in common with the other peripheral regions (see last section of this chapter). This high degree of external ownership is in part a consequence of regional policies pursued since 1945 and the present industrial structure '... may be interpreted as the outcome of the increasing inter-regional integration of regional economies attendent upon policies orientated towards the achievement of spatial equilibrium' (McDERMOTT, 1977a, 354).

Several other reasons exist for choosing Scotland, most of which were noted by Rich (1975, 33-4). First, as noted above, Scotland is a typical peripheral region. Second, it possesses a major urban centre which is lacking in the peripheral regions of East Anglia and the South West. The study of the region may therefore offer some insight into those forces operating in the other major conurbations (see CAMERON and EVANS, 1973). Third, it is a well defined region as detailed by Brown (1972, 32-3). Fourth, recent work has opened the way for more detailed research not least amongst these works is that of Rich himself which was '... apparently the first geographical study of change in the Scottish economy that adopts more than a purely verbal descriptive approach ...' (ibid., 175). Fifth, the industrial structure is not totally dominated by the traditional industries and therefore offers a range of both traditional and modern industries.

On a more pragmatic point, the availability of data determines the scope and depth of any analysis, and in this respect Scotland is better placed than most other regions. Thus, while there are strong grounds for analysing the structure of manufacturing industry in Scotland, the overriding factor is that of data availability. Data were made available by two national agencies, the Department of Employment and the Scottish Council (Development and Industry), which when combined with more specific data relating to new firms and their formation allowed a detailed appraisal of the processes operating in one peripheral region - Scotland. And, because of the nature of this region, the findings are probably applicable not only to other peripheral regions of the UK and possibly Europe, but also the more developed regions of the same countries.

2. MANUFACTURING INDUSTRY IN SCOTLAND

(a) An historical perspective

The industrial revolution, which in fact was more of a gradual change from the traditional craft methods to the technology of steam and industry (SMOUT, 1969, 247), marked a major break with the past. It was in many ways a total revolution represented as much by an ideological and social revolution (e.g. MARX, TAWNEY and WEBER) (2) as by a technological revolution. The birth of modern day capitalism and Western society was founded in the industrial revolution that 'started' in the eighteenth century. It was a period of technological development that was only possible with the secularization (placing something on a rational foundation) of society, a change that was not attendent with the economic developments of either the medieval or renaissance periods (LICHTHEIM, 1964, 402). It is important to realise then the totality of the industrial revolution and its dramatic impact upon, and interplay with, the society of the day.

Foremost in the industrial revolution was the United Kingdom, and the revolution affected all areas with the necessary resource base of fuel and of labour. Later with the developments of transport more areas were developed such that several major regional industrial centres existed. During the initial stages of the revolution, say, 1750 to 1830, Scotland, and especially the West of Scotland was well placed to take a lead in these changes. However, it would be wrong to assume that overnight that the West of Scotland became an industrial heartland. At the same time there were several equally important factors acting in the area's favour aiding its transition. In all, there were five main factors influencing the development of industry in the area. These factors acted together as a complex, and together promoted the area as an initial industrial centre. First, the dramatic increase in population, despite Scotland's having the highest infant mortality rate in Great Britain, provided the initial labour force for the first mines and factories. Second, improved transportation helped link both fuel and labour within the region and then with other regions giving it an initial comparative advantage. Third, world markets opened with the already expanding foreign trade centred on Glasgow. (3) Fourth, agricultural reform generally aided the situation. Fifth, and lastly, '... the crowning achievement of the age, the creation of machine-powered manufacturing industry' (SLAVEN, 1975, 5; see also, BEALES, 1957; DUGDALE, 1962, 195).

The West of Scotland was a highly favoured region that had many initial advantages and one which adapted from being a major textile region to one based on chemicals, iron, steel, shipbuilding and heavy engineering. Why did the region then fail to develop new industries in the 1920s? Why did it fail to adapt yet again, and develop a new industrial base? Unfortunately, the most recent study, that by Slaven (1975), did not examine these issues fully and did not evaluate, nor assign the relative importance played by capital (and its sources). Nor did he consider the development of transport (are inter- or intra-regional links equally important?). Nor the availability of engineering capacity (was there a shortage or surplus? The latter aided the linen-cotten change over.). And finally, what was the level of linkage? (how open was the economy?) (POLLARD, 1975, 427). It is answers to these, and similar questions that would help reveal why the West of Scotland declined, and more especially why it failed to unite both new methods and new products in new firms.

Several answers can be offered from the literature available and they help in the overall understanding of the present position of manufacturing industry in Scotland. The following reasons which are offered to explain the failure of the economy to adapt to new methods and products all stem from the industries upon which the area had based its previous prosperity.

First, the oligopolistic nature of control that existed in the major industries (MANNERS, 1972, 44) which was allied to a community of interests (SLAVEN, 1975, 193) (4) lead to a situation where all the 'entrepreneurial' (risk taking) decisions were taken by a few men. Such a situation does not allow many people to experience key managerial positions and hence deprived local people of the necessary training to become entrepreneurs (see PAYNE, 1974). It should be noted though that the industries in which Scotland was 'best suited' and specialised were ones in which there was (and still is) a low management to operative ratio and therefore tended to encourage the existence of a narrow decision base (see: WOODWARD, 1965).

Second, the growth of industry in Scotland was largely based upon local enterprise, invention and discovery, but often upon imported English capital (SLAVEN, 1975, 14). It is interesting to note that this was not the case in South Wales where a strong reliance was also placed upon both English capital and capitalists '... such as Guest, Bacon, Hamfry, Hill and Crawshay, who established the great ironworks of the Merthyr district, Dowlais, Plymouth, Cyfartha and Penydairen' (DUGDALE, 1962, 205).

Third, both the nature of control and source of capital were favoured by the type of industry (small batch and unit production) and the markets served. The final product of much of Scottish industry was delivered in its first years to the British, and later to an international market. Local production was geared in the main either to the single unit production of ships and heavy engineering items, or to the low level technology items of railway track. During the nineteenth and early twentieth centuries these industries generally relied on captive markets (based on the lack of competition and a community interest) which to some extent guaranteed their continued existence. With the growth of foreign competition and product substitution, these industries could not compete effectively, and this was mainly because of their now inherent high operating costs and relative inefficiency (SLAVEN, 1975, 193). (5)

The influence of the market went beyond simply encouraging inefficiency because its form possibly removed a necessary interface between the traditional and the new industries (LESER, 1954, 121). In a market where a single product is delivered the contact between producers and buyers is probably minimal. Furthermore, a single contract may not only occupy all of the productive capacity available in a plant, but also demand large capital resources as well. This situation would not encourage a plant owner to find new markets for any excess capacity he may have. Second, the interplay between producing a specialised item with limited market demand i.e. products are mono-purpose and mono-market, also means that surplus production cannot be channelled into new markets. Finally, a captive market ensured a steady income with both a minimum of effort and investment. These factors amongst others lead to a minimal level of contact with the market; a market that was rapidly changing and demanding new products made by new methods and from new materials. The large concentration in final products employing many thousands of workers also militated against the survival and development of industry in Scotland. However, in the West Midlands, for example, greater efforts lay with component production that allowed swift market changes and involved the investment of smaller amounts of capital. It was also an area more accustomed to the new large batch and continuous process production methods that were to become common after 1918 (see CAIRNCROSS, 1954, 220-1; SLAVEN, 1975, 193, 207, 226; LESER, 1954, 121; LESER and SILVEY, 1950, 169; FOGARTY, 1945, 165; and CARTER, 1971, 41).

These three factors: nature of control, source of capital and type of market served, acted together to further stifle the emergence of a new industrial base in Scotland. For example, captive markets would tend to encourage the slow adoption of new methods of production because of the highly interlinked nature of production and the reliance upon a common final market (SLAVEN, 1975, 195). This led to a complete failure to 'include' the new industries into the region's trading network (LESER, 1954, 121) and '... in adversity, retrenchment won out over new enterprise' (SLAVEN, 1975, 201). The failure of the motorcar industry, for example, to develop in Scotland was no fluke (LESER, 1954, 121; also see OAKLEY, 1949, 44-5; 1963, 24), and this is an area that requires further research (FIRN, 1977, 82, note 5). In fact, the switch made by Beardmore to pull out of the aircraft and motorcar industries typified the response of other industrialists to the then government's desire to reduce its involvement in manufacturing industry after 1918 (THOMSON, 1965, 67).

Sight must not be lost during this discussion that Scotland was not the only region not securing a major foothold in the new industries. In fact, Britain as a whole failed to attract and develop the newly emerging industries of the 1900-14 period (ALLEN, 1959). However, in the post-1918 period the South East, and especially London, rapidly developed as a major location for the new industries. The South East now holds a dominant position in these industries, but not necessarily in terms of direct production employment, but in terms of upper management positions ('decision and risk-taking positions'; see SCOTTISH COUNCIL (Development and Industry), 1969; EVANS, 1973; MASSEY, 1978). These new industries were dominated largely by new concerns often huge in size and operating vast production lines with low unit costs using labour along new lines. Such concerns were alien to existing practices in Scotland (J. and P. Coats being an exception), and Scottish management was not familiar with the new production techniques and planning procedures (LESER, 1954, 121). Still further, it is upon this already suspect industrial structure that has been 'placed' parts of international companies from a 'different trading culture' (JAMES, 1964; LEVER, 1974).

The development of industry based on local reserves of coal was also challenged, and new forms of power (electricity, gas and oil) released industry from its former resource based locations. This switch meant that new centres could develop with their growth being enhanced by the already extensive transport networks that existed throughout the country. Perhaps paradoxically, attempts to reduce the remoteness of the peripheral regions have acted in the reverse direction, and further enhanced the accessibility of the core

regions. (6) But nevertheless, the industrial structure of Scotland
was neither well placed, nor equipped for modern twentieth century
industry and this was still further compounded by the physical
(environmental) legacy of the industrial revolution (MANNERS, 1963;
EVERSLEY, 1965; HALL, 1970; GREEN, 1974).

These factors, location and a poor phsical environment, added to
the problems created by an oligopolistically controlled industrial
base dependent upon native invention and largely external capital
which had specialised in narrow and declining international markets.
These features are still evident today, and attempts to restructure
Scotland's industrial base may have only exacerbated the situation.

(b) Present day structure

Despite the large influx of new manufacturing plants into Scotland
from other regions of the UK and other countries, the employment
structure of manufacturing industry in Scotland has not changed
dramatically since 1952 (Table 2.1). In fact, the employment
structure of 1952 and 1975 are very similar (r_s = +0.772; $t_{0.01}$ =
2.624; t_c = 4.545; df = 14; one tailed). The main differences are
in electrical engineering (SIC 9) which has nearly trebled its
employment from 18,8000 to 52,900, and the numbers employed in
manufacturing have declined by a little over one hundred thousand.
Perhaps surprisingly the establishment of two large plants (5,000+
employees) in the vehicles order (SIC 11) made little impact on the
employment level in this order. This is because of the equally
large decline in the production of locomotive and railway track

Table 2.1
Scottish manufacturing industry, 1952-75

SIC		Employment ('000s)	
		1952	1975
3	Food, drink & tobacco	93.6 (3)*	99.0 (2)
4&5	Coal products/chemicals	37.5 (8)	31.8 (10)
6	Metal manufacture	66.8 (5)	43.2 (6)
7	Mechanical engineering	107.0 (2)	104.8 (1)
8	Instrument engineering	10.5 (15)	17.7 (14)
9	Electrical engineering	18.8 (13)	52.9 (4)
10	Shipbuilding	77.2 (4)	41.5 (7)
11	Vehicles	40.3 (7)	35.8 (8)
12	Other metal manuf.	27.8 (11)	24.9 (11)
13	Textiles	117.2 (1)	62.4 (8)
14	Leather & leather goods	4.7 (16)	3.1 (16)
15	Clothing & footwear	33.3 (9)	34.4 (9)
16	Bricks, pottery, glass	26.0 (12)	19.5 (13)
17	Timber & furniture	31.2 (10)	22.7 (12)
18	Paper & printing	51.5 (6)	48.9 (5)
19	Other manufacturing	16.3 (14)	16.1 (15)
Total		787.4	657.5

Source: FOTHERGILL and GUDGIN (1978c, 49-54).

*Rank position

13

equipment (mlh 384) and railway carriages, wagons and trams (mlh 385). There was also a large reduction in the numbers employed in textiles (SIC 13) of around sixty five thousand. Excepting these changes, the relative importance of each industry has remained much the same.

Employment figures give an approximate impression of the industrial structure of an area and should only be used as a starting point in any analysis. There may be features that have an important influence upon the formation of new firms that are hidden by these figures. This discussion, then, is concerned with those features of the present day industrial structure that are perhaps different from the other regions of the UK, and which are also of at least a priori importance in the new firm formation process.

There are a number of general categories under which an area's industrial structure can be viewed, and three of these are used here; age of industry, the type of employment, and the pattern of ownership. Within each of these categories the variations through space and between industry are also considered. More important still to this study are the conditions created in the local labour market by the industrial structure because one of the main themes of this study is the interplay between the local labour market and the formation of new firms.

Detailed observations of many aspects of the manufacturing economy in Scotland are sadly lacking and few, if any, try to develop any general appreciation of the whole manufacturing economy. Even the more recent studies have failed to advance our present meagre level of knowledge and in fact one study, that of Lea (1977), did not mention the existence of external ownership explicity in discussing manufacturing industry in Scotland. (7) The works that do exist tend to concentrate on selected aspects of the economy e.g. productivity (HART and McBEAN, 1961; SMYTH, 1961; BLAKE, 1976), the general (macro) economic structure (CAIRNCROSS, 1954; The ECONOMIST, 1965, 1978; McCRONE, 1965; ROBERTSON, 1967; JOHNSTON et al, 1971), and very few have attempted to link both the macro and micro economic approaches (for example see FIRN, 1975; McDERMOTT, 1976, 1977 1977a). The following discussion attempts to improve this situation, but makes no claims at being comprehensive.

An indication can be gained from the age of the industrial stock (year plants opened) as to which areas are the more dynamic and have been most recently developed. The patterns that emerge through space are as would be expected with the 'traditional' industrial areas possessing the older industrial plants. In contrast to this situation, the areas surrounding each of the major cities usually reveals a more youthful base. Similarly, the remaining and less well developed areas, in terms of industry, reveal even still more youthful industrial bases (Table 2.2). This table reveals the pattern of industrial development across Scotland as being one of a shift in the focus of industrial activity from the cities to their surrounding areas, and also to the more remote parts of Scotland.

Two questions immediately arise from these patterns. One, how has the pattern arisen, and what processes determine it today? The second would be to enquire as to whether there is any form of relationship between the age structure of an area and the emergence

Table 2.2
Age of manufacturing plants in Scotland by sub-region

Region/ Sub-region	Years					
	1900	1939	1950	1955	1960	1970
Strathclyde	22.5*	43.2	54.2	57.7	62.8	86.5
Glasgow City	24.5	52.5	65.1	70.4	75.1	91.1
Clydeside Con.	22.8	44.7	56.6	61.3	65.9	87.1
Outer Glasgow	20.8	37.9	48.7	52.8	57.3	83.4
Outer Strathclyde	21.8	37.0	45.7	48.7	54.9	84.7
Lothian	30.3	45.1	53.4	55.6	60.6	82.4
Edinburgh City	43.7	68.8	77.6	80.3	84.7	91.8
Outer Lothian	23.7	27.1	36.8	39.3	45.9	92.8
Grampian	26.5	46.3	55.1	58.8	64.6	80.9
Aberdeen City	26.5	44.3	55.1	60.0	64.8	80.5
Outer Grampian	26.6	49.5	55.0	56.9	64.2	81.7
Tayside	32.9	51.7	60.8	62.9	67.5	85.8
Dundee City	39.7	61.1	70.6	72.2	76.9	85.7
Outer Tayside	25.4	41.2	50.0	52.6	57.0	85.9
Fife	15.8	26.6	32.5	34.5	38.9	74.9
Central	25.9	43.9	50.6	55.4	57.8	87.9
South West	19.0	33.3	42.9	46.4	53.6	80.9
Borders	16.2	27.2	31.4	34.0	38.2	56.5
Highlands	10.6	20.7	29.8	32.9	39.9	64.9
Scotland	23.2	40.8	50.1	53.6	58.5	81.7

Source: Scottish Council (Development and Industry)

*Percentage of plants in existence prior to date stated

of new indigenous enterprises? The first of these questions is examined in Chapter Four and the second is considered in Chapters Eight and Nine. A decentralization of manufacturing investment such as described by these data is common to other areas and regions, and is in part the product of the balance between the number of plants opening and closing in the city and in the other areas. (8)

There are further features of this decentralization process that require further comment. For example, Rees (1979) in a recent study of technological change and regional employment shifts in North American manufacturing industry suggested that:

> ... as decentralization of production progresses,
> external economies (i.e. agglomeration economies,
> service infra-structure, and local linkages) can
> build up in the periphery and regional demand can
> grow to a critical threshold. At this point an
> industrial seed-bed effect can take place,
> particularly through the spin-off of small firms
> from 'lead-firms' and the migration of entre-
> preneurs to the new areas. In other words, a
> region that becomes the location for industries
> in the standardization phases of their product
> cycles can evolve as a focus of innovations.
> This is possible because small firms tend to be
> relatively more productive than large firms in

the generation of innovations. Traditionally the
Manufacturing Belt has served as the seed-bed of
the American manufacturing system. Because the
standardization of production technology has
permitted the dispersal of plants to more efficient
peripheral locations, there is a constant tendency
for the Manufacturing Belt's function as a
technological seed-bed to erode. (ibid., 49)

If this is also the case for Scotland, perhaps there is little to
worry about, and that market forces with the aid of regional
policies may result in a distinctly Scottish manufacturing economy.
However, this is not likely to be the case and in fact even in the
United States the evidence produced by Birch (1979b) certainly
challenges Rees' (1979) assertion. Though, it is undeniable that
Scotland has gained many plants operating in the new and high
technology sectors such as electronics and electrical engineering.
This situation is illustrated in Table 2.3 where the 'new' (recently
established) industries are evident (SIC 8, 9 and 19). The other
orders with a youthful plant stock are those experiencing both high
birth and death rates (SIC 12). One anomaly exists, the clothing
industry (SIC 15), and this reflects the build up of labour
intensive plants in Scotland since 1945 along the lines noted by
Erickson (1978) for the United States. Initially, then, one might
assume that the influx of investment into the new and expanding
sectors are beneficial to the economy and its future prospects, but
they are probably not totally efficacious.

Table 2.3
Age of manufacturing plants by
industrial order in Scotland, 1977

SIC	Median age (years) Plants*
3	43
4	49
5	19
6	57
7	27
8	14
9	11
10	59
11	19
12	14
13	46
14	42
15	14
16	24
17	30
18	63
19	11

Source: Scottish Council (Development and Industry)

*Means of calculation = age of plant (year opened)
is taken, and the median age is then calculated.

This doubt as to the either direct or indirect benefits of gaining new industrial investments begs still further questions. For example, where is the investment coming from? What is the nature of the employment created? Evidence is severely lacking for most regions of the UK (for an exception see TOMKINS and LOVERING, 1973, for an examination of the Welsh case) (9), but there is sufficient evidence to surmise that the situation in Scotland is similar to the other peripheral and assisted regions (see Chapter Four). The recent nature of much of the foreign investment is evident from Table 2.4, but how is this investment sectorally and spatially distributed, and perhaps more important still, what type of employment has been created by such investment?

Table 2.4

Age of manufacturing plants by the location
of ultimate ownership in Scotland, 1977

Location of ultimate ownership	Plants Mean	Median (Years)
Scotland		
Branch	52	49
Independent	46	29
Plant with HQ	50	36
England	43	23
Europe	20	9
N. America	24	12
Other World	18	13
Joint venture	32	9
All plants	45	22

Source: Scottish Council (Development and Industry)

An indication of the type of employment in each industry is given in Table 2.5. Large variations exist across industrial orders in the levels of operative workers required ranging from a little over 37 per cent in coal and petroleum products (SIC 4) to nearly 84 per cent in the clothing industry (SIC 15). Such variations reflect the nature of the production methods used in an industry, and hence the structure of employment in that industry. The numbers employed in each employment type category also vary from area to area within Scotland. For example, the level of administrative employment in manufacturing industry in the Lothian region is markedly higher than in, say, Dumfries and Galloway (Table 2.6). In fact, the level of administrative employment in manufacturing industry is larger in the old and central areas than in the outer lying areas. Though it is important to note that while in both the Borders and in Dumfries and Galloway (South West) there is relatively less manufacturing employment in administrative posts, those holding such posts in these two areas are more likely to be employed in Scottish owned plants (Table 2.7).

It would seem that the nature of ownership might prove an important feature of an area's industrial structure in determining its ability to produce new firm founders. Though it is perhaps

Table 2.5

Distribution of employment types by major industrial sectors for
manufacturing plants operating in Scotland, 1977

Employment Type

SIC	Administrative		Operative		Other		Total
3	9,721	15.37%	40,464	63.99%	13,053	20.64%	63,238
4	478	25.94	683	37.06	682	37.00	1,843
5	4,579	28.03	7,825	47.91	3,930	24.06	16,334
6	4,211	18.61	15,235	67.34	3,177	14.04	22,623
7	16,599	24.69	42,622	63.42	7,987	11.88	67,208
8	3,829	23.82	11,154	69.40	1,089	6.78	16,072
9	10,969	31.89	20,026	58.23	3,396	9.87	34,391
10	3,185	14.88	17,014	79.48	1,207	5.64	21,406
11	6,669	20.71	19,107	59.34	6,424	19.95	32,200
12	3,447	17.77	13,471	69.45	2,479	12.78	19,397
13	5,875	13.45	34,125	78.12	3,684	8.43	43,684
14	174	15.22	903	79.00	66	5.77	1,143
15	1,942	9.53	17,069	83.78	1,362	6.69	20,373
16	2,992	16.28	13,128	71.37	2,273	12.36	18,393
17	2,289	20.83	7,216	65.67	1,483	13.49	10,988
18	8,157	22.70	21,875	60.88	5,898	16.42	35,930
19	2,635	20.55	8,216	64.07	1,972	15.38	12,823
Total	87,607	20.02	289,933	66.24	60,162	13.75	437,702

Source: Scottish Council (Development and Industry)

Table 2.6

Distribution of employment types by region for manufacturing
plants operating in Scotland, 1977

Employment Type

Region	Administrative		Operative		Other		Total
Highlands	2,134	15.19%	10,040	71.47%	1,873	13.33%	14,047
Grampian	5,028	18.31	18,579	67.66	3,850	14.02	27,457
Tayside	7,301	19.55	25,651	68.71	4,379	11.73	37,331
Fife	6,142	21.82	18,370	65.27	3,620	12.89	28,142
Lothian	12,120	23.06	32,591	62.03	7,828	14.89	52,539
Central	5,340	19.98	17,044	64.02	4,258	15.99	26,622
Border	1,558	15.12	7,728	75.00	1,017	9.87	10,303
Strathclyde	46,821	20.13	153,379	65.96	32,302	13.89	232,502
South West	1,183	13.50	6,551	74.79	1,025	11.70	8,759
Scotland	87,607	20.01	289,933	66.23	60.162	13.74	437,702

Source: Scottish Council (Development and Industry)

Table 2.7

Distribution of administrative employment by region and the
location of ultimate ownership for manufacturing plants
operating in Scotland, 1977

Region	Location of Ultimate Ownership						Total
	Scotland	England	North America	Europe	Other World	Joint Vents.	
Highlands	627 (29.38%)	572 (26.8)	213 (9.98)	58 (2.71)	- -	664 (31.11)	2,134
Grampian	1,955 (38.88)	2,264 (45.02)	706 (14.04)	103 (2.04)	- -	- -	5,028
Tayside	3,686 (50.48)	1,531 (20.96)	1,893 (25.92)	184 (2.52)	- -	7 (0.09)	7,301
Fife	2,626 (42.75)	1,549 (25.21)	1,258 (20.48)	187 (3.04)	506 (8.23)	16 (0.26)	6,142
Lothian	3,644 (30.06)	7,736 (63.82)	685 (5.65)	32 (0.26)	- -	23 (0.18)	12,120
Central	2,201 (41.37)	2,480 (46.61)	143 (2.68)	87 (1.63)	51 (0.95)	358 (6.72)	5,320
Border	947 (60.7)	339 (21.75)	181 (11.61)	91 (5.84)	- -	- -	1,558
Strathclyde	14,788 (31.58)	20,560 (43.91)	10,239 (21.86)	1,155 (2.46)	15 (0.03)	64 (0.13)	46,821
South West	498 (42.09)	386 (32.62)	270 (22.82)	29 (2.45)	- -	- -	1,183
Scotland	30,972 (35.35)	37,417 (42.71)	15,588 (17.79)	1,926 (2.19)	572 (0.65)	1,132 (1.29)	87,607

Source: Scottish Council (Development and Industry)

unlikely that employment would have been created by other means, and so despite the apparent disadvantages of a major part of the economy being externally owned there are possible advantages in this situation (FIRN, 1975, 412; HOOD and YOUNG, 1976). The nature of either the advantages, or the disadvantages of external ownership depend upon the nature of the organisational control (HEALEY, 1979; HENDERSON, 1979, 9; see Chapter Five for an example of the textile industry) and the form of ownership itself (BANNISTER, 1977; HIRST, 1977). In spite of these complexities there are a series of more general statements that can be made as to the implications of external ownership. However, these comments cannot be divorced from the structure of the whole manufacturing economy, and this becomes increasingly evident during the following discussion.

External ownership of manufacturing industry in the peripheral regions is a common phenomena as was noted above, it is also one that would appear to be largely a post-1945 development (see Chapter Four). With the rise in the number of branch and subsidiary plants operating in Scotland only as a part of larger companies has meant that there has been a splitting of functions within these companies. In general this has led to the concentration of head-office activities in the South East, and especially London. This has led to a situation where the marketing, research and development, financing and other major decisions tend to be taken in London (see MORGAN, 1962; SCOTTISH COUNCIL (Development and Industry), 1969; BUSWELL and LEWIS, 1970). The long-run concentration of higher order economic activities in London and other major world cities (MANNERS, 1962) has tended to reinforce their advantages in terms of financial (see KERR, 1965, for Canada; McDERMOTT, 1977a, for the UK) and research contacts (see INHABER and PRZEDOWEK, 1974, for Canada; OAKEY, 1979a, for the electronics industry in the UK). This has further led to the concentration of government research contracts, and hence individuals with the access and the ability to use such information in the formation of new firms, in the same regions (DANILOV, 1963; HOLLAND, 1972; NAGPAUL and VASUDEVA, 1972).

There are other features that mark the difference between the central and peripheral regions (SELF, 1965), none more so, than the wage differential (HOLMANS, 1965; MacLEOD and WATKINS, 1969; see SEGAL, 1960; FUCHS, 1967). The existence of a labour cost surface would tend to reflect variations in the labour market (job opportunities) itself, rather than any absolute cost advantage in the periphery. It would seem reasonable to extend this argument by reasoning that the expansion of companies in Scotland in the form of branch and subsidiary plants can be accounted for in part by the labour cost element. Other important factors would be labour availability, the changing nature of the mass production process itself, and the shifts in labour requirements to female labour which is not only cheaper than male labour, but also 'strikes' less (DEPARTMENT of EMPLOYMENT, 1977a). Two industries that would have appeared to have taken direct advantage of this last situation are the electronics and electrical engineering (MASSEY, 1976, 1978a; SCOTTISH DEVELOPMENT AGENCY, 1979), and the clothing industries.

Furthermore, it would be equally wrong to argue that the build-up of externally owned plants in Scotland is a result of the distortions of the location cost surface made by regional assistance. The most

plausible explanation for the development of direct external
investment in Scotland would lie somewhere between the combination
of the changes in industry and its productive requirements, and the
strengthening of regional assistance (MASSEY, 1978a, 14; 1978b, 123).
No matter what the cause or reason for the development of the
externally owned sector of manufacturing employment in Scotland, it
represents an important feature of its present day (1977) industrial
structure.

The present ownership position today (1977) is very similar to
that analysed by Firn (1975) for 1973. In fact the only changes
that have occurred since that time are of degree, and the level of
external ownership appears to have increased marginally. As would
be expected the majority of plants are Scottish owned, but the
complete reverse is true of employment. This situation is detailed
in Table 2.8 (10) and it is shown that it has not changed greatly
since 1973. Some of the details of the changes shown in this table
(Table 2.8) are discussed in Chapters Four and Five. The number of

Table 2.8
Location of ultimate ownership in manufacturing
industry in Scotland, 1977

Location of ultimate ownership	Plants		Employment		Average size of plant
	No.	%	No.	%	
Scotland	2,886 (2,176)*	68.6 (71.6)	202,564 (243,440)	36.1 (41.2)	70.2 (111.9)
England	994 (644)	23.6 (21.1)	248,280 (235,150)	44.2 (39.8)	249.8 (365.14)
Europe	82 (44)	1.9 (1.5)	14,240 (12,560)	2.5 (2.1)	173.7 (285.45)
North America	222 (144)	5.3 (4.9)	86,396 (87,730)	15.4 (14.9)	389.2 (592.8)
Other World	6 (5)	0.1 (0.2)	626 (370)	0.1 (0.1)	104.3 (74.0)
Joint ventures	18 (24)	0.4 (0.8)	9,092 (11,450)	1.6 (1.9)	505.1 (476.7)
All plants	4,208 (3,041)		561,198 (590,700)		133.4 (194.2)

Source: Scottish Council (Development and Industry)

*These data are taken from Location of Ultimate Ownership of
Scottish Manufacturing Plants and Employment in 1973 in FIRN
(1975, Table 3, 402)

large plants (500 or more employees) has increased over the five
year period, 1973-77 (see Chapter Five) further reinforcing the
dependence upon large, externally owned plants (Table 2.9).
Unfortunately, it is not possible to further disaggregate the
location of ultimate ownership into single-plant companies, multi-
plant companies with Scottish headquarters, and branch plants as did

Table 2.9

Employment size distribution of manufacturing plants
operating in Scotland in 1977 by the location of
ultimate ownership

Location of Ultimate Ownership	Employment Size Group						
	10 or Less	11 - 24	25 - 99	100 - 199	200 - 499	500 or More	Total
Scotland							
Independent	3,247[a] (585)[b]	8,697 (511)	35,821 (736)	20,041 (149)	21,292 (74)	29,189 (27)	118,287 (2,082)
HQ	130 (18)	325 (19)	2,989 (52)	1,258 (9)	4,073 (14)	15,564 (11)	24,339 (123)
Branch	278 (37)	1,214 (69)	8,268 (159)	9,025 (66)	21,522 (69)	19,629 (21)	59,936 (421)
England	267 (41)	1,940 (110)	15,844 (301)	19,849 (143)	45,410 (144)	164,957 (115)	248,267 (854)
N. America	47 (7)	367 (22)	2,999 (49)	5,232 (37)	12,520 (36)	65,231 (45)	86,396 (196)
Europe	40 (7)	203 (12)	1,496 (28)	1,792 (13)	3,239 (11)	7,470 (8)	14,240 (79)
Other World & Joint Ventures	-	33 (2)	303 (6)	772 (6)	1,075 (4)	7,535 (5)	9,718 (23)
All Plants	4,009 (695)	12,779 (745)	67,720 (1,331)	57,969 (423)	109,131 (352)	309,575 (232)	561,183 (3,778)

Source: Scottish Council (Development and Industry)   a Employment   b Plants

Table 2.10

Location of ultimate ownership of Scottish manufacturing
employment by major industrial sectors, 1977

SIC	Scotland	England	Location of Ultimate Ownership North America	Europe	Other World	Joint Venture
3	47.7 (48.3)*	40.7 (44.5)	9.7 (5.7)	0.2 (1.5)	–	0.1 (–)
4	11.8 (15.4)	88.2 (80.2)	–	–	–	(4.4)
5	6.9 (11.8)	70.3 (63.2)	13.9 (12.1)	8.3 (10.7)	– (0.3)	0.04 (1.9)
6	17.1 (18.3)	80.5 (70.4)	1.3 (2.2)	–	–	1.0 (9.1)
7	38.9 (39.0)	24.9 (29.2)	30.9 (29.3)	2.2 (1.9)	– (0.4)	3.1 (0.3)
8	6.1 (16.9)	33.0 (21.1)	60.4 (60.7)		–	– (1.3)
9	12.8 (7.8)	45.8 (52.4)	31.1 (31.4)	10.3 (8.3)	–	0.1 (0.1)
10	14.4 (53.3)	78.8 (29.8)	1.9 (11.8)	0.04 (–)	–	– (5.1)
11	7.7 (9.8)	65.3 (53.3)	24.9 (36.4)	0.4 (0.5)	–	–
12.	52.6 (58.6)	37.4 (25.2)	6.9 (10.9)	2.7 (0.4)	0.2 (0.1)	0.2 (4.8)
13	74.1 (64.2)	21.8 (28.8)	3.2 (3.0)	0.8 (3.6)	–	– (0.4)
14	72.5 (88.0)	23.3 (12.0)	–	2.5	–	–
15	46.0 (48.2)	37.8 (38.0)	15.6 (13.8)	0.1 (–)	–	0.4 (–)
16	27.9 (37.1)	45.6 (48.1)	1.4 (1.2)	0.3 (–)	1.9 (–)	22.9 (13.6)
17	78.0 (87.2)	17.4 (12.4)	0.8 (0.4)	3.8 (–)	–	–
18	47.1 (55.0)	47.9 (39.4)	3.4 (2.5)	1.5 (0.8)	–	– (2.3)
19	25.7 (28.4)	35.9 (43.2)	27.5 (26.1)	9.2 (1.5)	0.7 (0.1)	0.9 (0.8)

Source: Scottish Council (Development and Industry)

* FIRN (1975, Table 6, 406)

Firm (1975, Table 5, 404), but later in Chapter Six (Table 6.2) it
is shown that many of the new externally owned plants which opened
in the 1968-77 period were branch plants. This would tend to
suggest that the relative importance of branch plants in the
Scottish manufacturing economy is increasing, and because of their
usually limited autonomy is possibly a disquieting development. (11)

   The distribution of external ownership is not spread evenly across
each of the industrial orders and is concentrated in those orders
that are expanding at the fastest rate (especially orders SIC 8 and
9) and those with high capital and technological input requirements
(SIC 4 and 5; see Table 2.10). Anomalies to this situation exist.
In both metal manufacture (SIC 6) and shipbuilding (SIC 10) the
dominant position held by English owned plants is a reflection of
the nationalised nature of both these industries. Irrespective of
the measure of external ownership, employment or turnover, the
picture is only marginally different (CROSS, 1980, 44).

Variations in the level of external ownership also exist within
Scotland. In both the Highlands and Strathclyde the importance of
Scottish owned plants is less than in either the Borders or Tayside
regions (Table 2.11). It is interesting to note that a complete
reversal has occurred in the Highlands which previously had the
highest level of employment in Scottish owned plants. The dramatic

Table 2.11
Percentage location of ultimate ownership of Scottish
manufacturing employment by planning region, 1977

| | | | Location of Ultimate Ownership | | | |
Region	Scotland	England	North America	Europe	Other World	Joint Ventures
South West	35.8 (37.6)*	42.6 (53.3)	19.5 (7.2)	2.1 (1.9)	–	–
Borders	67.7 (39.1)	18.1 (53.7)	9.6 (4.5)	4.6 (2.6)	–	–
Central	39.5 (37.6)	43.4 (42.0)	6.1 (9.9)	2.7 (2.9)	0.8 (-)	7.5 (7.6)
Fife/Lothian	35.7 (48.1)	49.9 (39.6)	11.6 (10.5)	2.1 (1.0)	0.1 (-)	0.5 (0.7)
Highlands	28.6 (55.4)	28.4 (20.4)	11.0 (17.5)	2.9 (1.0)	–	28.9 (5.7)
Grampian	45.0 (51.0)	41.7 (38.9)	9.6 (7.0)	3.2 (1.8)	–	0.3 (1.2)
Tayside	53.0 (55.3)	21.2 (18.6)	23.0 (24.2)	2.8 (0.8)	– (0.3)	0.1 (0.8)
Strathclyde	30.9 (36.2)	48.5 (42.5)	17.6 (16.7)	2.4 (2.7)	–	0.4 (2.0)

Source: Scottish Council (Development and Industry)

*FIRN (1975, Table 7, 408)

reversal is due to the opening of several oil rig construction firms employing many thousands of employees. These variations are also a function of both the industrial composition and the size and organisational form of the firms involved (see FIRN, 1975, 407). Still further disaggregation reveals that variations also exist within these regions and that all the older, traditional centres of manufacturing (Glasgow and Edinburgh) have a higher concentration of employment in Scottish and English owned plants. These two cities are then surrounded by the new industries that are dominated by externally owned firms and which are usually sited on the government sponsored industrial estates (see Chapter Four).

Hidden beneath the crude employment changes occurring between 1952 and 1975 there have been several dramatic developments in the manufacturing economy of Scotland. The shift in the location of ownership of manufacturing industry is perhaps the most important one. Concurrent with this change has been the growing awareness of the type of employment created by these post-1945 plants. Are these changes as dramatic as they first appear? It could be argued that the shift in the location of ultimate ownership has little material effect upon the nature of control. The oligopolistic form of ownership that existed during the nineteenth and earlier twentieth centuries in manufacturing industry in Scotland has been replaced by a more diffuse, but equally remote type of ownership. Complete enterprises have been replaced by parts of larger concerns, but in both periods the development of a broad management structure was, and is, not great. In the case of the former period this was a function of the product made e.g. boilers, vessels, etc., while in the second period it was also a function of the organisational structure of the firms involved. It could be suggested then that both the historic and contemporary forms of ownership exhibited by Scottish manufacturing industry were, and are not conducive to new firm formation. An analyses of the present position and one of previous periods might verify this hypothesis, and is at present under study (see FIRN, 1976). Further still, if this is the case, the process of new firm formation might not have changed in its basic form during the course of the industrial revolution up to the present time. What has changed is the institutional framework and the location of ultimate ownership of the industrial base, but these changes are unlikely to have directly affected the process of new firm formation itself.

The following discussion examines the formation of new manufacturing enterprises in a peripheral region with an externally owned manufacturing base. Of particular interest are their relative importance in employment creation, their characteristics, their location etc., and each of these are considered below. It is a wide ranging discussion and the analyses encompass the possible role of plant closures and contractions, and the industrial and geographic movement of founders in the new firm formation process. While it cannot claim to be a totally comprehensive study, it does offer an uptodate analysis, and opens-up and combines old lines of enquiry in an examination of the formation of new firms and their importance in the industrial development of Scotland during the period 1968-77.

25

NOTES

1. See Lichtheim (1964) where he discusses the notion introduced by
Hegel whereby history is seen as a continuous process, and the
explanation of processes occurs in stages. At each explanatory
stage an attempt is made to maintain an awareness of the whole
system, while at the same time being able to absorb all previous
explanations. Furthermore, to fashion both empirical and
theoretical explanation along such lines not only maximises the
chances for further additional increases in knowledge (CHURCHMAN,
1954, 172), but also helps check 'creeping parochialism' (LEBAS,
1977, 84). The adoption of an historic perspective also allows an
attempt at articulating the model of comparative functional analysis
outlined by Goldschmidt (1966). Such an analysis is based on the
assumption that processes or functions are universal - spatially and
temporally - and that institutions are responses to these universal
processes. The object of analysis is then moved away from the
institutions to the processes, and promotes the chance of
explanation as opposed to description. For specific geographic
examples of the value of historic perspective see Darby (1952),
Smith (1965) and Harvey (1967).
2. Marx (1867, 1903), Tawney (1929) and Weber (1931).
3. Glasgow was the main UK port serving the Canadian and USA
markets along with Liverpool. A large proportion of the trade
handled by Glasgow was of a trans-shipment nature and did not
necessarily represent goods produced in Scotland. I am indebted to
Mr. Alan S. Pitkethly for this information.
4. Slaven (1975, 193) noted that:
    The boards of the steel companies and the shipbuilders were
    shared by many men from both sides. Sir James Lithgow and
    Henry Lithgow were directors of Colvilles and of James
    Dunlop and Co., and Sir William Lithgow was chairman of
    Beardmore's. Sir James Lithgow was also a director of
    Fairfield Shipbuilding and Engineering Co., and Henry
    Lithgow, Sir Harold Yarrow and A.M. Stephen sat on the
    board of the Steel Company of Scotland. Conversely, a
    steelman like John Craig, chairman and managing director of
    Colvilles, also sat on the board of Harland and Wolff.
Such a pattern of control is unlikely to be conducive to either
opportunity seeking (de BONO, 1980, 33-35), or innovative behaviour
(KIRTON, 1980).
5. It must not be thought that the decline of shipbuilding is
totally due to international pressures because in '... the case of
shipbuilding the decline up to the mid-70's is more peculiarly
British' (FOTHERGILL and GUDGIN, 1978a, 28).
6. See Begg (1972, 50); Keeble (1976, 47); Manners (1972a, 2);
Smith (1954, 49); Loasby (1961, 309); Cameron and Reid (1966, 26-7);
Brown (1969, 778); Green (1974, 194); Cameron and Clark (1965, 197);
Toothill (1961); Keeble (1968, 37); and Scottish Council (Development
and Industry) (1962, 4-6).
7. One gauge of the number of studies of manufacturing industry in
Scotland is to count the number of entries in any of the major
bibliographies e.g. Hamilton (1968). It is seen that Scotland, in
common with the other peripheral regions (South West and North East
England, and Wales) and also surprisingly the West Midlands, are the
least studied areas in terms of published academic works. The
situation since 1968 has witnessed an improvement, but gaps still

exist. The area of greatest interest in recent times has been the level of foreign direct investment in Scotland and its possible influence upon the Scottish economy.

8. The decentralization of manufacturing activity has been noted in most of the major cities of the UK e.g. Birmingham (DEPARTMENT of ENVIRONMENT, 1977), Liverpool and Manchester (DICKEN and LLOYD, 1978), London (DENNIS, 1978), Glasgow (FIRN and HUGHES, 1974; HENDERSON, 1974). It is interesting to note that Stedman (1958) noted these processes in Birmingham in 1956 and in fact they were evident in Glasgow in the 1860s (DAVIDSON, 1967).

9. The study by Tomkins and Lovering (1973) is especially interesting because besides quantifying the level of external ownership and control in manufacturing industry in Wales they also consider the degree of autonomy at the plant level (ibid., 11).

10. In all tables where possible the comparable figures derived by Firn (1975) for 1973 are included.

11. See Henderson (1979) who shows that the branch plants in Scotland have a higher closure rate than those located in other regions of the UK.

3 The Data: Sources and Coverage

INTRODUCTION

The assessment of any phenomena relies on the existence and availability of a suitable body of information. Often no such body exists and so remedies must be sought. This study combines several bodies of information in a _pis aller_ fashion to assess the relative importance of new plants, and more especially new enterprises in providing new employment opportunities. While no assessment can be made at present as to the accuracy of the identified number of new plants, the overall representativeness of the source from which they were drawn can be made. An evaluation of the data bank of the Scottish Council (Development and Industry), then, can be made, and furthermore it is important to establish the coverage available on some of the variables contained in that data set. Two variables of key interest to this study are the year of opening of a plant and the level of administrative employment in an area or industry, and both of these are considered below in terms of their representativeness.

Two other main data sources are also used, the Department of Employment's local employment accounts (ERIIs and ACE) and their closure and redundancy records. Neither of these sources can be evaluated in terms of their accuracy and coverage, but the potential pitfalls in their usage can be highlighted to indicate their limitations. It is these three sources of data that form the major data inputs into the study and which are discussed below. Comment is also made in the case of the Scottish Council (Development and Industry) data as to how its coverage was improved.

1. SCOTTISH COUNCIL (DEVELOPMENT AND INDUSTRY)

Before any data source can be evaluated it is important to note the use to which the data is to be put. More explicitly, then, what is the 'problem' under examination? Initially it must be possible to identify new plants, and latterly new firms. To achieve these aims it must be possible to distinguish between plants in terms of their year of opening and status. The data bank of the Scottish Council allows plants to be identified on this basis. However, it should be added that after the 1974 national survey the question asking for the year of opening was removed from the questionnaire. This problem was solved by hand-printing this question on all questionnaires sent out during 1977 (approximately 10,000 in all).

The data bank of the Scottish Council represents a source of company information for use by the Council's employees in their promotion of Scotland and its industries throughout the UK and abroad. It is not therefore a data source specifically designed for statistical analyses. However, it represents the one major data source to which access is still possible and which holds a relatively wide range of variables for a large number of plants. Despite these initial advantages, the Scottish Council's data bank had, and still has, several weaknesses. Foremost amongst these weaknesses are its imperfect coverage for the smaller plants. An attempt was made to remedy this deficiency, and this is detailed below.

At the national level, and for each industry, the weaknesses of the Scottish Council's data bank do not represent major problems. If the data are disaggregated by spatial units other than at the national level (local office areas, districts and regions) or by industrial order at the local level deficiencies do appear. To reduce the size of these deficiencies and the biases they may introduce into any analysis an extension of the existing data bank was necessary. Those plants not already included in the data bank were identified by contacting district and regional councils who were asked to supply the names and addresses of manufacturing plants in their areas. The lists supplied by these bodies had usually been compiled using the Annual Census of Employment (ACE) records augmented by ad hoc surveys of local industry or by using the ratings records. In most cases these bodies were able to supply the information sought (CROSS, 1980, 53). In all 3,250 plants were contacted during this extension exercise, and of this total 1,602 plants had been previously contacted by the Scottish Council during similar exercises. This survey added a further 880 plants to the data bank and extended its plant coverage by 26.44 per cent. While these additions made a sizeable contribution to the number of plants covered, they did not add significantly to the level of employment covered. This is because most of the plants added were in the smaller size categories and usually employed 50 or less employees, and almost certainly less than 100. (1) It should be added that many of the plants from which replies were received had to be excluded as they did not fulfil the criteria of being predominantly a manufacturing concern i.e. more than 50 per cent of their turnover was derived from non-manufacturing activities.

The resultant data bank was found to contain a large number of plants for which their year of opening was not known. This was the case for a number of the larger plants and, thus, the volume of employment covered by this variable, year of opening, was low. Two related surveys were conducted to remedy this situation. The first covered all companies operating two or more plants in Scotland, and a second covered all plants employing 500 or more employees if not already covered by the first survey. This added a further 225 'year of opening dates' to the data bank, and improved the overall level of employment coverage on that variable.

A few other additions were made to the data bank from the Annual Census of Employment records and the closures and redundancy records both of the Department of Employment. It was from this plant based data set that both new firms and plants were extracted. Several features of this data set have a special importance to this study, and they are employment coverage at the local and industrial order levels, the coverage given by the year of opening, the employment type (administrative-operative-other) of a plant, and the size distribution of plants in each industrial order. Each of these facets of the data set are compared to official sources where possible in an evaluation of the suitability of these data for this study.

At the industrial order level there is a high degree of similarity (Table 3.1) though these two data sets are not for the same year. The Scottish Council data mainly relates to 1977 (64.89 per cent of cases), but it also includes employment data from previous years. While the relative importance of each order is similar in both data sets, the largest discrepencies occur in orders 10 (Shipbuilding) and 16 (Bricks and cement) and largely arises from two major causes. First, by the allocation of some types of rig construction to one rather than another order (involves Orders 7, 10 and 16). Second, the naval dockyards of Rosyth and the torpedo works of Faslane are not included and cause a shortfall of 6-7,000 employees in Orders 10 and 12 respectively. For reasons of national security these plants do not reply to 'non-governmental' surveys such as the one conducted by the Scottish Council.

Table 3.1
Distribution of employment by major industrial sectors:
Comparison of Scottish Council data for 1977 with
Department of Employment figures for 1976

SIC	Scottish Council No.	(%)	Department of Employment No.	(%)
3	74,051	13.2	90,800	14.9
4	2,153	0.4	2,800	0.5
5	24,366	4.3	28,600	4.7
6.	34,875	6.2	39,100	6.4
7	83,589	14.9	91,700	15.1
8	19,024	3.4	16,200	2.7
9	46,619	8.3	48,600	7.9
10	33,053	5.9	42,300	6.9
11	33,406	5.9	32,200	5.3
12	24,362	4.3	27,200	4.5
13	57,930	10.3	57,200	9.4
14	1,690	0.3	2,500	0.4
15	27,801	4.9	30,900	5.1
16	24,635	4.4	17,400	2.9
17	14,768	2.6	20,300	3.3
18	41,856	7.5	44,400	7.3
19	17,008	3.0	15,600	2.6
Totals	561,198		607,800	

Sources: Scottish Council (Development and Industry)
Department of Employment

Similarly, at the regional level (Table 3.2) and for the size distribution of plants for all industry (Table 3.3) there is a fairly high degree of agreement between the two data sources. Though, it is evident from Table 3.3 detailing the comparison of the size distribution of plants that there is a short fall in the number of plants with less than 99 employees. This deficiency, while expected, is less than would have been the case if the extention had not been made to the data bank. Undoubtedly, the data bank does have its deficiencies, but it is largely representative at the national level - Scotland. More important to this study, however, are its representativeness at the local level in terms of employment coverage and industrial structure. Comparisons made between the Annual Census of Employment (ACE) and the Scottish Council industrial order totals for each local office area reveal some of the deficiencies of the data.

Table 3.2

Comparison of regional manufacturing employment totals: Annual Census of Employment (1976) and the Scottish Council data (1977)

Region	Annual Census of Employment		Scottish Council		Difference
	No.	(%)	No.	(%)	(%)
Borders	13,300[a]	2.19	13,200	2.35	+0.16
Central	36,100	5.93	33,000	5.88	-0.05
South West	11,400	1.88	9,900	1.76	-0.12
Fife	40,300	6.63	33,700[b]	6.00	-0.63
Grampian	37,500	6.17	36,900	6.57	+0.40
Highland	14,700	2.42	15,700	2.79	+0.37
Lothian	66,800	10.99	64,100	11.42	+0.43
Strathclyde	342,000	56.25	307,700	54.82	-1.43
Tayside	45,800	7.53	47,100	8.39	+0.86
Totals	608,000		561,300		

Sources: Scottish Council (Development and Industry)
Department of Employment

[a] All figures are rounded to the nearest hundred because ACE figures are presented thus by the Department of Employment.
[b] Nearly the whole of the differences between the ACE and Scottish Council totals for Fife can be accounted for by the failure to include the Rosyth dockyards in the latter total.

First, employment totals derived from each data source, ACE and the Scottish Council data bank, were compared for each local office area. This comparison revealed that in 88 of the 121 local office areas there was a strong degree of agreement between the two data sources. In most of these cases Scottish Council coverage was in excess of 80 per cent. Part of the discrepancy for the remaining 33 local office areas stems from the comparison of 1976 ACE totals with 1977 Scottish Council employment totals. It is likely that the coverage is in fact better than is indicated by these totals because more than 20,000 employees lost their jobs during 1977. Admittedly, this decline was in part compensated by the expansion and opening of other plants, but the overall effect would be to depress the level cover.

Table 3.3
Manufacturing units by employment size:
A comparison of Scottish Council data for 1977
with the Business Statistics Figures for 1975

| | Scottish Council | | | | |
| Employment | Plants | | Employment | | Mean |
Size-Group	No.	(%)	No.	(%)	Size
11 - 19	505	16.37	7,551	1.36	14.95
20 - 99	1,572	50.97	72,961	13.09	46.41
100 - 199	423	13.72	57,969	10.40	137.04
200 - 499	352	11.41	109,133	19.59	310.04
500 or more	232	2.50	309,575	55.52	1,334.36
Totals	3,084		557,189		180.67

Source: Scottish Council (Development and Industry)

| | Business Statistics Office | | | | |
| Employment | Plants | | Employment | | Mean |
Size-Group	No.	(%)	No.	(%)	Size
11 - 19	1,426	29.59	20,437	3.35	14.33
20 - 99	2,276	47.24	100,288	16.44	44.06
100 - 199	490	10.17	68,563	11.24	139.92
200 - 499	399	8.28	125,010	20.49	313.31
500 or more	227	4.71	309,575	48.48	1,302.69
Totals	4,818		610,009		126.61

Source: Business Statistics Office

Second, independent comparisons were also made between the ACE totals on the one hand, and the employment totals for those plants possessing a year of opening data and an employment breakdown on the other. The first comparison indicated that the coverage was marginally less than for those plants with employment totals. When each individual plant with a full employment breakdown into administrative, operative and other employment was taken and compared, the level of coverage was less comprehensive. In fact, there were only 45 local office areas in which Scottish Council coverage was greater than 75 per cent. Though a further fifteen areas fell into the 70-75 per cent coverage category. This would suggest that the coverage for both the employment totals, and for the year of opening variable was reasonable, and might be used with caution. For the type of employment variable coverage however was less comprehensive. By disaggregating each of these three comparisons, and when mapped-out, areas with 'good' and 'poor' coverage emerge. One area dominates these maps, Glasgow. Five of the local office areas that comprise Glasgow City have 'poor' coverage in all three cases (Kinning Park, Maryhill, Parkhead, Partick and Springburn). The 'poor' coverage afforded to Glasgow City by the data available would not appear to unduly bias the data because other areas to the periphery of both Glasgow and Edinburgh, and in the outer lying areas of the Highlands also figure in the 'poor ' coverage category. And while the distribution of 'good' and 'poor' is not random, there is no undue bias favouring one single set of areas at the expense of any others.

Another feature important at the local level is the industrial structure of each area. Comparisons were made between the ACE industrial order totals for each of the 121 local office areas for 1976 with the records of the Scottish Council. The comparison of industrial order totals can, and is used as a surrogate measure for the size distribution of plants at the local level. While this measure is undoubtedly crude, it does give some form of indication of further possible weaknesses of the data used. In 38 of the 121 local office areas no major deficiencies exists, and employment coverage was 76 per cent or more in these cases. Of the remaining 83 local office areas, 45 had 'poor' coverage for only one industrial order and in a further 22 this was the case for two industrial orders. The balance, 16 local office area, had 'poor' coverage in three or more industrial orders and 13 of these areas were in the Glasgow Conurbation area (Alexandria, Barrhead, Bridgeton, Clydebank, East Kilbride, Glasgow South Side, Johnstone, Maryhill, Paisley, Parkhead, Partick, Port Glasgow and Springburn).

Perhaps more important than the immediate distribution in terms of the numbers of industrial orders with 'poor' coverage is the actual orders themselves. Two orders dominate if the number of times an order is mentioned with 'poor' coverage is recorded for all of the 121 areas, and it is then totalled. These orders are food, drink and tobacco (SIC Order 3) and mechanical engineering (SIC Order 7), both of which are represented by large numbers of small plants. It could be argued that those areas recording 'poor' coverage in these orders are also deficient in terms of the numbers of small plants identified in these areas. This situation tends to add a bias in favour of the more recent industries (e.g. electronics and plastics) and may complicate further analyses. Furthermore, it is amongst the ranks of these small plants that most of the new firms are to be found. Thus, 'poor' coverage in these orders would also suggest deficiencies in the number of new firms identified. Such deficiencies would tend to underestimate the birth rate of new firms in the data deficient areas. Despite this problem, the findings of the research reported in the following chapters lie in the realm of the possible and the probable, and therefore suggests that these deficiencies do not restrict the uses to which these data can be put. Furthermore, the results compare favourably with official estimates (SDD, 1978).

In a final assessment, the size distribution of plants in each industrial order in the Scottish Council data was compared with those of the Business Statistics Office. Two comparisons were made between all plants with employment data and the year of opening on the one hand, and the BSO data on the other. The details of these comparisons are listed in Table 3.4. The BSO figures are for 1975 and are the ones most recently available. (2) The results of these comparisons reveal that the Scottish Council data does have some deficiencies especially in those orders in which small plants are of relative importance. Because of these deficiencies, the Scottish Council data are aggregated up to the local office area level in further analyses. However, one attempt is made to construct a spatially disaggregated industrial model (see Chapter Nine) for the

Table 3.4

Comparison of the size distribution of plants in each Industrial Order:
Business statistics office and the Scottish Council

SIC[a]	Similar	Different	Significance (not different) 0.05	0.01
3 all[b]	-	Yes		
Yest[c]	-	Yes		
5 all	Yes	-	x	x
Yest	Yes	-	x	x
6 all	Yes	-	x	x
Yest	-	Yes		
7 all	-	Yes		
Yest	-	Yes		
8 all	Yes	-	x	x
Yest	Yes	-	x	x
9 all	Yes	-	x	x
Yest	Yes	-	x	x
10 all	Yes	-	x	x
Yest	Yes	-	x	x
11 all	-	Yes		
Yest	- Yes	-	x	-
12 all	-	Yes		
Yest	-	Yes		
13 all	- Yes	-	x	-
Yest	-	Yes		
14 all	Yes	-	x	x
Yest	Yes	-	x	x
15 all	-	Yes		
Yest	-	Yes		
16 all	Yes	-	x	x
Yest	- Yes	-	x	-
17 all	-	Yes		
Yest	-	Yes		
18 all	-	Yes		
Yest	-	Yes		
19 all	Yes	-	x	x
Yest	Yes	-	x	x

Sources: Scottish Council (Development and Industry)
Business Statistics Office.

a: SIC 4 is excluded because of the BSO figures use only two size categories.

b: all = all of those plants that can be allocated to an industrial order and for which employment data are available are allocated to six employment size categories and are compared by chi-square tests with the BSO distributions for 1975.

c: Yest = as above, but only those plants are used for which the year of opening is also available along with the employment data.

34

electronics and electrical engineering industry.

Despite these weaknesses, the Scottish Council data represents a unique collection of variables for a large number of manufacturing plants in Scotland. These data are best regarded as a very large sample of all manufacturing plants and given the often low response rates to such surveys, it is surprisingly representative and offers 'good' coverage in many areas and for most industries. On a more pragmatic note, these data represent the only records available that could accommodate the type of analyses detailed in this study. The problems of biases and the attempts to reduce their size must be one of acceptance because no alternative source of information is either available, or accessible. (3) Furthermore, MacLennan and Parr (1979) have recently noted that:

> ... the development of theoretical approaches may
> have outstripped our capacity for empirical
> investigation. This has been due, in part, to the
> quality of regional and inter-regional statistics
> which, though considerably improved in recent years,
> are still inadequate for the kinds of analyses that
> need to be undertaken ... (ibid., xv)

These sentiments are echoed by both Firn (1973) and Swales (1979). Use of the Scottish Council data, while not providing direct output information, does add several 'new' variables to the study of new firms and their formation e.g. year of opening, employment type, etc. In this respect this study can be regarded as innovatory, and is an attempt to examine some of the ideas suggested in recent works (FIRN, 1975; MASSEY, 1978a; SEGAL, 1979).

Throughout the analysis then, caution must be exercised and is voiced where the data might 'explain' the phenomena under study. While these deficiencies do not restrict the analysis in its preliminary stages, they do prove insurmountable in the later stages where an attempt is made to combine features of the new firm formation process with those of the local labour market. Overall, however, the benefits of using these data are considered to be greater, than the losses.

2. THE LOCAL EMPLOYMENT ACCOUNTS OF THE DEPARTMENT OF EMPLOYMENT

Both the quality and usefulness of the local employment accounts of the Department of Employment for industrial research has been questioned (LLOYD and DICKEN, 1968, 307) and debated (KEEBLE and HAUSER, 1971). And two recent texts by Buxton and Mackay (1977, 47-84) and Allen and Yuill (1978, 78-136) detail the methods of how the local employment accounts are constructed, and how these methods have changed through time. This section therefore does not detail these methods, but instead highlights only those features that may materially affect the analyses.

During the ten year period, 1968 to 1977, the local employment accounts underwent two major changes. First, the 1958 method of industrial classification was modified and a new method was introduced in 1969. Second, in 1971 a switch occurred from the card count enumeration method to an annual census of manufacturing plants.

Employment fluctuations in 1971 might then be a product of this
switch in the enumerating methods rather than being either an
employment gain, or loss. However, from the records of the
Department of Employment it is possible to construct two series of
local employment accounts for each of these years, and so the size
of the error introduced by these changes can be assessed. This type
of comparison was conducted for both 1969 and 1971 to gauge the
changes, and the error that they might introduce. Correlation
coefficients were calculated between the two series of local
employment accounts for each of these years and are detailed in
Tables 3.5 and 3.6. However, use of the local employment accounts
at the industry level accounts does create problems e.g. Wood (1976, 89) and
Allen and Yuill (1977, 253; 1978, 125), but they do not constitute a
problem for this study. It is only the sector totals that are used
when the whole period is considered in the components of employment
change analyses which are reported in the next chapter (Chapter Four).

Table 3.5
Correlation coefficient matrix showing the coefficients
between the sector totals at the local office area level
in Scotland: The 1958 and 1968 based SIC classificatory
system

		1958 SIC Sector Totals				
		Primary	Manuf.	Construct.	Service	Total
1968	Primary	0.9997				
SIC	Manuf.		0.9999			
Sector	Construct.			0.9999		
Totals	Service				1.0000	
	Total					1.0000

Source: Department of Employment

Table 3.6
Correlation coefficient matrix showing the coefficients
between the sector totals at the local office area level
in Scotland: The card count and ACE enumerating systems
for 1971

		ACE Sector Totals				
		Primary	Manuf.	Construct.	Service	Total
Card	Primary	0.9766				
Count	Manuf.		0.9994			
Sector	Construct.			0.9916		
Totals	Service				0.9992	
	Total					0.9993

Source: Department of Employment

Elsewhere in the study, the local employment accounts have been
used for single years (post-1971; Chapter Nine) and therefore does
not cause any problems. In this chapter, the 1976 industrial order
totals can be compared with the Scottish Council data because of the
change in the method of their compilation. Under the card count
system industrial order totals could be subject to fairly large

errors, especially in the smallest areal units (see Chapter Nine). However, under the annual census, where each plant in an area reports its employment total to the Department of Employment, the resulting employment totals are not subject to the same margin of error, though caution is still necessary in some cases (DEPARTMENT of EMPLOYMENT, 1978). Thus, the comparison between industrial order totals for each local office area was possible using 1976 data, but it is doubtful that this would in fact have been the case for the first years the census was conducted. For example, the problem of double job holding creates a problem in that employment positions are counted and not employees in an area (see ALDEN, 1971; DEPARTMENT of EMPLOYMENT, 1978). However, these errors do not adversely affect the analyses presented here.

3. THE CLOSURE AND REDUNDANCY RECORDS OF THE DEPARTMENT OF EMPLOYMENT

To date only a few studies have made use of the Department of Employment's closure and redundancy records (e.g. FIRN, 1976; McVEAN, 1979a). Firn's study, for example, used them in a secondary fashion to augment the already created GURIE data bank (Glasgow University Register of Industrial Establishments; see FIRN, 1970). Other studies have used similar records, but they have mainly been concerned with plant closures (GRIPAIOS, 1977a and 1977b; DENNIS, 1978; CAMERON, I., 1979). This study would appear to be introducing a new source of data into industrial research, and its usefulness for research purposes, and more especially the present research programme, is evaluated here.

The closure and redundancy records of the Department of Employment represent a centrally held register (in the case of Scotland) detailing the loss of employment in all industries by whatever means. Two of the three categories of job loss are used in this study, the third, the _temporary_ loss of employment (short-time working and similar) is not used. For inclusion as either 'a closure' or 'a redundancy' at least ten to twenty workers must loose their jobs respectively, though these criteria do not appear to be rigidly adhered to. McVean notes that it appears '... that the coverage overall redundancies is more extensive in Scotland than in England and Wales so that missing observations are less important in the former case' (ibid, 1979, 1).

When a plant closes or makes workers redundant, the manager of the local employment office is usually notified (IPM, 1980, 68). In turn, the manager notifies the Department of Employment and it is from these returns that the records are compiled. Their maintenance therefore relies upon both the plant shedding workers and the local employment office manager reporting the occurrence. Undoubtedly this 'chain-method' of reporting employment loss is open to error. For example, redundancies might not be notified to the local office. However, the local manager sometimes augments the direct notices of redundancies received with his own personal knowledge of the situation.

A further complication can be introduced with the existence of the Temporary Employment Subsidy (TES) which can lead to the situation where two returns are made to the Department of Employment. One reports the loss of employment and the closure of a plant (if applicable; Form ED 955 followed by the monthly progress reports; ED 956) and the other is an application for government aid to help retain those workers under threat of redundancy (Form HR1). There is therefore the possibility that a redundancy or closure might be recorded when in fact TES has been granted to the firm, and hence no employment loss occurred. Every effort is made by the Manpower Services Commission, the part of the Department of Employment directly responsible for maintaining the records, to prevent erroneous entries of this kind.

For each entry in the records, the address of the plant is recorded along with the number of female and male jobs lost. Other variables covered are the size of the labour force prior to closure or contraction, the reason for the employment loss, the date of the loss, industrial activity, and in some cases the location of ultimate ownership (see CROSS, 1980). The last variable was not present in all cases and was augmented with the records of the Scottish Council from previous national surveys and company directories e.g. Who Owns Whom, Kompass, Dun and Bradstreet, Jordan Dataquest.

Another complication arises from the actual use of these records. In their raw state these records can have several entries for the same plant in the same year. This situation can arise where a plant, which may or may not be an independent firm, makes workers redundant on several occasions in the same year. Using the records without any form of modification would overstate the number of plants making workers redundant. This problem was overcome by aggregating all such cases, and so the actual number of plants making workers redundant could be established. Adopting this procedure, of course, means that the number of employees made redundant in any one instance is inflated. However, comparisons between both the raw and modified data reveals that there is no material difference between the two data sets (see Chapter Five).

A final series of complications arise from the fact that the data refer to notifications rather than to actual redundancies. It would appear that the actual numbers of jobs lost is less than numbers recorded on the notification forms. The Manpower Services Commission are at present investigating this discrepancy. Finally, McVean (1979) in discussing this data source noted that notification was voluntary prior to 1976 and this situation continues for small plants. However, the main problems of under-notification occur in the construction, distribution, and commerce sectors. And even though the Employment Protection Act requires the notification of redundancies of ten or more workers, the problem with redundancies from small plants still remains.

From these data it is possible to derive the numbers of workers made redundant by plant closure or contraction for individual years (within the constraints of the data). For many other studies using data for two non-consecutive years has meant that it is the difference between two years separated by a varying number of years is measured and therefore underestimates the real impact of plant contraction on the local labour market. Furthermore, it is

hypothesised in Chapters Five and Six that the level of employment
turbulence (level of involuntary quits) in an area might influence
the number of new firms formed in an area. These data are the only
means of deriving such values for each local office area. (4) Other
data sources do exist and if access was granted to them similar
figures could be derived from them. Yet even these records, the
Annual Census of Employment and SCOMER (Scottish Manufacturing
Establishments Records), only record one employment figure for each
plant per year, but this total may fluctuate throughout the year and
will go unrecorded unless the plant employs 200 or more employees.
In the case of these medium and large plants, their fluctuating
employment totals are noted in an independently maintained set of
records that are not combined (as yet) with either ACE, or SCOMER.
The closure and redundancy records thus represent the only available
source of data that allow some form of employment turbulence figures
to be derived.

These records have the further advantage in that with minor
modification they can be used to perform a components of employment
analysis (Chapter Four). They also provide a valuable insight into
the nature of plant contraction and the speed with which plants move
between employment size categories. In addition the difference
between the major ownership categories can be considered (Chapter
Five), and further extend the studies of corporate change across
space and through time (see DICKEN and LLOYD, 1977; SMITH, 1978;
Chapter Five). While these records have their weaknesses in terms
of the closure of small plants and hence inner city areas, the
flexibility offered by other features of the data makes their use
productive.

4. DATA SOURCES: A CONCLUSION

Neither the simple derivation of 'facts', nor the reduction of
measurement error are sufficient justifications for the use of any
data source (see ACKOFF et al, 1962; DRAY, 1964). Yet, if the
empiricist philosophy of Locke is adhered to, a philosophy that
underlies the inductive method, no incentive exists to restrict
observation to anything less than the whole universe (MEDAWAR, 1969,
29). It is therefore important to construct an a priori image of
the real world based on the findings and failures of previous
studies, an image of the possible and the probable. The assembled
data then represent a series of 'facts' seen as relevant to the
problem under examination. All three data sources detailed here are
regarded as some of the relevant data to the study of new firm
formation.

Further to this discussion, McCrone (1965, 123; 1967) has stressed
the many deficiencies of the statistics available at the regional
level, while Johnston et al (1971) noted that:

> ... private investigators have often had to try to
> fill the gaps in official data, and that their
> calculations have sometimes to use second-best
> rather than ideal methods ... (Yet) ... Scotland
> is better served than any other region of Britain
> ... (ibid., 30)

This study continues in this tradition and attempts not only to extend previous studies of manufacturing industry in Scotland (e.g. LEA, 1977; TURNOCK, 1979), but also to contribute to the understanding of regional development using Scotland as an example (e.g. FIRN, 1975; 1977).

These data, detailed above, represent second-best in many cases, yet they possess advantages that, while not removing their inadequacies, certainly reduce them in the light of the objectives of the study. In addition to these three data sources others are used to extend the analyses, and comments as to their relevance and quality are reserved to the respective sections where used.

NOTES

1. I am greatly indebted to the Scottish Council (Development and Industry) for funding the extension to their data bank and to its staff for helping. A special thanks is due to Elaine Edwards, Elspeth Wills, Aileen Taylor, Anne Veitch, Flo Medlam, Colin Dale, Lindsay Aitken, and Sharon who stamped every envelope.
2. The BSO figures used were kindly supplied by the Scottish Office and will form Table 91 in the forthcoming Annual Abstract of Statistics for Scotland.
3. Three other sources exist, and they are the records of the Health and Safety Executive (formerly the Factory Inspectorate), SCOMER, and ACE. Access to the Health and Safety Executive records was sought and while the regional office in Scotland was willing to make their records available their decision was overruled by the Executive's head-office in London. In fact, in the series of correspondence held with the Executive it was noted that the Scottish Council's data were more complete and uptodate than their own records (LAIDLAW, 1977, personal communication). The remaining two sources of plant based data are not available because of the Statistics of Trade Act of 1947 under whose auspices these data are collected. It is also worth noting that while access to any one of these sources of plant based data would have provided a more comprehensive picture for a single year (or period in the case of the Health and Safety Executive records), none of them by themselves would allow the identification of new firms, the nature of ownership, the type of employment in each plant etc. Thus comprehensive coverage has been sacrificed for more detailed information for a smaller number of plants. And while government data is likely to be comprehensive, it is not free from inaccuracies (FIRN, 1975, 400). For a discussion of confidentiality and government statistics see Wynn (1978).
4. Pearson and Greenwood (1978, 408) note, however, that employment lost by both plant closure and plant contraction represent approximately 30 per cent of the total movement of individuals between employment positions in a local labour market. These data, it can be suggested, represent employment turbulence in a relative sense between areas, and could therefore be used in the manner suggested.

4 Scotland: The Components of Manufacturing Employment Change, 1968-77

INTRODUCTION

In assessing the size and hence the relative importance of new manufacturing firms, it is necessary to determine both the size and relative importance of the other components that account for changes in employment. It is the purpose of this chapter to undertake such an analysis.

The components of change approach as an employment accounting procedure has been generally accepted as being a useful starting point for most employment change studies (WOOD, 1977, 5-6; 1978, 8; KEEBLE, 1978, 321-2). Recent studies of either full (GUDGIN, 1974; 1978; FIRN and HUGHES 1973, 504) or partial (LLOYD and MASON, 1977; DICKEN and LLOYD, 1978; WOODWARD, 1978; NRST, 1975; SCOTTISH DEVELOPMENT DEPARTMENT, 1977; DEPARTMENT of EMPLOYMENT, no date; DENNIS, 1978; SCOTTISH ECONOMIC BULLETIN, 1977, 14-25; and SMITH, I., 1978) components of change analyses provide ample evidence for this belief. Such studies also provide useful material for comparative purposes, but such analyses must be treated with caution because of the varying nature of the data sources they have used. Despite these limitations these studies are used in a comparative manner where ever possible, and form an important part of this chapter. The scale adopted in the comparisons is mainly the Standard Region and in all cases the studies have been conducted within the United Kingdom. While this approach is still subject to many problems in that these studies use a 'wide range of definitions, sectors, sources and time-periods ...' (FIRN and SWALES, 1978, 201), it avoids the complications created by international comparisons, and so minimises the potential stumbling blocks noted by Sjoberg (1955, 110), Smelser (1968, 62-4), and Vallier (1971, 208). Yet, it cannot be assumed, without reservation, that the 'events and situations we wish to explain are comparable' (SMELSER, 1968, 63) because the set of reference points adopted for the study may not hold for the different Standard Regions used (SJOBERG, 1955). For example I.R. Carter (1974, 280) suggests that there are different cultural differences between England and Scotland, and that Scotland is more than an antediluvian province of England (ibid., 297; see POLLARD, 1975, 427). In spite of this problem, the comparisons are made in a qualitative rather than a quantitative fashion. But even this use of other findings is questionnable because of its simple-to-complex approach of reasoning (CHURCHMAN, 1964, 162-3). This last comment raises a huge area of debate and is dealt with elsewhere by

Kempthorne et al (1964), Slater (1975), Castells and de Ipola (1976), and Gregory (1978) amongst others.

This chapter divides into several main areas of discussion. Initially, the nature of the data is discussed as it may affect the components of employment change analyses presented here. Added to this section is a consideration of the various spatial scales at which the components of employment change can be detailed. Each of the components are then detailed at the National level, and here, brief comment is also made of the possible impact of both North Sea oil and regional policy. One component, the loss of employment by both plant closure and contraction, is examined extensively in Chapter Five. In that chapter several hypotheses are formulated concerning the potential importance of both plant closure and contraction in affecting the rate (number) of new firm formations. The remaining two sections of this chapter consider the spatial variations in the components of employment change at four different levels. Comparisons with other studies are made in these sections where ever possible, and explanation is sought at the scale that the process is operating. A summary and conclusion unites the main findings of the foregoing analyses, and outlines the next stage of the analysis.

1. DATA: ESTIMATIONS AND AREAL UNITS

(a) Estimations

It is thirty years since Kaplan (1948) considered the range of data required to obtain a comprehensive picture of the number of entries and exits of firms to and from the total manufacturing population of plants. He stated that a study of these two components was only possible:

> If we could register every new enterprise, whether incorporated or not, with the record of its starting position - initial investment, number of owners and their former connections, number of employees, and other relevant data on its size and character - and if we had a similar registration for every business that closed, then we might draw some dependable conclusions on the relation between size and survival capacity. (KAPLAN, 1948, 54)

Unfortunately these data are not available, and all studies are therefore based on some form of sample. In some studies the samples used have nearly approximated the total population of plants (for Liverpool and Manchester, DICKEN and LLOYD, 1978; for the East Midlands, GUDGIN, 1974; 1978), while in others they have been defined within certain limits (for Glasgow, FIRN, 1970). It is important as a consequence of the paucity of the data available to define the population to which the results are to apply, and in many cases even to decide which population the sample used actually relates (RIDGMAN, 1975, 9). The use of the closure and redundancy records maintained by the Department of Employment immediately introduces a degree of error. For example, these records represent the loss of employment of either ten, twenty or more employees. The consequence of the adoption of these lower limits would therefore tend to underestimate the number of small plants closing in the main cities (Glasgow, Edinburgh, Dundee and Aberdeen). Suffice to say, the figures derived from the closure and redundancy records must only be regarded as best estimates, and not as an actual measurement of these components of manufacturing employment change. Similar weaknesses could be documented for the data used to estimate the number of openings, and even the size of the manufacturing employment shift at the local office area level using ER II and ACE records (RICH, 1975, 188; ALLEN and YUILL, 1978, 119; and section two of Chapter Three). But, despite the weaknesses of the data used, they provide the best available means for directly measuring the components of manufacturing employment change. Unfortunately, one of the components of change could not be measured, that of in situ expansion of plants existing throughout the study period. It is therefore necessary to estimate the size of this component from the knowledge of the other main components i.e. total employment change, employment gained due to openings, and employment lost due to both closures and redundancies. Even by adopting this procedure not all of the problems are solved because it is still not known how many plants both opened and closed during the 1968-77 period. However, there appears to be no immediate answer to this problem (i.e. data not available), and it is doubtful that the 109 plants identified as having opened and closed during the period are representative of all those plants existing for similar short intervals during the study period.

This study is not alone in being obliged to make some form of estimation. For example, Gudgin (1974; 1978), in his study of the East Midlands, estimated the status of some plants (ibid., 1974, 438) and the 'employment lost in those establishments which were in production in 1948 but which closed before 1967' (ibid., 1978, 58). In the sections that follow where the in situ expansion component has been estimated and found to be either misleading or meaningless, it has been omitted.

(b) Areal units

The choice of a geographic unit for the purpose of defining the study area or as representing the basic, 'best' unit for data aggregation is a universal problem faced by all geographic studies (HAGGETT, 1965, 177). This problem has been noted in various studies (CHISHOLM, 1960; DUNCAN et al, 1961), and has been recently reconsidered (OPENSHAW, 1976, 36-7; COOMBES et al, 1978). The search for the 'best' or 'base' geographic unit would probably prove as illusive as Winnie-the-Pooh's and Piglet's search for a woozle, and so the definition of the 'best' geographic unit would appear to depend upon the nature and scope of the study itself. The best geographic unit is therefore a product of the processes under study and the availability of data.

In the introduction to a recent statistical text, Johnston (1978, 2) asks the first of his two fundamental geographic questions: 'Are there relationships between phenomena in various locations?' He could have qualified this by two further questions asking about the problems of scale linkage and standardization. The problem of scale linkage concerns the transferring of patterns and processes noted as operational at one spatial level to another (HOARE, 1975, 43). As a consequence, this may lead to possibly spurious conclusions e.g. findings derived from national level linkage studies suggest that industries '... that have a high volume of goods moving between industries (and, by extrapolation, between firms within those industries) encourages their spatial proximity' (ibid.). The basis for such an extrapolation is weak, and has more in common with the circular arguments used to explain the localization of the metal industries in the West Midlands than common sense (WOOD, 1973, 1). Because of this problem, Hoare (1971, 37) in a study of the impact of London airport, believed it was '... crucial to examine the problem on a number of different geographical scales, from the local borough to that of the South-East as a whole'. This study, for this reason and for several other reasons outlined below, adopts a similar procedure and the geographical scales used range from the local employment office of the Department of Employment to that of Scotland as a whole.

Scale standardization has been the focus of recent attention, yet despite the work of Openshaw (1977, 470) '... it has yet to be established to what extent it is important to make allowance for the size of unit for which data is available' (sic, NORCLIFFE, 1970, 1.37). In recognition of Openshaw's warning, it is all the more necessary to link the '... appropriate level of analysis ... in the hypothesis formulation phase of the research' (SAWICKI, 1973, 114). Sawicki concludes that because the unit of analysis determines the results, it is important to use several analytical levels (ibid., 112 and 114). This study adopts several analytical levels likewise, but even a multi-level analysis does not reduce the problem of the random disturbing variable (BLALOCK, 1964, 99; HOARE, 1971, 39).

Perhaps the most important reason why several levels of analysis have been adopted is because of the express need to link the emergence or non-emergence of the new enterprises to other changes in the manufacturing economy, changes that are affected by forces operating at a level higher than, say, the local community. In effect, this means the reversing of Massey's (1975, 90) tree diagram of locational choices which was based on empirical work. The basic argument used to justify such an approach rests in part upon the concept of 'seed bed growth' (BANNOCK and DORAN, 1978, para. 5.2). In essence this concept postulates that the emergence of completely new manufacturing firms is a function of the industrial structure of the immediately surrounding area. Consequently, factors affecting the local industrial environment may in turn affect the number of new manufacturing firms emerging. And while the opening and closure of a few small manufacturing plants may not dramatically change the local industrial environment, the opening or closure of a large employer may create a completely new local situation. The processes that have caused these changed local circumstances would certainly not have found their origin locally, but would have been created by changes at either the regional, national or international level. Such changes are possibly a product of increased international competition, and hence a decreased demand for local products, and also the changing use of space made by modern manufacturing industry (MASSEY, 1976; MASSEY and MEAGAN, 1977; MASSEY, 1978a, 7; MASSEY, 1980). It would therefore appear necessary to combine these levels of analysis as the latter clearly may affect the former (see CHINITZ, 1961, 284 and 288).

The final levels of analysis used were as much a product of the above reasoning as they were of pragmatic considerations of data handling (COLLINS, 1972, 100). The areal objects used in the analysis were not simple 'areal aggregates' (CHAPMAN, 1977, 55), but have some degree of self-containment and represent functioning entities (COOMBES et al, 1978, 1182). The two lowest levels used are the employment office (also called the employment exchange area or local office area - henceforth written as LOA) and the travel-to-work-areas (also called labour market areas - henceforth written as LMA or TTWA) of the Department of Employment. The LOA is an administrative unit which is '... centred on a separate town and in approximate terms corresponds to labour market areas for those towns' (GUDGIN, 1978, 74). In Gudgin's (1978) study of the East Midlands there were 37 LOAs (the West Midlands, for example had 58 LOAs in 1966, WOOD, 1976, 74), while in Scotland there were 135 LOAs open at some point during the study, but this total was reduced to 121 because of LOA amalgamations.

The next level of analysis uses the LMAs as defined by the Department of Employment and are subject to the limitations of aggregating LOAs. This procedure amalgamates 79 LOAs to produce 20 LMAs which with the remaining 'self contained' LOAs gives 62 LMAs. Other studies have produced varying numbers of LMAs for Scotland because they have used different criteria and data. For example, Smart (1974, 310-1) produced 45 LMAs (for criteria used see SMART, 1974, 261-77), while Lever (1978, 308) produced 31 LMAs (for criteria used see LEVER, 1978, 307). Neither of these figures are either correct, or incorrect because they depend upon the criteria adopted. It is interesting to note that Lever (1978, 308) produces more LMAs for the East Midlands (26) than for the West Midlands (22) despite the large differences noted in the number of LOAs between the two areas (21 in all). Furthermore, the difference noted in the number of LMAs for Scotland are of degree and not of kind because they represent attempts to define areal units that are less arbitrary than the economic planning regions (for England, see JOHNSON, SALT and WOOD, 1974, 33) or similar administrative areas (COOMBES et al, 1978, 1183).

Before proceeding to the next level of analysis, it is useful to define what an LMA represents. Even though the topic has attracted much attention (KERR, 1954; GOODMAN, 1970; HALL et al, 1973; SMART, 1974), the definitions emerging differ only slightly and the generally accepted definition '... is that of an area in which most workers can respond to job opportunities and change their jobs without changing their residences' (JOHNSON, SALT and WOOD, 1974, 35). The LMA is therefore similar to the Daily Urban System (DUS) or Standard Metropolitan Labour Area (SMLA) except that the latter have different criteria for defining their areal extent (see JOHNSON, SALT and WOOD, 1974, 40; HALL, 1974, 386-7).

The third and fourth levels of analysis represent a compromise situation between the individual LMA and the whole of Scotland. These two levels are made up of the nine administrative regions and a disaggregation of some of these regions - Strathclyde, Lothians, Tayside and Grampian - into their main centres and the outer lying areas. In the case of Strathclyde, disaggregation has led to five levels ranging from Glasgow City made up of eleven LOAs to the whole of Strathclyde (53 LOAs). The resulting series of units, especially in the case of Glasgow City, outer Glasgow and the Clydeside conurbation, approximate the main economic functional units of Scotland in terms of 'within Scotland migration' (HOLLINGSWORTH, 1970; ROBERTSON, 1978) and self-contained employment centres.

The final level of analysis is the whole of Scotland which is used for two main reasons. First, it probably represents the initial level of search when a new location is sought for either a complete relocation or an expansion by the establishing of a branch or subsidiary plant by a firm. Scotland also represents a distinct economic unit whose location and boundary, one would assume, would be perceived with greater accuracy than those of the other assisted regions (GREEN, 1977, 9-13). Second, in order to perform even the most simple of comparisons with findings of most other studies (the exception being GUDGIN, 1974; 1978), the results must be presented at the regional level.

2. COMPONENTS OF MANUFACTURING EMPLOYMENT CHANGE

(a) The national accounts

Before comparing the composition and changes of manufacturing employment in Scotland to those of four other regions, industrial South Wales, the East Midlands, the Northern Region, and Cleveland County, it is first necessary to consider the Scottish situation in isolation. During the period under study, 1968-77, the level of manufacturing employment in Scotland decreased by over one hundred thousand (14.93 per cent decline) leaving marginally more than six hundred thousand people employed in manufacturing industry by 1976. Much of this decline would have been expected given the nature of manufacturing industry in Scotland in the period (Chapter Two).

The net employment change for the period understates the full nature of the decline because the gross level of employment change far exceeds net change (GUDGIN, 1978, 63). The composition of manufacturing employment in 1977 is presented in Table 4.1. Two series of figures are shown because of the methods of allocation used to construct the table. The major figures (all plants) represent the complete allocation of all plants and employment. This means the total figures for 'permanent plants' includes those plants and their employment that could not be allocated to either a pre-, or post-1968 year of opening date. By adopting this procedure the relative importance of the employment contribution made by the opening of new plants of all types is slightly depressed. In order to correct for this situation, the figures have been recalculated using only those plants for which a year of opening is available. Having made allowance for this possible source of error, there is little difference between the two sets of figures.

The table suggests the overriding importance of the permanent manufacturing plants existing throughout the study period in providing employment. Yet, despite this relative and absolute importance of the permanent stock of plants, the employment contribution made by the opening of new plants, especially 'immigrant' plants, is not inconsiderable. Immigrant plants, as can

Table 4.1
Composition of manufacturing employment in Scotland in 1977

	All Plants	Employment %	Plants with dates*	%
Permanent stock of plants	507,060	90.35	466,201	89.59
All new plants (1968-77)	54,138	9.65	54,138	10.40
Branch (local	4,308	0.77	4,408	0.83
Branch (non-local)	37,636	6.71	37,636	7.23
New enterprises	12,194	2.17	12,194	2.34
Total	561,198		520,339	

*Employment totals are used only where the year of establishment is available in all cases unlike in the preceding column where all plants for which a year of opening is not available has been allocated to the permanent stock of establishments.

be seen, provided more than 37,000 jobs and it is probable that this total understates their contribution in direct employment terms. Two pieces of evidence can be offered to support this statement. First, it appears to be generally accepted that most manufacturing firms move or open a branch plant for reasons of expansion (CAMERON and CLARK, 1966; COLLINS, 1966; KEEBLE, 1968; SPOONER, 1972; DEPARTMENT of TRADE and INDUSTRY, 1973). Second, the data presented in Table 6.17 suggests that the level of employment created by immigrant plants is likely to reach 50-55,000 based on the growth records of the earlier immigrant plants opening in the 1968-71 part of the study period. It is also interesting to note that the employment created by new firms (12,194) will probably not decline despite the expected closure of at least half of the number of new firms. This situation is likely to occur if the growth of the surviving new firms equals that attained by the equivalent population of new firms opening in the preceding ten year period, 1958-67 (Table 4.3).

If one considers the level of employment created by immigrant plants still further, and assumes it as being equivalent to the number of jobs 'created' by regional policy, there is a marked similarity between the Moore and Rhodes estimates and those derived from this study. Moore and Rhodes (1977, 73) estimate that the regional policy effect on Scotland for the period 1968-76 as being 33,000 new jobs. If one adopts the Moore and Rhodes (1974, 233) assumption that approximately '... three-quarters of (this) employment came from the establishment of new factories, largely by firms operating from other regions ...', and then allow for the effect of North Sea oil, there is little difference between the Moore and Rhodes estimate of 24,750 new jobs and that derived from this study - 27,939 new jobs. (1) However, because these two employment totals appear similar it does not imply that they were in fact a product of regional policy. Moreover, it is probable that the changes both within industry and in regional policy itself have had an equal influence in 'creating' the employment totals mentioned above (MASSEY, 1977b, 456). The possible importance of regional policy in creating employment in Scotland is considered in a later

Table 4.2

Manufacturing employment created by the opening of new manufacturing
plants in Scotland, 1968 - 77: A consideration by
initial and present employment totals.

Employment Year of Opening	Present Year (1977)	Number of Plants involved
1968	888 - 4,706*	79
1969	605 - 3,431	56
1970	1,130 - 3,380	69
1971	1,230 - 6,161	70
1972	2,982 - 7,001	82
1973	800 - 2,042	68
1974	826 - 1,991	52
1975	442 - 1,092	35
1976	600 - 924	39
1977	1,016 - 1,016	33
Total	10,519 - 31,744	583

Source: Survey

* The 79 plants opening in 1968 for which data are available employed a
total of 888 employees on opening and by 1977 they employed 4,706
employees.

Table 4.3

Manufacturing employment created by new firms in Scotland
opening during the periods 1958 - 67 and 1968 - 77.

Period	No. of new firms	Employment (in 1977)
1958 - 1967	232[a]	13,240[b]
1968 - 1977	504	12,194

Source: Scottish Council (Development and Industry)

a. Employment data are not available in 10 cases.
b. This total will be depressed because of the change in the status of
   some indigenous firms due to their merger with, or take-over by
   externally owned firms. (see SMITH, I., 1978)

chapter (Chapter Six), and was introduced into the discussion at
this stage to illustrate the spatial scale at which some processes
operate i.e. the regional level. Another illustration of regional
level processes is made in Chapter Five in connection with the loss
of employment.

Despite the valuable information that may be inferred from knowing
the composition of manufacturing employment at one moment in time,
little knowledge is gained as to the real dynamics of manufacturing
employment change. In order to gain some knowledge of an area's
employment dynamics it is necessary to know, besides the features
noted above (Table 4.1), how much employment was lost by plants
either closing or contracting, and how much employment was gained by
plants expanding. This information in the form of both measurements
and estimates is presented in Table 4.4. The gross employment
change exceeds the net employment shift by at least 90,000 (measured
values - henceforth written as mv), but it is in fact probably
nearer to 145,000 (estimated value - henceforth written as ev).
This large discrepancy of 55,000 is partially due to the incomplete
coverage of the closures and redundancy data collated by the
Department of Employment (see Chapter Three). And it is because of
this discrepancy that the calculated expansion figure is depressed
to less than half its expected value. The expected value is based
on the summing of the calculated expansion values of the 87 LOAs
where it proved possible to calculate such a value.

Table 4.4

Scotland: Components of manufacturing employment change, 1968-77

Components	Employment Measured	Estimated
Total lost:	195,922	(248,500)[a]
Plant closures	82,719	(123,500)
Plant contraction	113,203	(125,000)
Plant openings total	54,138	(70,833)
Plant expansion (in situ)	35,946[b]	(71,829)
	(74,853)	
Net employment shift	-105,838	

[a]Estimates derived from year average values between 1969-74
(Scottish Economic Bulletin, 1977, 22).
[b]Value obtained by subtracting total employment shift (105,838)
from the total employment lost (195,922) and subtracting
employment created by openings (54,138) from that total.
However, this figure understates the employment created by
expansion as it is depressed by the understatement of the
number of jobs lost (approximately 50,000 too low) and an
overestimation of the total employment shift (see Chapter 3 on
ER II Card count and Annual Census of Employment). A third
expansion figure has thus been produced by aggregating the
expansion figures for the 87 LOAs (of a total of 121) where
expansion values have been obtained. The two larges errors
occur in Glasgow City (10 LOAs) and in Edinburgh City (3 LOAs)
where the net employment decline exceeded gross employment
decline due to the coverage of the closure and redundancy data
(see Chapter 3).

It would appear that between 130,000 and 140,000 new jobs were created over the ten year period, and the expansion of permanent plants provided 50 per cent or more of this new employment. The relative importance of the expansion of the permanent stock of plants varies according to which figure is used, the calculated, or the expected, or the estimated. For the purposes of this discussion the expected expansion and measured openings figures are used. The relative importance of the four sources of new employment is shown in Table 4.5. Unfortunately the expansion figure can not be disaggregated by either status, or ownership in order to give some indication of the source of this new employment (see SCOTTISH COUNCIL (Development and Industry), 1977).

Table 4.5
Sources of new manufacturing employment in Scotland, 1968-77

Source	Employment	
	Total	%
Total new employment	128,991	100.00
Openings total	54,138	41.97
New firms	12,194	9.45
New branches of Scottish firms	4,308	3.34
Immigrant plants	37,636	29.18
Permanent plants expansion	74,853	58.03

Sources: Scottish Council (Development and Industry)
Scottish Development Agency
Department of Employment
Regional and district councils
New town development corporations
Chambers of Commerce
Ports authorities

Neither the presentation, nor description of a single area's employment accounts can explain or even suggest why changes, such as those noted above, actually occur. It is the aim of the remainder of this chapter to begin to explain why these changes have occurred. One part of the explanation considers the reasons why employment was lost, and this explanation also serves to illustrate the importance of considering the Scottish economy as an integral part of the UK economy (Chapter Five). A comparison of the components of employment change for Scotland with those of the East Midlands, the Northern Region, Industrial South Wales, and Cleveland County also forms part of this explanation, and is detailed in the following section.

(b) A comparison with some of the UK regions

The object of this section is to compare the components of employment change where possible the findings of this study at the planning regional level (and in one case below this level) with those of other regions. Unfortunately sophisticated statistical comparisons between various series of results from independent enquiries are not possible because of the constraints of the differing data sets used. The result of four other studies are thus reported here to suggest possible similarities between them, but at all times it is important to recognise their weaknesses for direct comparisons.

Table 4.6 presents the findings of these studies. The main focus of attention is on the relative and absolute importance of new firms to new immigrant plants in providing new employment opportunities. All of the studies have used different data sources, each with their problems of accuracy and definition. Two features of the regions must also be considered at this juncture: first, the absolute size of the manufacturing labour force; and second, whether their manufacturing base was expanding or declining during the study period. Manufacturing employment in Scotland has declined continually since the war, while the other three regions have on average grown consistently, if one ignores the slight decline that has occurred in all regions in the 1973-75 period.

Yet, despite these limitations, one general finding is that in Scotland, in Industrial South Wales, in the Northern Region, and in Cleveland County, there is a dependence upon immigrant plants for providing the bulk of new employment through openings. In complete contrast to this situation, the East Midlands relied more heavily upon employment created by the opening of new firms. A similar situation was noted by Firn and Swales (1978, 208) in their comparative study of the West Midlands and Central Clydeside conurbations. While the findings of this brief comparison do not validate the basic hypothesis examined by Firn and Swales (1978, 203), they do tend to support Gudgin's (1978) idea that:

> ... industrial birth-rates are higher in the core
> regions and this means that their industrial
> structures will almost constantly be the most
> favourable. A final step to complete the
> explanation would account for higher birth-rates
> in the core regions. ... potential causes might
> be a history of greater commercial intensity and
> of greater economic security. In the peripheral
> areas greater dependence on primary activities
> and primary processing was historically less
> secure, and perhaps as a result co-operative and
> communal activities were more important. (ibid.,
> 301)

Unfortunately, the other three main components of employment change, closures, in situ contraction and expansion, are not fully explored by the studies listed in Table 4.6, and so no comment can be made on them. Furthermore, the focus of this study is the absolute and relative importance of new firms in regional development, and consequently less importance is placed upon the variations between the other components of employment change. The major concern with the other components of employment change is neither their relative, nor absolute size, though this is important, but the manner in which they may affect the rate (number) of new firms formations. Again, none of the studies listed consider directly the impact of one or more components of employment change on the others because they have been in essence employment accounting exercises of an exploratory nature.

A conclusion that can be drawn from these regional comparisons, and one with great relevance to this study, is that there appears to be a distinct core-periphery pattern with respect to the relative importance of new enterprises in the creation of new employment

Table 4.6

Components of manufacturing employment change: Regional comparisons.

Region	Period	Openings Ind(1)	Openings Imm.(2)	Closures	Contraction	Expansion
(a) Northern	1961-71	8[a]	92			
		2,000	23,000			
(b) Scotland	1968-77	22.5	77.5	82,719	113,203	74,853
		12,194	41,944			
(c) E. Midlands	1947-67	52	48			
		65,240	60,580	134,800		107,180
(d) Scotland	1950-74	221,500		206,900	175,000	125,300
(e) Cleveland County	1965-76	25.1	74.9	9,955		-16,704
		3,848	11,474			
(f) Industrial South Wales	1966-74	16.7[b]	83.3			
		(10)[b]	(50)			(40)

Sources: (a) – N.R.S.T. (1977)
          (b) – This study
          (c) – Gudgin (1974, 1978)
          (d) – Scottish Economic Bulletin (1977)
          (e) – Storey and Robinson (1979)
          (f) – Woodward (1977)

a. Percentage contribution made either indigenous or immigrant (includes local branch plants as well) plants opening of the total employment created by all plants opening.

b. Percentage contribution to all employment created during the 1966-74 period in Industrial South Wales.

opportunities. Such a conclusion must however be treated with caution because of the variety of data sources used and time periods studied. The only data source that would allow direct regional comparisons without the complications of data or temporal variability would be the Annual Census of Employment initiated in 1971. The Department of Employment is at present conducting such a study and will be published shortly (early 1980). However, even this data set has its drawbacks, and is not accessible because it is covered by the Statistics of Trade Act of 1947 (see TRADE and INDUSTRY, 1977, February 11th; DEPARTMENT of EMPLOYMENT - personal communication, 1977b).

(c) Regional and sub-regional accounts

The various components of employment change are described and examined at two aggregate levels in this section, the regional (9 areas) and the sub-regional levels (19 areas). Subdividions have been made in the four major regions by removing their main cities thus Strathclyde, Lothian, Tayside and Grampian have been further broken down into Glasgow, Edinburgh, Dundee and Aberdeen and their surrounding areas. Each of these regions and sub-regions has been constructed by the initial grouping of the employment accounts of each of the Department of Employment's local office areas which also form the basis of the local accounts presented in the next section.

The absolute and percentage employment shifts for each of the regions and sub-regions are detailed in Table 4.7 and Maps 4.1 and 4.2. The most striking feature of the table is the decline of manufacturing employment in almost all areas. In contrast to this overall decline is the growth of manufacturing employment in three regions, Fife, the South West and the Highlands and Islands, and two sub-regions, outer Grampian and outer Lothian. Yet, only three of these five areas made significant absolute increases in their manufacturing employment levels, Fife (8,737 increase), Highlands and Islands (6,426), and outer Lothian (2,163). The sources of this growth is different in each of the three cases and is considered in the next section.

Beyond the simple dichotomy of either growth or decline, is the distinct pattern formed by the relative sizes of the decline itself. All four of the major cities, Glasgow, Edinburgh, Dundee and Aberdeen, are major centres of decline. Further out and away from these cities both the absolute and relative sizes of the decline decrease. The nature of the decline has a distinct core-periphery pattern in which the suburban areas have declined to a lesser extent than the cities upon which they are centred. This pattern of suburban 'growth' has been noted at various times in previous studies in Scotland (CAMERON, 1973, 136; FIRN and HUGHES, 1973, 501-2; SCOTTISH DEVELOPMENT DEPARTMENT, 1977) and has been a main feature of the industrial growth of other major cities e.g. Amsterdam (KRUIJT, 1979), Paris (CAMERON, 1977, 147), Toronto (KERR and SPELT, 1958, 11-13; COLLINS, 1972, 85), Leicester (GUDGIN, 1974, 264), London and the South East (KEEBLE and HAUSER, 1972; KEEBLE, 1972a; 1972b; 1976, 269-73; WOOD, 1974, 142-9) and appears also to be the case in the United States (KING, 1975; ERICKSON, 1976; 1978).

The build-up of manufacturing employment in the suburban areas is

Table 4.7

Changes in manufacturing employment in Scotland, 1968 - 76:
Regional and sub-regional accounts.

Region	Employment ('000s) 1968	1976	Shift	Percentage Change
Strathclyde	421,285	341,173	-80,112	-19.02
Glasgow City	167,030	119,630	-47,400	-28.38
Outer Glasgow	163,466	135,795	-27,671	-16.93
Clydeside	330,496	255,425	-75,071	-22.71
Outer Strathclyde	90,789	85,748	- 5,041	- 5.55
Lothian	83,216	65,478	-17,738	-21.32
Edinburgh	56,233	36,332	-19,901	-35.39
Outer Lothian	26,983	29,146	+ 2,163	+ 8.02
Tayside	57,758	45,849	-11,909	-20.62
Dundee	42,681	31,109	-11,572	-27.11
Outer Tayside	15,077	14,740	- 337	- 2.24
Grampian	39,936	36,515	- 3,421	- 8.57
Aberdeen	27,302	23,384	- 3,918	-14.35
Outer Grampian	12,634	13,131	+ 497	+ 3.93
Central	41,564	36,140	- 5,424	-13.05
Fife	30,088	38,825	+ 8,737	+29.04
Borders	16,296	13,303	- 2,993	-18.37
South West	10,769	11,365	+ 596	+ 5.53
Highlands & Islands	7,946	14,372	+ 6,426	+80.87
Scotland	708,858	603,020	-105,838	-14.93

Source: Department of Employment

Map 4.1

Scotland: Employment Change, 1968−76
Regional & Sub−regional Accounts.

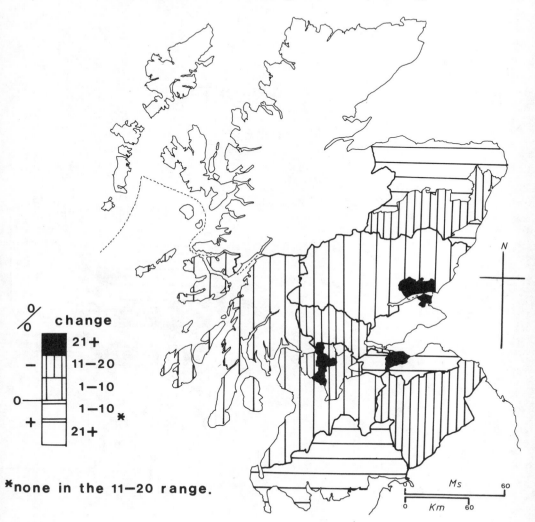

%
% change

21+

11−20

1−10

1−10 *

21+

0

*none in the 11−20 range.

N

Ms   60

0   Km   60

Map 4.2

Scotland: Employment Change, 1968–76.
Accounts for Travel to Work Areas.

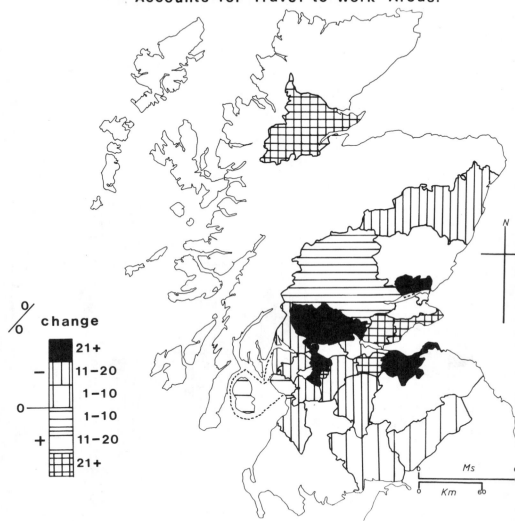

due to the differential impact of the various components of employment change. In essence, therefore, the difference in the employment performance between the cities and their surrounding areas is due to differences in the birth/death and expansion/ contraction components and the gain/loss of migrant plants. Yet, the development of suburban zones as areas of manufacturing importance had often been seen as a decentralization of manufacturing activity from the city centre (MOSES and WILLIAMSON, 1967; KERR and SPELT, 1958, 14). A decanting of industrial growth from the 19th century centres of manufacturing activity to the urban periphery. This has meant that:

> ... for many decades surburban and satellite areas around large cities have not only experienced rapid growth of indigenous firms (whatever their first origins), but have also provided a benign environment for the growth of new firms and for the attraction of increased investment from other regions. (WOOD, 1974a, 135)

It would therefore appear:

> ... legitimate to enquire whether other processes of change and sources of growth originating in the fringe zone itself have now achieved greater significance for the explanation of manufacturing trends. (ibid., 134)

Wood then continued, and considered that it was:

> ... no longer sensible to regard outer metropolitan areas merely as industrial satellites of the central city. (ibid., 135)

The results of disaggregating the shifts of manufacturing employment for each of the regions and sub-regions (Table 4.8) reveals overwhelming support for these comments (see SCOTTISH DEVELOPMENT DEPARTMENT, 1978). However, it would be misleading not to discuss the importance of the relocation of plants from the city centre. And although it has not been possible to derive accurate statistics for the movement of plants, it was possible to gain some indication of the relative importance of the movement of plants in accounting for either employment gain or loss in the inner city, or in the suburbs from work undertaken by the Scottish Development Department (1977). The loss of employment due to the relocation of plants from both Glasgow and Edinburgh is shown in Table 4.9. It is apparent that there is a difference in the importance of the relocation of plants in accounting for employment loss in these two cities. For Glasgow 6.42 per cent of all employment lost was due to plants leaving the city, while for Edinburgh the comparable figure is 14.57 per cent. Thus, relocation accounted for a larger share of employment lost in Edinburgh (31.12%) than in Glasgow (11.09%). The situation in Manchester was similar, where 7.07 per cent of all employment lost was due to plant relocation, and 9.59 per cent of plants closing moved out of the city. A major difference between the Scottish and Manchester cases is the greater importance of employment contraction of plants in the Scottish cases than was the case of Manchester in accounting for employment lost (LLOYD and MASON, 1978, 80). Detailed consideration of the relocation of plants in both Glasgow and Edinburgh has been made elsewhere (Glasgow:

Table 4.8

Components of manufacturing employment change in Scotland, 1968 - 77: Regional and sub-regional accounts.

Region	Employment 1968	1976	Shift	Closures	Redundancies	Openings	Expansion
Glasgow	167,030	119,630	-47,400	-20,869	-19,827	+ 3,960	+15,383[a]
Outer Glasgow	163,466	135,795	-27,671	-17,978	-32,410	+10,456	+12,261
Clydeside	330,496	255,425	-75,071	-38,847	-52,237	+14,416	+ 1,597
Outer Strathclyde	90,789	85,748	- 5,041	-11,915	-18,055	+ 4,386	+20,543
Strathclyde	421,285	341,173	-80,112	-50,762	-70,292	+18,802	+54,582[a]
Edinburgh	56,233	36,332	-19,901	- 4,449	- 2,389	+ 1,405	+ 6,567[a]
Outer Lothian	26,983	29,146	+ 2,163	- 3,866	- 3,922	+ 3,152	+ 6,799
Lothian	83,216	65,478	-17,738	- 8,315	- 6,311	+ 4,557	+13,366
Dundee	42,681	31,109	-11,572	- 5,544	-10,338	+ 2,228	+ 2,082
Outer Tayside	15,077	14,740	- 337	- 2,023	- 1,309	+ 1,319	+ 1,676
Tayside	57,758	45,849	-11,909	- 7,567	-11,647	+ 3,547	+ 3,758[a]
Aberdeen	27,302	23,384	- 3,918	- 2,030	- 2,471	+ 2,321	+ 2,594
Outer Grampian	12,634	13,131	+ 497	- 739	- 1,604	+ 748	+ 352
Grampian	39,936	36,515	- 3,421	- 2,769	- 4,075	+ 3,069	+ 1,935
Central	41,564	36,140	- 5,424	- 4,622	- 5,673	+ 2,936	+11,486[a]
Fife	30,088	38,825	+ 8,737	- 2,578	- 7,004	+ 6,853	
Borders	16,296	13,303	- 2,993	- 1,994	- 2,498	+ 4,353	+ 989
South West	10,769	11,365	+ 596	- 650	- 807	+ 1,064	
Highlands and Islands	7,946	14,372	+ 6,426	- 2,081	- 3,876	+ 8,572	+ 3,811
Scotland	708,858	603,020	-105,838	-82,719	-113,203	+54,138	+74,853[b]

Source: Department of Employment.   Scottish Council (Development and Industry), Survey.

a.   These data do not allow the direct calculation of an expansion employment figure in these cases, estimates are used in most cases using average values from the Scottish Development Department (1977) study of industrial change in the four main cities, 1966 - 71.

b.   See Table 4.5 for derivation.

Table 4.9

Manufacturing employment lost in Glasgow and Edinburgh, 1966-71

| | | Employment Lost | | |
	Plant Closures	Plant Moves from City	Stationary Contraction	Total Lost
Glasgow	20,609	2,572	16,865	40,046
Edinburgh	5,484	2,437	8,803	16,724

Source: Scottish Development Department (1977, part of Tables 1 and 2)

HENDERSON, 1974; Edinburgh: SESDA, 1973; GHODGERI, 1974) and further elaboration is not particularly relevent to the present discussion.

In switching the attention from the cities themselves to their surrounding areas, the importance of new plants i.e. plants moving into the area from outside Scotland or completely new firms, is evident in accounting for recent employment growth of these areas. It is important to note that the redundancy totals are the 'complete' redundancy totals for each of the ten years of the study period. By using this accounting procedure the importance of redundancies may be inflated. However, there is no evidence that the plants declining during the period made dramatic recoveries, and then laid-off employees in yet further instances. In fact, where the same plant has been recorded as making employees redundant more than once it has been the case of reducing the labour force still further, rather than reducing a labour force that increased in size having been reduced earlier. In this case it is assumed that the accounting procedure has not led to any undue bias in the importance of redundancies in accounting for employment lost. Moreover, it allows an estimate of employment turnover, which is hypothesised as being a potentially important factor in the formation of new firm founders. That issue aside, the failure of the cities to either attract plants or develop new firms does not hold for either Aberdeen or Dundee, both of which gained more employment from the opening of new plants than their surrounding areas. The four areas surrounding each of the major cities therefore form two distinct groups. The areas surrounding both Glasgow and Edinburgh declined less than the cities upon which they are centred because their manufacturing population not only decreased to a far lesser extent, but they also achieved a far higher degree of 'success' in attracting and developing new plants. This situation is in direct contrast to the position found in both Aberdeen and Dundee. The surrounding areas for both of these cities fared better in employment terms because their stock manufacturing population declined less than the cities upon which they are centred.

It is tempting to conclude therefore that the processes developing the suburban areas surrounding Glasgow and Edinburgh have been operating for a much longer time period than in the areas surrounding both Aberdeen and Dundee. In fact, the balance between Glasgow and its surrounding area is such that the surrounding area is now more important than the city itself in employment terms. Edinburgh has not yet reached this position, but the relative (and absolute) importance of its surrounding area has increased over the period uch that in 1968 it accounted for 32.43 per cent of all manufacturing employment in the Lothian region and by 1976 this level had increased to 44.51 per cent. While the forces operating to spatially readjust the distribution of industry may be internal to industry, one should not underestimate the effect of national policies in encouraging this patten of suburban growth. For example, East Kilbride and Cumbernauld near Glasgow and Livingston near Edinburgh act as major focii for incoming industry. These new towns possess distinct advantages over other areas because of their financial and administrative/executive autonomy which allows them to operate with a greater degree of flexibility than, say, the councils of either Glasgow or Edinburgh. Furthermore, the proliferation of industrial estates around the periphery of Glasgow has had a strong influence on the specific siting of incoming plants. In fact, by the early 1960s the Scottish Industrial Estates Corporation:

> ... had constructed estates at Blantyre, Carfin, Carluke, Carntyre, Chapelhall, Coatbridge, Craigton, Hillington (with the North Cardonald extension), Larkhall, Newhouse, Queenslie, Thornlibank and a small development at East Kilbride - all of which are contained in an area 20 miles long by 10 miles wide. (WELCH, 1970, 142-3)

The influence of institutional policies in both directing and augmenting industrial investment should not therefore be underestimated (WOOD, 1974a, 142; 1974b, 25). However, it is possible that these institutional measures are in fact harnessing forces that are operating independently of the administrative and legal framework they impose (MASSEY, 1978a, 14). For example, Davidson (1967, 18) noted that after 1850, a major split occurred between the location of work place and residence such that even at this early date the development of suburban Glasgow was occurring. Similarly, Smart (1974, 245) details a parallel development for London and also noted that the earliest '... suburbs beyond convenient walking distance of the City ...' favoured the middle-class because the fares were beyond the means of the manual workers. But by 1860:

> ... growing numbers of working men travelled to work by public transport as successive Victorian Acts of Parliament required railway companies to run cheap workman's trains. Together with the trams, which offered much lower fares than the omnibus, these made possible a much wider dispersal of working-class housing away from employment areas. (ibid.,245)

The point being made here is that institutional planning has had (and is having) a direct impact upon the development of housing and in the provision of a mass transport system. Furthermore, the suburban development of industry has not happened in isolation or independently of other changes, and in fact the recent 'rounds' of industrial investment are attempting to make the best possible use of the factors of production, the distribution of which has been changing.

The changing distribution of industry can be interpreted as a response by industry itself to the real or apparent changes in the distribution of comparative advantages for production. An evaluation of the comparative advantages (in spatial terms) has meant that the previously locationally restricting supply factors of production often no longer apply. The result of this situation might increase the locational flexibility exhibited by industry. Moreover, two other factors must be considered at this juncture. Technological change, for example, can have a dramatic impact upon the very nature of production itself. Though it is perhaps important to note that the bulk of the Research and Development effort of industry is focused upon short-reach applied work and is mainly concerned with modifying the product and its constituent parts. Process changes have also occurred and these have allowed the nature of productive employment to have changed.

> Skillful decomposition of activities, and an
> education and occupational training system well
> tuned to the pattern of decomposition, permit a
> great reduction in the amount of knowledge that
> must be specific to any particular activity.
> (NELSON et al, 1967, 12)

The electronics industry is often offerred as one example of this deskilling process (FIRN, 1975, 411; MASSEY, 1978a, 9; SCOTTISH DEVELOPMENT AGENCY, 1979), yet evidence is largely lacking in this area (see TOWNSEND et al, 1978). Some evidence exists from work undertaken in the United States though this work is not necessarily transferrable to the UK situation (BRIGHT, 1958, 189; NELSON et al, 1967, 140 and 145; for UK see THOMAS, 1979).

With a possible reduction of the demands made by industry for skilled labour, the emphasis changes to a direct requirement for labour, skilled or otherwise. The readily available supply of labour is not restricted to any one area, but this supply does possess a broad distribution. But allied to the tight labour markets that have existed in the South East and in the West Midlands and the regional policy inducements that have existed since 1945, the distribution of this labour is largely restricted to areas such as South Wales, North East England, Northern Ireland, and Scotland. The demand for labour has also been shown to be a major locating factor for new industrial investment, and when combined to the new demands for industrial land help to explain the rise of suburban centres of manufacturing. Demands for land in the major urban centres has risen through time and as a consequence the supply of land has decreased in these areas, thus increasing the price of the remaining land (see CAMERON, 1973, 126-8; FIRN and HUGHES, 1974, 485-93). In this context I. Carter (1974) has noted that:

> The activities of private industrial estate
> developers and a changing attitude on the part of
> Glasgow Corporation now means that very many more
> prepared sites within the city can be offered to
> industrialists, than at any time since the war.
> (ibid., 25)

If the inner city still remains the preferred location by industry, therefore, and that suburban sites represent a second best location, one would expect that during the 1965-77 period (1965 being the end

Carter's study period) that a resurgence of interest in the inner city would have occurred. There is no evidence of any such resurgence occurring at the present time, but it is possible that this is too short a time period to expect any changes to have occurred.

These two points, the demand and supply of both labour and land, serve to illustrate part of the process of the growth of manufacturing industry in the suburbs. Furthermore, this changing demand/supply situation has not been localised and is probably best explained within a wider spatial context. Contrary to expectations, at the local level the impact of rent differentials does not appear to be of major importance. In the West Midlands, for example, Barbara Smith (1972, 37-9) has commented upon the lack of rent differentials between the conurbation and the overspill areas. And she attributes the lack to the increased supply of industrial land in the conurbation (due to increased demand and to the closure of plants) and the '... need for the overspill authority, first, to recoup its outlays on the factory, land and site facilities and, second, to obtain some extra to help finance the rest of the town development ...' (ibid., 39). The impact of non-domestic rates upon industry appears inconclusive (SMITH, 1972, 57; JACKMAN, 1978), but may have a localised effect. At a regional or national level rent differentials appear to exist (LOGAN, 1966, 456; SMITH, D.M., 1969, 123), but their importance in either promoting, or in prohibiting industrial investment is not known (see SMITH, 1966; TAYLOR, 1971; McDERMOTT, 1973). Also at the local scale there are also the policies and attitudes of the city corporation towards new industry which may be important. In both Birmingham (SMITH, 1972, 45-6) and Edinburgh (BARLOW COMMISSION, 1940, evidence, 227, q.2416), for example, there seems to have been an ambivalent position backed by the naive belief that '... the region (or city) has grown and adapted for the last 200 years - why should it stop doing so now?' (WOOD, 1973, 1).

The interplay between a city and its surrounding area, and the interplay between the whole city region and the national economy has therefore been instrumental in shaping the growth and subsequent development of manufacturing industry in suburban locations. Part of these relationships have been influenced by institutional forces, especially in terms of housing and of road network provision, and also by the provision of inducements and statutory restrictions upon the location of new industrial investment in all regions of the UK. Set between the city/suburbs and city region/national relationships and the influences of institutional measures, lies the important affect of population movement both within cities (LAMONT, 1979) and within a nation (SCOTTISH COUNCIL (Development and Industry), 1966; JACK, 1968; HOLLINGSWORTH, 1970; JOHNSON, SALT and WOOD, 1974). The establishment and continued growth of the suburban manufacturing centres has made them a major location of industrial growth, and this pattern is unlikely to change in the near future. It is perhaps then to these centres that present intraregional policies could turn and attempt '... to harness the considerable growth capabilities of the metropolitan fringe, rather than remain preoccupied with the more difficult task of attracting firms from farther afield.' (WOOD, 1974a, 151).

The above discussion however does not explain the growth of industry in either Fife or the Highlands and Islands region. Increases in manufacturing employment in the Highlands and Islands region is almost wholly due to the establishment of several large rig construction firms e.g. McDermott Scotland, M-K Shand, Highland Fabricators etc. Employment created by these types of firms is not permanent and is related to the demand for rigs and associated equipment from mainly the North Sea. Moreover, the nature of the rig production puts its into a fabrication/construction nature, and as such is liable to large fluctuations in employment as various aspects of the work progresses. It is likely that employment in these construction yards has 'peaked' (MACKAY and MACKAY, 1975, 133) and so a gradual decline will occur over the next few years and manufacturing employment in the Highlands will return to the levels existing prior to the North Sea oil boom i.e. 8,000.

Part of the Highlands growth has also been due to the opening of a major aluminium smelter at Invergordon. The choice of Invergordon was the result of political, at both regional and national levels, and economic decisions and can only be interpreted in a national context. During the mid 1960s it had become apparent that the UK demand for aluminium would increase dramatically over the next 10-20 years, while the level of UK aluminium smelting would remain very low. This low level of smelting capacity was seen as a major industrial weakness and one that should be rectified in the national interest. As a result of these deliberations three smelters were opened, one of which was at Invergordon. The history of the Invergordon case and the details leading up to its designation are detailed elsewhere (MANNERS, 1968; WARREN, 1972, 419-21; 1973, 196-208). In this case the employment created can be regarded as near permanent.

In direct contrast to the Highlands, the growth of manufacturing employment in Fife has in part been due to the opening of plants (6,853), while the main growth has been the result of plants expanding their work forces (11,486). It seems reasonable to assume that the bulk of the employment growth from expansions is due to the buildup of employment plants opening in Fife during the preceding 5-10 years (see CAMERON, 1971, 431; SCOTTISH ECONOMIC BULLETIN, 1978, 17-18). The buildup of industry in Fife over the 1945-67 period is detailed elsewhere (POCOCK, 1970, 127-8; McNEIL, 1973, 176-7; McNEIL, 1974). Each of these studies shows the decline of coal mining employment and the infusion of new industrial development mainly through the opening of branch plants (57 or 67.1 per cent of all plants opening in the 1958-71 period).

Two of the remaining three regions, Central and Borders, experienced declining levels of manufacturing employment. Both regions were, and still are dominated by declining industries, though this is true to a lesser extent for the Central region. For example, 66.1 per cent or 9,140 of all employees in manufacturing industry in the Borders worked in textiles (SIC Order 13) in 1977. Alongside this concentration, the Borders has 'attracted' several large electronics plants such that the electrical engineering industry now employs 1,200 people. Similarly, the Central region contains several of the major declining industries, metal manufacture (SIC Order 6) and textiles (SIC Order 13) which together employ 7,803 or 22.5 per cent of the total manufacturing labour force. Again, this declining element of the Central region's economy has been partially offset by the growth of chemicals and related industries (SIC Orders 4 and 5), glass production (SIC Order 16), and the 'attraction' of a few instrument engineering plants (SIC Order 8). It would appear from Table 4.9 that the opening of new manufacturing plants is more important than the expansion of existing plants in the provision of new employment in both of these regions, Central and Borders. If one now includes the South West region, which has experienced a net increase in manufacturing employment, a distinct pattern emerges. All three of these regions are now experiencing greater employment growth from the opening of new plants than from the expansion of the existing ones, and this would also appear to be the case in both Aberdeen and Dundee. In the last two cases however the employment gains are probably more a product of their fortuitous location in relation to the North Sea rather than anything else. The point being that the gain of new plants in both Aberdeen and Dundee and the Highlands can be regarded as resource orientated locations (NORCLIFFE, 1975, 51) and are thus operating outside the restrictions of most other locational factors.

The growth of employment through the opening of new plants in the Borders, the South West, and the Central regions can be seen as an extension of the patterns depicted by the locations chosen by plants opening in Scotland over the 1945-68 period. Welch (1970) noted over this period that of the plants entering and were still operating in 1968:

> ... 170 or 46.96 per cent of all incoming establishments were located less than 20 miles from Central Glasgow and 285 or 78.73 per cent between 0 and 40 miles from that point. Of the remaining 77 or 21.27 per cent which were located more than 40 miles from Central Glasgow, 26 were sited in two centres; Glenrothes and Dundee (16 and 10 respectively), and the remaining 51 were scattered over the North East and Southern Scotland. (ibid., 139)

While in the ten year period following the study period of Welch, a similar pattern has emerged but with far less emphasis upon the Clydeside conurbation. During the 1968-77 period, the Borders, the Central, and the South West regions have all gained more immigrant plants than they did during previous periods. It is thus tempting to suggest that tight labour markets existing in the previously developed areas had encouraged the search for new, but equally suitable locations. As a result, more plants have located in the three regions in question. Furthermore, the balance between the expansion and the opening of plants is in favour of the former in providing most of the new employment opportunities in the previously developed areas e.g. Fife, outer Glasgow, etc. Thus, the provision of new employment in these areas is dependent upon the expansion of existing but recently located industries. Whereas other areas with possible a generally declining stock of plants gains most of its new employment from the opening of new plants in the first instance, a period which would be followed by the subsequent expansion of these plants. It would appear that the balance between new employment supplied by either the expansion or the opening of new plants is

largely dependent upon the previous industrial investment in each
region prior to the present study period. The bulk of new
employment would appear to be gained from the continued growth of
recently established manufacturing plants rather than from the
opening of new manufacturing plants.

In turning to the loss of manufacturing employment, it is plant
contraction rather than plant closure that accounts for the bulk of
all employment lost in the five non-city centred regions: Central,
Fife, Borders, South West and Highlands. In fact, this is also the
case for both Tayside and Grampian, though not for outer Tayside.
From Table 4.8 it would appear that if the amount of new employment
is balanced against the employment lost by the closure of existing
plants, the previously less industrial regions have fared much
better. What is more, in the case of Fife, the Borders, the South
West, and the Highlands new employment created by openings exceeds
employment lost due to plant closures, and it is these new plants
that would tend to expand over the next 5-10 years. It could be
concluded that it is these regions that will best be able to
maintain their existing levels of manufacturing employment based on
their present favourable openings/closures differential. Table 4.8
also reveals that these four regions had a favourable openings/
closures differential, while Table 4.10 suggests that they all
gained more new employment opportunities from openings than would
have been expected. The Central region being the only exception.

This section has examined the components of manufacturing
employment change at the regional and sub-regional levels, and has
explained where possible the patterns that exist. It was also
pointed out that many of the employment changes in Scotland over the
1968-77 period were a product of processes operating at both the
city-region and national levels. The areal units used however
necessitated generalisations in comparing, for example, the city
centre and their surrounding areas. Within the surrounding areas
there are variations that have been averaged out due to aggregation.
The components of employment change at the local office area level
are considered below, and reveal marked local variations.

(d) Local accounts

The marked variations in performance (2) between the regions and sub-
regions are the product of large local variations. It is the object
of this section to discuss these local variations in performance at
the local office area level. As with the previous section greater
emphasis is placed upon the provision of new employment by the
opening of new plants, but that does not exclude the other
components of change on which comments are also made.

At the local level, to which all of the comments in this section
will be addressed, several stricking features emerge. First, of the
106 spatial units used in this local level analysis, there has been
an increase in manufacturing employment in 47, while there has been
a decrease in the remaining 59 (Map 4.3). The total employment
increase of the 47 expanding areas is 37,726, while the
corresponding figure for the declining areas is 141,822 jobs lost.
Second, only eleven of the expanding areas increased their level of
manufacturing employment by 1,000 or more: these were Broxburn

Table 4.10

Comparison of observed and expected levels of new employment created by the opening of new plants in Scotland, 1968 - 77: Regional and Sub-regional accounts

Region	Employment No.	%	Employment from Plant Openings Observed	Employment from Plant Openings Expected*	Difference
Glasgow	167,030	23.56	3,960	12,755	− 8795
Outer Glasgow	163,466	23.06	10,456	12,484	− 2028
Clydeside	330,496	46.62	14,416	25,239	− 10823
Outer Strathclyde	90,789	12.81	4,386	6,935	− 2549
Strathclyde	421,285	59.43	18,802	32,174	− 13372
Edinburgh	56,233	7.93	1,405	4,293	− 2888
Outer Lothian	26,983	3.81	3,152	2,063	+ 1089
Lothian	83,216	11.74	4,557	6,356	− 1799
Dundee	42,681	6.02	2,228	3,259	− 1031
Outer Tayside	15,077	2.13	1,319	1,153	+ 166
Tayside	57,758	8.15	3,547	4,412	− 865
Aberdeen	27,302	3.85	2,321	2,084	+ 237
Outer Grampian	12,634	1.78	748	964	− 216
Grampian	39,936	5.63	3,069	3,048	+ 21
Central	41,564	5.86	2,936	3,172	− 236
Fife	30,088	4.24	6,853	2,295	+ 4558
Borders	16,296	2.29	4,353	1,240	+ 3113
South West	10,769	1.52	1,064	823	+ 241
Highlands	7,946	1.12	8,572	606	+ 7966
Scotland	708,858		54,138	54,126	

Source: Department of Employment, Scottish Council (Development and Industry). Survey.

* Expected on the basis of employment levels in 1968
  Does not take into account either industrial, or plant size structure.

Map 4.3

MANUFACTURING EMPLOYMENT
CHANGE IN SCOTLAND, 1968-76.
SOURCE: DEPT. of EMPLOYMENT.

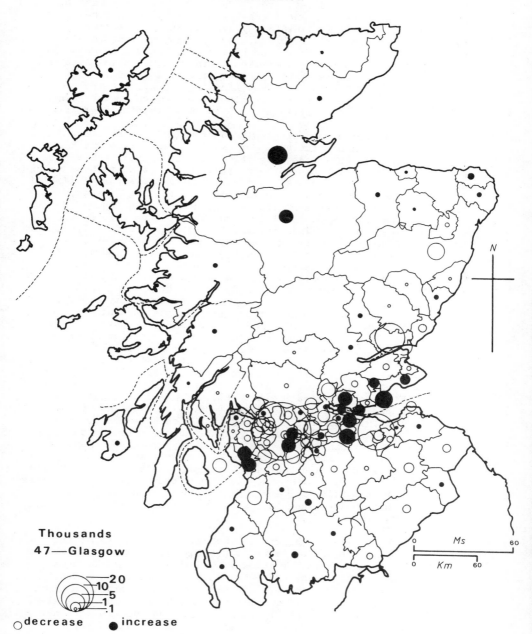

Thousands

47—Glasgow

20
10
5
1

○ decrease   ● increase

(2,688) and Livingston (3,462) in West Lothian; Dumfermline (2,527), Inverkeithing (1,202), and Kirkcaldy (4,180) in Fife; the new towns of Irvine (1,806) and East Kilbride (2,721); Invergordon (4,287) and Inverness (1,939) in the Highlands; and Cambuslang (1,656) and Kilwinning (2,289) in Strathclyde. Two other areas expanded by nearly a 1,000 employees and these were in Fife: Glenrothes (921) and Leven (958). It is immediately evident that the better performance of the outer Lothians, for example, was the result of employment growth in Broxburn and Livingston, and was not equally spread throughout the outer Lothians. Other areas in the Lothians did record increases in their manufacturing employment levels - Haddington (254), Tranent (46) and Linlithgow (147, now in the Central region) - but were negligible in comparison to the gains made at Broxburn and at Livingston in the West Lothian District.

The above apportionment of growth can similarly be made for the other regions. In Strathclyde, for example, Cambuslang and East Kilbride are located in the area termed outer Glasgow, while Irvine and Kilwinning are in outer Strathclyde. The growth of these four areas on aggregation tends to partially cancel the areas of decline in these two outer areas. In Strathclyde, excluding Glasgow, thirteen local areas have recorded large declines in their manufacturing employment levels (losses of 1,000 or more jobs). These declines occurred in Airdrie (-3,784), Alexandria (-1,643), Clydebank (-9,004), Coatbridge (-2,533), Hamilton (-2,569), Johnstone (-1,891), Kilmarnock (-1,997), Larkhall (-1,302), Motherwell (-1,360), Paisley (-3,247), Renfrew (-2894), Wishaw (-1,496), and Saltcoats (-2,202). The level of manufacturing employment in these thirteen areas decreased by a total of 35,922, only 11,478 less than the total decline of Glasgow City itself. It is therefore important to note that although the absolute decline of Glasgow City is far greater than any other area, in percentage terms its decline has been no more dramatic than has occurred elsewhere. Table 4.11 details the percentage increase or decrease in manufacturing employment for each of the 106 local areas, and it is apparent that the 28.38 per cent decline of Glasgow City is not an isolated case. In fact, six areas adjacent or nearly adjacent to Glasgow City have suffered similar relative sized declines e.g. Airdrie (-32.07 per cent), Clydebank (-38.19), Coatbridge (-23.34), Hamilton (-25.63), Larkhall (-39.09), and Wishaw (-25.28). The nature of the decline in these six areas varies according to the structure of their industry. The loss of employment by plant contraction is more important in all six cases than the loss by plant closure. Both Clydebank and Coatbridge have older industrial bases than the other four areas. And the closure of plants in these two areas in accounting for employment loss is relatively more important than in the other four areas (Airdrie, Hamilton, Larkhall and Wishaw).

If one extends these analyses to include all of the older and larger manufacturing areas (areas employing approximately 10,000 or more people in manufacturing industry and this excludes Bathgate, East Kilbride, Dunfermline and Glenrothes) a similar situation is revealed. In only one case are closures more important than plant contraction in accounting for employment loss, and this is Paisley. Nine further areas are added by using these criteria and together with the six areas noted above and the four major cities they

Table 4.11

Percentage employment change at the local level
in Scotland, 1968-76

Percentage size of employment change		No. of local office areas
	41+	2
	31 - 40	10
Decline(-)	21 - 30	21
	11 - 20	16
	1 - 10	10
	NO CHANGE	
	1 - 10	12
	11 - 20	9
Increase (+)	21 - 30	8
	31 - 40	6
	41+	12
Total		106

Source: Department of Employment

account for 354,121 or 58.72 per cent of all manufacturing
employment in Scotland (in 1976). The point being made here is that
decline of manufacturing employment is not only found in the inner
city, but is in fact occurring in all of the older industrial areas.
The balance between plant closures and plant contractions in
accounting for employment lost is a product of the industrial
structure, the size distribution of plants in an area, and the age
of investment they represent. For example, in Kilmarnock 9,685 or
66.57 per cent of the manufacturing workforce are employed in only
six plants. Consequently, both the fortunes of Kilmarnock and the
balance between plant closures and plant contractions in accounting
for employment lost is influenced by, if not dependent upon, the
actions of these six large plants (each employing 700 or more
employees). A similar situation also exists, though to varying
degrees, in each of the other eight areas (Alloa, Ayr, Falkirk,
Greenock, Johnstone, Motherwell, Paisley, and Renfrew). The
inclusion of Johnstone and the exclusion of Bathgate might appear
arbitrary especially as they are both dominated by a major vehicle
assembly plant that employs most of the local workforce (62.21 per
cent in the case of Bathgate; 71.81 per cent for Johnstone). The
difference between these two areas lies in the age of the
manufacturing plants. In Bathgate 34.78 per cent of plants were
open prior to 1939, while in Johnstone the same figure is 57.14 per
cent, and·it is on this basis that Johnstone was included and not
Bathgate.

The comments made above have been related to both the size and
direction of employment change and only a few brief comments have
been made as to the relative importance of either plant closures or
plant contractions in accounting for employment loss. In the
remainder of this section the balance between employment lost by
closure and that gained by the opening of new plants is considered.
The number of new employment opportunities created by the expansion
of plants existing throughout the study period has been calculated

for each of the local office areas by subtracting the net employment
lost from the gross employment loss and then by subtracting the
employment created by the opening of new plants from that total
(Equation 4.1). The method used earlier to correct for the problem

$$\text{In Situ Expansion} = \text{Gross Employment Change} - (\text{Net Employment Change} + \text{Employment created by the opening of new plants})$$

Eq. 4.1 Means of calculating the level of _in situ_ expansion

underestimation of employment lost by both plant closures and plant
contractions was derived for the national, and not the local level
(Table 4.5). At the local level there are further complications
that relate not to the errors inherent in the data itself, but to
the number of manufacturing plants in each area. The problem arises
from the distorting effect that one large individual plant can exert
on a small population of plants in an area. While if the same plant
were placed in a larger population, its overall influence would be
reduced. In essence this can be regarded as the 'law of large
numbers' effect (HARVEY, 1969, 246-7) which '... tends to average
out random fluctuations in areas with sufficiently large numbers of
plants, but elsewhere the random fluctuations can dominate
employment change. The randomness is derived from the unpredictable
variations in the distribution of entrepreneurs and in the ability
or success of managements with individual firms.' (GUDGIN, 1978, 76-
8).

It follows on from the above, and is perhaps more important to
note, that while the actions of an individual plant are of
importance, it should not '... become pivotal in our studies'
(CULLEN, 1976, 407). Research should be nomothetic in its approach
and attempt to derive '... statements that have some general
applicability' (NORCLIFFE, 1977, 18). Such an approach does not
rule out the study of the individual, but would tend to emphasise
the search for a '... conceptual framework (that) will allow ... (a)
... transition between structure and actor' (CURRY, 1978, 45). The
point being made here is not purely a conceptual one, but one of
direct methodological importance. By the inclusion of local office
areas whose employment change is the result of the growth or the
decline of one plant with areas whose employment change is the
result of a combination of the growth and decline of many plants is
confusing two types of approach, and two types of behaviour. On the
one hand, individual behaviour is being described, while on the
other hand, group actions are being considered. The combination of
both of these types of employment change within one single spatial
system of local areas for a common analysis is problematic for the
derivation of statements with a general applicability.

Two further points need to be added to this discussion concerning
the types of areal units used and the size of plants operating
within the manufacturing economy of Scotland. First, the number of
plants and the level of manufacturing employment in an area is a
product of the boundaries of that area. There is therefore a
problem of aggregating individual plants into spatial units. One
can optimize the spatial units used in order to draw boundaries to
include a minimum population of plants (OPENSHAW, 1977). However,

Table 4.12

Dominant components of manufacturing employment gain and loss in
Scotland, 1968 - 77: Local accounts

Dominant Components of Employment Change	No. of Local Office Areas		
	Expanded	Contracted	Total
Openings GT Expansion - Map 4.4	14	31	45
Expansion GT Openings - Map 4.4	30	29	59 = 104[a]
Closure GT Contraction - Map 4.5	17	27	44
Contraction GT Closure - Map 4.5	25	30	55 = 99[b]

a: Data are not available in one case, and in the case of Thurso the
level of employment created by expansion and openings is equal.
b: Data are not available in seven cases.

Table 4.13

Dominant component mixes of manufacturing employment change in
Scotland, 1968 - 77: Local accounts

Dominant Components	No. of Local Office Areas		
	Expanded	Contracted	Total
Openings & Contraction - Map 4.7	5	14	19
Expansion & Contraction - Map 4.8	20	15	35
Expansion & Closures - Map 4.9	10	12	22
Openings & Closures - Map 4.10	6	15	21
Totals	41	56	97[a]

a: Data are not available in nine cases.

71

Map 4.4

COMPONENTS OF MANUFACTURING
EMPLOYMENT CHANGE:LOCAL ACCOUNTS,
SCOTLAND, 1968—77.

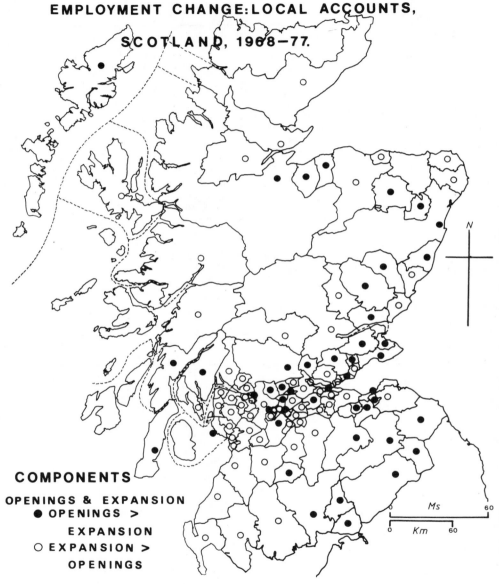

COMPONENTS

OPENINGS & EXPANSION
- ● OPENINGS >
- EXPANSION
- ○ EXPANSION >
- OPENINGS

Map 4.5

COMPONENTS OF MANUFACTURING
EMPLOYMENT CHANGE: LOCAL ACCOUNTS,
SCOTLAND, 1968—77.

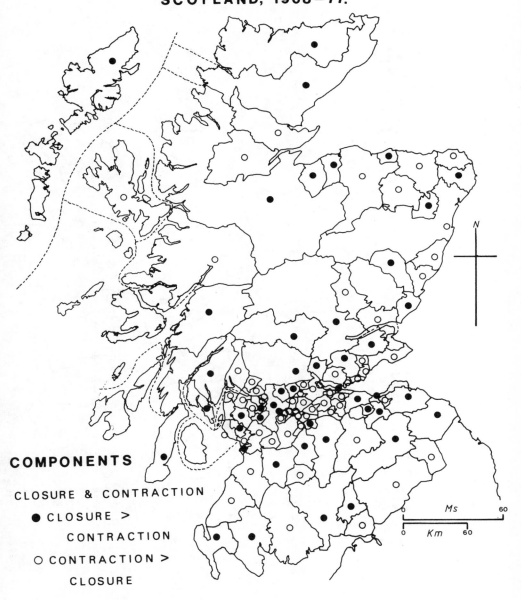

COMPONENTS

CLOSURE & CONTRACTION

● CLOSURE >
   CONTRACTION

○ CONTRACTION >
   CLOSURE

Map 4.6

Components of Manufacturing Employment Change: Local Accounts, Scotland, 1968–1977.

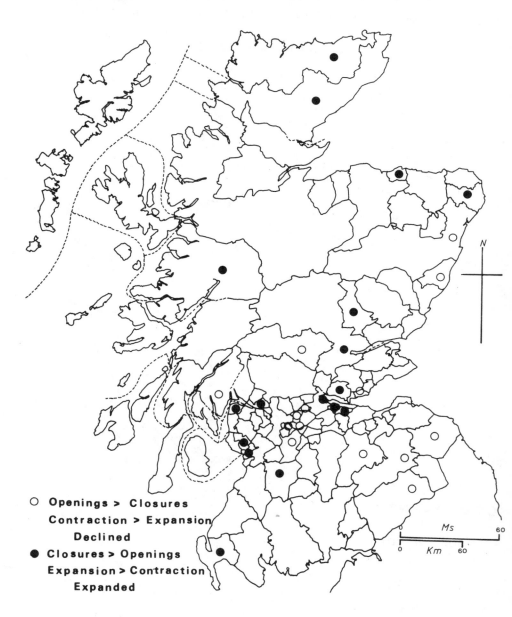

O **Openings > Closures**
  Contraction > Expansion
     Declined
● **Closures > Openings**
  Expansion > Contraction
     Expanded

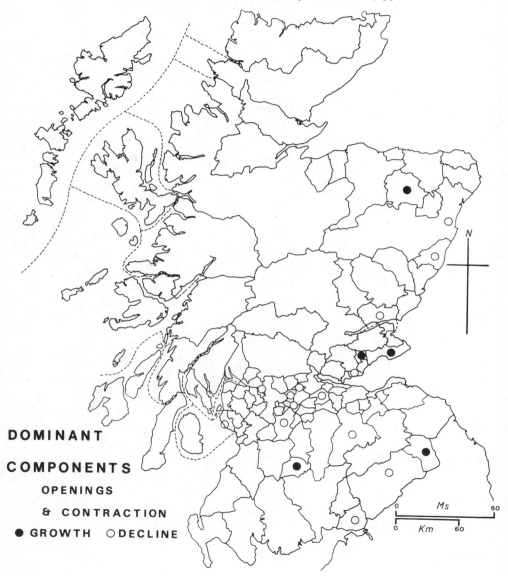

Map 4.7

COMPONENTS OF MANUFACTURING
EMPLOYMENT CHANGE: LOCAL
ACCOUNTS, SCOTLAND, 1968—77.

N

DOMINANT

COMPONENTS

OPENINGS

& CONTRACTION

● GROWTH ○ DECLINE

Ms

0   60

Km

0   60

Map 4.8

COMPONENTS OF MANUFACTURING
EMPLOYMENT CHANGE: LOCAL
ACCOUNTS, SCOTLAND, 1968—77.

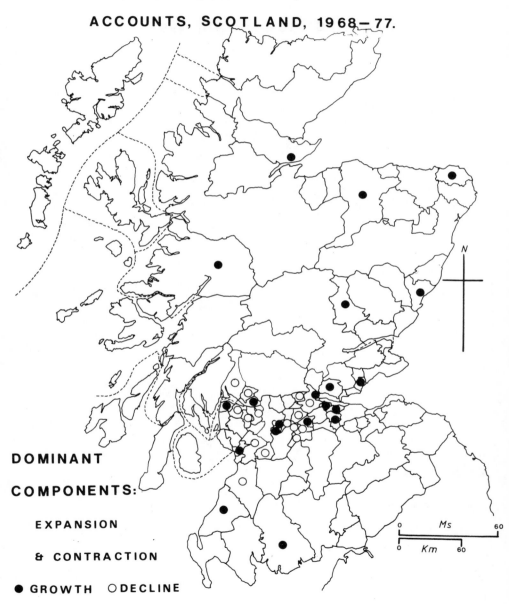

DOMINANT

COMPONENTS:

EXPANSION

& CONTRACTION

● GROWTH ○ DECLINE

Map 4.9

COMPONENTS OF MANUFACTURING
EMPLOYMENT CHANGE: LOCAL
ACCOUNTS, SCOTLAND, 1968—77.

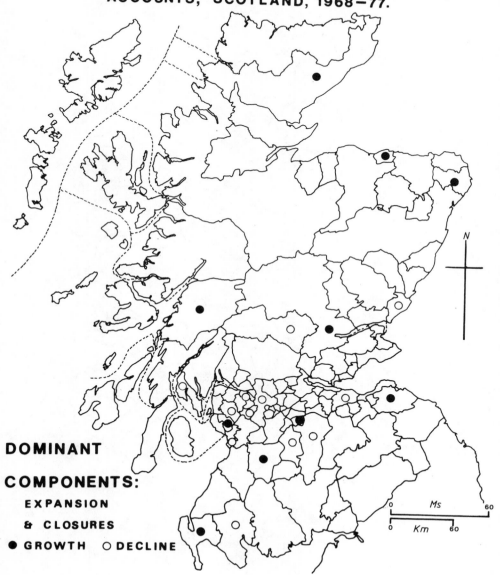

DOMINANT

COMPONENTS:
EXPANSION
& CLOSURES
● GROWTH ○ DECLINE

N

Ms
0   60
Km
0   60

Map **4.10**

COMPONENTS OF MANUFACTURING
EMPLOYMENT CHANGE: LOCAL
ACCOUNTS, S.COTLAND, 1968—77.

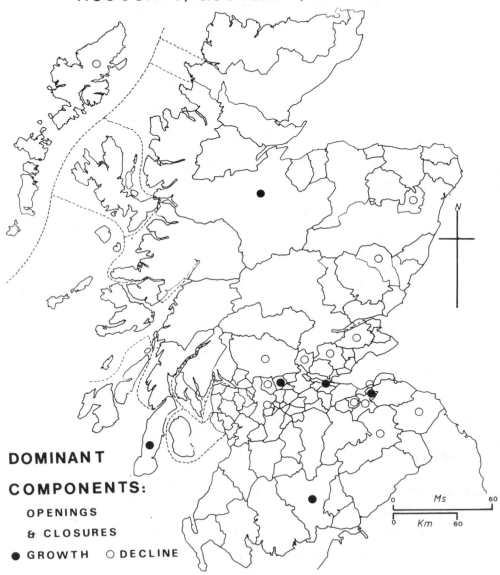

DOMINANT

COMPONENTS:
  OPENINGS
  & CLOSURES
  ● GROWTH ○ DECLINE

such a procedure would pay little or no regard to the operation of the labour market, or other economic forces. It would therefore follow that while the local area comments qualify the general statements made in the previous section, as spatial units of analysis they are not necessarily the most appropriate level for analysis.

The second point concerns the size distribution of manufacturing plants operating in Scotland. Whether either the number of plants employing 500 or more employees, or the numbers they employ is increasing, does not detract from the fact that they employ at present 309,575 (3) (or 295,711 (4)) or 55.52 per cent (or 48.48 per cent) of the total manufacturing labour force. Thus any actions these plants may undertake is bound to have an impact at all levels, local or regional. And so in any instances where employment levels have changed, the actions of large plants will almost invariably be important.

At this juncture, then, several questions can be posed: Where is the creation of new employment by the opening of plants greater than the provision of new employment by the expansion of the existing stock of plants, or vice versa? Where is the loss of employment by the closing of plants more important than that lost by the contraction of the existing stock of plants, or vice versa? Furthermore, is there any relationship between the number of plants opening and closing within an area? And, which combination of components is most likely to result in an overall expansion of the manufacturing employment base? Some of these questions are answered by the data presented in Tables 4.12 and 4.13 which detail the dominant components of either employment gain or loss at the local level and in Maps 4.4 - 4.10. Perhaps the most striking feature to emerge from these tables and maps is the importance of changes in the employment of the plants existing throughout the 1968-77 period. The opening of new plants has undoubtedly made an important contribution to employment creation and employment change, but the bulk of employment change has resulted from the expansion, contraction, and closure of plants. Though in the short term this mix of components may result in the greatest numbers of jobs being created, it is unlikely in the long term that this component mix would in fact ensure the continued growth of an area. It seems generally agreed that the opening of new plants and more especially the formation of indigenous firms is important to an area's development (BEESLEY, 1955, 49; BAUMOL, 1968, 69; LIGGINS, 1977, 94; FIRN and SWALES, 1978, 299). Yet, despite assurance that indigenous firms are so important to an area's development, there is a distinct lack of empirical evidence (except GUDGIN, 1974, 1978) and few, if any, attempts at deriving a theory of new firm formation and entrepreneurship (except BAUMOL, 1968, 70-1; LEIBENSTEIN, 1978, 39-55). It is to both of these topics that the following two chapters (Chapters Six and Seven) address themselves.

Only one traditional industrial area, Clydebank, had any of its components dominated by the action of one firm, where the Marathon Shipbuilding Co. (UK) Ltd dominated employment created by the opening of new plants. However, for the present analysis this case is not regarded as a new plant because it represents a change in ownership rather than a completely new investment. In fact the dominant position held by Marathon had decreased by 1977 as its labour force then was only a third of its 1973-74 level. All of the other areas where the action of a single plant dominated any of the components were largely non-industrial and rural. For both Inverness and Invergordon the actions of two plants in either case were responsible for their large employment gains from openings, 3,830 and 3,756 respectively. Perhaps rather surprisingly the gain of employment from a single indigenous firm dominates all employment gained in two places, Burntisland in Fife and Campbeltown on the Kintyre peninsula. Moreover, in both of these cases the firms were shipbuilding concerns. Other areas where the opening of single branch plant dominated the supply of new employment were Annan, Kirkcaldy, Inverurie, Saltcoats, Portree and Brechin.

Turning to consider where the loss of employment is dominated by the closure of a single plant, only six areas emerge: Blairgowrie, Cupar, Kilburnie, Troon, Brechin and Helensburgh. In the cases of both Blairgowrie and Helensburgh the total loss of employment by plant contraction is also due to the actions of one plant. The erratic and dominant actions of one or two plants is mainly restricted to rural areas and is similar to the findings of Gudgin (1978). He noted that:

> In the more rural areas the importance of new firms
> is relatively low, again largely because their
> impact is overshadowed by incoming branch plants or
> subsidiary firms. (ibid., 84-5)

As would be expected at such a disaggregated level, the variations are great, but several distinct patterns do appear to exist. For example, the areas where employment created by the opening of indigenous firms is more important, in absolute employment terms, than the opening of other plants, tended to be in the previously non-industrial areas. Areas such as Thurso, Wick, Fort William, Campbeltown, Dunoon and Rothesay would fall into this category. There were also previously industrial areas where this was the case e.g. Ayr, Loanhead, Linlithgow, Paisley and Musselburgh. Plant openings generally tended to be more important than the expansion of existing plants in areas where the existing industrial base was relatively small, and was still receiving the inward movement of plants e.g. Dunfermline, Glenrothes, Dalkeith, Tranent, Selkirk, Peebles, Hawick and Kelso. Perhaps rather surprisingly, in both Dundee and Aberdeen the greatest supply of new employment came from the opening of new, non-indigenous plants largely concerned with North Sea oil. The reliance upon the expansion of the existing manufacturing base therefore still remains the major supplier of new employment in the older industrial areas such as Glasgow, Edinburgh, Renfrew, Paisley, Barrhead, Falkirk and Denny. Other areas that have attracted large amounts of incoming industry e.g. Irvine, East Kilbride and Livingston (all new towns) were all experiencing major gains from both the expansion and the opening of plants, but the former process has made the major contribution to employment provision over the 1968-77 period. In contrast to this situation both Cumbernauld and Glenrothes generated more employment from plants opening rather than from plant expansion.

Employment lost by plant closures also shows two distinct distributions. First, there are those areas that represent the old

traditional industrial tracts which are declining as a direct result
of the reduction of their industrial base e.g. Glasgow, Edinburgh,
Rutherglen, Paisley and Barrhead. Second, there are those areas
with a small industrial base and whose plants tend to be small e.g.
Inverness, Forres, Nairn, Thurso, Wick, Fort William, Campbeltown
and Rothesay. A third element of this distribution is the
employment lost due to plant contraction which also has a distinct
distribution. Encircling the traditional manufacturing zones of
Glasgow lie the areas that have received much of the initial
incoming manufacturing industry and are therefore strongly
represented in the 'newer' industries. This would include the areas
of Dumbarton, Alexandria, Johnstone, Port Glasgow, Hamilton, East
Kilbride, Cambuslang, Uddington, Wishaw and Cumbernauld. A similar
position also exists in Fife, West Lothian, the Falkirk-Grangemouth
area, and perhaps rather surprisingly in both Aberdeen and Dundee.

Based on the above observations, the four elements of employment
change considered here can be combined into four sets of dominant
components of employment change (as in Table 4.14): openings and
closures, openings and contraction, expansion and closures, and
expansion and contraction. In each case these component mixes
accounted for the greater proportion of both employment gain and
employment loss. A most striking distribution emerges when the
expansion and the contraction of existing plants are the two most
important components of employment change. If consideration is
restricted to the Central Lowlands, the employment shifts in the
areas encircling Glasgow can be largely accounted for by these two
components, the exapnsion and the contraction of existing plants.
The limits of this horseshoe shaped zone run from Helensburgh and
Alexandria in the north west, to Newmilns in the south, goes north
east to Airdrie and Denny, taking in the block of zones running from
East Kilbride to Shotts, and south to Larkhall. In the remoter
areas, the actions of a few firms can account for the expansion or
contraction of employment e.g. Invergordon, Fraserburgh, Fort
William, Blairgowrie, and even Dunfermline and Kirkcaldy (see Map
4.8). The remaining three component mixes of manufacturing
employment change do not reveal distinct patterns. This is partly
due to there being fewer areas in each category, but even so, this
does not detract from the fact that there appears to be an
underlying national pattern. A pattern centred on the older
industrial areas, their surrounding areas, and the more recently
developed areas.

Table 4.14
Dominant component mixes of manufacturing
employment change: A categorization by the
age and size of an area's industrial base

| Age of Industrial Base | Dominant components of manufacturing employment change | | |
| | | Industrial Base | |
		Large	Small
New	Openings	Contraction	Closure
Recent	Expansion	Contraction	
Old	Expansion	Contraction/Closure	

Source: See text

It could then be suggested that there are relationships between an individual component, the combined components of employment change, and the overall age of an area's industrial base. Thus, just as an individual firm goes through growth phases at birth (e.g. WEBSTER, 1975, 430; 1976, 29; 1977, 58) and after its survival during the first few years (JAMES, 1973, 68-9), so do the areas containing large groups of firms. A simple typology can then be derived for this situation and is detailed in Table 4.14. The basic idea behind Table 4.14 is that the buildup of manufacturing industry in a region does not reveal spatial continuity at the sub-regional, or local level e.g. a shifting from the inner city to the surrounding suburbs. It is the discontinuous development of industry within a region that leads to the spatial variations in the various components of employment change noted in this chapter. Furthermore, the most important component underlying these variations is the spatial discontinuity in the emergence of new enterprises and the location of new branch and subsidiary plants (see Chapter Six). Of course, the use of a plant's age does not imply it holds any set position within an exact life framework, but for present purposes it can be used as a surrogate for the employment growth potential of a firm.

3. SUMMARY AND CONCLUSIONS

This chapter has examined the various components of manufacturing employment change and has shown by the use of various levels of analysis that either the growth or the decline of an areas' manufacturing employment total is a product of several components. Moreover, it has been shown that the major components accounting for the greater part of either employment gain or loss have a distinct spatial distribution. The distribution of the expansion and contraction of plants suggested a possible association with the age of the plants in the area. The point being that the component mixes that accounted for the employment changes at the local level are not purely a result of four major components operating during the study period, but are a direct consequence of that area's history of industrial development. The lack of continuity of industrial development tends to favour the overall dominance of employment change by a single component. This is the case, for example, in Fife, in West Lothian, and in the South Eastern periphery of Glasgow where in the 1950s and 1960s most of the new employment was created by the opening of new plants. These new plants were also locating in 'new' locations with little previous local industry. By the late 1960s and early 1970s a sizeable industrial base in these areas had been established, and so the balance of new employment created shifted from the opening of new plants to the expansion of the recently established ones. Similarly, the loss of employment in such areas could likewise be described (for a UK view see KEEBLE, 1976, 155-6).

Other factors causing variations in the relative importance of the components of employment change relate to the industrial structure and size distribution of plants in an area, and ceteris paribus, an areas' industrial age. One relates to whether or not an area is represented by the declining industrial sectors which tend to be represented by older firms. Another feature of concern here is the size-distribution of plants which is especially important where a single plant dominates the labour market. To illustrate the possible importance of these factors, in 1976-77, 37 local areas had 50 per cent of their manufacturing employment in plants employing 500 or more employees. Also in 1976-77, 33 local areas had 50 per cent of more of their manufacturing employment in only one industrial order.

The overall importance of indigenous firms in providing new employment appeared minimal especially when compared to the East Midlands (GUDGIN, 1978, 86). Variations exist at the local level, and indigenous firms were more important in rural areas. It is to this topic that Chapter Six turns and is the focus of the remainder of the study: the attempted explanation of the formation of new firms and the spatial variations in their emergence. While Chapter Five examines the possible influence of the closure and contraction of plants on the emergence of new indigenous firms.

NOTES

1. Total employment created by all immigrant plants opening during the period = 37,636. Total employment created by plants related to North Sea oil and employing 200 or more employees in 1977 = 9,697* Regional Policy Effect = 37,636 - 9,697 = 27,939.
*Employment total of the eleven largest plants directly related to the development of the North Sea oilfields.
2. Performance is used here to denote the changes in the levels of employees in manufacturing employment.
3. Source: Scottish Council (Development and Industry), 1977.
4. Source: Business Statistics Office (BSO), 1975.

5 Aspects of Employment Decline and Its Potential Role in the New Firm Formation Process

1. EMPLOYMENT DECLINE: AN EXAMINATION AND AN EXPLANATION

The decline of a region's manufacturing base represents a situation of gross employment loss which is greater than the net employment loss. In Scotland, for example, manufacturing industry declined by 105,838 jobs over the period 1968-77, but 195,922 jobs were actually lost. Yet even the knowledge of these figures indicates nothing of either the industrial or the organisation differences that they may hide. It is necessary to disaggregate the elements that make-up this employment decline to reveal any of the differences that may or may not exist. By adopting this approach it is shown that the Scottish owned manufacturing sector is declining at a faster rate (compared to the rate of the externally owned sector) than would be expected. The increase in external ownership is in part a product of the declining Scottish sector rather than to the absolute growth of its externally owned counterpart. In fact, the tables presented below tend to suggest that if foreign investment had not taken place in Scotland during the study period the level of employment decline may have doubled.

There have been few studies that have considered employment lost by either plant closure or by plant contraction. Of the studies that do exist, many have considered branch plants (ATKINS, 1973; SANT, 1975; TOWNROE, 1975; CLARK, 1976; SLOWE, 1977; HENDERSON, 1979) and were concerned with aggregate employment changes and plant survival, rather than the reasons behind such changes. Other studies have considered closures either in specific industries (CROOK, 1964; TAYLOR, 1971, 84, 88, 94-6), or as an option open to multiplant companies (RAKE, 1972, 930). General studies of plant failure and closure are rare and the few that do exist are limited. Woodruff and Alexander (1958, 48), for example, present general reasons for failure, but their observations are based on only ten closures. Collins and Roberts (1977, 2-3) also list general reasons for business failure, but these relate to all businesses, and their study of 73 closures (bankruptcies and liquidations) included only one manufacturing company. Likewise, Allsopp's (1977) interesting text on Survival in Business spends only two short chapters on the reasons for closure (Chapters 2 and 3, 14-19 and 20-32 respectively), while the remaining nine chapters are devoted to the avoidance closure, which is in fact the main object of the book. It would appear that only a little is known of the reasons for plant closure (1) and contraction, though more is known of the magnitude of

employment lost due to plant closure and contraction. Before
considering the reasons for employment loss, the nature and
magnitude of manufacturing employment lost is described, then the
two are combined in an assessment of the absolute and relative
importance of each reason in accounting for employment loss.

The objectives of this chapter are threefold. First, to present
employment accounts showing the nature and magnitude of the decline.
Second, attempt to explain why employment has been lost. In this
explanation explicit attention is drawn to the roles of external
ownership and the UK economy in the decline of employment. And
third, a series of situations arising from either plant closure, or
contraction are then highlighted to illustrate how they may
influence the rate of new firm formation.

(a) Employment decline: An examination

The aggregate decline of manufacturing industry in Scotland has been
marked since 1966. Prior to 1966 most of the traditional industries
had started to decline (metal manufacture, shipbuilding and textiles),
but it was only in shipbuilding that the major part of the decline
had occurred by 1966. The period since 1966 has been one of
continuous decline, and the only employment increases have occurred
in instrument and electrical engineering, and clothing and footwear.
As would be expected, the largest _gross_ employment losses have
occurred in those orders in which the largest _net_ employment
declines have been recorded.

It is evident from Table 5.1 that within the time period studied
employment turnover varied greatly between the orders (expressed as
the percentage of the total labour force leaving over the period,
1968-76). Employment turnover values such as these and the net
balance between gross employment loss and gain reflect features of
each order. First, they indicate whether or not the order is
declining in absolute terms as for example in the case or orders 6
(metal manufacture) and 13 (textiles). And second, they suggest
that those orders with a 'high' employment turnover rate, but are
not necessarily declining (Orders 9, electrical engineering and 15,
clothing and footwear), are dynamic in creating new employment via
the opening of new plants (branch plants or completely new
enterprises) and the expansion of existing plants. Furthermore, the
high employment turnover rate noted in some cases may be a result of
the production process itself.

While little further understanding of employment loss can be
gainded from solely considering gross employment change, an advance
can be made if gross employment loss is split into two constituent
parts:

    (1)   Employment lost due to plant closures, and
    (2)   Employment lost due to plant (_in situ_) contraction.

This split, which in many ways could be considered arbitrary, can be
seen as a situation that represents either permanent (plant closure)
or temporary (plant contraction) employment loss. The arbitrary
nature of the split stems in part from the recording of a complete
production line closure as a plant contraction rather than as a
closure. This situation may arise where a manufacturing

Table 5.1

Employment shifts within each standard industrial order in Scotland, 1968 – 76.

SIC	Employment 1968	('000s) 1976	Shift (%)	Estimated[a] Gross Loss	Gross Gain	Employment Turnover Rate %
3	94	90.8	− 3.2	23,374	20,174 b	24.86
4	3	2.8	− 0.2	27	−	0.90
5	31	28.6	− 2.4	3,061	661	9.87
6	47	39.1	− 7.9	13,530	5,630	28.79
7	108	91.7	−16.3	64,558	48,258	59.78
8	15	16.2	+ 1.2	4,394	5,594	29.29
9	48	48.6	+ 0.6	23,419	24,019	48.79
10	46	42.3	− 3.7	19,418	15,718	42.21
11	39	32.2	− 6.8	11,039	4,239	28.31
12	30	27.2	− 2.8	8,686	5,886	28.95
13	86	57.2	−28.8	31,742	2,942	36.91
14	3	2.5	− 0.5	723	223	24.1
15	30	30.9	+ 0.9	12,956	12,956	40.19
16	23	17.4	− 5.6	7,815	2,215 b	33.98
17	26	20.3	− 5.7	5,508	−	21.85
18	56	44.4	−11.6	13,876	2,276	24.78
19	17	15.6	− 2.4	5,205	2,805	30.62
Total	699	607.8	−91.2	248,431	157,231	35.54

Source: Department of Employment.

a. For method see Table 4.4

b. Figures not meaningful

establishment produce more than one product and operates on several, unrelated production lines such that they operate physically independently of each other. The contraction of the labour force at such a plant could therefore be the product of either an overall shedding of labour (a temporary loss of employment), or the closure of one production line (a permanent loss of employment). A further disaggregation of the plant contraction figures would reveal the size of this misallocation and one which is performed below in the explanation of employment loss.

Despite the probable misallocation of employment lost under the conditions outlined above, it is doubtful if a complete plant closure has been misallocated in this way. However, it should be noted that the distinction often drawn between employment lost by either plant closure or plant contraction is not clear cut, though this is rarely stated (e.g. KEEBLE, 1976, 122-5; DENNIS, 1978). This lack of precision in allocating employment to one of two categories is of greater significance than just a problem of data accuracy. It indirectly introduces the role of multiplant companies in the process of employment loss and hence, the operations of supraregional influences in shaping the development of manufacturing industry in Scotland. This topic is considered more fully in the following two sections.

The split of employment lost into plant closure and contraction is shown in Table 5.2. It is interesting to note that for most other components of employment change studies for which data are available the closure of plants in accounting for the loss of employment has (with the exception of Edinburgh, Dundee and Aberdeen - SDD, 1977) been usually greater than that lost due to plant contraction. A caveat must be made at this point because most other components of employment change studies have been of major conurbations and not of whole regions (an exception being GUDGIN, 1974; 1978). When the components of employment change are spatially disaggregated to the sub-regional and lower levels, the importance of closures increases but only exceeds plant contraction in accounting for employment loss for Glasgow City. Further comments were made on the lower levels of analysis in the final section of Chapter Four.

In only seven of the seventeen orders listed in Table 5.2 are plant closures more important than plant contractions in accounting for employment loss. The variations both between and within orders are due to a series of reasons and forms the focus of the next section, but a few comments are necessary before examining the ownership and the size distribution structure of plant closures and contractions. There are several general observations one can make based on these figures (Table 5.2). First, one might expect less employment to be lost by closures in those orders dominated by very large establishments. For example, Vehicles (Order 11, especially mlhs 381 and 383) is dominated by a few very large establishments, each representing massive capital investments. It is also doubtful that the closure of these plants would be allowed considering their importance in employment terms and the dominance they exert over their immediate labour market areas. (2) Conversely, such plants would be more likely to make workers redundant, or rather than make workers redundant they would operate on a part-time/short-time

Table 5.2

Employment lost by manufacturing industry in Scotland, 1968 - 77:
A consideration by industrial order

| SIC | Employment lost by plant: Contraction | | Closure | | Total |
	No.	%	No.	%	
3	7,796 (154)*	42.3	10,638 (151)	57.7	18,434 (305)
4	13 (1)	61.9	8 (1)	28.1	21 (2)
5	1,243 (26)	51.5	1,171 (26)	48.5	2,414 (52)
6	7,449 (125)	69.8	3,221 (41)	30.2	10,670 (166)
7	34,739 (315)	68.2	16,174 (155)	31.8	50,913 (470)
8	2,663 (43)	76.9	802 (19)	23.1	3,465 (62)
9	13,164 (140)	71.3	5,305 (48)	28.7	18,469 (188)
10	12,620 (88)	82.4	2,694 (24)	17.6	15,314 (112)
11	7,297 (43)	83.8	1,409 (19)	16.2	8,706 (62)
12	4,467 (92)	65.2	2,383 (64)	34.8	6,850 (158)
13	10,004 (168)	40.0	15,029 (170)	60.0	25,033 (338)
14	140 (6)	24.6	430 (15)	75.4	570 (21)
15	2,956 (56)	31.1	6,552 (107)	68.9	9,508 (163)
16	2,315 (70)	37.6	3,848 (99)	62.4	6,163 (169)
17	1,059 (37)	24.4	3,285 (77)	75.6	4,344 (114)
18	2,885 (53)	26.4	8,058 (53)	73.6	10,943 (106)
19	2,393 (59)	58.3	1,712 (35)	41.7	4,105 (94)
Totals	113,203 (1,476)	57.8	82,719 (1,126)	42.2	195,922 (2,602)

Source: Closure and redundancy records of the Department of Employment

* No. of establishments involved.

working basis. The latter course of action is the more likely because of possible labour relations problems and also the need to maintain a large trained workforce ready to return to full production at short notice. It could therefore be argued that the costs of maintaining the labour force are exceeded by potential training costs of new employees. Furthermore, it is generally only the major companies that can operate such a policy as most single plant companies do not possess this flexibility. It would appear that the level and complexity of the production process in determining the decision whether to completely close or to make employees redundant is of paramount importance. The status of the plant appears important in that most single plant companies do not possess the financial strength achieved by companies operating on a multiregional or multinational scale.

Second, it would be expected that the declining orders where Scottish ownership is highest in terms of employment, the number of closures would also be the highest. Nearly 80 per cent of Scottish owned manufacturing establishments are independent companies and operate at a single site (Table 5.3). If textiles (Order 13) are taken as an example, this point can be further illustrated. The large number of Scottish owned independent plants is evident from Table 5.4, and hence there exists a possible inflexibility of response of the whole order in periods of decreased demand. The loss of employment in textiles due to closures is concentrated in the following four minimum list headings (mlh):

(1)   412 (Spinning and doubling on the cotton and flax
         systems)
(2)   414 (Woollen and worsted)
(3)   415 (Jute)
(4)   417 (Hoisery and other knitted goods)

Table 5.3
Location of ultimate ownership in manufacturing industry
in Scotland, 1977

Location of ultimate ownership	Employment No.	%	Plant mean size	Establishments No.	%
Scotland					
Branch/subsid	59,936	10.68	142	481	11.43
HQ at site	24,341	4.34	197	134	3.18
Independent	118,287	21.07	57	2,271	53.97
England and rest of UK	248,267	44.24	291	993	23.59
Europe	14,240	2.54	180	82	1.95
North America	86,396	15.39	441	222	5.28
Other World	626	0.11	125	6	0.14
Joint Venture	9,092	1.62	505	18	0.43
Total	561,198		149	4,207	

Source: Scottish Council (Development and Industry)

It is important to realise that the figures in Table 5.4 hide not
only a diverse range of products and production systems, but also
many patterns of plant organisation and control. An examination of
the jute industry reveals its domination by two Scottish firms - Tay
Textiles Ltd and Sidlaw Industries Ltd - who operated 19 plants in
1977 (11 in Dundee; see LEVENSON, 1979).

Table 5.4
Location of ultimate ownership in the textile industry
in Scotland, 1977

Location of ultimate ownership	Employment No.	%	Plant mean size	Establishments No.	%
Scotland					
Branch/subsid	17,560	30.3	197	107	21.2
HQ at site	4,717	8.1	277	18	3.6
Independent	20,635	35.6	81	281	56.3
England and rest					
of UK	12,640	21.8	178	82	16.3
Europe	502	0.9	84	6	1.2
North America	1,876	3.2	268	7	1.4
Total	57,930		130	504	

Source: Scottish Council (Development and Industry)

Tay Textiles Ltd developed by a series of takeovers staged over
the last ninety years (in 1888, 1900, 1924, 1932, 1938, 1960 and
1963) and have recently converted three existing jute mills to
polypropylene extrusion and weaving (in 1969, 1971 and 1974). The
latter plants represent the 'new' element of the firm and an attempt
to switch from jute weaving and sewing to the use of man-made fibres.
Sidlaw Industries Ltd (Scott and Robertson) was created by a major
merger and then a takeover. First in 1921, Jute Industries Ltd
amalgamated with a number of old established family jute firms to
form what is now Sidlaw Industries Ltd. And second in 1972, Sidlaw
Industries Ltd took over the mills belonging to the South Mills
Group. In the last ten years they have also opened two new plants
in Dumfrieshire (in Sanquhar, 1971; in Kirkconnel, 1974).

Against this background of reequiping and new developments, these
two companies closed 18 plants and made over 4,000 employees
redundant over the 1968-77 period. Both firms have conducted
drastic rationalisation programmes and have concentrated production
at fewer sites. They have also shed surplus labour with the advent
of new technologies, increased competition, and changing demands.
The decline of the jute industry to a position of now employing only
6,700 (in 1976) and its gross loss of nearly 5,600 jobs over the
1968-77 period must be balanced against the historic development of
the two companies (at least 8 plants predate 1900) and their attempt
to survive in a changing world market (Tables 5.5a and 5.5b for the
four selected mlhs). (3)

Similar illustrations could be made of other industries. For
example, the decline of Scottish Brick Ltd was marked by a reduction

Table 5.5a

Employment lost due to plant closures in the textiles
industry: Selected mlhs.

| mlh | Employment | | | | | Plants | | | | |
| | Scottish | | Other | | | Scottish | | Other | | |
	No.	%	No.	%	Total	No.	%	No.	%	Total
412	1,381	100	0	0	1,381	12	100	0	0	12
414	1,708	75.9	541	24.1	2,249	26	81.3	6	18.7	32
415	3,147	100	0	0	3,147	29	100	0	0	29
417	2,969	82.5	629	17.5	3,598	45	81.8	10	18.2	55
Total	9,205		1,170		10,375	92		16		108
Total for Whole Order	12,020		3,009		15,029	143		27		170

Source: Closure and redundancy records of the Department of Employment.

Table 5.5b

Employment lost due to plant contractions in the
textiles industry: Selected mlhs.

| mlh | Employment | | | | | Plants | | | | |
| | Scottish | | Other | | | Scottish | | Other | | |
	No.	%	No.	%	Total	No.	%	No.	%	Total
412	1,250	80.2	309	19.8	1,559	12	85.7	2	14.3	14
414	1,228	74.7	415	25.3	1,643	39	92.9	3	7.1	42
415	2,406	98.7	31	1.3	2,437	36	97.3	1	2.7	37
417	1,963	100	0	0	1,963	27	100	0	0	27
Total	6,847		755		7,602	114		6		120
Total for whole order.	8,705		1,299		10,004	153		15		168

Source: Closure and redundancy records of the Department of Employment.

of its operating sites from 25 to 15 over the 1968-77 period. This could be seen as a result of the company being taken over in 1969 by NCB (Ancilliaries) Ltd. (4) In fact five sites were closed within two years of the takeover. The purpose of these examples is to illustrate the importance of knowing not only how much employment was lost and whether it was due to either plant closures or plant contractions, but also how that industry was owned and how those changes, if any, have affected the industry as it stands today. The importance of knowing the ownership status of a plant is not simply to extend an ownership analysis, but to place a plant's closure or contraction into a notional, yet reasonable, spatial decision making framework (HEALEY, 1979). The question being, not where did the decision take place, but in what spatial context was it taken.

The rest of this section is devoted to an examination of the size distribution, ownership structure, and types of the plants that have either closed or contracted over the study period. The size distribution of plants either closing or contracting over the 1968-77 period is shown in Table 5.6a and is complemented by Table 5.6b which shows the associated levels of employment lost by the various employment size categories. From Tables 5.6a and 5.6b it is evident that nearly 80 per cent of <u>plants</u> (892) closing employed less than 100 employees. While over 80 per cent of <u>employment</u> lost (63,235) by plants closing employed less than 500 employees. The situation with plants making employees redundant is almost completely the reverse. More than 60 per cent of <u>plants</u> (889) making employees redundant employed more than 200 employees at the time of the contraction, and likewise almost 65 per cent of <u>employment</u> lost (71,418) by plants contracting employed more than 500 employees. It would appear therefore that there are possible two populations of plants. Those that are able to reduce their labour force and those, because of their already 'small' size, that are not able to contract their labour force without severely limiting the operations of the

Table 5.6a
Employment loss: Size distribution of plant closures
and contractions in Scotland, 1968-77

Employment size group	Plants:			
	Closing		Contracting*	
	No.	%	No.	%
10 or less	149	13.27	5	0.35
11 - 24	309	27.52	36	2.51
25 - 99	434	38.65	255	17.78
100 - 199	145	12.91	249	17.36
200 - 499	68	6.06	423	29.49
500 - 999	15	1.34	225	15.69
1,000 - 1,999	3	0.27	154	10.74
2,000 - 4,999	0	-	55	3.84
5,000 - 9,999	0	-	29	2.02
10,000 or more	0	-	3	0.21
Total	1,123		1,434	

Source: Closure and redundancy records of the Department of Employment
*Actual size of establishment prior to making employees redundant

Table 5.6b
Employment loss: Size distribution of plant closures
and contractions in Scotland, 1968-77

| Employment size group | Employment lost by plant: | | | |
| | Closures | | Contractions | |
	No.	%	No.	%
10 or less	971	1.18	27	0.002
11 - 24	5,327	6.47	334	0.30
24 - 99	21,481	26.08	5,332	4.82
100 - 199	20,021	24.31	8,953	8.09
200 - 499	20,762	25.21	24,645	22.27
500 - 999	9,646	11.71	20,470	18.49
1,000 - 1,999	4,156	5.0	20,803	18.79
2,000 - 4,999	0	-	18,056	16.31
5,000 - 9,999	0	-	10,766	9.72
10,000 or more	0	-	1,323	1.19
Total	82,364		110,709	

Source: Closure and redundancy records of the Department
of Employment

whole company. An indication of the size of the labour force prior
to the contraction occurring is shown in Table 5.7 (see MACKAY, et
al, 1971, 372). It appears that few plants employing less than 100
employees (296 or 20.6 per cent of all plants making employees
redundant) make employees redundant due to contraction. This
situation may be the result of the inability of these smaller plants
to make employees redundant to effect savings without having a
direct impact upon the 'normal' operations of the plants. It is
therefore more likely that these smaller plants would be forced to
close in such a situation. Yet, a small, but not insignificant
number of plants were able during the period to make reductions of
35 per cent and greater in their total workforce and survive.

Even though the size distribution noted above in Table 5.7 reveals
that it is the larger plants that are making employees redundant,
the actual number of employees being made redundant is in fact small
in most cases. This would tend to indicate a marginal trimming or a
natural wastage (beyond retirement and resignations) of the labour
force rather than a series of infrequent disinvestment decisions (in
terms of labour). The introduction of the location of ultimate
ownership further subdivides the total number of plants contracting
(Tables 5.8a and 5.8b). These data indicate that there are no
significant differences between redundancy size distributions of
English and North American plants, while there would appear to be a
significant difference between the Scottish distribution and their
English and North American counterparts. The Scottish distribution
of redundancies (by size, number of employees made redundant by
plant contraction) is almost wholly concentrated in redundancies of
under 100 employees (89.63 per cent). The comparable figures for
such a concentration is lower in the case of English (73.23 per cent),
North American (70.66 per cent), and other world (78.26 per cent)
plants. However, it is important to note that over half (52.8 per
cent) of the employment shed by Scottish owned plants is also
concentrated in the under 100 employees lost category. This is in

Table 5.7

Employment size group of plants making employees redundant in Scotland, 1968 - 77.

Employment Size Group	Mean (1)	No.	%	Mean (2)	No.	%	Mean (1)/Mean (2) expressed as a %
10 or less	8	5	0.35	5	27	0.002	62.5
11 - 24	19	36	2.51	9	334	0.30	47.4
25 - 99	60	255	17.78	21	5,332	4.82	35.0
100 - 199	145	249	17.36	36	8,953	8.09	24.8
200 - 499	327	423	29.49	58	24,645	22.27	17.7
500 - 999	693	225	15.69	91	20,470	18.49	13.1
1,000 - 1,999	1,364	154	10.74	135	20,803	18.79	9.9
2,000 - 4,999	3,021	55	3.84	328	18,056	16.31	10.9
5,000 - 9,999	6,336	29	2.02	371	10,766	9.72	5.9
10,000 or more	11,073	3	0.21	441	1,323	1.19	3.9
Total		1,434*			110,709		

Source: Closure and redundancy records of the Department of Employment.

*Total labour force figures are not available for 42 plants that were responsible for making 2494 employees redundant.

Table 5.8a

Location of ultimate ownership of plants contracting in Scotland, 1968 - 77. (i) Plants.

Redundancy Size Group	Location of Ultimate control								Total	
	Scotland		England		N. America		Other World			
	No.	%	No.	%	No.	%	No.	%	No.	%
10 or less	132	14.88	21	5.30	10	5.99	1	4.35	164	11.13
11 - 24	272	30.67	74	18.69	25	14.97	5	21.74	376	25.53
25 - 99	391	44.08	195	49.24	83	49.70	12	52.17	681	46.23
100 - 199	63	7.10	56	14.14	22	13.17	3	13.04	144	9.78
200 - 499	21	2.37	37	9.34	17	10.18	2	8.69	77	5.23
500 - 999	5	0.56	10	2.53	5	2.99	0	-	20	1.36
1,000 or more	3	0.34	3	0.76	5	2.99	0	-	11	0.75
Total	887		396		167		23		1,473	

Source: Closure and redundancy records of the Department of Employment.

Table 5.8b

Location of ultimate ownership of plants contracting in Scotland, 1968 - 77: (ii) Employment.

Redundancy Size-Group	Location of Ultimate Control									
	Scotland		England		N. America		Other World		Total	
	No.	%	No.	%	No.	%	No.	%	No.	%
10 or less	992	2.14	156	0.38	72	0.31	7	0.39	1,227	1.09
11 - 24	4,732	10.23	1,299	3.15	462	1.97	90	5.12	6,583	5.84
25 - 99	18,710	40.43	10,365	25.11	4,475	19.05	679	38.62	34,229	30.34
100 - 199	8,715	18.83	7,989	19.35	3,523	14.99	417	23.72	20,644	18.29
200 - 499	6,298	13.61	10,877	26.35	5,173	22.02	565	32.14	22,913	20.31
500 - 999	3,598	7.77	6,392	15.48	3,317	14.12	0	–	13,307	11.79
1,000 or more	3,233	6.99	4,205	10.19	6,470	27.54	0	–	13,908	12.33
Total	46,278		41,283		23,494		1,758		112,813	

Source: Closure and redundancy records of the Department of Employment.

marked contrast to both the English (28.64 per cent) and North American (21.33 per cent) levels of employment lost in redundancies of 100 employees or less made by plants contracting. The figures for the Rest of the World are not fully compared because of their small relative and absolute size in terms of the number of plants involved (1.56 per cent of 1,473). One caveat must be added to the above discussion and it relates to both the number and size of redundancies made by plants over the period, 1968-77. In constructing Tables 5.8a and 5.8b the number of redundancies made by each plant in one year has been added together. Thus plants making 10 employees redundant five times in the year would be recorded as a redundancy of 50 employees and not five redundancies of 10 employees. The two distributions of these data of with and without aggregation were compared and found not to be significantly different (CROSS, 1980, 168-9). It is assumed, therefore, that the aggregation has not unduly biased the data in any way.

The reduction of the labour force at a plant varies according to the size of that labour force, the location of ultimate ownership (5), the industry, and possibly through time. Yet, irrespective of these variations, the loss of employment means a contraction in the size of that plant (in terms of employment) and a shift in the employment size distribution of the population of plants that are contracting. The two employment size distributions of the plants prior to and after contraction is shown in Table 5.9.

Table 5.9

Employment size distribution of plants contracting:
A comparison of plant sizes before and after contraction

Employment size group	Before contraction No.	%	Mean plant size	After contraction No.	%	Mean plant size
10 or less	5	0.35	8	55	3.84	6
11 - 24	36	2.51	19	65	4.53	18
25 - 99	255	17.78	60	285	19.87	58
100 - 199	249	17.36	145	252	17.57	147
200 - 499	423	29.49	327	368	25.66	322
500 - 999	225	15.69	693	202	14.09	703
1,000 - 1,999	154	10.74	1,364	129	8.99	1,356
2,000 - 4,999	55	3.84	3,021	49	3.42	2,976
5,000 - 9,999	29	2.02	6,336	26	1.81	6,166
10,000 or more	3	0.21	11,073	3	0.21	10,632
Total	1,434			1,434		

Source: Closure and redundancy records of the Department of Employment

There are several features to note from this table: first, the moderate increase in the number of plants employing less than 100 employees (7.8 per cent) and the commensurate decline of those employing more than 100 employees. And second, the negligible effect on the number of plants employing more than 2,000 employees. However, the latter feature is dependent upon the employment size groups used. It should be noted also that the increased number of

plants employing less than 100 employees has not been just a process
of plants moving downwards from the immediately preceding (and
higher) employment group, but also a movement from even higher ones
as well. If one considers those plants in the 100-199 employment
size group which on declining entered a lower employment size group,
but not necessarily the one immediately below (25-99). The
situation as shown in Table 5.10 is revealed. The 25-99 employment
size group has been further subdivided into three smaller employment
size groups to gauge the degree of spread within the whole size
group. It is evident from the table that most plants (62 per cent)
did not move far down the size group (below 75 employees), but
several did contract to end in employing less than 50 employees (14
in all). The number of plants leaving the 100-199 employment size
group is perhaps surprising given that the mean size of plants in
that size group was 145 and that the mean size of employment lost is
36 (or 24.8 per cent of the total labour force, see Table 5.7). The
importance of plant contraction in affecting the size distribution
of plants will be returned to later along with the other features of
employment loss that may influence the process of new firm formation.

Table 5.10
Plants moving down from the 100-199 employment size group

New employment size group	No.	%	No.	%
10 or less	1	1	3	0.04
11 - 24	4	4	68	0.92
25 - 49	9)	9)	318	4.28)
50 - 74	24)95	24)95	1,525	20.54)7,355 or 99.04
75 - 99	62)	62)	5,512	74.22)
Total	100		7,426	

Source: Closure and redundancy records of the Department of
         Employment

A final element of employment loss to be considered in this
section is the size distribution of plants. Several important facts
emerge from the size distribution of plants that closed over the
1968-77 period. First, the overwhelming importance of plants
employing less than 100 employees in accounting for the bulk of
closures (79.44 per cent). The concentration of closures below the
100 employees level would tend to be expected given the large number
of small plants operating at any one time is equally large (76.83
per cent BSO or 73.34 per cent Scottish Council (Development and
Industry)). If the employment size distribution of the closures is
subdivided by the location of ultimate ownership (Tables 5.11a and
5.11b) and is compared to the size distribution of plants described
earlier (Table 2.9) the only apparent significance is in the
ownership category. Further comparisons were made between the
employment size distributions of plants with their location of
ultimate ownership in either Scotland, or England. The first series
of comparisons made use of the complete size distributions i.e. all
plants identified as operating in 1977 and all plants that closed in
the 1968-77 period. Comparisons conducted on this basis revealed
that the distributions were significantly different. In a second

Table 5.11a

Location of ultimate ownership of plants closing in
Scotland, 1968 - 77: (i) plants closing.

Employment Size Group	Location of ultimate ownership								Total	
	Scotland		England		N. America		Other World			
	No.	%	No.	%	No.	%	No.	%	No.	%
10 or less	137	16.16	10	4.17	2	8.33	0	-	149	13.27
11 - 24	250	29.48	54	22.50	3	12.50	2	18.18	309	27.52
25 - 99	321	37.85	104	43.33	4	16.67	5	45.45	434	38.65
100 - 199	91	10.73	44	18.33	7	29.17	3	27.27	145	12.91
200 - 499	42	4.95	20	8.33	5	20.83	1	9.09	68	6.06
500 or more	7	0.83	8	3.33	3	12.50	0	-	18	1.61
Total	848		240		24		11		1,123	

Source: Closure and redundancy records of the Department of Employment.

Table 5.11b

Location of ultimate ownership of plants closing in
Scotland, 1968 - 77: (ii) Employment lost.

Employment Size Group	Location of ultimate ownership								Total	
	Scotland		England		N. America		Other World			
	No.	%	No.	%	No.	%	No.	%	No.	%
10 or less	882	1.76	70	0.27	19	0.38	0	-	971	1.18
11 - 24	4,302	8.61	933	3.55	57	1.15	35	2.98	5,327	6.47
25 - 99	15,661	31.34	5,314	20.25	210	4.23	296	25.17	21,481	26.08
100 - 199	12,596	25.20	6,045	23.03	1,010	20.35	370	31.46	20,021	24.31
200 - 499	12,749	25.51	5,829	22.21	1,709	34.44	475	40.39	20,762	25.21
500 or more	3,788	7.58	8,057	30.69	1,957	39.44	0	-	13,802	16.75
Total	49,978		26,248		4,962		1,176		82,364	

Source: Closure and redundancy records of the Department of Employment.

series of comparisons all of those plants employing ten or less employees in both the distributions were excluded. It was decided to exclude these small plants in order to reduce the errors that may be introduced into the analysis that arise from the near impossibility of being able to produce accurate data for these small plants. Even when this precaution was taken the comparison for distribution of English owned plants showed no change, and was still significantly different. The exclusion of the smaller plants was not expected to make any difference to the comparison of the English employment size distributions because the number of plants in this category for plants operating in 1977 (41 in all) or closing during the 1968-77 period (10 in all) was small. This situation was not however the case with the two Scottish employment size distributions. In fact, the second comparison for the Scottish distribution revealed no significant difference.

It could be concluded from these comparisons that more English owned plants employing less than 100 employees closed than would have been expected given the employment size distribution of English owned plants in 1977. One conclusion that can be drawn from the second Scottish comparison is that the employment size distribution of plants closing was as would be expected given the employment size distribution of Scottish owned plants in 1977. The reservations that must be placed on the use of these data in the above fashion are considered in Chapter Three (Table 3.3).

This section has illustrated some of the benefits of apportioning employment loss to either plant closure, or plant contraction. It was also shown through a consideration of the size of plants closing and the number of employees made redundant by plants contracting how different sized plants respond to stress. Some plants were able to shed excess employment, while others were forced to close. This picture was further complicated when the location of ultimate ownership was introduced. Overall, however, it was the size of the plant that was of overriding importance in determining whether it either closed, or contracted. Some multiplant companies were shown to have conducted drastic rationalisation programmes. And in order to understand the changes in the textiles industry, for example, it was shown that it was important to know how that industry was organised and the role of multiplant companies in the industry.

Knowledge of how many plants either closed or contracted gives some indication of how various aspects of manufacturing industry are responding to different trading conditions. The following section goes some way to explain why employment was lost i.e. why plants closed and contracted. Using both of these sections measuring and explaining employment loss, the final section considers in a slightly speculative fashion how plant closures and contractions might influence the formation of new firms. These discussions suggest several hypotheses and in Chapter Nine an attempt is made to measure some of the factors involved at the local level e.g. number of small plants closing, volume of redundancies, etc., and so further examine these hypotheses.

(b) Employment decline: An explanation

The object of this section is to give some indication of the range of possible reasons that may account for employment loss. In all, twenty seven reasons for employment loss emerged from the closures and redundancy records of the Department of Employment. The reasons used represent the ones noted on the individual forms, and do not therefore form part of any predetermined series of categories. Described first in this section are the wide range of reasons accounting for plant closures and contractions in Scotland. These reasons are shown to vary not only by plant size, but also by industry and by plant ownership. Comparisons are made with other studies in which the reasons for either plant closure or contraction have been noted. Two reasons for plants closing and contracting, merger and acquisition and rationalisation, are then further considered. These two processes are used to illustrate the potential importance of multiplant companies in the spatial restructuring of manufacturing industry in Scotland.

Despite there being twenty seven recorded reasons for employment loss, eight main ones emerge. And of these, two are of paramount importance, fall in demand and the shedding of surplus labour. Both of these reasons one would expect to vary with the buoyancy of the economy especially with respect to the contracting of plants. In fact, the yearly fluctuations in the level of employment lost due to plant contractions generally reflects the variations in the numbers of employees made redundant due to a fall in demand and, to a lesser extent, the shedding of surplus labour. However, in order to assess the relative importance of the various reasons upon different types of plants the figures detailed in Table 5.12 were further disaggregated by the location of ultimate ownership. The result of this disaggregation is shown in Tables 5.13a and 5.13b. The purpose of the disaggregation is to compare the behaviour of Scottish manufacturing plants and that of externally owned plants. While these comparisons are not wholly justified as neither all Scottish employment, nor plants are independent single plant enterprises, they do in fact form the bulk of the Scottish owned sector. This assumption appears valid as the importance of independent single plant enterprises was possibly more important during the study period than today. For example, for 1973 Firm (1975, 404, Table 5) estimated that 68.81 per cent of employment and 91.22 per cent of plants under Scottish ownership were to be found in independent single plant enterprises. The position in 1977 was somewhat different with only 58.39 per cent of employment and 79.28 per cent of plants under Scottish ownership were in independent single plant enterprises. It should be noted that although these figures are derived from the same data source they are not directly comparable. However, despite their lack of direct comparability it is tentatively assumed that they are both relatively accurate statements for their respective years, 1973 and 1977.

Based on this assumption, it is possible to pose several questions. For example: Do the reasons for employment lost by either plant closure or contraction differ between Scottish and non-Scottish owned plants? Second: Are the reasons for closure, size or industry specific? And third: Are the reasons for employment lost by plant closure similar to those noted elsewhere?

In order to compare the reasons for employment loss between Scottish and non-Scottish owned manufacturing plants Spearman's

Table 5.12

Reasons for manufacturing employment loss in Scotland, 1968 - 77.

	Reason	Employment lost by plant:		
		Contraction	Closure	Total
1.	Conc. production elsewhere	3,389 (55)[a]	9,150 (87)	12,539 (142)
2.	Fall in demand	59,200 (858)	24,335 (285)	83,535 (1,143)
3.	Conc. on fewer items	5,942 (113)	2,016 (22)	7,958 (135)
4.	Voluntary Liquidation	5,030 (10)	8,798 (126)	13,828 (136)
5.	Uneconomic production	1,914 (19)	14,862 (134)	16,776 (153)
6.	Surplus labour to requirements	26,919 (259)	4,208 (58)	31,127 (317)
7.	Introduction of a new process	2,921 (28)	0 (0)	2,921 (28)
8.	Merger/Aquisition Take-over	1,275 (23)	3,448 (46)	4,723 (69)
9.	Lack of capital	157 (7)	481 (16)	648 (23)
10.	Death of Managing Director etc.	26 (2)	567 (39)	593 (41)
11.	Redevelopment CPO.	0 (0)	975 (31)	975 (31)
12.	Act of God fire etc.	979 (13)	696 (17)	1,675 (30)
13.	Financial difficulties	1,679 (23)	2,669 (64)	4,678 (87)
14.	Site being rebuilt	75 (3)	0 (0)	75 (3)
15.	Premises unfit	13 (1)	969 (15)	982 (16)
16.	Bankrupt	0 (0)	59 (4)	59 (4)
17.	Lack of skilled labour	48 (2)	486 (12)	534 (14)
18.	Asset stripping	0 (0)	13 (1)	13 (1)
19.	Excessive transport costs	4 (1)	532 (7)	536 (8)
20.	Government action	184 (5)	459 (4)	643 (9)
21.	Excessive material costs	39 (2)	150 (4)	189 (6)
22.	Mismanagement	47 (2)	139 (3)	186 (5)
23.	Sale of premises	0 (0)	108 (3)	108 (3)
24.	Voluntary redundancies	1,084 (6)	0 (0)	1,084 (6)
25.	Lack of materials	1,227 (32)	282 (9)	1,509 (41)
26.	End of lease	16 (1)	235 (11)	251 (12)
27.	Site too isolated	0 (0)	32 (3)	32 (3)
	Totals	112,168 (1,465)	76,009 (1,001)	188,177 (2,466)[b]

Source: Closure and Redundancy Records of the Dept. of Employment.

a. Number of plants involved.
b. These data are not available in 136 cases.

Table 5.13a

Reasons for manufacturing plant contraction in Scotland, 1968 - 77: Location of ultimate ownership.

Reason	Location of Ultimate Ownership					
	Scotland	England	N. America	Other World	Total Non-Scottish	Total
1[a]	1,057 (23)[b]	1,749 (23)	347 (7)	144 (1)	2,332 (32)	3,389 (55)
2	22,946 (510)	21,672 (222)	12,964 (109)	1,331 (16)	36,254 (348)	59,200 (858)
3	3,073 (78)	2,027 (24)	626 (8)	216 (3)	2,869 (35)	5,942 (113)
4	3,707 (7)	1,323 (3)	–	–	1,323 (3)	5,030 (10)
5	633 (14)	61 (3)	1,220 (2)	–	1,281 (5)	1,914 (19)
6	8,968 (141)	12,041 (87)	5,886 (30)	24 (1)	17,951 (118)	26,919 (259)
7	557 (18)	339 (5)	2,014 (4)	–	2,353 (9)	2,921 (28)
8	674 (15)	542 (7)	59 (1)	–	601 (8)	1,275 (23)
9	157 (7)	–	–	–	–	157 (7)
10	26 (2)	–	–	–	–	26 (2)
11	–	–	–	–	–	–
12	326 (8)	447 (4)	206 (1)	–	653 (5)	979 (13)
13	1,509 (20)	156 (2)	–	14 (1)	170 (3)	1,679 (23)
14	54 (2)	21 (1)	–	–	21 (1)	75 (3)
15	13 (1)	–	–	–	–	13 (1)
16	–	–	–	–	–	–
17	–	–	19 (1)	29 (1)	48 (2)	48 (2)
18	–	–	–	–	–	–
19	4 (1)	–	–	–	–	4 (1)
20	154 (4)	30 (1)	–	–	30 (1)	184 (5)
21	39 (2)	–	–	–	–	39 (2)
22	18 (1)	–	29 (1)	–	29 (1)	47 (2)
23	–	–	–	–	–	–
24	1,026 (5)	58 (1)	–	–	58 (1)	1,084 (6)
25	511 (21)	592 (8)	124 (3)	–	716 (11)	1,227 (32)
26	–	16 (1)	–	–	16 (1)	16 (1)
27	–	–	–	–	–	–
Total	45,452 (880)	41,074 (392)	23,494 (160)	1,758 (23)	66,716 (585)	112,168 (1,465)

Source: Closure and redundancy records of the Department of Employment.
a. See Table 5.12 for reasons. b. Number of plants contracting.

103

Table 5.13b

Reasons for manufacturing plant closures in Scotland, 1968 - 77: Location of ultimate ownership.

Reason	Location of Ultimate Ownership				Total Non-Scottish	Total
	Scotland	England	N. America	Other World		
1[a]	2,697 (43)[b]	5,561 (38)	568 (4)	136 (1)	6,453 (44)	9,150 (87)
2	14,044 (199)	7,400 (76)	2,660 (6)	231 (4)	10,291 (86)	24,335 (285)
3	1,202 (18)	540 (3)	274 (1)	-	814 (4)	2,016 (22)
4	6,923 (113)	1,739 (11)	-	136 (2)	1,875 (13)	8,798 (126)
5	8,531 (97)	5,852 (34)	397 (2)	82 (1)	6,331 (37)	14,862 (134)
6	1,902 (33)	1,627 (21)	204 (3)	475 (1)	2,306 (25)	4,208 (58)
7	-	-	-	-	-	-
8	2,624 (34)	824 (12)	-	-	824 (12)	3,448 (46)
9	344 (13)	147 (3)	-	-	147 (3)	491 (16)
10	567 (39)	-	-	-	-	567 (39)
11	975 (31)	-	-	-	-	975 (31)
12	548 (14)	148 (3)	-	-	148 (3)	696 (17)
13	2,596 (55)	379 (8)	24 (1)	-	403 (9)	2,999 (64)
14	-	-	-	-	-	-
15	809 (11)	60 (2)	31 (1)	69 (1)	160 (4)	969 (15)
16	59 (4)	-	-	-	-	59 (4)
17	347 (10)	139 (2)	-	-	139 (2)	486 (12)
18	13 (1)	-	-	-	-	13 (1)
19	246 (3)	286 (4)	-	-	286 (4)	532 (77)
20	459 (4)	-	-	-	-	459 (4)
21	150 (4)	-	-	-	-	150 (4)
22	30 (2)	109 (1)	-	-	109 (1)	139 (3)
23	108 (3)	-	-	-	-	108 (3)
24	-	-	-	-	-	-
25	201 (6)	34 (2)	-	47 (1)	81 (3)	282 (9)
26	216 (9)	-	19 (2)	-	19 (2)	235 (11)
27	-	32 (3)	-	-	32 (3)	32 (3)
Total	45,591 (746)	24,877 (223)	4,177 (20)	1,176 (11)	30,418 (255)	76,009 (1,001)

Source: Closure and redundancy records of the Department of Employment.

104

coefficient of rank correlation was computed for the distributions shown in Tables 5.13a and 5.13b. In each case there was found to be no significant difference between the Scottish and non-Scottish distributions of total employment lost (r_s = 0.6963; t_{calc} = 4.85; at 0.01 level of significance), and both employment lost due to plant closures (r_s = 0.658; t_{calc} = 4.098; at 0.01 level) and plant contractions (r_s = 0.771; t_{calc} = 5.41; at 0.01 level). This is perhaps somewhat surprising given the disparity in the nature of the plants compared. The similarity is continued when the number of plants closing is ranked by the reason for closure for both Scottish and non-Scottish owned plants (r_s = 0.6661; t_{calc} = 4.189; at 0.01 level) and is found not to be significantly different. The rankings of the number of plant contractions by reason and again split by plant ownership - Scottish and non-Scottish - are suspect because of the subjectiveness of defining entries for each category. For example, should one plant making workers redundant on ten occasions be entered as ten individual instances or just one? Or, if all the redundancies occurred in the same year, what is the correct number of entries to be made? No simple answer exists to these questions, and any solution that is arrived at would be arbitrary. One solution would be not to attempt a comparison, but to indicate their similarity in terms of employment lost, and their dissimilarity in terms of the size of redundancies made (Tables 5.8a and 5.8b). If a direct comparison is made it would most probably result in revealing a similarity. The reason being that although the number of redundancies made will be less, and their size will be greater than the redundancies made by their Scottish owned counterparts the overall distribution of plant contraction decisions would be much the same. In fact, if the figures in Table 5.13b are used there is found to be no significant difference between the two distributions (r_s = 0.8382; t_{calc} = 6.874; at 0.01 level). This discussion as to either the similarities or the differences between Scottish and non-Scottish owned plants in their closure rate and associated levels of employment loss is returned to in the following section.

When the plants that closed are classified by the reason for closure, and then expressed by their respective employment size groups, two distinct populations emerge (Table 5.14). First, there are those plants that employed less than 200 employees at closure, and whose reasons for closure ranged over all of the twenty seven reasons. The vast majority of plants in the latter category were in fact concentrated in only six reasons (638 or 69.35 per cent of plants employing less than 200 employees). While the second population of plants, those employing 200 or more employees, are almost exclusively restricted to the same six reasons (74 or 91.36 per cent of plants employing 200 or more employees). These distributions would tend to suggest that the larger the plant, and hence its likelihood to be part of a multiplant company, the lower the probability that the plant would close due to 'freak events' e.g. the death or retirement of the managing director, lack of capital etc. However, it should be remembered that the closure of a plant is rarely due to a single reason, but is the outcome of a series of interrelated events. For example, the closure of a plant due to uneconomic production might be the result of decreased demand such that the relative running costs increase and make production uneconomic. Furthermore, this situation may lead to the axeing of a production line, and the shedding of the resulting surplus labour.

Table 5.14

Reasons for, and the size distribution of, manufacturing
plants closing in Scotland, 1968 - 77.

Reason	Employment Size-Group of Plant Closing							Total
	10 or less	11 - - 24	25 - - 99	100 - - 199	200 - - 499	500 - - 999	1,000 or more	
1	5	26	29	18	6	2	1	87
2	25	65	127	38	24	6	0	285
3	0	6	7	6	3	0	0	22
4	12	43	46	17	5	2	1	126
5	12	29	51	23	15	3	1	134
6	8	12	29	4	4	1	0	58
7	0	0	0	0	0	0	0	0
8	5	9	21	8	2	1	0	46
9	3	8	4	1	0	0	0	16
10	20	13	5	1	0	0	0	39
11	8	16	4	3	0	0	0	31
12	2	4	9	2	0	0	0	17
13	10	18	30	4	2	0	0	64
14	0	0	0	0	0	0	0	0
15	1	4	7	3	0	0	0	15
16	2	1	1	0	0	0	0	4
17	3	0	1	7	1	0	0	12
18	0	1	0	0	0	0	0	1
19	0	0	5	2	0	0	0	7
20	1	0	2	0	1	0	0	4
21	0	1	3	0	0	0	0	4
22	1	1	0	1	0	0	0	3
23	0	1	2	0	0	0	0	3
24	0	0	0	0	0	0	0	0
25	3	2	3	1	0	0	0	9
26	3	6	2	0	0	0	0	11
27	1	2	0	0	0	0	0	3
Total	125	268	388	139	63	15	3	1,001[b]

Source: Closure and redundancy records of the Department of Employment.

a. See Table 5.12 for reasons.
b. Data are not available in 125 cases.

A subsequent concentration of production of that item at another site may then occur. It is therefore evident that employment recorded as lost under one reason may in fact be the cumulative outcome of three or four reasons.

A similar situation is found with both the size of redundancies made, and the size of plants making employees redundant (Table 5.15). It was noted earlier that the size of plants making employees redundant tended to be the larger ones (e.g. 61.99 per cent employed more than 200 employees, Table 5.7), but nonetheless the overall distribution is similar to the one noted for plant closures. However, despite the concentration of plant contraction under only six reasons (91.81 per cent or 1,345 of 1,465 of all cases), the same problem arises with their interpretation, and should be considered as a possible indication of the reasons for employment·loss (see Chapter Three). It is perhaps salutary to note at this juncture that the loss of employment due to the fall in demand conceals the loss due to the failure of a single sales order in a number of cases. From the closure and redundancy records, 56 redundancy <u>decisions</u> (6.53 per cent of all redundancy decisions within the category "fall in demand", Reason No. 2, or 3.82 per cent of all decisions) were the result of single sales order failures. Even though this small number of single sales order failures only accounted for 3,357 of all jobs lost by plant employment (4,111 jobs if the 12 plant closures are also included), it is conceivable that this total was in fact greater. This is because the loss of a sales order may have caused cash flow problems for the firm, and they are commonly the cause of a firms failure (COLLINS and ROBERTS, 1977).

The overall situation is not immediately clarified by further disaggregation by industrial order. However, if the reason for employment loss is disaggregated by industrial order, and reference is made to the location of ultimate ownership the position becomes clearer. For example, if one considers instrument engineering (SIC Order 8, see Tables 5.25a and 5.25b in the next section in this Chapter), an industry that lost 3,434 jobs over the period 1968 - 77, several interesting features emerge. The number of jobs lost ·due to closures is not great in absolute terms (771), but of this total 692 employees were formerly employed by Scottish owned firms. A total far in excess (in excess by 643) of what would be estimated given the ownership structure of that order. Furthermore, those jobs lost due to financial problems (Reasons 9 and 13) were all in Scottish owned firms. It could be inferred from this that the availability of capital may be a possible problem in either setting up or continuing in business in this industry. Such a suggestion would gain general support from the survey findings presented later (Chapter Eight), and would also agree with the findings of Draheim et al (1966, 48-9). As has been stated earlier, the reasons for employment loss are only indicators, and should be treated as being suggestive rather than conclusive. It has also been noted that companies that fail due to apparent lack of capital could have in reality failed because they were unable to manage their funds - which were often sufficient - adequately (ALLSOPP, 1977; COLLINS, 1977). The implication of such variations between estimated and observed numbers of employees losing their jobs is considered in the following section in terms of its potential role in the new firm formation process.

Table 5.15

Reasons for, and the size distribution of, employees made redundant
by manufacturing plants contracting in Scotland, 1968 - 77.

Reason	10 or less	11 – – 24	25 – – 99	100 – – 199	200 – – 499	500 – – 999	1,000 or more	Total
1[a]	4	12	30	7	2	0	0	55
2	88	224	410	77	49	7	3	858
3	30	21	49	8	5	0	0	113
4	2	0	2	0	1	2	3	10
5	1	6	11	0	0	0	1	19
6	21	58	116	36	17	8	3	259
7	6	7	12	0	1	1	1	28
8	1	8	11	2	1	0	0	23
9	1	2	4	0	0	0	0	7
10	1	1	0	0	0	0	0	2
11	0	0	0	0	0	0	0	0
12	1	3	5	3	1	0	0	13
13	3	7	5	7	1	0	0	23
14	0	1	2	0	0	0	0	3
15	0	1	0	0	0	0	0	1
16	0	0	0	0	0	0	0	0
17	0	1	1	0	0	0	0	2
18	0	0	0	0	0	0	0	0
19	1	0	0	0	0	0	0	1
20	0	1	4	0	0	0	0	5
21	0	2	0	0	0	0	0	2
22	0	1	1	0	0	0	0	2
23	0	0	0	0	0	0	0	0
24	0	1	3	1	0	1	0	6
25	4	9	17	2	0	0	0	32
26	0	1	0	0	0	0	0	1
27	0	0	0	0	0	0	0	0
Total	164	367	683	143	78	19	11	1,465[b]

Source: Closure and redundancy records of the Department of Employment.

a. See Table 5.12 for reasons.
b. Data are not available in 11 cases.

The remainder of this section is devoted first to a series of comparisons with other empirical work that has considered the reasons for plant closures. While the second part considers the direct spatial implications of two processes of industrial change, acquisition activity and rationalisation, that operate at a regional and national level. This could indicate the importance of setting such processes with direct regional implications, within a national context. Both of these processes were briefly considered earlier in a Scottish context with specific reference to the activities of two firms in the textile industry.

Few studies have considered the reason for plant closure and the subsequent loss of employment, and is in fact an area seen as requiring much urgent research (WOOD, 1977). The studies that have been conducted are largely qualitative, and only three studies have presented any quantitative results. First, Lloyd and Mason (1978, 87) found that urban redevelopment in the guise of compulsory purchase orders (CPO) affected 12.93 per cent of all plants closing in Inner Manchester. This figure includes all plants closing and transferring production from Inner Manchester, and it falls to 7.26 per cent if only complete closures are considered. Plant closures due to redevelopment were all found in Glasgow City and they were all in Scottish owned plants. In all they accounted for 11.88 per cent of all plant closures and 4.67 per cent of employment lost due to plant closures. Such a finding would tend to agree with the findings of the Manchester based study that "... as a reason for closure, the direct impact of the issue of CPO is relatively small." (ibid., 87).

Second, Wedervang (1965, 175) expected an exit-rate (plant closure rate) of 2 - 3 per cent per annum due to problems of succession in small firms. All of the plants closing in Scotland due to the death or retirement of the managing director were in Scottish owned plants. This is not surprising given that such firms were both small and largely represented independent family concerns. Such closures accounted for 3.89 per cent of all plant closures in Scotland, and 5.23 per cent of closures of Scottish owned plants. One must remember with respect to the last two figures that the closures here are due to the death or retirement of the managing director (see CHURCHILL, 1955, 16), and does not therefore include all closures due to problems of succession. Furthermore, it should be noted that the closure and redundancy records from which these figures have been extracted are compiled with a plant size distribution bias in favour of the larger plants. This situation could mean that the absolute importance of plant closures due to succession might be underestimated.

Other studies have considered the succession/inheritance problem but not in relation to plant closures. Oxenfeldt (1943, 27), for example, has estimated that two out of five new enterprises are the outcome of succession. While Kaplan (1948, 56) has estimated that one third of pre-war discontinuancies were due to changes in ownership rather than being due to liquidations. Furthermore, Crum (1953, 23) has noted the data definition problems caused by successions and later notes (ibid., 121) that firms arising from successions are more successful in terms of survival rate than completely new enterprises. In a UK context, Boswell (1973, 185) has commented upon the problems of succession on the death of the owner in the light of the Bolton

Report (1971). This report noted that:

> Estate duty obviously increases the difficulty of passing on a
> family business to one's children. It may undermine the
> entrepreneur's motivation to invest and develop the business,
> particularly as he gets older and is forced to calculate the
> risks of new development against the certainty that an
> increasing proportion of any profit he makes will go to the
> Estate Duty Office. (ibid., parag. 13.69, 225).

Yet, it seems strange that the Bolton Report saw succession as being
so potentially important to small firms when Boswell (1973, 91-2)
found it only to exist, and not to be of paramount importance in
either theory or practice.

One can only conclude that the problems of succession and inheritance
are probably important, and in fact are not the preserve of small
companies (see DONALDSON, 1973, 164). The variations that exist
through time (BOSWELL, 1973, 92-3) and between countries may well
reflect the existence of different social and economic conditions.
One would therefore expect not only variations, but also fluctuations
to exist in terms of plant closures due to succession. However, what
is most remarkable is the fact that problems of family succession
exist in any form today given the supposed impact of the Companies
Acts of the mid-19th century (THOMSON, 1950, 139-40) and the almost
inexorable growth of industrial concentration (PRAIS, 1976; JEWKES,
1977).

The third, and final study of closures with which a comparison can
be made is that of Rake (1972). Rake's study (1972, 930) considered
the actions of forty four multi plant firms with their headquarters
in the East Midlands. He found that these forty four firms closed
115 plants, established another 148 and acquired a further 189. An
exact comparison can not be made because the closure of Scottish
owned plants could not be further subdivided into the closure of
independent, of branch, or of subsidiary plants. If this had been
possible it is probable that similar results to those of Rake would
have been obtained given the example of the jute industry

Table 5.16
A comparison of the reasons for branch and subsidiary plant
closure: Scotland and the East Midlands

Reason	Rake's Findings		Branch/Subsidiary Plants Closing under Non-Scottish Ownership			
			All Plants		Plants Employing 100 or more at closure	
	No.	%	No.	%	No.	%
Rationalisation	53	46	48	18.82	20	24.39
Declining Demand	25	22	86	33.73	29	35.37
Technological Obsolescence Labour Problems Lease falling due	35	30	5	1.96	1	1.22
Other	2	2	116	45.49	32	39.02
Total	115		225		82	

Source: Closure and redundancy records of the Department of Employment
        D. J. Rake (1972, 930).

noted earlier. However, Rake's results are compared above to the reasons recorded for the closure of "known" branch and subsidiary plants whose location of ultimate ownership lies outside Scotland. There appears to be little similarity between the findings of this and Rake's study (Table 5.16). The difference between the three series of figures may be a result of the sample bias existing in the Rake's study. His sample was dominated by companies operating in dyeing and finishing, other textiles and hosiery, and under-represented in other manufacturing and the engineering industry (RAKE, 1972, 138-42). There are also many other complications in comparing Rake's findings and those derived from the closure and redundancy records, and it is best to conclude that a difference exists rather than to attempt to derive any statements from the differences noted.

One main conclusion to be made from this brief comparison of studies of plant closures is that too few studies exist to allow meaningful comparisons to be made. Many of the reasons cited by the qualitative studies, most of which have concentrated upon small or small new businesses, have derived reasons that have been centred upon managerial failure (COVER, 1933; BARBEE, 1941, 20; WOODRUFF and ALEXANDER, 1958, 48). Such factors could be seen as being unique, and hence possibly random, while the reasons cited above could be interpreted as being general reasons for plant closure or contraction within which these unique reasons are subsumed (FREDLAND and MORRIS, 1976, 9). Another major conclusion is that research into plant closures in the UK is generally lacking, and where it has been considered, (e.g. GRIPAIOS, 1977a, 1977b; DENNIS, 1978), only cursory mention is made to the actual reason for the employment lost.

The final part of this section considers two processes that have resulted in the closure of plants, concentration of production at another site (rationalisation) and acquisition activity, both of which have been the subject of recent research and speculation. While it can be concluded from the foregoing consideration of both the nature and reasons for closures that "... failure is not related to location ..." (FREDLAND and MORRIS, 1976, 12), it cannot likewise be concluded that "failure" does not have locational implications. The processes noted here have direct spatial results though the forces that brought them about are invariably aspatial. Rationalisation and acquisition activity are considered together, not because they are necessarily linked, though there is a strong probability that they are, but because they have had similar spatial consequences. Furthermore, they can be considered as forces with an origin lying outside Scotland and acting to restructure a local economy. In Tables 5.17 and 5.18 the magnitude of employment loss and the number of plants involved in both of the processes under consideration are outlined.

First, in spatial terms, three cities have been "hardest hit" by these two processes, Glasgow (18 acquisition decisions and 56 rationalisation decisions causing employment loss), Edinburgh (6 and 12) and Dundee (2 and 11). These are also areas where the present levels of employment in plants that were established prior to 1900 is highest (Table 2.4). For example, 43.7 per cent of plants operating in Edinburgh City in 1977 were established either in, or before 1900, while for the remainder of the Lothian Region the level is 23.7 per cent. The respective figures for employment are, rather

Table 5.17

Impact of acquisition activity on manufacturing industry in Scotland,
1968 - 77:   A consideration by the location of ultimate ownership.

Plant Fate:	Location of Ultimate Ownership			Other World	Total
	Scotland	England	N. America		
Contraction	674 (15)*	542 (7)	59 (1)	0 (0)	1,275 (23)
Closures	2,624 (34)	824 (12)	0 (0)	0 (0)	3,448 (46)
Total	3,298 (49)	1,366 (19)	59 (1)	0 (0)	4,723 (89)

Source: Closure and redundancy records of the Department of Employment.
* Number of plants involved.

Table 5.18

Impact of rationalisation activity on manufacturing
industry in Scotland, 1968 - 77:   A consideration
by the location of ultimate ownership.

Plant Fate:	Location of ultimate ownership			Other World	Total
	Scotland	England	N. America		
Contraction	1,057 (23)*	1,749 (23)	347 (7)	144 (1)	3,389 (55)
Closures	2,697 (43)	5,561 (38)	568 (4)	136 (1)	9,150 (87)
Total	3,754 (66)	7,310 (61)	915 (11)	280 (2)	12,539 (142)

Source: Closure and redundancy records of the Department of Employment.
* Number of plants involved.

surprisingly, exactly the same. In terms of the location of ultimate
ownership a distinctive pattern exists for two of the cities, and
while the third, Dundee, is an exception, it is found that the
ownership patterns for employment in both Edinburgh and Glasgow are
dominated by both Scottish and English owned plants. The levels
being 38.8 and 56.5 per cent, and 41.2 and 54.5 per cent respectively.
The position in Dundee is more typical of the country as a whole, but
even still Scottish ownership of manufacturing employment is well
represented in the city (47.4 per cent Scottish; 21.8 per cent
English; 27.3 per cent North American). It is important to note that
Dundee received two very large North American owned plants in 1946
prior to the general build up of industry in the areas ajoining the
existing major urban centres.

Based upon these two pieces of information, and the knowledge that
a sizeable proportion of English owned manufacturing industry was
operating prior to 1900 (22.05 per cent of all plants and 38.2 per
cent of all employment), the distribution of rationalisations, in
particular, is perhaps then not surprising. Several underlying ideas
need to be clarified at this point. First, it is assumed that plant
age and technological (product and process) obsolescence are related.
There is some general support for this statement, for example, from
the work on decline of industry in the inner city areas (KEEBLE, 1976;
MASSEY and MEAGAN, 1977, 17). And this assumption can be further
extended with the introduction of the ideas of the corporate (JAMES,
1973) and product life-cycles (LEVITT, 1965). However, despite these
additions, the conclusion remains the same, that neither a plants age
or size commits it to immortality. In fact, the success and continued
survival of some old established companies could be due to their
unwitting adaption to the changing corporate environment through time
(JAMES, 1973, 74). There would appear to be no method by which firms
surviving by either positive, or passive adaption could be identified.
Yet, while acknowleging these complexities, the concepts of the
corporate and product life-cycles, and this is the second point, would
suggest that industrial investment does have a definite life-span.
Thus, unless the initial rounds of industrial investment, which were
city centred, were replaced by investment in successive rounds, the
city centres in the long term would suffer some form of decline.
Subsequent rounds of investment have in fact preferred suburban and
small town locations. The net result has been the decline of the
major cities, and the growth of the areas peripheral to the existing
urban centres and of the smaller free standing towns. This position
is further accentuated by the variations that exist in the formation
of new manufacturing enterprises between the city centre and its
suburbs, and between the urban and the rural areas. It could then be
suggested that the locational shifts in the emergence of new enterprises
is in fact a response to the locational shifts of new fixed capital
investment in manufacturing industry.

Hence, the dominant position of Scottish and English owned manufacturing industry in the inner city, and their subsequent involvement
in the two processes of interest here is not surprising given these
observations. One can only assume that the decline of the inner city
is, at least in part, a symptom of the spatial and corporate restructuring of manufacturing industry in the whole of the UK. The
influence of government measures in this restructuring process via
the IRC etc. can not be fully assessed, but it would appear that the

spatial (WOOD, 1974a, 142) and industrial (McDERMOTT, 1976, 319) structure of present day manufacturing industry in the UK has been influenced by successive regional policy measures.

The overall point being made here is that these two processes could be interpreted as being part of the spatial restructuring process operating within the whole UK economy. Its spatial expression is bound up with previous industrial investment whose response to the then regional variations in locational and industrial advantages was somewhat different from today. Consequently, one would then expect the areas dominated by an industrial structure of a previous "round" of investment to decay, and possibly be replaced by subsequent rounds of investment. If, however, subsequent rounds of investment differ in their nature to previous rounds in terms of physical and labour inputs, their location may also differ. It would appear that this has been the case within Scotland (see Tables 2.2, 2.3 and 2.4), and the patterns of industrial decay we are witnessing now is part of the continued decline of previous rounds of industrial investment. Such a situation, if the above observations are correct, would add some empirical justification to Nevin's (1966, 46) observations on the possible nature of regional economic decline.

(a) Employment Decline: A Summary

The main points are:

1. The gross loss of employment due to both plants closures and contractions exceeds net employment loss.
2. Plants whose ownership lies outside Scotland account for over 50 per cent of employment loss, of which nearly 70 per cent was due to plant contractions.
3. The large number of small plants closing i.e. employing less than 100 employees, is assumed to reflect their inability to reduce their employment size without directly affecting the viability of the firm. Larger plants it would appear possess a greater degree of flexibility in that immediate running costs may be reduced by a marginal adjustment of the labour force, while at the same time not adversely affecting the viability of the plant.
4. As a corrollary of 3, the majority of employment lost by plants contractions was the result of the actions of plants employing 500 or more employees.
5. Despite the large size of most plants making employees redundant, the size of the majority of plant contractions made is less than 100 employees. This would tend to suggest that the labour force of these larger plants is being marginally adjusted rather than being radically altered, and might therefore indicate marginal short-term cost adjustment.
6. Most of the redundancies made by non-Scottish owned plants were greater than 100 employees each time. Thus non-Scottish plants made fewer actual redundancy decisions than their Scottish owned counterparts, but they were generally larger. This situation is not surprising given the employment size distribution of both Scottish and non-Scottish owned plants. (See Table 2.9).
7. The closure of manufacturing plants directly affects the employment size group they are in at closure by reducing its population by one. Similarly, the contraction of the labour

(7. cont'd) force at a plant will also affect the employment size group the plant is in at the time of contraction. The decline of the labour force may not only lower the position of the plant within an employment size group, but it may also remove it from the size group altogether. Such a removal is not always confined to the direct transfer of the plant to the smaller, and immediately preceding employment size group. In fact, this transfer process moves plants both in to the immediately smaller employment size groups and those preceding the latter ones as well. The reverse process is also probably occurring with those that are growing (Chapter Six). Each employment size group has therefore its own components of change occurring at all times such that the total population may remain static, its members will be constantly changing.

8. Most of the plants closing that were Scottish owned employed less than 100 employees. Moreover, given the employment size distribution of Scottish owned plants and the complementary distribution of Scottish owned plants closing, it is found that there are no significant differences between the two. The conclusion being that the number and distribution of Scottish owned plants closing is as would be expected given the present (1977) employment size distribution of Scottish owned plants.

9. Of the twenty-seven different reasons recorded for the loss of employment, eight account for the bulk of employment lost by either plant closure or contraction (fall in demand; surplus labour to requirements; uneconomic production; voluntary liquidation; concentration of production elsewhere; concentrated on fewer items; merger/aquisition/takeover activity; and, financial difficulties).

10. The range of reasons accounting for employment loss by either plant closure or contraction are found not to differ significantly between the major location of ultimate ownership categories.

11. The reasons for the closure of plants employing less than 200 employees range over all of the twenty-seven reasons, but the majority are concentrated under only six of them. Those plants that employed 200 or more employees on closing are almost exclusively accounted for by the same six reasons (see No. 9.).

12. The reasons for plant closure recorded by the Department of employment are similar to those noted by other studies.

13. Both the closure and contraction of plants operating in Scotland is in part related to the changes occurring within the UK economy, and the direct action of multiplant firms. These processes were found to have had a direct spatial impact in Scotland which appears to be related to the distribution of plants both by age and by ownership. This situation was illustrated with reference to both rationalisation and acquisition activity in Scotland over the study period, 1968 - 77.

2. EMPLOYMENT DECLINE: ITS POSSIBLE ROLE IN THE NEW FIRM FOUNDER FORMATION PROCESS.

The closure and contraction of individual plants will result in varying numbers of employees being made redundant. This in itself may result in some new firms being established. However, the overall loss of employment will also affect other aspects of manufacturing industry. For example, the ownership structure of an industry may change as a result of employment loss. In turn, this may have further repercussions for, say, a single industry's organisation. In the long term, these changes may influence the emergence of the opportunities that encourage the formation of new firm founders. If the number of managerial positions, or the context of existing managerial jobs were to change as a result of shifts in the ownership structure of an industry there may be an indirect influence upon the numbers of new firms set up by employees presently employed in that industry.

There are numerous other possibilities of how the loss of employment may influence the emergence of new firm founders both locally and nationally. A closure and contraction of a plant for example, may have a severe disruptive effect upon the purchasing patterns within a key industry e.g. shipbuilding (GIBB and QUINCE, 1978). The three effects of employment decline considered here are in relation to how they might influence the new firm founder formation process: (i) ownership structure of industry; (ii) plant size distribution; and (iii) employment stability. Of key interest is how employment decline on the actual formation of new firms, or these firm's subsequent success, or failure. These three aspects are also used to highlight the interlinked nature of the components of employment change, and how they might influence one another.

(a)   The impact of employment decline on the ownership structure of manufacturing industry in Scotland and its possible role in the new firm founder formation process.

Little evidence exists to give any firm indication of the employment ownership structure of manufacturing industry in Scotland in 1968. The second half of the study period is covered by two other studies. Both of these studies have used the same data base for different years, Firn for 1973 (1975) and Campbell for 1976 (1977). Cautious use of these two earlier studies would give some indication of what changes have occurred over the last five years (1973 - 77), but offers no insight into the preceding five year period. An attempt can be made, however, to estimate the employment ownership pattern for 1968 in order to give some indication of any changes that have occurred over the last ten years, 1968 - 77. The 1968 ownership pattern can be roughly estimated by using the results of two surveys undertaken at that time. First, the results of a survey of North American owned plants operating in Scotland in 1969 are used (FORSYTH, 1972). And second, an ownership survey undertaken by the Scottish Council (Development and Industry) provides data for 1967. In fact the EEC (1975) made use of these data in order to analyse the level of foreign inward investment into Scotland.

The basic method used in constructing the 1968 ownership structure revolved around discounting the numbers of jobs gained by the opening of new plants from the 1977 employment total for each of the four ownership categories. To this total was then added the total employment lost by both plant closures and contractions (double entries being removed from the latter total). Each of the five methods are minor variants of this method. For example, methods A, B, and E all adopt the level of North American employment noted by the Scottish Council (Development and Industry) in 1967, while method C uses the employment level derived by Forsyth (1972). Other variants involved the use of the direct levels of employment lost or gained over the period such as in D, while the other methods use estimates based on the method used earlier (Table 4.5). In the case of method E, each of the plant opening components were scaled against Scotland because the employment created by non-Scottish owned plants had been understated (see Chapter Six, employment data are not available for 47 incoming plants which might have employed as many as 6,000 employees in 1977). Table 5.19 details the actual employment totals for each of the methods used and for the other ownership studies.

The resulting ownership structure is an average of each of the above methods, and should be regarded as being a rough approximation of the 1968 ownership situation. Despite the caution with which these figures should be judged, the general premise that there has been a decline in the level of manufacturing employment under Scottish ownership during the 1968 - 77 period appears valid. If the derived ownership structure is then applied to employment lost by both plant closures and contraction for each industrial order an estimate can be made of the expected employment loss given the various ownership levels of each order. Such an estimate is based on the assumption that all plants operating in any order are equally well, or badly managed as any other, and that they use the same technologies to produce the same goods. Moreover it is also assumed that all plants react in the same way to the changing economic conditions.

If the 'average' ownership structure is applied to all employment lost, it is found that Scottish owned plants would have been expected to loose 89,928 jobs. Yet, Scottish owned plants actually lost 96,256 jobs; a difference of 6,320. Two of the major other ownership categories made gains where losses were expected. The exception was in North American plants which lost 5,730 more jobs than expected. English and Rest of the World plants made gains of 7,863 and 5,098 jobs above the expected losses. A 'gain' being the difference between the observed and estimated employment losses. If less employment was lost than expected, a gain was made.

The observed and estimated employment losses calculated on the above basis are presented for each of the four ownership categories for both plant closures and contractions across each of the industrial orders (SIC 3 - 19, Tables 5.20a and 5.20b). Probably the main feature to note is the Scottish position over closures where 12,165 more jobs were lost than might have been expected. In fact, overall, Scottish owned industry did better than expected in only four orders (Orders 7, 9, 14 and 15). It should be noted that the ownership structure of 1973 is used because of the problems and errors that would have been encountered in attempting to derive a full industrial ownership structure for 1968. Furthermore, even if a structure had been derived it would have been inaccurate for each of the succeeding nine years. The inaccuracy arising from the continually changing ownership pattern due to continual expansion, contraction, opening, and closure of plants. Thus the 1973 ownership structure was chosen both for its accuracy relative to any derived structure, and as a compromise representing an 'average' position between the ownership structure of 1968 and 1977.

Table 5.19

Location of ultimate ownership of manufacturing employment in Scotland, 1968 - 77: Employment estimates.

Source/Method	Location of Ultimate Ownership				
	Scotland	England	No. American	Other World	Total
A	323,239	250,936	71,595	47,493	693,263[a]
B	347,317	250,936	71,595	23,415	693,263[a]
C	298,954	289,030	91,810	29,063	708,857[a]
D	282,318	299,570	98,929	21,260	702,077[a]
E	356,362	257,486	71,595	23,415	708,858[a]
Average	321,638	269,591	81,105	28,929	701,263
Firn for 1973	248,280	202,564	87,730	24,380	590,700[b]
Campbell for 1976	221,400	199,260	86,940	32,400	540,000[b]
This study for 1977	202,564	248,280	86,936	23,958	561,198[b]

a. Total from SCOMER and Department of Employment. b. Total from the Scottish Council (Development and Industry)

METHODS:
A. Correction estimates only: Firn (1975); SC(DI); E.E.C. (1975).
B. As above with downward estimate for other world employment total.
C. Firn (1975); Forsyth (1972) and correction as above.
D. Discounting of employment from plant openings from present ownership totals, then the employment lost by plant closures and contractions were added on. No allowance made for expansion.
E. Estimations made of employment lost by plant closing and contracting but not for employment in plants opening. SC(DI).

Table 5.20a

Estimated and observed employment losses made by the closure of manufacturing plants in Scotland, 1968 - 77: An industrial analysis.

SIC	Scotland O - E*	England O - E	N. America O - E	Other World O - E	Total Non-Scottish O - E	Total
3	- 1,504	+ 317	+ 1,032	- 15	+ 1,334	10,638
4	- 7	+ 7	-	-	+ 7	8
5	- 315	+ 223	+ 3	+ 84	+ 310	1,004
6	- 1,015	+ 943	+ 39	+ 30	+ 1,012	3,033
7	- 2,061	- 1,970	+ 3,275	+ 756	+ 2,061	16,174
8	- 643	+ 169	+ 470	-	+ 639	802
9	- 41	+ 195	- 618	+ 470	+ 796	5,305
10	- 984	+ 529	+ 318	+ 1	+ 848	2,694
11	- 289	+ 151	+ 108	+ 6	+ 265	1,409
12	- 352	+ 426	- 149	+ 74	+ 351	2,383
13	- 884	+ 476	+ 354	+ 38	+ 868	15,029
14	+ 92	- 88	-	+ 6	- 82	430
15	- 505	+ 169	+ 40	- 708	- 499	6,552
16	- 1,297	+ 278	+ 54	+ 966	+ 1,298	3,848
17	+ 81	- 68	- 5	- 8	- 81	3,285
18	- 1,795	+ 1,392	+ 274	+ 121	+ 1,787	8,058
19	- 646	+ 101	+ 375	+ 167	+ 643	1,712
Total	-12,165	+ 3,251	+ 5,570	+ 1,988	+10,809	82,364

Source: Closure and redundancy records of the Department of Employment.

*Observed - Estimated. For full table see CROSS (1980), p.219.

Table 5.20b

Estimated and observed employment losses made by the contraction of
manufacturing plants in Scotland, 1968 - 77: An industrial analysis.

| | Location of Ultimate Ownership | | | | | |
| SIC | Scotland | England | N. America | Other World | Total Non-Scottish | Total |
	O - E*	O - E	O - E	O - E	O - E	
3	− 698	+ 194	+ 746	+ 23	+ 575	7,693
4	+ 2	− 2	−	−	− 2	13
5	− 283	+ 7	+ 126	+ 64	+ 197	1,243
6	− 1,414	+ 1,242	+ 90	+ 74	+ 1,406	7,449
7	+ 5,037	− 6,102	− 502	+ 1,566	− 5,038	34,739
8	− 97	+ 355	− 272	−	+ 83	2,663
9	+ 334	+ 313	− 1,672	+ 1,028	− 331	12,877
10	− 4,928	+ 3,659	+ 625	+ 5	+ 4,289	12,620
11	− 43	+ 377	− 391	− 67	− 81	7,297
12	+ 168	+ 99	+ 14	− 281	− 168	4,467
13	− 1,292	+ 1,208	− 6	+ 80	+ 1,282	10,004
14	− 27	+ 22	−	+ 4	+ 26	140
15	+ 697	− 318	+ 170	− 474	− 622	2,956
16	− 302	− 1,199	+ 5	+ 546	− 648	2,315
17	− 87	+ 119	+ 8	− 41	+ 86	1,059
18	− 900	+ 780	+ 98	+ 19	+ 879	2,885
19	− 131	− 151	+ 21	+ 256	+ 126	2,393
Total	− 3,964	+ 215	− 940	+ 2,802	+ 2,077	112,813

Source: Closure and redundancy records of the Department of Employment.
* Observed − Estimated. For full table see CROSS (1980) p.220.

The importance of the tables lies not in their recording of discrepancies between the series of estimated and observed values but in their sign, either positive or negative. The overwhelming direction of the signs for Scottish owned industry is negative which would tend to suggest that Scottish owned industry has contracted to a greater extent than would have been expected. It must be stressed that such a statement is based on a series of assumptions that immediately bias the analysis against Scottish owned industry. This bias is caused by the high proportion of Scottish owned plants employing less than 100 employees (83.3 per cent) and an equal dependence on single plant, independent companies (79.3 per cent). It could be suggested that the apparent decline of the Scottish owned sector to a greater extent than was expected is a result of both its organisation and its plant size distribution.

This situation can be partially resolved by analysing the plant size distribution of the other major ownership categories. The results of such an analasis reveal that relatively more Scottish owned plants employing more than one hundred employees closed than might have been expected. In 1977, 43.69 per cent of all plants employing one hundred or more employees were Scottish owned, yet 60.01 per cent of closures in this size category over the 1968 - 77 period were Scottish owned. This would tend to indicate that the relatively greater loss of employment by Scottish owned plants vis a vis their English or North American owned counterparts is not purely a product of the greater importance of smaller plants in Scottish owned industry. However, it should be noted also that the branch and subsidiary plants opening in Scotland over the 1966 - 1975 period did in fact have a higher closure rate than those established in other regions of the UK (HENDERSON, 1979, 13-5).

The decline of Scottish owned industry could have important implications for the formation of new firm founders. It is generally assumed that the locally owned manufacturing unit whose destiny is controlled from the plant itself, forms a more suitable incubator environment for the potential new firm founder (6). Such an assumption is based on the notion that an independent unit is integrated and possess all the facets of a larger firm, but in a much reduced form in one place. Thus, the individual employee, and potential new firm founder, employed in such independent firm, which is often small, is more likely to take risk taking decisions. Furthermore, it could also be argued that employees in these firms are more likely to have direct experience of all areas of the firm's operations than those employed in large plants. However, this assumes that idea and motivation to establish a new firm both occur while employed in the firm immediately prior to founding. The idea to establish a new firm and the various steps taken to establish it can take several months, and often much longer (DELANO et al, 1966, 112-3; WATKINS, 1976; RITCHIE et al, 1979.). The hypotheses below, therefore, do not necessarily relate to the incubation of the idea or ability to establish a new firm, but more the conditions most likely to launch an individual into self employment. Given that this might be the case, it could then be hypothesised that the declining share of total manufacturing employment in Scottish owned plants might have a detrimental effect upon the number of incubator environments for potential new firm founders. The second hypothesis is an extension of the first, and states, the closure of Scottish

owned plants will effect a specific plant size distribution. The
implication being that not only is the level of Scottish ownership
declining, but it is also declining in the incubator plant size band.
It is generally assumed to be those plants employing less than 100
employees (COLLINS, 1972, 73, used less than 11; GUDGIN, 1978, 226-7,
used less than 100) form the most likely incubators of new firm
founders.

Of course, the decline of Scottish ownership has not been confined
to the closure of small independent plants, but has also affected
the larger plants as well. The decline of Scottish ownership amongst
the larger plants due to acquisition activity may also have an
adverse affect upon new firm founder formation. Leigh and North
(1978a, 239), for example, conclude from their study of acquisition
activity that the:

> ... trend leading to the spatial concentration of ownership
> does lead to a corresponding concentration of ultimate
> control, but not necessarily to a matching centralization
> of middle-management functions.

And for Scotland noted:

> ... a high proportion of cases where the acquired firm kept
> the highest degree of managerial independence post-
> acquisition. (ibid., 239)

Of relevance to this discussion is the possible regional concentration
of control functions which over time may favour the region's which
contain the acquiring company's headquarters (THORNGREN, 1970;
TORNQVIST, 1971; GODDARD, 1973, 1978; FIRN, 1975; GODDARD and SMITH,
1978). There is the possibility therefore that a disproportionate
increase of administrative functions may occur at the headquarter
sites (TORNQVIST, 1973, 87) at the expense of the newly acquired
plants. Not only may such a situation act as a factor to increase
forced migration external to the firm because of the decreased
number of local job opportunities or er ̣urage 'promotional migration'
within the firm (GLEAVE and PALMER, 1978, 9-10). But also, it may
decrease the population containing potential (aspirant) new firm
founders. It could be tentatively concluded that the apparent
decline in the level of Scottish owned plants may have a long term
influence on the formation of new firms and their founders.

(b) The impact of employment decline on the size distribution of
     plants in Scotland and its possible role in the new firm
     founder formation process.

As employment is lost by either plant closure or contraction, the
overall size distribution of plants is affected. The net result is
the wholesale removal of some plants by closure, or the downward
movement of other plants. These changes in the size and number of
plants in turn means some workers are made redundant. The working
conditions of those remaining employed in the declining plants may
change. Three possible effects of employment decline are considered
here as it has a direct impact on the size distribution of plants,
and a possible indirect effect upon the formation of new firm
founders.

Perhaps the most immediate and dramatic impact of employment decline on the size distribution of plants is that of the wholesale removal of a plant by its closure. It was stated earlier in this chapter that the vast majority of plants that closed employed less than 100 employees, and most of these were Scottish owned. If it was possible to undertake a detailed components of change analysis for the plants in the employment size groups of less than 200 employees it would be possible to delimit the number of static (non growing) potential incubator firms. However, it is more likely that plants static in terms of numbers employed (a surrogate measure for growth) do not in fact make the "best" incubators. It is more likely that the expanding small plant will act as an incubator (JAMES, 1973). To what extent the closure of plants, especially those employing less than 200 employees, has upon the formation of new enterprises is not directly considered in this study. Nonetheless it is hypothesised that <u>where the number of smaller plants (less than 200 employees) is either decreasing or is made up of a majority of static or contracting plants, the less the likelihood that new enterprises will be formed by their employees</u>.

The second aspect is a direct extension of the above, and it concerns the number of plants contracting their labour force and hence moving down the size distribution of plants. It is hypothesised that <u>if a plant is contracting it is unlikely to provide the necessary environment for the formation of new firm founders for those employees remaining employed at the plant</u>. Again, it was shown earlier that the contraction of a plant's labour force should not be interpreted as the simple downward movement of a plant to the immediately preceding employment size group. It is possible for a plant to lose more than 30 per cent of its labour force. A plant suffering such a loss, it seems reasonable to suggest, would have to radically reorganise its operations. Such re organisation might create, under a general strategy of retrenchment, less favourable conditions for new firm founder formation. The plant has 'lost its way', and may therefore not immediately attract the more staff. In fact, the initial decline of a plant might encourage some employees to choose to leave, and to work elsewhere. These individuals may establish new firms as they are likely to be the more able and ambitious employees. However, there is little evidence to support this suggestion.

The third aspect of the changing size distribution of plants concerns the larger plants in the economy (those employing 500 or more employees). Two aspects are of interest here: first, the changing number due to plant expansion, plant contraction, etc.; and second, their changing ownership patterns. These two aspects are detailed in the table below (Table 5.21). Most of the movement in this size category has been due to both plant expansion and acquisition activity. The increase in the number of English owned plants is largely due to acquisition activity. For example, the formation of British Shipbuilders in 1977 transferred eight formerly Scottish plants employing 500 or more employees to English ownership (TRADE and INDUSTRY, 1978, 191).

The changes in the constituent members of the 500 or more employee size group and the related changes in ownership may have important consequences for the number of new enterprises being formed. The contraction of a large plant may result not only in the shedding of

123

Table 5.21

The components of ownership change amongst plants
employing 500 or more employees in Scotland, 1973 – 77.

Location of Ultimate Ownership	1973[a]	1977[b]	Net Change	Plants[c] Opening	Plants[d] Closing	Plants[e] Contracting	Other Gains
Scotland	70	59	-11	1	6	9	+ 3
England	98	115	+17	1	5	12	+33
N. America	39	45	+ 6	1	1	5	+11
Other World	14	13	- 1	1	0	0	- 2
Total	221	232	+11	4	12	26	45

Sources: a. Firn (1975, Table 4, 404).

b. Scottish Council (Development and Industry).

c. Scottish Council (Development and Industry) and surveys.

d. and e. Closure and redundancy records of the Department of Employment.

surplus labour, but also the closing of a whole product division, and hence the possible removal of skilled technical and administrative employees as well. The loss of highly skilled employees, which is generally avoided by most firms, may in some cases release employees on to the labour market with sufficient ability and desire to establish their own firm. Furthermore, the redundancy payments made to such workers, it could be assumed, would be sufficient for them to set up their own enterprises. In fact, in some cases the readily available funds may encourage some individuals to at least consider setting up their own firm. In the cases where divisions have been closed there may be an increased likelihood of partnerships or groups establishing new enterprises. However, from the data held on both closures and redundancies there is no means of distinguishing between the overall removing of surplus labour, the closing of a section, or the division of a plant. The above situation could also arise following the change in ownership through acquisition.

Further changes may also result from acquisition, and they concern the the organisation of the firm. Several questions can be posed: first, what appears to happen to the R and D facilities of a firm on acquisition? And second, in what possible ways is the organisational structure of the firm altered following acquisition activity? For example, on acquisition are the newly acquired company's R and D facilities absorbed within the new parent company? Does this then lead to the closure of the newly acquired company's R and D facilities, and then release skilled workers on to the labour market? No conclusive evidence exists to date on this topic. However, Hood and Young (1976, 285) noted the gradual build up of R and D investment in North American plants, but made no comments on the case of acquired plants. Similarly, Leigh and North (1978b) do not consider this aspect of acquisition activity, but do consider the transfer of skilled and professional job opportunities. In fact they go on to state:

> Aquisition which transferred a promising new product away
> from an acquired firm for development and production
> elsewhere is also arguably negative to the regional
> economy, representing the loss of its 'seed bed' firms
> and industries. (ibid., 174)

The extent of acquisition activity affecting the rate (number) of new enterprise formations either positively or negatively is neither known, nor will be resolved by this study, but it can still be concluded that acquisition activity could have some influence on the formation of new firm founders.

The second influence of acquisition activity would not necessarily emerge by the loss of employment at the newly acquired firm, but may exhibit itself by the more subtle changes in business style that may occur post-acquisition. Leigh and North (1978a, 238-9) provide some evidence on the shifts in managerial control and functional responsibilities, but not on the subtleties of the changing organisational structure within the newly acquired firm. However, the management of the acquired firm may not only have its own structure changed, but also it must discover its own role within the larger structure of its new parent company. It could be hypothesised that if the management of the acquired firm are subjected to new restrictions that may frustrate their ability to manage, the situation may soon arise where such pressures occur that the higher management are 'forced' to leave. One could also hypothesise that such a situation may be more frequent when the acquisition has been part of a diversification programme and so new products, production methods, and management methods are being encountered for the first time. Again this study can not fully answer these questions, but evidence is presented later (Chapter Eight) relating to this issue (Tables 8.2 and 8.4).

A final aspect concerns one of the general properties of these large plants (and firms of which most of the large plants form a part) and that is their career and management development policies. For example, if an individual's career progress within a firm is frustrated due to personal failing or those of the management review procedure; or, if an individual's job security is threatened because the firm is failing; or, if promotion is offered to an individual but requires a move to another area, the individual may be inclined to leave the firm to pursue their career either with another firm, or even by working for themselves (see HERZBERG et al, 1967, 46-9; SCOTT, 1976, 106). In a declining plant or firm it would appear a priori, reasonable to suggest that career prospects are less attractive than in a rapidly growing company. Career advancement and prospects could then be placed in a growth/decline of plant setting, or even on an old/new plant basis. It could be tentatively argued that the older firms tended to employ large numbers of manual, and often highly skilled workers and generally had a small range of job opportunities, e.g. shipbuilding, heavy engineering, etc. By contrast, in the new firms, including those entering Scotland from elsewhere, there is possibly a wider range of job opportunities. This wider range could exist both at the plant and within the whole company. The overall result may be twofold: first, labour might be attracted from the old to the new firms. And second, the desired level of career advancement of individuals may exist (SYKES et al, 1974, 9 and 46-8). Could this possible transfer of the more ambitious and motivated labour from old to new firms be harnessing local enterprise within firms established by existing companies? If this were the case, it might reduce the number of potential new firm founders available to establish new firms. In fact, it might well be the case that the infusion of new companies with a diversity of job opportunities may in the long run develop an employment skill structure more favourable to new enterprise formation, but this is, of course, open to conjecture.

It has been suggested that the closure and contraction of individual plants possibly have a direct effect upon the formation of new firm founders. These effects were shown how they could influence the employment environment of individuals, and how in turn this may encourage, or discourage these individuals to change their employment positions. Overall, it is suggested that there is a dynamic interplay between new firm formations, the closure and contraction of plants and their associated employment loss, and the intervening labour market. No matter what employment strategy an individual adopts, at some stage he will pass through the labour market which presents a series of employment options. The hypotheses presented here indicate that the employment strategy pursued by an individual is in part dependent upon the way employment was either lost, or threatened. The formation of new firms is therefore seen as a reflection of the labour market and the forces acting on that market.

(c) The impact of employment decline on the stability of employment in Scotland and its possible role in the new firm founder formation process.

The lack of employment stability may encourage individuals to set up an enterprise for themselves. However, this is unlikely given the capital and experience generally required to establish a new enterprise. Moreover, the initial development of a career is often required before one might consider working for oneself (see Chapter Eight). It could then be tentatively hypothesised that <u>in a labour market where the number of secure job opportunities are both large in number and diverse, the greater the probability of new firm founders being found.</u> The converse of this hypothesis might be usefully employed to explain the low rate (small number) of new firms established in some labour market areas in Scotland.

If, as is hypothesised above, the stability of the labour market and the rate (number) of new firm formation are related, then those features of the manufacturing environment that affect the stability of the labour market could also affect the rate (number) of new firms formed. Two features of the employment size distribution appear to be related to employment stability within a labour market. First, Gleave and Palmer (1978, 22) found that labour turnover was related to firm size (7) (MACKAY <u>et al</u>, 1971, 372 and 385) which in turn may be related to migration (GLEAVE AND CORDEY-HAYES, 1977). And second, the impact and importance of large employers in a labour market may endow that labour market with specific features beyond the situation described by Chinitz (1961). The loss of employment by a large employer could have a direct impact in terms of the reduced spending power of the community and perhaps more importantly, the level of required inputs from local industry may also fall. The downward multiplier may have a dramatic affect upon the whole labour market (RABEY, 1977).

Evidence presented above suggested that plants owned by non-Scottish based concerns tended to contract their labour forces rather than to completely close a plant. Moreover, the plants whose ownership lay outside Scotland tended to be larger than their Scottish owned counterparts and in addition to this, the number of employees made redundant tended also to be larger. It could be hypothesised that <u>due to the nature of the production techniques used in many non-Scottish owned plants and the market their products are intended for, endow their immediate labour market areas with an employment structure less stable than might be the case if they were independent plants.</u> This point should be qualified because Atkins (1973) and Clark (1976) have indicated the stability of the labour force of branch plants in comparison to the situation in their parent plants. These studies used total employment for both the parent and branch plants on a yearly basis, and were not concerned with either within-year-employment fluctuations, or labour turnover. The total employ-ment of a plant may remain static, while it has a labour turnover rate of 10-15 per cent (see BALMER, 1979). The hypothesis, therefore, is concerned not with year-on-year employment, but with the actual nature of the recruitment and the loss of labour by a plant throughout the whole year. Parsons (1972, 176-9 and 255-6) considered the impact of labour turnover on the productivity of paper and board mills and upon iron foundaries, and he found that in both cases a large proportion of the workforce had been employed for less than a year (Table 5.22). In some cases over the three year period of the firms Parsons' studied had turnover rates in excess of 50 per cent. It should be added that such turnover rates of the magnitude noted above are not uncommon (BARTHOLOMEW, 1973).

Table 5.22

Labour turnover: An example

Industry	Percentage Employed Less Than One Year			
	Mean	Median	Range	Sample Size
Paper and Board	16.3	16	7 - 28	10
Foundries	19.5	20	12 - 28	17

Source: Tables 7 - 10 and 9 - 7 in Parsons (1972, 176 and 256).

Unfortunately, comparative statistics are rare, but it could be surmised that with an increase in the skill factor of the job opportunities available the level of labour turnover will decrease. (8) The degree of gainful employment that exists in branch plants might possibly be less than is present in headquarter facilities or in plants possessing a large variety of employment opportunities, hence there would probably be a commensurate difference in the levels of labour turnover at any three of these plants. It could then be hypothesised, but not without reservation, that the level of labour turnover is related to the levels of skills required to perform a task and the likelihood of promotion to a position where such skills may be learnt. If an employment structure exists in a labour market such as to promote labour due to one of the above reasons, the level of new firm founders would be low. It is assumed therefore that to found a new enterprise a minimum degree of experience is required, and this can be obtained only by remaining in at least one occupation (especially managerial) prior to founding a firm for a number of years. Any factors affecting this later assumption will then also affect the rate (number) of new firm founders formed.

3. SUMMARY AND CONCLUSIONS

Employment lost at the local level by both plant closure and contraction does not occur in isolation. It is the response to a wide range of reasons, and is often caused by factors not directly connected with the local area, or even the immediate region. Irrespective of the cause of the employment lost, individuals are thrown out of work. And those that remain to work in the contracting plants may do so under changed operating conditions. Overall, the labour market receives a series of blows when jobs are lost.

However, the impact goes beyond the individual. It was suggested that with some forms of employment loss there are long term effects and several of these have been detailed. In each case the key area of interest was the possible impact upon the formation of new firm founders. Whilst these arguments are speculative at this stage, the general theme still remains relatively sound: the human resource base of an area is affected by the changes of individual employers.

And, if these individual changes in aggregate turn out to be an overall trend, there may be long term effects upon an area's economic vitality. Three of these long term effects were detailed here and suggest the need for a far greater scrutiny of employment loss. Perhaps in the interests of a regional economy, plants should not be allowed to close, nor should jobs be supported in failing plants. Policy responses could be couched in such a way to allow a slow rundown of a plant's labour force. These policies might include a company compensation scheme (9), or the transfer out of company ideas and employees into new firms. The rationale for such a policy stance would be the immediate social consequences of closing major plants e.g. the steelworks of Consett, Corby and Shotton would fall into this category, and the longrun economic consequences if major employers were allowed to close overnight in an area.

NOTES

1. The major exception to this statement are the studies concerned with small firms: see KAPLAN, 1943; OXENFELDT, 1948; CLARKE, 1972; and BOSWELL, 1973.
2. For example, the BL plant in the Bathgate travel-to-work area employed nearly 29 per cent of the total employed manufacturing labour force in 1976-77.
3. The information on these two companies came from personal communication with: (a) H. S. Crighton, Esq., Tay Textiles Ltd., and (b) J. Mair, Esq., Sidlaw Industries Ltd.
4. This company is a joint venture between the National Coal Board and Tilling Construction Ltd.. This and other information concerning Scottish Brick Ltd. was supplied by J. H. Press, Esq., Scottish Brick Corporation Ltd..
5. See Chapter Two for a consideration of the location of ultimate control and ownership, and this, and Chapters Seven, Eight and Nine as to how it might affect the rate (number) of new firm formations.
6. New firm founder is used in preference to entrepreneur because of the latters many meanings, and hence is open to as many interpretations (see THWAITES, 1977).
7. Firm size is defined as the proportion of an industry's labour force employed in firms with less than 100 employees.
8. Turnover rates of skilled employees are also a function of the demand for skilled labour (MACKAY et al, 1971, 170).
9. Company compensation scheme is one by which an existing firm sheds excess employees and equipment and sets up a new firm. The products of this firm are then marketed, in the initial stages, by the existing firm which set it up.

6 The Opening of New Manufacturing Plants in Scotland, 1968-77

Employment created by the opening of new plants was shown earlier (Chapter Four) to be of major importance, and in all provided 41.97 per cent or 54,138 of all new employment created (128,991) over the 1968 - 77 period. The contribution made to the latter total by 'original' or 'indigenous' enterprises is not great, in fact only 9.45 per cent or 12,194 of all new employment created came from this source. This chapter considers employment created by the opening of all new plants, and analyses the main features of these plants and their associated employment. The chapter is divided into several sections and describes the structure of these new plants with respect to three characteristics:

    (a)   source (indigenous, local branch, and non-local branch);
    (b)   size (measured in terms of employment); and
    (c)   type of activity.

Emphasis is placed on the indigenous enterprises and the descriptive analyses are used to suggest relationships and to derive hypotheses for their later consideration and testing in this, and in Chapters Eight and Nine.

1.   THE SOURCE OF NEW MANUFACTURING PLANTS IN SCOTLAND, 1968 - 77.

The opening of a manufacturing plant in a town or region may originate from a variety of sources. First, a new plant can represent the end result of an often protracted gestation period which precedes the establishment of new enterprise (1). These plants, often the product of local initiative, are termed indigenous enterprises in this study and while not being the dominant supplier of new employment, they can be seen to represent "... an area's industrial vitality and prosperity." (KEEBLE, 1976, 119-20).

   The second source of new plants are the local firms themselves. Such firms often set up branch or subsidiary plants in their immediately surrounding area, or within their local region. This source of new plants is recorded in a truncated form for this study because the branch and subsidiary plants set up by Scottish owned concerns outside Scotland are not recorded. It is probable that the number of branch or subsidiary plants set up outside Scotland is very small; during the 1945 - 65 period, for example, only 28 plants fell into this category (HOWARD, 1968, 40). Such a situation, Taylor (1975, 321) has noted, may reflect the action space of these firms, which if "... frozen at the regional scale, the information and decision spaces would probably be frozen at a local scale" and that "... such a proposition would explain the parochialism of industrial location decisions and why of 16 ironfoundries in the West Midlands conurbation that had considered setting up branch or relocating their works in 1968, 11 had considered no location away from that which they occupied in the West Midlands industrial complex." A similar line of argument could be used also to explain the low number of plants set up by Scottish based and Scottish owned firms elsewhere in the UK and recent evidence collected by McDermott (1977, 5) would tend to support such an argument.

The third, and final source of new plants is from direct investment in Scotland by companies based elsewhere within the UK or the rest of the world. This source is by far the most important for employment created by plant openings and provides nearly 70 per cent of employment from all openings (37,636 jobs). The procedure used to aportion employment to a non-Scottish source means that the totals derived from this source are not directly comparable to those obtained by Howard (1968). Several examples can be quoted to explain this variation. First, in 1956 a now large electronics firm was established in Edinburgh by two Scottish brothers, one of whom had returned from Canada to set up the enterprise. For all intents and purposes it was an indigenous enterprise, but for the Howard Report it would have been recorded as investment made from abroad. This company was subsequently taken-over by a large English electronics company and is therefore recorded for this study as an English owned enterprise (MASSEY, 1976, 20-1). Second, a firm moved from England, yet its ultimate ownership and control lay in Canada. For this study, such a plant is recorded as representing inward investment from Canada. Third, an indigenous enterprise which was set up in the Borders in 1962 and which was taken-over in 1969 by a large English electronics company is recorded as an immigrant plant. Other examples exist and there is no method of checking how many entries of this type there are in either the Howard Report or in the DTI/SDD/IDD (2) records. However, these examples do illustrate the point that industrial movement figures are not all that they appear, and while they no doubt give a good general picture, in detail they may be suspect. The records used for this third source of new employment have been augmented by the DTI/SDD/IDD records, but in all cases before a plant was included, it was cross-checked with the plant itself. The resultant series of plant is probably more accurate than single source official figures, and also more comprehensive.

It might appear arbitrary to include plants that have moved across a regional border as an opening whilst excluding those plants that have moved and crossed local and sub regional boundaries. There are two main reasons for adopting this procedure. First, plants moving across the regional border represent additions to the total stock of manufacturing plants in that region. It is also possible to derive relatively accurate statistics for such movements. Second, plants moving across local and sub regional boundaries represent both a loss and a gain at the local level i.e. the total stock of plants in the region has not been changed by its movement. On a more pragmatic note it proved impossible to derive accurate within-Scotland plant movement statistics. It was possible to derive some idea as to the level of movement, but was impossible to measure it accurately.

Furthermore, other work has been undertaken in Scotland to make up for this deficiency e.g. Scottish Development Department (1977, see Table 4.10), Henderson (1974), and Bull (1978), and even still, these studies are far from perfect (see Chapter Eight; FAGG, 1979).

Further to this discussion, it is equally arbitrary to exclude the consideration of plant expansion by the physical extension of a site and likewise the movement of productive capacity between existing sites. Both therefore cause neither a plant opening, nor a plant closure (see RAKE, 1972; NORTH, 1974; HEALEY, 1979). The three sources considered here represent a distinct part of the process of new employment creation. The rationale behind considering this single, though important source of new employment lies in its element of 'newness'. A. E. Oxenfeldt (1943, 30-1) developed a typology for classifying new firms, two of his categories are considered here, completely new enterprises and extensions. Extensions are taken to cover those firms that can be called 'extenders' and 'proliferators' (JONES, 1974, 17-21) i.e. there are those firms that extend and expand their existing facilities, and there are those that expand by the establishment of new plants. The balance between the two expansion options depends upon the importance of external economies in the operations of the firm, and is an issue that is of no concern to the discussion here (JONES, 1974, 20-1).

The concept of newness, though most applicable to completely new enterprises, can be used to cover all new plants. But it must be remembered that new enterprises differ from established firms and the branch and subsidiary plants of established firms in several major ways e.g. pricing policy, methods of production, level of investment, and the employment size. However, new plants irrespective of their source will probably have some impact upon the local or regional economy in several ways e.g. the allocation of resources, outlets for investment goods and investable funds, introduction of new products and new methods of production, intensity of competition, waste resources and also the economic and social advancement of individuals (OXENFELDT, 1943, 17-22). There is also the possibility of the interplay between both of these sources of new employment (ALEXANDER, 1973; GERMIDIS, 1977, Vols. I and II), though it is more likely that there is a lagged response in such a relationship (see Chapters Seven and Eight). The point being made here is that new plants possibly represent a major source of new industrial ideas and methods for some regional economies, and as such play a larger role in long term regional development than the existing stock of plants (see OAKEY, 1979b). Furthermore, it was shown in Chapter Four that it was probably the date of establishment (and the period of investment) that determined the subsequent components of manufacturing employment change. Hence, the key overall component in all employment change is the opening of manufacturing plants, and therefore an understanding of the present sources, sizes, types and location of new plants might allow a degree of predictive modelling of a generally qualitative nature (HAGGETT, 1972, 440-1). Thus in an attempt to understand the development of a region's economy it would appear necessary to at least enumerate one of the potentially most important factors in a regions' development, or the lack of it, the opening of new plants.

Turning from the rationale and the three sources of plant openings

of interest in this chapter, the remainder of this section outlines
the relative importance of each of these sources. In the case of
direct inward investment from abroad, the location of the source has
been further subdivided by the location of ultimate ownership and
the location of headquarter facilities (Tables 6.1 and 6.2). Table 6.1
reveals that while employment from all Scottish sources is important
(16,502 or 30.48 per cent), the bulk of employment from plant openings
has come from direct investment from abroad (37,636 or 69.52 per cent).
Of the investment coming from outside Scotland there are two major
and three minor sources. Investment from England and the USA are by
far the most important sources of inward investment accounting for
15,887 (29.33 per cent) and 14,884 (27.49 per cent) of employment
from non-Scottish plant openings respectively. The only major
discrepancy between these two major sources of investment lies in
the number of plants each of these sources accounted for, 195 came
from English sources while only 74 came from USA sources. The
three minor sources of inward investment are from France (3,208 jobs
or 5.93 per cent), from Holland (1,050 or 1.94 per cent), and from
Canada (1,039 or 1.92 per cent).

While the establishment of externally owned plants in Scotland
over the period is by far the most important supplier of new employment
it is necessary to know the possible location of control which is
often distinct from the location of ultimate ownership. The location
of control in this context is taken as the location of the headquarters
facilities whose responsibility it is to directly oversee and
administer the functions of the newly opened plant. Of course, the
nature of control at a plant and its relationship to the parent or
holding company varies between industries and from company to
company such that:

> ... definitions of the location of ultimate control obviously
> hide more than they reveal, and ultimately there is no
> alternative but to pursue more detailed studies at the company
> level. (FIRN, 1975, 400)

Hence, most of the discussion in this section refers to ownership
and not control, because control can reside at different places
within an organisation's control hierarchy. Yet, it should be
noted that the geographic dispersion of a firm's productive capabilities has necessitated the separation of a firm's production and
administrative functions (CHANDLER and REDLICH, 1961, 6). Suffice it
to say, the decision to locate a new incoming plant in Scotland
comes from outside Scotland and that the overall benefit of the
build up of such plants is open to question (CROSS, forthcoming, 1981;
STOREY and ROBINSON, 1979b).

The location of the headquarters of those externally owned plants
opening in Scotland during the 1968 - 77 period are detailed in
Table 6.2. As would be expected, the overwhelming dominance of the
South East and East Anglia is evident and within this area, London
forms the major focus. Other studies considering the location of
headquarters have noted a similar dominance of the UK corporate
hierarchy from London (BUSWELL and EVANS, 1970; EVANS, 1973; LLOYD
and DICKEN, 1977, 369; GODDARD and SMITH, 1978). Nevertheless, two
studies (GODDARD and SMITH, 1978, 1083; and LEIGH and NORTH, 1978a,
239 and 1978b, 167) suggest that due to the distance of Scottish

Table 6.1

Manufacturing employment created by the opening of new plants
in Scotland during 1968 - 77: Location of ultimate ownership

Location of Ultimate Ownership	Male	Employment	Female		Total	
Scotland (Indigenous)	7,208}[a]		4,133}		12,194 (504)[b]	
Scotland (Other)	2,363}	9,571	976}	5,109	4,308 (50)	16,502 (554)
England	9,494		5,717		15,877 (195)	
N. Ireland	83		121		204 (5)	
W. Germany	127		89		276 (5)	
France	2,798		60		3,208 (3)	
Italy	26		16		42 (1)	
Belgium	15		6		21 (1)	
Holland	411		639		1,050 (10)	
Denmark	70		92		162 (2)	
Norway	110		121		231 (6)	
Sweden	31		74		105 (2)	
Iceland	2		1		3 (1)	
Switzerland	178		35		213 (2)	
Iran	-		-		- (1)	
U.S.A.	9,444		3,814		14,884 (74)	
Canada	151		698		1,039 (9)	
Japan	16		5		21 (1)	
Australia	30		90		120˙ (1)	
Joint Ventures	26		23		179 (2)	
Totals	32,583		16,710		54,138 (875)	

Sources: Scottish Council (Development and Industry)
           Scottish Economic Planning Department/Department of Trade and
              Industry
           Survey.

a.   Employment levels in 1977.

b.   Number of plants involved.

Table 6.2

Location of head-quarters of externally owned manufacturing plants opening in Scotland during 1968 - 77.

| Location of Headquarters | Location of Ultimate Ownership | | | | Total |
	U.K.	U.S.A.	Europe	Rest of World	
Scotland	394[a] (3)[b]	177 (1)	-	-	571 (4)
Northern	313 (2)	-	-	30 (1)	343 (3)
Yorkshire & Humberside	353 (11)	514 (1)	13 (1)	19 (1)	899 (14)
North West	1,181 (16)	-	-	-	1,181 (16)
W. Midlands	161 (14)	29 (1)	-	-	190 (15)
E. Midlands	699 (9)	20 (1)	-	-	719 (10)
South East & East Anglia	6,899 (83)	3,851 (26)	2,729 (6)	-	13,479 (115)
South West	847 (6)	-	-	-	847 (6)
Wales	35 (1)	- -	-	-	35 (1)
N. Ireland	2 (2)	-	-	-	2 (2)
Totals	10,884 (147)	4,591 (30)	2,742 (7)	49 (2)	18,266 (186)
Totals not applicable[c]	5,197 (53)	10,293 (44)	2,569 (26)	1,131 (10)	19,190 (133)
Grand Total[d]	16,081 (200)	14,884 (74)	5,311 (33)	1,180 (12)	37,456 (319)

Sources: Scottish Council (Development and Industry), Survey.

a. Employment totals at 1977.   b. Number of plants involved.   c. Categories used in this table not applicable.

d. Excludes two joint ventures.

owned plants from company headquarters there may be a need for these plants to maintain a higher level of autonomy. The balance between branch and semi-autonomous plants is indicated in Table 6.2 by the number of plants in the two rows of totals for those plants with and without UK headquarters. Over a quarter of the English owned plants (26.5 per cent) are in fact 'single-plant' companies despite their non-Scottish ownership. Unfortunately, a breakdown of the total population of plants into branch and subsidiary plants is not possible (for the 1973 position see FIRN, 1975, 404, Table 5), but it would appear that there has been an overall increase in the branch plant element of the externally owned sector.

In terms of employment generated by incoming plants, the bulk of direct control appears to be located outside Scotland and the most frequent location for headquarter facilities in the South East of England and more especially London. The continued build up and subsequent reliance upon employment created by inward investment is obviously disturbing in relation to the long term development of the region. It was shown in Chapter Two (Table 2.5) that the build up of the externally controlled sector in Scotland is mainly a post 1945 phenomena, and the question must then be raised: Is the present inflow of plants likely to continue? M. E. C. Sant (1975) studying industrial movement in the 1945 - 71 period concluded that:

> ... there seem no strong grounds for believing that
> industrial mobility will fall in the foreseeable
> future (except during short-term cyclical fluctuations)
> nor that it will increase dramatically. (ibid., 183)

If the inflow of plants was to continue at the present, or a higher level and thereby match the employment requirements seen as necessary to provide full employment in Scotland (McROBBIE, 1963, 411), it might end the possibility of producing a viable and distinctly Scottish manufacturing economy (see JOHNSON and CATHCART, 1978, 6-7; and the inflow of mobile investment appears to be decreasing, CRAWFORD, 1978; NORMAN, 1978). Furthermore, the apparent increase in the number of multiplant firms (PRAIS, 1976; also see JEWKES, 1977) might lead to a decrease in the number of potential firms 'able' to invest on a multi-regional basis. Thus a situation may be reached whereby multi-plant firms would tend to extend existing facilities that had formerly 'moved' into the region, and they might also increase the level of product switching amongst plants (BEHRMAN, 1969, 73). However, it could be argued that the locational trends noted earlier (Chapter Four) reflect recent past and present locational preferences, while future preferences may well be different, and radically so. The point being that the opening of new plants by a multi-plant company is a necessary, though possibly wasteful part of its growth, and that most production sites do have a limited life span (RAKE, 1972; HEALEY, 1979; Chapter Five). Despite the uncertainties of incoming plants, they continue to dominate the provision of new employment, and the period since 1945 has been one of dependence upon these plants for the creation of new employment (HOWARD, 1968, parag. 30, 8; SCOTTISH ECONOMIC BULLETIN, 1977, 15).

While incoming plants have taken most of the headlines and provided the bulk of new employment from openings, the openings of indigenous enterprises and local branch plants have also acted as important suppliers of new employment. Indigenous enterprises provided 12,194 new jobs, and local branch plants 4,308 new jobs. Neither of these totals are large in comparison to the 37,636 new jobs created by incoming plants, but in many cases they represent the product of 'within' region initiative and enterprise. In several respects, employment from these two sources, local branch plants and indigenous enterprises, could be seen as representing what new employment might have been created in the absence of incoming plants. Such a statement would tend to deny the existence of secondary or multiplier effects of incoming plants, the extent of which has not been fully explored apart from a few linkage (JAMES, 1964; MOSELEY and TOWNROE, 1973; STEWART, 1973; LEVER, 1974) and employment impact studies (SALT, 1967; GRIME and STARKIE, 1968; JONES, 1968). The relationship between incoming plants either within this (1968-77), or an earlier period with the emergence of new enterprises must not be ruled out as a possibility as well (Chapter Eight). While the number of branch plants established by Scottish owned firms appears very small in comparison with, say, the East Midlands where Gudgin (1978, 58 and 61) found that local firms established 434 branch plants over the 1947-67 period. This apparently low number of branch plants is also reflected in the plant types noted by Firn (1975, 404, Table 5) where the vast majority of Scottish owned plants were single-plant companies (91.22 per cent in 1973, and 83.33 per cent in 1977).

In summary, the new employment outlined in this section has arisen from three sources each of which has been the product of different factors. First, the expansion and possible diversification of both local and non-local firms, and second, the creation of completely new enterprises. The expansion of non-local firms has resulted in this instance in the locating of branch and subsidiary plants in Scotland mainly concerned with market and labour considerations (FORSYTH, 1972; BLACKBOURN, 1974, 263; SCOTTISH DEVELOPMENT AGENCY, 1979, 31 and 33). Branch and subsidiary plants established by local firms again represents expansion (KEEBLE, 1971, 29), but of the local stock and as such denotes retained expansion i.e. has not led to the setting-up of branch plants outside Scotland. The final source, that of new enterprises, is a product of a whole gammut of factors covering a broad spectrum of variables and these are discussed in this and the remaining chapters.

2. THE SIZE OF NEW MANUFACTURING PLANTS IN SCOTLAND, 1968-77.

This section divides into two sections. The first considers the size of plants opening and is itself split into two sections that examine the two distinct populations of plant openings, new indigenous enterprises and other plant openings (local and non-local branch and subsidiary plants). The second details the size of new plants in 1977 by employment, and their rate of growth by employment within each employment size-group and industry.

(a) The initial size of new indigenous enterprises in Scotland, 1968-77.

As one would expect, new indigenous enterprises usually start as very small concerns employing less than ten employees. It must be remembered that this size of entry must be seen within its historic context. Firms establishing in the 19th and early 20th Centuries tended to be larger than today (OXENFELDT, 1943; THOMSON, 1950, 139-40; DAHMEN, 1970, 13-23; TRADE and INDUSTRY, 1978, 622). There are two main ways of considering completely new enterprises and their initial size. One is in relation to factors of supply (availability of capital and the associated features of the enterprise's founder(s)). The second concerns the nature of competition in the whole of manufacturing industry, and also within each industrial order. Of course, it is unreal to separate both of these approaches as they come to much the same conclusions.

The environment into which a new enterprise emerges might act to fashion the size and subsequent success of that enterprise. Each industry represents a complex collection of competing and complementary firms, and the emergence of a new enterprise will in part affect this situation. The new enterprise will complement some firms and directly compete with others. There is then the possibility that the existing stock of firms into which the new enterprise emerges would react to the new competitor by maintaining a fixed level of output, a position expected by the new enterprise (Sylos's Postulate, see MODIGLIANI, 1958, 217). Thus, the entry of a new enterprise would increase the total capacity for the product and hence reduce prices. The new enterprise would therefore proceed if, and only if, the post-entry price was to exceed the average cost of production:

> ... and this permits established firms to hold their price
> above their average cost by an amount equal to the fall in
> price which potential entrants expect to result from the
> introduction of additional capacity. (CURWEN, 1976, 74-5).

Other actions and opinions exist on this topic (WILLIAMSON, 1963; STIGLER, 1966; SHERMAN and WILLETT, 1967; PASHIGAN, 1968). However, Wenders (1971, 18) noted after redefining the limit price that:

> If there is any kind of collusion going in the industry,
> the most profitable reaction for the established firms is to
> contract or expand output depending on the situation. It
> is never profitable for them to follow Sylos's Postulate and
> do nothing.

Thus allied to the economies of scale, the potential changes in prices might affect the minimum efficient scale at which a new enterprise may enter the industry, and thereby retard entry. Yet, despite the absolute and industry specific economies of scale (STIGLER, 1966, 220), many new firms enter most industries each year and large numbers of 'small' firms (employing less than 200 employees) persist from year-to-year (STEINDL, 1945; NORCLIFFE, 1970, 2.19). It would appear that at any given time there is a finite population of competing firms that can exist in any one industry and that the highly skewed distribution of plants reflects variations in the types of production used and markets served. Furthermore, the objectives of establishing a new enterprise vary from founder to founder and are often redefined after being established and having experienced business life for a number of months.

It is not surprising to note that although the industry as an aggregate may react by changing prices to maintain a fixed market price, it is unlikely that such price changes are seen as impeding entry in any way (see BAIN, 1966, 21-2 for three types of impeded entry). Moreover, as Kinnard and Malinowski (1959) point out:

> The business man thinks in terms of the local community or at most the local metropolitan area. It is this level at which decisions to enter into business are made and at which the efforts and representations of industrial development commissions bear fruit. For most small businesses, this is also the limit of their market, both for products and labour. (ibid., 6)

The entry of an enterprise into an industry is often a protracted affair starting in the classical 'garden shed' (EDWARDS and TOWNSEND, 1964) on a part-time basis and operating with minimal capital. Many new enterprises might therefore fail to be recorded such that the ones that are recorded may represent partially successful firms i.e. they have succeeded in employing at least one full-time employee. Already then, many new enterprises may have failed before being recorded. Furthermore, from the situation described in the West Midlands (WRIGHT, 1866, 454 quoted in WISE, 1949, 62; BEESLEY, 1955, 49) it could be inferred that many small enterprises emerge only when work is available and are intermittent sources of income for their owners.

The point being made here is that the general approach offered by the economist to the entry of new enterprises is largely unrealistic in terms of the new enterprise itself and its environment. Furthermore, the assumption, as with much of theoretical economics,

> ... that life takes place on the head of a pin should be regarded as one of its less convincing abstractions. (MASSEY, 1974, 17)

By introducing space and the probability of the non-profit maximising nature of many new enterprises, the importance of long-run average cost curves and minimum efficient scale decrease in importance. And, the assumption that a new enterprise initially manufactures a product, which is often not the case, and that the costs of production are uniform or at least similar, would appear illfounded. The real costs of production are learnt with experience.

In summary, the above discussion has attempted to indicate that there are a variety of reasons why new enterprises start operations on a small scale and one must keep in mind the newly acquired life-style element of the founder. Michael Scott (1976; 1978, 10-11), for example, found that the need for independence was evident in over half of the new firm founders interviewed (also see McCLELLAND, 1961; and SCHATZ, 1971, for a critique) and that sociological and psychological reasons should be given, perhaps not equal, but at least greater acknowledgement than has hitherto been the case by both economists and industrial geographers.

The initial sizes of plants opening in Scotland over the period 1968-77 can be plotted in log-probability form. If the distribution were lognormal it would appear as a straight line. By plotting the numbers employed at opening (size) against the frequency of occurrence (probability, both logged) one can derive two useful measures relating to the initial distribution (see CROSS, 1980, 257-59).

> The first is that the geometric mean (approximating to both
> the median and mode of the distribution) can be read immediately
> by tracing across from the 50 per cent point on the vertical
> axis, to the line on the graph, and then down to the horizontal
> axis.   ... This measure of the average is much more useful
> than the arithmetic mean which, in such cases, is strongly
> influenced by the few largest firms (3). The other useful
> feature is that the variance (i.e. spread) of the distribution
> is indicated by the steepness of the line. The steeper the
> line the smaller the variance. (GUDGIN, 1978, 92 and 94).

From Table 6.3 the very small size of new plants is evident. However,
reservation must be placed upon each of these mean values for three
reasons. First, the varying time periods used for each of the studies
may render the values incomparable. To assume that conditions prevailing
in Norway in the mid 1930s and 1940s and in Ontario in the early 1960s
were the same as those in Scotland in the 1970s or for the 1950s and
1960s in the East Midlands is not necessarily sound. For example,
during the 1924-61 period the mean average size of manufacturing
plants (excluding textiles and mining) increased from 87.5 to 149.0
employed persons for plants employing more than 10 persons (CHISHOLM,
1962, 170). It is possible, therefore, that during the same time
period the size of new plants has also changed.

Table 6.3

Comparisons of initial employment size (geometric mean) of new
plants opening in Scotland during the 1968 - 77 period
compared with other studies.

Area Covered	Period	Establishment Type	Geometric Mean	Source
Scotland	1968-77	New Indigenous Enterprises [a]	2.7	
Scotland	1968-77	New Indigenous Enterprises [b]	5.0	This Study
Scotland	1968-77	New Branch and Subsidiary Plants	43.7	
Leicestershire	1947-67	New Independent Firms	3.5	Gudgin (1974, 86
East Midlands	1947-67	New Independent Firms	5.5	1978, 94 and 96)
Ontario	1961-65	All New Plants	6.0	Collins (1972, 68)
Norway	1930-37	All New Plants	4.4	Wedervang (1965, 200)

a.   Survey of indigenous enterprises, n = 191.
b.   Survey of (part) all new plants, n = 396.

Second, the definition used for either an entry or opening are
different in each of the studies. This study is able to split all
openings into two source categories as discussed earlier in this
chapter. Most other studies have not, or have not been able to do

this; both Collins (1972) and Wedervang (1965) used an all embracing definition covering all plants opening during their respective study periods. Gudgin's (1974, 1978) study rests somewhere between these two extreme positions and his definition of new firms covers two main types of origin: "... establishment by individuals; and establishment as a subsidiary by an existing firm or consortium of firms." (ibid, 1978, 141). It is likely that the inclusion of plants that are not founder-based would tend to inflate the mean size of plants (however expressed) opening (COLLINS, 1972, 67-8 and 90; GUDGIN, 1978 94). The effect of including branch and subsidiary plants of non-local firms on the mean size of all openings can be gauged by considering the mean employment size of migrant plants. During the 1966-71 period the minimum mean size of a migrant plant was 61 while the maximum was 175 (short and long-distance migrant plants respectively, KEEBLE, 1976, 138, Table 6.4). It is easy to imagine the effect of including several such plants upon the mean size of completely new enterprises.

Finally, the third major problem of comparing these four studies is the data bases used in each instance. The most complete data set was used by Collins (1972), but even his analyses excluded the very smallest plants (less than 2 employees). F. Wedervang (1965, 21) included all firms exploying 6 or more employees. The use of Factory Inspectorate records (now the Health and Safety Executive) by Gudgin (1974, 1978, 94) introduces several problems in that they only refer to operatives and also the first employment figure recorded could often be for several years after the actual plant opening (GUDGIN, 1974, 528; 1978, 94 and 312-13; also see NORCLIFFE, 1970, Appendix 5; LLOYD and MASON, 1976). However, it should be noted that the deficiencies in Gudgin's data were decreased by the execution of a large (1,250) questionnaire survey. The present study, whilst not using a comprehensive data base, does not suffer from the temporal or definitional problems of the other studies and what is more, the survey method used represents the 'best' available data source.

Despite these problems, the geometric mean size of all the studies are remarkably similar. This is especially so considering the possible distorting effect of including local and non-local branch and subsidiary plants in the analysis for Scotland. The probably explanation of why the mean (geometric) initial employment sizes are comparable despite the inclusion of branch and subsidiary plants by other studies is because the other studies, notably Collins (1972), were using near complete data sets. An effect of using a complete data set would be to increase the number of new, very small indigenous plants and thereby dilute the distorting affect of including branch plants. It was therefore all the more important for this study to be able to distinguish between the various sources of new plants because a complete data set was not available (Chapter Three).

(b) The initial size of new local and non-local branch and
     subsidiary plants (openings) in Scotland, 1968-77.

As would be expected the initial employment of either local or non-local branch and subsidiary plants and those plants relocating in Scotland are much larger than the new indigenous enterprises (Table 6.3). This expected initial employment size difference would appear to be a direct result of the expansion of existing production facilities of the parent company. It therefore represents investment with an explicit purpose and assured financial backing. The various facets of the decision making process and the factors considered in making a locational decision have been studied elsewhere (TOWNROE, 1971; GREEN, 1974; NORTH, 1974; COOPER, 1975). These studies have revealed that the three main factors in locating industry <u>during their respective study periods</u> were the availability of land (sites), of labour, and of government grants. A recent survey by Northcott (1977) confirms the findings of these earlier studies and presents data which suggests that government grants have encouraged an increase in the capital intensity of investment (see CHISHOLM, 1970; BROWN, 1972, 313). And another recent study (TOWNSEND et al, 1978, 1,359) notes that associate with the newness of these branch and subsidiary plants is a "... lack of apprenticeship schemes and openings for juveniles."

The nature of the branch and subsidiary plant opening, irrespective of their source, is in direct contrast with their indigenous counterparts. Both the indigenous and branch/subsidiary populations of new plants represent the outcome of two largely different sets of circumstances and are often set up with completely different goals in mind. Furthermore, a 'positive' location decision has been made on the part of the branch plant, while the location of an indigenous enterprise is invariably the subject of only a passive location decision. While both types of plant, indigenous and branch/subsidiary, may be the product of different circumstances, they belong to the same population of manufacturing plants and are subject to potentially similar operating conditions. Other differences are noted below in discussing other features of new plants.

(c) The present size of new indigenous enterprises in Scotland, 1968-77.

In considering the present size of new indigenous enterprises one measure is used, total employment. The rate of employment change (increase or decrease) is also examined by means of three formulae. While they all measure the same phenomena, the rate or degree of employment change, the second and third measures offers a refinement of the first.

The two most usual approaches used to consider employment size distributions are the allocation of each plant to a series of employment size categories. And second, the cumulative frequencies of employment and size plotted as Lorenz curves. (see CROSS, 1980, 266-271) A Lorenz curve is constructed by plotting of the cumulative percentage of plants (x-axis, abscissa), starting at the smallest employment, against the associated cumulative percentage of employment (y-axis, ordinate). The distribution produced by plotting either employment or turnover is highly skewed, and reveals a concentration of both employment and turnover in only a few plants. For example, there are 22 indigenous enterprises employing 100 or more employees accounting for only 4.37 per cent of all indigenous establishments, but at the same time account for 29.98 per cent of the total employment (Table 6.4). And so, even at this early stage the distinct concentration of employment in only a few plants emerges. It is therefore evident that quite a few of the indigenous enterprises established during the ten year period (1968-77) experienced rapid growth rates, whilst the vast majority have remained very small,

Table 6.4

Employment size-group in 1977 of new independent manufacturing
companies (NIMCs) and new manufacturing units (NMUs) set-up in
Scotland during the 1968 - 77 period.

Employment Size-Group	Plants				Employment			
	NIMCs	%	NMUs	%	NIMCs	%	NMUs	%
10 or less	220	43.65	83	22.37	1,208	9.91	235	5.6
11 - 24	153	30.36	62	16.71	2,607	21.38	1,049	2.5
25 - 99	109	21.63	126	33.96	4,723	38.73	6,719	16.02
100 - 199	17	3.37	45	12.13	2,093	17.16	5,912	14.09
200 - 499	4	0.79	38	10.24	993	8.14	11,859	27.63
500 - 999	1	0.19	12	3.23	570	4.67	7,769	18.52
1,000 or more	-	-	5	1.35	-	-	8,401	20.03
Totals	504[a]		371[b]		12,194		41,944	

Sources: Scottish Council (Development and Industry)
Department of Employment
Survey.

a.   These data are not available in 5 cases

b.   These data are not available in 47 cases.

e.g. 74 per cent of new enterprises employed 24 or less employees at
the end of the period. The remainder of this section considers this
rate of growth in greater depth, but the initial discussion centres
on the more wide ranging aspects of plant growth.

The Law of Proportionate Growth or Gibrat's Law (1931) concerns the
process of firm (plants) growth.

> According to this law, the probability of a given proportionate
> change in size during a specified period is the same for all
> firms in a given industry - regardless of their size at the
> beginning of the period. For example, a firm with sales of
> $100 million is as likely to double in size during a given
> period as a firm with sales of $100 thousand. (MANSFIELD,
> 1962, 1,030-1)

Even though this law forms an integral part of many models formulated
to explain the shape of the size distribution of firms, few studies
appear to have provided any empirical verification to support it. In
the study by Singh and Whittington (1968, 92) it was found that "...
both the mean and dispersion of growth rates are independent of the
size of the firm" but did not find any support for the dispersion of
growth rates being the same for all size-classes of firms. It should
be remembered though that this study was restricted to only four
industrial orders (Shipbuilding, Non-electrical engineering, Food,
and Clothing and Footwear) and only used data from public companies
quoted on the UK stock exchange (ibid., 19). Similarly, Mansfield's
study (1962) was also restricted to four industrial orders (Steel,
Petroleum, Tyres, and Automobiles) and, perhaps more importantly,
derived his data from a series of directories (ibid., 1,044-5). This
though does not reduce the utility of his study as directories have
been used in both England (e.g. TAYLOR, 1970) and the USA (e.g. LEONE,
1971; STRUYK and JAMES, 1975) and have been shown to be accurate.

Further problems also exist. Not only do many studies use different
forms of data relating to either firms or plants, but they also
calculate the size or class of growth differently. Perhaps more
important than these problems is the fact that the discussion here
relates to new indigenous enterprises and the growth of local and non-
local branch plants. This population may possess distinct characteristics in terms of the rate of growth. It is however probably more
satisfactory to isolate this population of new plants from the
permanent stock of plants as was done by Collins (1972). Yet, the
removal of the very recent additions and the calculation of growth
rates for the remaining plants, those existing throughout the study
period, is somewhat arbitrary. The problem arises from the inclusion
of plants opening in the years just prior to the study period. For
example, it was shown in Chapter Four (see Map 4.8) that those areas
receiving immigrant plants in the years immediately prior to 1968 gained
most of their new employment opportunities from the expansion of these
very same plants. The solution to this problem would be to exclude
those plants opening in, say, the preceding five year period. This
procedure would remove those plants during their period of employment
'build-up' which is experienced by most firms.

On the basis of the above it might be argued that the law of
proportionate growth might best be applied to certain subsets of the

total population of plants (other than specific industries). This is in fact in accordance with Gibrat's (1957) own ideas when he stated:

> The sphere of application cannot be limited a priori. We must always look to see if there is any chance that the law applies and then make our calculation. (ibid., 65)

In effect, then, the few studies cited above did exactly this, testing Gibrat's law on a series of data relating to the complete distribution of a population of manufacturing plants. Furthermore, similar subsets of the total number of manufacturing plants might be abstracted and tested in a similar fashion e.g. those plants operating at, or above the minimum efficient scale of production in an industry.

The remainder of this section first details the three formulae used to calculate employment growth rates, and then reports the results of applying these three formulae. The three formulae used are as follows:

$$G_1 = E_n/E_i \qquad \ldots \text{ eq. 6.1}$$

$$G_2 = E_n/E_i \times t \qquad \ldots \text{ eq. 6.2}$$

$$G_3 = E_n - E_i/E_i \times t \qquad \ldots \text{ eq. 6.3}$$

G_1 = Growth rate/Degree of employment change (in the case of G_2 and G_3 this is the rate of growth per annum).

E_n = Total employment in 1977.

E_i = Total employment at the end of the first year of operating (this then means, for example, that firms opening in January or December of the same year report their employment totals for the end of the same year).

t = Length of time the plant has been operating (1978 minus the year of opening).

Formula (or equation) 6.1 has been used elsewhere by Wedervang (1965, 208-10) and in a slightly modified form by Collins (1970, 124; 1972, 54 (4)). The main drawback with using this formula in this instance is that the time period is variable because only a relatively small number of plants (for which data are available) opened at the beginning of the study period (51 indigenous enterprises or 12.88 per cent and, 25 or 14.71 per cent of the branch plants). This was not a problem with the two studies previously cited as they were considering the growth of plants present throughout the whole period of their respective studies.

The second formula (eq. 6.2) introduces the element of time (annual rates of growth), but does not allow for distortions that may be introduced by the growth of the very smallest plants. This equation was used by Gudgin (1974, 202; 1978, 160) and he noted two distinct advantages in its use. First, the Factory Inspectorate records used in his study are collected by visits to plants once every 4-5 years and so the difference between initial and final employment could

145

vary from a minimum of twelve years to a maximum of twenty-eight years. The subsequent discounting of initial from final employment would then lead to inexact measures of employment for various time periods. Second, this measure of growth "... tends to a lower limit of zero, and thus has the further advantage of allowing logarithms to be taken without prior transformation to avoid negative values." (ibid., 1974, 202)

An extension of the second formula by the inclusion of the initial employment to derive a measure of the actual employment gained by the plant over the period of operating yields a measure of the rate of employment growth (eq. 6.3). In fact, the difference between the first two formulae (eqs. 6.1 and 6.2) are marginal as the only change that occurs is that the former formula is divided by the number of years the plant has been operating. Furthermore, both these formulae do not measure growth rates but merely the amount the employment at a plant has increased. The results from both these formula are therefore difficult to interpret. None of these problems occur when the third formula (eq. 6.3) is used and what is more, the measure produced by the third formula is easy to interpret and actually measures the annual increase in the numbers employed assuming a simple growth rate. A simple growth rate is one in which the rate of growth and hence increase in employment always refers back to the original level of employment. For example, if an enterprise employs 3 employees at opening and 10 employees after ten years the increase in employment is seven. Thus every year the increase is 0.7 employees or 23 per cent of 3, the initial employment i.e.

Year:	1	2	3	.	.	.	.	.	10
Employment:	3	3.7	4.4	.	.	.	.	.	10

If a compound growth rate was used the subsequent gains in employment each year would be taken into consideration in calculating the subsequen annual employment totals. Thus, in the example given above 23 per cent of 3.7 would be calculated rather than 23 per cent of 3 for the increase in employment between the second and third years. And as Gudgin (1974, 202) notes that the simple growth rate "... is preferred to a compound interest formulation since data is (sic.) available only at end points of long periods, and there is no reason to assume that in the short-term exponential growth is an accurate description of what occurred between the end points." This is well supported by the fact that 141 (or 24.91 per cent) of all new plants opening in the 1968-77 period employed less employees in 1977 than they had at some other times during the few years they had been operating.

Two aspects of employment growth are examined; first, the initial employment size-group to consider the relationship between initial size and growth rate; and second, the rate of employment change by each industrial order (SIC). Changes in employment size-group are also depicted by a series of matrices which describe the movement of new enterprises between each size-group.

For the purposes of the discussion in this section the median measurement of employment change is referred to. This measure is chosen in preference to the mean (average) growth rate because of the distortions extreme values have on the latter measure of employment change. Irrespective of the method used to calculate the change in employment by the initial employment size-group (Table 6.5), there is a distinct decline in the rate of growth from the largest to the smallest size-groups (see Table 6.13). Such a finding supports those of other studies that have considered the rate of growth of permanent (COLLINS, 1972, 56; GUDGIN, 1974, 192) and of all plants (WEDERVANG, 1965, 210). The complete tables for each equation with the mean growth rate, standard deviation, number of cases in each size category, as well as the median growth rate are presented elsewhere (CROSS, 1980, 630-43).

When growth rates are derived for each of the main industrial orders (Table 6.6) there appears to be a certain degree of discrepency between each of the methods used. If Spearman's rank correlation

Table 6.5

Median rates of employment change in new indigenous enterprises calculated by three different formulae for twelve employment size-groups.

Employment Size-Group	Median Employment Growth Rate Formulae					
	1		2		3	
(1) 1 - 5	4.0	(1)*	30.0	(1)	25.0	(1)
(2) 6 - 10	3.0	(3)	22.5	(2)	16.0	(2)
(3) 11 - 15	3.16	(2)	18.33	(3)	11.33	(3)
(4) 16 - 20	2.53	(4)	13.41	(4)	6.75	(4)
(5) 21 - 30	1.67	(7)	11.88	(6)	3.67	(7)
(6) 31 - 40	1.81	(5)	12.31	(5)	5.0	(5)
(7) 41 - 50	1.75	(6)	9.9	(8)	3.75	(6)
(8) 51 - 70	1.0	(11)	6.48	(10)	0.0	(11)
(9) 71 - 100	1.22	(9)	6.12	(11)	0.52	(9)
(10) 101 - 150	1.39	(8)	10.7	(7)	2.7	(8)
(11) 151 - 250	0.74	(12)	6.06	(12)	-1.44	(12)
(12) 251 +	1.05	(10)	7.36	(9)	0.36	(10)
	2.22		13.31		6.73	

* Rank position.

coefficients are computed to assess the degree of similarity between the three series of measures it is found they do not in fact appear to differ greatly. The series of rank correlation coefficients are listed in Table 6.7. In calculating these values allowance is not made for tied values. . Though Siegal (1956, 210) has noted that the effect of tied values tends to be relatively insignificant. However, they do tend to inflate the value of the computed r_s value. Furthermore, the test of similarity here is to help assess the level of agreement between the three measures of growth and is not intended as an exact measurement of their association.

It is also important to recognise at this stage that the three measures of growth are not measuring exactly the same aspect of growth, but only certain parts of its features. For example, formula 6.1 is merely a measure of the size of the magnitude that the present employment total (in 1977) is larger or smaller than the

Table 6.6

Median rates of employment change in new indigenous enterprises
calculated by three different formulae for each of the seventeen
major industrial orders.

Median Employment Growth Rates

S.I.C..	Formulae: 1		2		3	
3	1.89	(12)*	15.0	(6)	6.22	(10)
4	2.63	(7)	12.0	(9)	7.5	(6)
5	3.0	(2)	18.0	(3)	12.0	(3)
6	1.68	(14)	8.5	(16)	3.0	(15)
7	2.63	(7)	20.0	(2)	13.0	(2)
8	2.71	(6)	9.0	(14)	6.0	(11)
9	4.33	(1)	20.65	(1)	15.83	(1)
10	3.0	(2)	12.0	(9)	8.0	(5)
11	2.79	(5)	9.36	(11)	5.25	(12)
12	3.0	(2)	15.0	(6)	10.0	(4)
13	1.83	(13)	8.25	(17)	2.25	(17)
14	1.93	(11)	15.25	(5)	7.25	(8)
15	1.53	(15)	9.2	(13)	3.2	(14)
16	1.33	(16)	8.75	(15)	2.5	(16)
17	1.5	(17)	9.33	(12)	3.29	(13)
18	2.0	(10)	15.63	(4)	7.13	(9)
19	2.23	(9)	14.86	(8)	7.5	(6)
	2.22		13.31		6.73	

* Rank position

Table 6.7

Test of similarity between the three measures of employment
growth for each of the seventeen major industrial orders.

Measures Correlated from the 3 formulae used:	Spearman's Rank Correlation Coefficient (r_s)	Value of 't' (t)
Eq. 1 with Eq. 2	+.5662	2.6380
Eq. 2 with Eq. 3	+.8811	7.2151
Eq. 1 with Eq. 3	+.7904	4.9969

Df. = 15   all significant at the 0.01 level (one tail)

employment total at the end of the first year of operating. Whereas,
formula 6.3 is a measure of employment gain per year and it expresses
this gain as a proportion of the initial employment total. The
second formula (eq. 6.2) lies somewhere between these two positions.
On reflection then, it is not surprising that the degree of
similarity between the three series of measures are not greater.

The final aspect of employment change is that of movement between
the initial employment size class, the one entered on opening, and

the present one. Table 6.8 reveals that the use of size classes, however defined (the ones used here are the same as those used by GUDGIN, 1974, 1978), will result in information being lost, but it does not mask the overwhelming direction of movement and that movement is 'up' into larger size categories i.e. across the matrix from left to right. Tables 6.9 and 6.10 detail this movement for indigenous enterprises using two final employment totals, the present one (as in 1977) and the maximum numbers employed since opening. Transition probabilities or the likelihood of a plant moving from one size class to another can be derived from these tables (CROSS, 1980, 287). If these probabilities are multiplied by a hundred, the resultant figure is the percentage of plants in that cell of the row total (see GUDGIN, 1974, 218-22, Tables B3.1 - B3.4). The main feature that makes this matrix different from those of Gudgin, Collins (1972, 59-60, Tables 4.9 - 4.12) and Wedervang (1965, 246-7, Tables X-2a and 2b) is the very small probability of a plant remaining in the size class entered at opening. However, the likelihood of an enterprise remaining in the employment size class entered at opening increases with a movement down the diagonal (top-left to bottom-right). It should be remembered that the employment ranges of the upper size classes are quite large, and hence likely to hide any employment growth. The actual shape of the distribution within the matrix is similar to those Wedervang, but this unlikely to be of any significance.

Table 6.8

The changes in total numbers employed by new indigenous enterprises considered by employment size class and actual numbers employed.

Direction of Movement	Employment Size Class[a]		Actual Employment Totals[b]	
	No.	%	No.	%
Downward (Contraction)	15	3.79	29	7.32
Static (No Change)	83	20.96	41	10.35
Upward (Expansion)	298	75.25	326	82.32
Totals	396		396	

a. Plants are allocated to a series of employment categories and are then further assigned to another three categories depending upon whether the employment at the plant had increased, decreased, or remained static since opening.

b. Plants are again allocated on the basis of employment size but not to specific employment categories. Further allocation is on the basis of any change of employment at that plant and not upon whether it has changed employment size categories.

It has shown that while most new indigenous plants start life as very small concerns, often employing ten or less employees at the end of the first year of operating (71.9 per cent), and they exhibit a high rate of employment growth. In common with other studies of employment growth of permanent plants it was found that it was the smaller plants that exhibited the greatest rates of employment growth. However, this growth in absolute numbers is relatively small and only a few new firms go on in the initial years to employ considerable

Table 6.9

1968 – 77 Structural tally matrix for new indigenous enterprises.

Initial Size[a]	1	2	3	4	5	6	7	8	9	10	11	12	13	14	15	16	17	Total
1[b]	8	5	11	4	8	5	3		1									45
2		7	9	10	8	9	5	2										51
3			12	15	20	22	9	4	2	1					1			86
4		1	2	11	11	9	14	5	1	1	2	1						58
5		1	3		14	19	12	5	4	1								59
6				1	1	4	11	10	2	2								31
7						1	8	11	8	5								33
8			1				1	1	1	1	2							11
9							1	1	6	3	2	1						14
10									1	3				1				4
11											1							2
12												2						2
13																		0
14																		0
15																		0
16																		0
17																		0
Total	8	14	38	41	62	69	64	45	26	18	5	4	0	1	1	0	0	396

Source: Survey

a. Not a fixed year of entry. Year of entry varies over the complete ten year period, 1968 – 77.

b. For clarity the employment size categories are presented here:

1 = 1; 2 = 2; 3 = 3-4; 5 = 5-7; 6 = 8-12; 7 = 13-19; 8 = 20-31; 9 = 32-49; 10 = 50-79; 11 = 80-124; 12 = 125-199; 13 = 200-315; 13 = 316-500; 14 = 501-799; 15 = 800-1,249; 16 = 1,250-1,999; 17 = 2,000+ (GUDGIN, 1978, 164).

Table 6.10

1968 – 77 Structural tally matrix for new indigenous enterprises

Initial Size [a]	Maximum size attained during the 1968 – 77 period																	Total
	1	2	3	4	5	6	7	8	9	10	11	12	13	14	15	16	17	
1 [b]	7	5	11	4	8	5	4		1									45
2		7	9	8	9	10	4	3			1							51
3			10	15	19	22	12	4	2	1					1			86
4				12	8	11	15	3	5	1	2	1						58
5					14	21	13	6	4	1								59
6						5	11	10	2	3								31
7							7	12	7	7								33
8								7	2	2								11
9									7	3	3	1						14
10										3				1				4
11											2							2
12													2					2
13																		0
14																		0
15																		0
16																		0
17																		0
Total	7	12	30	39	58	74	66	45	30	21	8	2	2	1	1	0	0	396

Source: Survey

a. Not a fixed year of entry. Year of entry varies over the complete ten year period, 1968 – 77.
b. For employment size-groups see Table 6.9.

numbers of employees. Three industrial orders, on which nearly all the measures of growth agreed, chemicals and allied industries (order 5), mechanical engineering (Order 7), and electrical engineering (Order 9) revealed the greatest rates of employment growth. Enterprises entering the latter orders tended to be relatively small. While those enterprises entering the food, drink and tobacco (Order 3), the instrument engineering (Order 8), and the textiles (Order 13) industries had slow growth rates and tended to be entered by larger plants. Though this feature was not explicitly considered in this section, it is further explored later in this chapter. Further to these aspects of new indigenous enterprises, the resultant employment size distribution after only a few years is skewed with the concentration of employment in a handful (22 in all) of seemingly 'successful' companies.

(d)   The present size of new local and non-local branch and
      subsidiary plants in Scotland, 1968-77.

While new indigenous enterprises form the main focus of the analysis, branch and subsidiary plants represent important additions to the permanent stock of plants. Also these plants offer a means of comparison and help to illustrate the differences between new indigenous enterprises and other types of new plants. And, likewise, this section covers those aspects covered in the immediately preceding one.

A largely inverse relationship between the initial employment size class and the rate of growth of branch plants appears to exist (Table 6.11). If the employment size groups are ranked from the largest to the smallest and correlated with the rates of growth ranked in a similar manner, a negative rank correlation coefficient is obtained. Table 6.12 details these results for both indigenous and branch plants. Despite the apparently higher growth rates of the small plants, the size distribution of the branch plants, measured by either employment (CROSS, 1980, 267-9) or turnover (ibid., 271) is highly skewed in favour of a few large plants.

When the rate of employment change is viewed across each of the major industrial orders (Tables 6.13 and 6.14), the fastest growing plants opened in the electrical engineering (Order 9), the vehicle (Order 11), and other manufacturing industries (Order 19). The small number of branch and subsidiary plants in the last two of these three orders though makes their position as orders containing fast growing plants rather dubious. On the other hand, the slowest growing plants were found in the instrument engineering (Order 8), the shipbuilding and marine engineering (Order 10), and the bricks, pottery, glass and cement industries (Order 16). Again, the inclusion of Order 10 is questionnable because it is based on only one observation. Perhaps of more interest is the contrast between the orders with fast and slow growing plants for both indigenous and branch plants. For example, the textiles industry contained relatively slow growing indigenous plants, while some of the fastest growing branch plants are found in this order. This contrast serves to illustrate the variations that can occur in one order and suggests that different methods of production are possibly being employed either in intensity of use, or scale of operation.

Table 6.11

Median rates of employment change in new local and non-local branch and subsidiary plants calculated by three different formulae for sixteen employment size groups.

Employment Size-Group	Median Employment Growth Rates Formulae					
	1		2		3	
1[a]	55.0	(1)[b]	275.0	(1)	270.0	(1)
2	8.0	(2)	40.0	(3)	35.0	(3)
3	5.5	(3)	42.0	(2)	36.0	(2)
4	2.07	(7)	12.35	(7)	6.78	(8)
5	2.0	(8)	12.22	(8)	7.0	(7)
6	1.5	(10)	9.38	(10)	2.75	(9)
7	2.82	(4)	17.4	(5)	8.17	(6)
8	1.67	(9)	8.7	(11)	2.51	(10)
9	1.32	(12)	8.35	(12)	1.56	(11)
10	1.04	(13)	6.22	(13)	0.23	(13)
11	2.28	(6)	20.28	(4)	11.67	(4)
12	1.37	(11)	9.84	(9)	1.37	(12)
13	0.61	(14)	4.88	(14)	-3.35	(15)
14	–		–		–	
15	2.41	(5)	16.85	(6)	9.85	(5)
16	0.54	(15)	3.23	(15)	-2.77	(14)
	1.76		11.19		5.25	

Source: Survey.

a. For employment size groups see Table 6.9.

b. Rank Position.

Table 6.12

Test of similarity between employment size class and the rate of employment growth (Change).

Growth Formula Used:	Indigenous Enterprises		Branch Plants	
	Spearman's Rank Correlation Coefficient	Value of 't'	Spearman's Rank Correlation Coefficient	Value of 't'
1	-.6964	3.4989	-.9091	6.9018
2	-.6304	3.6056	-.8986	6.4767
3	-.5492	3.2665	-.9161	7.2244
	Df. = 10		Df. = 13	

all significant at the 0.01 level (one tail)

153

Table 6.13

Median rates of employment change in new local and non-local branch and subsidiary plants calculated by three different formulae for each of the seventeen major industrial orders.

Median Employment Growth Rates
Formulae:

S.I.C.	1	2	3
3	1.46 (12)*	8.5 (11)	3.23 (9)
4	-	-	-
5	2.14 (4)	12.11 (5)	4.5 (6)
6	1.5 (11)	6.0 (13)	2.0 (12)
7	1.76 (8)	11.71 (6)	3.76 (8)
8	1.86 (5)	5.29 (14)	1.75 (13)
9	4.12 (1)	23.58 (1)	18.91 (1)
10	0.54 (15)	3.23 (15)	-2.77 (15)
11	3.14 (2)	15.71 (3)	10.71 (2)
12	1.63 (9)	9.38 (10)	2.63 (10)
13	1.85 (7)	16.4 (2)	7.4 (4)
14	-	-	-
15	1.25 (13)	9.92 (9)	2.25 (11)
16	1.04 (14)	6.76 (12)	0.4 (14)
17	1.86 (5)	11.14 (7)	5.14 (5)
18	1.58 (10)	11.09 (8)	4.09 (7)
19	2.28 (3)	15.56 (4)	7.6 (3)
	1.76	11.19	5.25

Source: Survey

* Rank position.

Table 6.14

Test of similarity between the three measures of employment growth for each of the seventeen major industrial orders

Measures Correlated from the 3 formulae used	Spearman's Rank Correlation Coefficient (r_s)	Value of 't' (t)
Eq. 1 with Eq. 2	+.7375	3.9373
Eq. 2 with Eq. 3	+.9464	3.6055
Eq. 1 with Eq. 3	+.8196	5.1575

Df. = 13   (all significant at the 0.01 level - one tail)

The final series of tables (Tables 6.16 and 6.17) show that most branch plants increased their employment since opening and have usually moved 'up' at least one employment size-group. It is also evident from the tally matrices that the dispersion of growth rates is more restricted amongst branch plants than amongst their indigenous enterprise counterparts. This difference between the two sources of new plants is to be expected given the differences in the initial mean employment size (Table 6.3), and the scales and methods of production employed.

Table 6.15

The changes in total numbers employed by new local and non-local branch and subsidiary plants considered by employment size class and actual numbers employed.

Direction of Movement	Employment Size Class[a]		Actual Employment Totals[b]	
	No.	%	No.	%
Downward (Contraction)	19	11.18	30	17.65
Static (No Change)	34	20.00	11	6.47
Upward (Expansion)	117	68.82	129	75.88
Totals	170		170	

Source: Survey
a. and b. See footnotes to Table 6.8.

In an attempt to indicate some of the present size and growth features of new branch plants, this section has illustrated the present size distribution by employment. Furthermore, it has been shown how these plants' employment levels have changed since opening and how they vary between industrial orders and initial employment size groups. Mention was also made of how these features of branch plants, size and growth, differed from indigenous enterprises. These differences can in part be attributed to industrial structure, but in the main are probably a product of their widely differing origins. The individual entrepreneur (new firm founder) has rarely got a large capital resource base to draw upon as have many of the branch and subsidiary plants. Also, the entrepreneurial decision must be considered within the personal circumstances of the entrepreneur. It is equally important to place the decision that leads to the setting up of the branch plant within the context of its parent, or even its holding company. Thus to expect that either of these populations of new plants would be similar in any respect other than describing a skewed cumulative size distribution would prove ill founded because of the widely differing origins and aspirations behind their creation (COLLINS, 1972, 72).

3. THE INDUSTRIAL TYPE OF NEW MANUFACTURING PLANTS IN SCOTLAND, 1968-77.

Here, attention is first focused on accounting for the number of plants opening and their associated levels of employment in each major

Table 6.16

1968 – 77 Structural tally matrix for local and non-local branch and subsidiary plants

Initial Size [a]	Employment Size Category in 1977																	Total
	1	2	3	4	5	6	7	8	9	10	11	12	13	14	15	16	17	
1 [b]									2									2
2				1		1		1										3
3			2	2	2	2	5	3		1		2						19
4			1	1	4	2	2	2										12
5					2	6	4	2	1	3								19
6						10	3		4		2	1	1					21
7			1		1		3	2	3	6		1	1			1		18
8							3	2	6	3	2	1	1					18
9							3		9	6	2	3	1					24
10								1	3	2	6							12
11										1	1	2	4	2				10
12												1	2	1				4
13											2	3	1					6
14																		0
15														1				1
16																	1	1
17																		0
Totals	0	0	4	4	9	21	23	13	28	22	15	14	11	4	0	1	1	170

Source: Survey

a. Not a fixed year of entry. Year of entry varies over the complete ten year period, 1968 – 77.
b. For employment size-groups see Table 6.9.

156

Table 6.17

1968 – 77 Structural tally matrix for local and non-local branch and subsidiary plants.

Initial Size	\	\	\	\	\	\	\	\	\	\	\	\	\	\	\	\	\	\
						Maximum size attained during the 1968 – 77 period												
	1	2	3	4	5	6	7	8	9	10	11	12	13	14	15	16	17	Total
1ᵇ									2									2
2			2					1										3
3				1	2	1	5	2	1	1		1	1					19
4				2	5	2	2	2	3	1		1						12
5					2	6	3	2	3	3	1							19
6						8	4	1	6	1	2	1	1					21
7							4	2	3	6	1	1	4				1	18
8								5	6	3	1	1	2					18
9									11	6	3	2	1					24
10										6	6	3	1					12
11											2	2	4	2				10
12												1	2	1				4
13													4	2				6
14																		0
15																1		1
16																1		1
17																		0
Total	0	0	2	4	9	19	18	16	27	26	15	11	15	5	0	2	1	170

Source: Survey

a. Not a fixed year of entry. Year of entry varies over the complete ten year period, 1968 – 77
b. For employment size-groups see Table 6.9

157

industrial order. Second, the rate of new enterprise formation (number of enterprises per 1,000 employees per annum) in each industrial order (S.I.C.) is then further explored by 'testing' a series of hypotheses. The hypotheses themselves can be regarded as denoting the standard hypotheses i.e. they associate either changes or attributes of an industry with the number of new enterprises entering and surviving in each major industry. Unlike the preceding sections, this one is not split between indigenous and branch plants, but considers them both together. Though the bulk of the section concentrates upon new indigenous enterprises and does not consider the various aspects of plant/investment mobility by industrial order in any detail.

The wide range of industrial orders entered by both indigenous enterprises and branch plants is detailed in Table 6.18. This table also charts the levels of employment generated by the opening of all plants and the balance between male and female employment. Before considering the rate of entry of indigenous enterprises by industry and suggesting several possible avenues explaining the variations between each industrial order, it is perhaps important to note some of the salient features of this table. Despite the large variety of industrial activities entered by new plants, a few industrial orders dominate. In the case of indigenous enterprises five industrial orders (Orders 3, 7, 12, 13, and 19) (6) account for over 60 per cent of all employment created by their opening (7,652 or 62.75 per cent). For the branch plants there are again five major orders (Orders 7, 9, 13, 15, and 16) (7) which collectively account for over 65 per cent of all employment created by these plants (27,648 or 65.92 per cent).

Two further features of this table, Table 6.18, are of direct interest. The first item concerns the nature of the employment created by the opening of these new plants. For example, there is a heavy reliance upon a high labour requirement (in some cases) for the production methods used by the branch plants. It is therefore perhaps not surprising that sectors such as textiles, apparel, metal fabrications, and electrical equipment (electronics) - all characterised by a substantial labour requirement - are all well represented (ERICKSON, 1978, 18). Of course, there is an interplay between the supply (availability) and cost of labour on the one hand and the changing labour requirements of industry on the other (Chapter Four). One example of this relationship is:

> ... where there has been a transition from electro-mechanical
> to semi-conductor products, the female proportion of employees
> increased as direct male labour was shed. ... In companies
> where electronic products have been produced from start-up,
> the proportion of female labour has decreased against
> technical and professional manpower requirements as direct
> labour content in the products has been reduced by component
> integration and manufacturing automation. (SCOTTISH
> DEVELOPMENT AGENCY, 1979, 47)

The direct availability of labour has had a strong influence in attracting investment to Scotland. The wage differential was also important and it has been argued that this is no longer the case (NORCLIFFE, 1975). However, data do exist to suggest that a wage

Table 6.18

Male and female manufacturing employment created in Scotland by the opening of new plants during the period 1968 - 77 by industrial order.

SIC	Indigenous Enterprises			Local/Non-Local Branch and Subsidiary Plants			All New Plants		
	Male	Female	Total	Male	Female	Total	Male	Female	Total
3	513	880	1,442[a] (35)	1,606	1,078	2,694 (32)	2,119	1,958	4,136 (67)
4	6	3	9 (1)	-	-	-	6	3	9 (1)
5	78	47	131 (13)	856	279	1,235 (16)	934	326	1,336 (29)
6	260	82	342 (9)	1,077	284	1,281 (9)	1,337	286	1,623 (18)
7	1,835	215	2,116 (64)	8,569	632	10,289 (48)	10,404	847	12,405 (112)
8	113	75	178 (15)	1,017	464	1,481 (12)	1,150	539	1,659 (27)
9	411	280	711 (32)	2,097	2,759	5,326 (45)	2,508	3,039	6,307 (77)
10	397	27	424 (11)	626	84	740 (6)	1,023	111	1,164 (17)
11	204	25	263 (14)	171	155	326 (6)	375	180	589 (20)
12	1,171	293	1,681 (88)	1,875	864	2,883 (34)	3,046	1,157	4,564 (122)
13	297	742	1,171 (44)	1,900	1,364	4,044 (39)	2,197	2,106	5,215 (83)
14	46	28	74 (5)	95	66	161 (3)	141	94	235 (8)
15	88	617	759 (20)	351	3,628	4,884 (35)	439	4,245	5,643 (55)
16	175	90	282 (24)	2,876	179	3,105 (32)	3,051	269	3,387 (56)
17	767	154	967 (34)	152	29	181 (7)	919	183	1,148 (41)
18	243	101	403 (28)	686	344	1,030 (15)	929	445	1,433 (43)
19	584	475	1,242 (68)	1,421	447	2,283 (21)	2,005	922	3,525 (89)
	7,208	4,134	12,194 (504)	25,375	12,576	41,944 (371)	32,583	16,710	54,138 (875)

Sources: Scottish Council (Development and Industry), Survey.

a. Employment level in 1977. The male and female totals do not sum to this total in all cases as the breakdown was not available in some instances.

b. Number of plants.

differential does in fact exist (Table 6.19). However, the differential does reveal a degree of convergence over the 1970-78 period (DEPT. of EMPLOYMENT GAZETTE, 1979). In terms of regional development, the aim to erode wage differentials may be interpreted as being a positive sign towards regional equity, but this is not necessarily desirable for regional development. Three pieces of research would tend to support this view. First, the employment created by incoming plants does not necessarily mean an increase in the average (mean) wage level; 39 per cent of workers interviewed by Townsend et al (1978, 1,357) took a reduction in gross pay on being employed in a newly opened branch plant. Second, while incoming plants may increase the average income of an area there are strong possibilities that these income gains are not evenly distributed (SUMMERS et al, 1976, 47-71). On the same theme, the net balance between public and private gains from incoming industry are strongly in favour of the latter (SHAFFER, 1972, 94). Third, and at a more general level, MacLeod and Watkin (1969) noted that:

> An important concomitant of low average earnings ... is a high concentration of the distribution pattern which means in practice fewer opportunities to achieve higher individual earnings. ... A low dispersion of earnings may give the impression of greater equality in the distribution of earnings but it may also give the impression of dull uniformity both in the opportunities which the region affords to those who live there and in those aspects of the regional environment which depend upon private expenditure for their development. (ibid., 98)

It would appear that the compression of the income range within an area might not be wholly advantageous and apart from reducing the possible multiplier effects (KEEBLE, 1976, 204-5), it might also affect the number of potential entrepreneurs in an area by limiting the ability of individuals to save seed capital.

In summary it is possible to conceive of a situation whereby the infusion of external investment upon a host region might not be in either the short or long-term interests of that region. Of great relevance to this study are the long-term implications of inward investment over a 20-25 year period upon the present (1968-77) rate of new firm formation. It would appear that the likelihood of an improved range of job opportunities is unlikely to improve with time in these plants (HOOD and YOUNG, 1976, 285-6; SCOTTISH DEVELOPMENT AGENCY, 1979, 46; also see JEWKES et al, 1958, 191-6; SHAPERO et al, 1965, 7-16), and so the benefits of inward investment would seem to be minimal. The situation with indigenous enterprises is less likely to be so clear cut because of the small scale at which they generally operate. Furthermore, their impact in employment terms is much less than that of the larger plants that tend to be externally owned (see Tables 2.9 and Table 5.21).

A second element, and one raised elsewhere (FIRN and HUGHES, 1974, 505-14; FIRN, 1975, 398), concerns the entry of new enterprises into growing and declining industrial orders. J. R. Firn (1975, 398) noted that "... new local enterprises set-up by local entrepreneurs are biased toward those industrial sectors that are in decline both locally and nationally." This analysis concerned the setting-up of new

Table 6.19

Spatial variations in labour costs for selected occupations.

Location	Works Manager	Senior Draughtsman	Quality Control Manager	Production Operatives		
				Skilled	Semi-Skilled	Unskilled
1[a]	£10,135[b]	£5,835[b]	£ 6,544[b]	£121.00[c]	£99.00[c]	£94.50[c]
2	7,352	4,832	6,048	83.51	76.12	63.52
3	9,200	5,536	6,270	88.75	80.00	70.32
4	7,704	5,275	5,500	88.09	78.98	65.70
5	7,927	5,161	5,875	85.00	74.75	77.82
6	7,500	4,949	5,545	90.00	83.13	68.07
7	8,475	4,790	6,080	84.50	73.50	73.00
8	9,345	5,364	6,481	77.60	64.89	68.23
9	10,008	5,642	6,712	103.57	86.54	75.50
10	-	6,000	10,140	-	-	-
11	7,584	4,906	6,000	79.51	78.51	56.40
12	8,250	5,000	5,600	89.17	80.95	64.78

Source: Reward Regional Surveys Ltd., 'National Analysis of Salaries and Wages', Autumn, 1979.

a. 1 = Grampian; 2 = South and West Yorkshire; 3 = Manchester; 4 = Nottingham/Derby; 5 = Mid/North Staffordshire; 6 = Wolverhampton/Outer Birmingham; 7 = Leicestershire/Northamptonshire; 8 = South Buckinghamshire/East Berkshire; 9 = Hertfordshire/North London; 10 = Central London; 11 = South Hampshire/Dorset; 12 = Cornwall, Devon, and South West Somerset.

b. Annual salary; c. Weekly wage.

enterprises in the Clydeside conurbation during the period 1958-68.
During this period the number of expanding industries (in terms of
employment at the mlh level) was far greater than at the present
time. At the local level (Scotland) there were 41 expanding
industries and 6 static ones, while at the national level (UK) there
were 48 expanding industries and one static one. Today, the situation
is somewhat different with only half as many expanding industries.

Tables 6.20 and 6.21 detail the distribution of entrants by either
growing or declining sectors by employment. The second table,
Table 6.21, offers a refinement of the first, Table 6.20, and reveals
that the two distributions are probably not significantly different.
Two caveats need to be added to these observations. First, the use
of the crude minimum list heading (mlh) categories to indicate
industrial growth or decline probably hide more than they reveal. It
is evident that within each mlh there is a wide range of industrial
activities some of which will be expanding, while others are
contracting. Furthermore, to measure the growth or decline of an
industry by using employment is surely open to question and it would
probably be better to use some measure of liquidity or profitability
(HUTCHINSON et al, 1975, 147; HUTCHINSON, 1978, 7). The only
rationale for using employment totals are their availability rather
than any innate merit they may possess (see ALEXANDER and LINDBERG,
1961, 80). Despite these problems, it would appear that there are
no great differences in either of the sources of new enterprises.

Table 6.20

Distribution of employment in the new manufacturing plants
set-up in Scotland, 1968 - 77;   Allocated to categories
of growth or decline and to origin of enterprise.

Origin of Enterprise	Percentage of Employment			
	National (UK)[a]		Regional (Scotland)[b]	
	Contracting	Expanding	Contracting	Expanding
Indigenous	76.69	20.31	71.83	28.17
Branch/Sub-sidiary	83.94	16.06	76.82	23.18

a. 21 mlhs growing   b. 22 mlhs growing

Underlying the above discussion is the idea that the expansion
of the numbers employed in an industrial activity indicates a
concurrent growth in demand for that industry's products or services.
If, then, demand is increasing, the existing numbers of firms meeting
this increased demand will increase their output to match this new
level of demand. Of course, in the initial stages demand might
tend to outstrip supply, and so leave open some unsatisfied
markets (8). It is into these markets that new enterprises could
sell their products. Moreover, the likelihood of both succeeding
and surviving in an expanding market is possibly far greater because
inter-firm competition would tend to be less severe than in a static
or declining market situation. Thus, one might expect a priori
that the number of firms entering and surviving in an expanding
industrial order to be greater than elsewhere, and that the

Table 6.21

Distribution of plants set up in Scotland, 1968 - 77; Allocated to categories of growth or decline and by origin of enterprise.

Employment Growth Groups (%)		Origin of Enterprise	
		Indigenous	Branch
Growth	40 +	9.23	15.63
	20 - 39	16.26	11.56
	10 - 19	0.0	0.0
	0 - 9	1.76	2.19
	Static	1.54	1.88
	0 - 9	27.69	19.69
	10 - 19	21.32	20.94
Decline	20 - 39	17.58	21.56
	40 +	4.62	6.56

$x^2 = 17.487$
at 0.01 level - not significantly different
at 0.05 level - significantly different

entrepreneur would consider his chances for success to be much greater in a growing market. Why then do many new indigenous enterprises enter apparently declining sectors?

There are a series of hypotheses that can be formulated in an attempt to account for these sectoral variations. Most hypotheses derived by earlier researchers have tended to concentrate upon measuring different facets of the barriers-to-entry and very few have considered the supply of entrepreneurs. For example, Collins (1972, 70-3) derived four hypotheses related to different aspects of the barriers-to-entry. However, one of his hypotheses did concern the supply of entrepreneurs and stated that:

> ... within every industry each employee, since he already possesses experience and first-hand information concerning that form of economic activity, is a potential entrepreneur in that industry. Under this assumption the number of births in any sector would be directly proportional to the total employment of that sector. (ibid., 70)

To this end it might then be best to split the hypotheses considered into at least those related to the barriers-to-entry and those concerned with the supply of entrepreneurs.

The measure used to express the rate of entry relates the number of new enterprises opening in an order to the numbers employed in that order. To express this figure as a standardised value, the entry rate of new enterprises is expressed as the number of new enterprises per thousand employees per annum. Of course, this is a somewhat arbitrary as it will be seen later that there is often more than one founder behind each new enterprise (see Chapter Eight,

Tables 8.14 and 8.15). In fact, in more than 50 per cent of the enterprises (54.45 per cent) covered by the survey of new entrepreneur-based-enterprises were set-up by two or more founders. A more accurate measure of the number of potential founders per 1,000 employees in an industry might be to use the number of founders rather than the number of enterprises. In fact, Johnson and Cathcart (1978, 19) did use the number of founders in this situation and found that it made no difference (see note to Table 6.22). Their study, however, used incorporation statistics and considered only 74 new enterprises. While the survey of new enterprises for this study yielded usable data for 191 new enterprises which did not significantly differ from the total identified population of new enterprises. And there is no evidence to suggest that the average number of founders for each industry (however expressed) would be directly transferrable from the survey to the total population. In the end, the entry rates were calculated by using the first method and the results are shown in Table 6.22. The associated death rates are also recorded in this table, but these refer to all plants closing because it is not possible to distinguish between totally independent and the remainder of Scottish plants closing. It is these entry rates that are used in the following analyses.

Table 6.22

Average birth and death rates of new enterprises and plants in Scotland, 1968 - 77.

S.I.C.	Entry Rate[a]	Exit Rate[b]
3	0.036	0.127
4	0.050	0.050
5	0.043	0.767
6	0.018	0.066
7	0.057	0.090
8	0.094	0.106
9	0.074	0.081
10	0.023	0.035
11	0.035	0.040
12	0.303	0.217
13	0.051	0.136
14	0.167	0.467
15	0.069	0.297
16	0.104	0.391
17	0.148	0.287
18	0.050	0.105
19	0.453	0.207
Mean	0.104	0.204
Median	0.035	0.040
Std. Dev.	0.114	0.193
Std. Error	0.028	0.048

a. Entry rate = No. of new indigenous enterprises per 1,000 employees in 1968 per annum
b. Exit rate = No. of plants closing per 1,000 employees in 1968.

(Adjustment was made to the rate of entry to allow for the number of founders for each industrial order. Thus a measure of the number of founders per 1,000 employees in 1968 per annum was calculated. This was then rank correlated with entry rate as presented above; $r_s = +.9424$; $t = 10.91$ and for this reason, that of very close similarity, the above entry rate was used in all subsequent calculations in this Chapter.)

(A) An examination of some hypotheses:

a. <u>Barriers-to-entry</u>. Three major groups of hypotheses were derived and they are concerned with the barriers-to-entry, factors of supply, and the characteristics of each industrial order. The first series of hypotheses directly concern the factors that may impede or retard the emergence of new enterprises. Five main sub-hypotheses were developed and these are:

1. The rate of entry of indigenous enterprises is directly related to the cost of entry. It is therefore expected that the less it costs to set-up in an industry the greater will be the number of enterprises setting-up in that industry.

2. The rate of entry of indigenous enterprises is inversely related to the proportion of employment in plants employing 500 or more employees in an industry (CHINITZ's HYPOTHESIS).

3. The greater the proportion of plants employing between 11 to 19 employees in an industry the higher the rate of entry.

4. A higher rate of entry will be found in those industries experiencing the greatest degree of expansion or the least degree of contraction.

5. Industries in which small plants are able to enter and survive have the highest rates of entry.

The results of examining these five sub-hypotheses are detailed in Table 6.23. While all of the hypotheses are shown to have been correct in predicting the direction of the relationship, in only two cases are the relationships significant at the 0.05 level and only one of these is also significant at the 0.01 level. A few words of explanation are required to justify these hypotheses.

The cost of setting-up a new business is obviously a vague notion. In an attempt to assess these costs, the survey, reported in Chapter Eight, sought data relating to the sum initially invested at the very beginning of the enterprise's existence. These data were available in 179 cases (93.72 per cent of the 191 respondents) and the median cost of entry is used here. The median value is used in preference to the mean as it is not subject to the same distortions of mean values. For the purposes of the hypotheses then it was assumed that the cheaper it was to enter an industry the more enterprises would be set-up in that industry. It is also probable that the lower the cost of entry the fewer the number of sources of finance would be needed. This then would lead to greater dependence upon personal finance, and a greater independence of action not restricted by any institutional checks.

Plant dominance and industrial concentration have often been seen as factors that result in two major influences which act to suppress

Table 6.23

Rank correlation for hypotheses relating to sectoral variations in entry rates: Barriers-to-entry.

SIC	Entry Rates 1968-77	Cost of Entry (Median)	Plant Dominance (Employment)	Prop. Small Plants	Industry Expansion 1968-1977	Size at Entry M1*	M2*
3	14	3	9	9	1	1	2
4	11	4	5	2	10	17	17
5	13	8	7	13	4	16	16
6	17	2	6	14	11	13	5
7	9	10	8	7	17	6	6
8	6	5	3	5	2	15	10
9	7	8	4	12	5	14	15
10	16	1	2	8	13	10	6
11	15	11	1	3	8	8	10
12	2	12	12	4	12	11	10
13	10	7	14	17	15	5	3
14	3	5	17	6	13	7	4
15	8	17	15	16	3	3	1
16	5	13	13	15	16	2	8
17	4	16	16	1	6	11	9
18	11	14	11	11	7	4	10
19	1	15	10	10	8	9	10
Spearman's Rank Correlation Coefficient	-.5576	-.5429	+.0192	-.2424	-.0931	-.0123	
't' values	2.602	2.504	0.80	0.9677	0.3623	0.0476	
Significance Level	0.01 Yes 0.05 Yes	No Yes	No No	No No	No No	No No	No No

* M1 = Mean size at entry;   M2 = Median size at entry

the rate of entry. First, the dominance of an industrial order by a few large plants would tend to indicate that the minimum size for efficient production is large, and would therefore prohibit entry by individuals (see PRATTEN, 1971; SILBERTSON, 1972; SHAW and SUTTON, 1976). One can counter this argument and suggest that while an industry may be dominated by a few large plants there will always be scope for the small enterprise serving either the geographically isolated (NORCLIFFE, 1966) or the highly specialist market (PRAIS, 1976, 12-3).

A second influence of large enterprises concerns the supply side of entrepreneurs. It has been noted by Cooper (1970b, 75) that "... firms with less than 500 employees had a spin-off rate eight times as high as firms with more than 500 employees." To this he adds: "... past entrepreneurship generates new small firms that seem uniquely suited to function as incubators." (ibid., 75) In another paper Cooper (1970a, 59) suggested that both the market and technology of the incubator organisation (former employer of new firm founder) were also important. This position is largely confirmed by work undertaken elsewhere e.g. Northern Region (JOHNSON and CATHCART, 1979), East Midlands (GUDGIN et al 1979) etc..

The use of plant dominance as a measure of a barrier-to-entry would seem to be more important as a measure of inhibiting entrepreneur (new firm founder) development. Though it should not be regarded as a closed issue. For example, Chinitz (1961) recorded that the:

> ... average establishment in the apparel industry ... has one-sixth as many employees as the average establishment in primary metals. (ibid., 284)

He continues,

> ... multi-unit firms account for 82 per cent of the employment in primary metals, while they account for only 28 per cent of employment in apparel. Now you may have as much management per dollar of output in primary metals as you have in apparel, but you certainly do not have as many managers who are also risk-takers and this is my definition of an entrepreneur. (ibid., 284)

This concept introduces not only that of plant dominance, but also ownership and control. Return is made to this latter aspect in the series of hypotheses relating to the characteristics of each industrial order (Table 6.25; also see Chapter Eight).

At the other extreme, it is often assumed that the rate of entry is related to the number or proportion of small plants in an industrial order. Most studies have used the proportion of small plants or the employment they account for as an indication of the ease of entry. They argue that a large number of small plants in an industrial order reflects the ease with which new firms can enter and survive in that industry (WEDERVANG, 1965, 178-9; GUDGIN, 1978, 137; GUDGIN and FOTHERGILL, 1978, 6; JOHNSON and CATHCART, 1978, 18; 1979) (9). However, this is not necessarily the case, Collins (1972, 70) more correctly notes that the rate of entry decreases with increasing size. One would therefore expect higher rates of entry in industries with larger numbers of small plants. At first sight this appears contradictory. Yet, the numbers of small plants does not necessarily reflect the ease of entry, but may reflect the 'newness' or 'youthfulness' of an industry amongst other possible factors.

There are several extensions to this line of argument. First, it could well be that small plants breed more new, small plants. Such a premise would gain support from the arguments of both Chinitz and Cooper. In extending this notion still further, Gudgin and Fothergill (1978, 11) considered variations in the number of small plants (10) on a regional basis and considered that "... birth rates are highest in the South East. It also seems likely, although by no means proven, that they are lowest in the Assisted Regions other than Scotland." Hence, those areas with higher birth rates will always tend to have the largest proportion of small plants.

A second facet of the importance of small plants could, in a few circumstances, reflect the 'newness' or 'youthfulness' of an industry. S. J. Prais (1976, 15-6), for example, "... lists ten trades accounting for the greater part of the rise in numbers (of small plants) in the decade 1958-68. ...   ... many of these trades are 'modern', in that they include scientific instruments, electronic apparatus, plastics fabrication and printing ... ." He notes later that this influx of new firms will have little effect upon concentration (ibid., 208) and so the overall employment impact of small plants in these new industries may appear minimal, and therefore hides their, and the orders youthfulness. If either the mean or median age of plants are computed for a series of employment groups a steady decrease in the average age of plants with decreasing size is evident, i.e. more recent the year of opening date. Though this distribution is far from perfect, it does indicate the youthfulness of the smaller employment size groups (Table 6.24) (11) and therefore supports the inductive arguments of Gudgin and Fothergill (1978). While both the degree of plant dominance and the population of small plants are both correlated only the former measure is significantly correlated (Table 6.23). The only other significant correlation was found between the rate and cost of entry.

The remaining two hypotheses relate the expansion rate of the permanent stock of plants and the average (mean and median) employment size at the end of the first year of operating and the rate of entry. It is assumed that those industries experiencing growth would attract and allow new enterprises to survive (see arguments to entry into growth and declining sectors above). Contrary perhaps to expectations, a negative relationship is obtained. This is dissimilar to the findings of Collins (1972, 70), and supports neither Gudgin's (1978, 139), nor Johnson and Cathcart's, findings (1978, 18). The last two studies, Gudgin's and Johnson and Cathcart's, seem to have measured industrial growth by the total employment change in all plants and so their expansion rates would have been dependent, in part, upon the rates of entry into each industry. A relationship might however exist between expansion of each industry and the rate of entry if the former was measured over the period of incubation i.e. during the period that the entrepreneur gained his/her experience and conceived the idea to set-up the new firm. There would appear to be no studies to date that conduct such an analysis (12), and would it be only possible if the entry rates during that pre-formation period were

Table 6.24

The average age of manufacturing plants in Scotland, 1977:
An analysis by plant size and the location of ultimate ownership.

Employment Size-Group	Branch	Scotland Independent	Location of Ultimate Ownership H.Q.	England	Europe	North America	Other World	Joint Venture	Total
1-10	[a]37/13[b]	23/9	25/13	30/13	7/5	2/2	-	-	24/9
11-19	40/13	14/17	36/41	18/8	4/4	9/9	-	4/4	37/13
20-24	54/28	43/31	16/14	35/10	18/4	10/5	-	6/6	41/25
25-99	56/41	56/28	44/41	38/18	17/6	19/9	13/13	15/7	49/31
100-199	68/57	63/54	58/54	50/29	14/12	31/11	10/10	21/8	54/42
200-499	74/71	89/94	86/101	54/30	19/15	25/15	34/34	30/6	62/43
500-999	97/53	70/75	77/71	62/56	27/21	32/19	-	134/133	62/35
1,000-1,999	117/108	81/72	144/144	84/73	26/32	43/27	-	35/35	75/65
2,000-3,999	29/29	69/72	78/69	57/69	-	26/26	-	5/5	54/47
4,000-9,999	-	-	-	60/37	-	52/31	-	-	60/37
	62/49	46/29	50/36	43/23	20/9	14/12	18/13	32/9	45/22

Sources: Scottish Council (Development and Industry)
          Survey

a.   Mean Age   b.   Median Age.

known as well. Knowledge of this entry rate would allow the expansion of permanent plants to be calculated. Such an analysis would·
be feasible for Scotland using the Scottish Manufacturing Establishment
Record (SCOMER) to which access is restricted by the Statistics of
Trade Act of 1947 (see SCOTTISH ECONOMIC BULLETIN, 1977).

The final hypothesis considers size of new firms at entry and the
rate of entry in an industry. Here it is assumed, in a similar way
to the cost of entry, that the smaller the initial size a firm can
be in an industry, the easier it would be to enter that industry.
Negative relationships were obtained for both the measures of initial
size, but both of them were not significant.

In examining these five hypotheses, which are explicitly concerned
with the barriers-to-entry, it was found that the rate of entry was
related to the level of initial investment and possibly to the level
of plant dominance of both an area (GUDGIN, 1978, 211-27; GUDGIN and
FOTHERGILL, 1978, 2) and an industry. Furthermore, the dominance of
either industry or an area by a single or a series of large plants
would appear to impart a certain type or level of trading (JAMES, 1964;
MOSELEY and TOWNROE, 1973; LEVER, 1974a, 1974b; SMEATON, 1975, 1977;
SCOTTISH DEVELOPMENT AGENCY, 1979, 52). They may well be important
in encouraging new businesses if sub-contract work is available.
Other possible characteristics of plant dominated areas were noted
earlier (Chapter Five) e.g. labour turnover, level of redundancies,
etc.. The remaining variables hypothesised as being related to the
rate of entry were found to be weakly correlated in the direction
hypothesised, but were not statistically significant.

b. Industrial Characteristics. The next series of hypotheses concern
the rate of entry and its level of association with several characteristics of each industry. Three main hypotheses are proposed as
being important:

1.   There is a negative relationship between the rate of entry and
      the age of the permanent stock of plants in an industry. The
      complementary hypotheses proposing a relationship between the
      rate of entry and the age of employment in an industry is less
      certain and therefore the hypothesis is non-directional. It
      is then hypothesised in the latter case that there is a
      difference between the two ranked distributions. (NORCLIFFE,
      1977, 34)

2.   Those industries experiencing a high exit rate will also
      experience a high rate of entry. Furthermore, this direct
      relationship will be most pronounced amongst those industries
      with the highest closure rates amongst small plants.

3.   It is expected that there is a direct correlation between
      the level of employment under Scottish ownership (however
      expressed) and the rate of entry.

These three hypotheses, the results of the examination of which are
detailed in Table 6.25, lie between the ideas of entry impedence and
the supply of entrepreneurs. The rationale behind each of the
hypotheses is detailed below.

Table 6.25

Rank correlation for hypotheses relating to sectoral variations
in entry rates: Industrial characteristics.

SIC	Entry Rates 1968-77	Permanent Plants Plant Age	Emp. Age	Exit Rates[a] 1968-77	Exit Rates[b] 1968-77	Owner Emp.[c] 1973	Scot. Plants[d] 1968
3	14	6	8	9	8	7	8
4	11	4	7	15	17	14	13
5	13	11	13	1	10	15	12
6	17	3	2	14	14	12	14
7	9	9	10	12	12	9	10
8	6	13	12	10	9	13	11
9	7	16	15	13	13	17	15
10	16	2	1	17	16	6	16
11	15	12	13	16	15	16	17
12	2	13	11	6	5	4	3
13	10	5	4	8	7	3	7
14	3	7	6	2	1	1	1
15	8	13	17	4	3	8	6
16	5	10	9	3	2	10	4
17	4	8	5	5	4	2	2
18	11	1	3	11	11	5	9
19	1	16	15	7	6	11	5
Spearman's Rank Correlation Coefficient	−.4718	+.01	+.5895	+.7243	+.3149	+.7708
't' value	2.072	0.3892	2.8708	7.269	1.285	8.5469
Significance Level 0.01	No	No	Yes	Yes	No	Yes
0.05	Yes	No	Yes	Yes	No	Yes

a.   Total number of plants closing expressed as a number closing per
     1,000 employees in the industry in 1968.
b.   Total number of plants closing that employed 100 or less employees
     at closure expressed as a number closing per 1,000 employees in
     the industry in 1968.
c.   Level of employment under Scottish ownership ranked.
d.   Number of plants under Scottish ownership in 1968 expressed as a
     number per 1,000 employees in the industry in 1968.

Introducing the age of either employment or plants is a vague notion and can be considered in a number of ways. First, it could represent a high turnover rate within an industry. Or second, the industry might be new and therefore have a low average age. Or third, there may be a direct relationship between the youthfulness of an industry and its ability to 'produce' new firms. In any event, there is a fairly strong inverse correlation between age and the rate of entry. The strength of the relationship decreases, and its direction is reversed when the age of employment is used instead. Why this is so is not clear, but it is probably a reflection of using employment levels relating to 1977 and attributing their existence to a former period i.e. does not allow for expansion during the 1968 - 77 or any earlier period. There is also the complication that a single plant can dominate this employment distribution e.g. Ferranti and NCR in electronics, and BL (formerly British Leyland) and PSA Peugot-Citreon (formerly Chrysler (UK) Ltd.) in motorvehicles. Unfortunately no other studies exist to compare these findings. The study by Crum (1953) using tax returns data is mainly concerned with the age of the corporate system and the evidence he produces (ibid., 53-82) does tend to support the above statements (also see ALLA, 1974, 99; SAVAGE, 1979, 93-4).

In many respects the turnover rate of plants i.e. the entry and exit rates, are responsible for the age structure of each industry. And it is found that the exit rate is strongly correlated with the entry rate, and even more so when the exit rates of the smaller plants (those employing 100 or less employees on closure) are used. Perhaps what is disturbing is that the exit rate is higher than the entry rate. While this situation may be so in reality, it might also be a function, in part, of the quality of the data used. However, both the data used and the results obtained compare favourably with other, mainly official data sources (see Chapter Three) and with other studies.

A similar relationship to the above was noted by Collins (1972, 73, r_S = +.3474). In Collins' analysis the exit rate exceeded the entry rate in those industries that tended to have a poor expansion record. The exception to this being the clothing industry. Yet, if the correlation between exit rate and expansion is measured a weak positive value is obtained (Collins' study, r_S = +.0286; this study r_S = +.1005, t = 0.471), and both are neither significant, nor in the direction hypothesised. The marginally stronger relationship for Scotland may be due to the inclusion of plants opening and closing during the period 1968-77, and only being recorded as closures. This is an obvious weakness and would tend to inflate the exit rate. In other studies, such a plant would be included in both the exit and entry rates and would therefore inflate both rates equally, and would not distort any correlation values.

The final hypothesis in this group concerns the level of Scottish ownership in each industrial order. Again, this variable is deeply rooted in ones used earlier e.g. plant dominance, and is considered in general terms elsewhere (Chapter Two). In essence it is postulated that the increase in external ownership decreases the number of risk-taking managerial positions (Chinitz's entrepreneurs) in the economy. This, then, might reduce the potential pool of local entrepreneurs. While the correlation is not significant, it is still fairly high and in the direction hypothesised (Table 6.26). In an attempt to clarify the possible role of ownership still further, the number of Scottish owned plants for 1968 was calculated. This was achieved by discounting the number of plants opening from the total number of plants in each order in 1977, and then adding to that total the number of plants that had closed over the period. The final total was then expressed as the number of Scottish owned plants per 1,000 employees in each order. These ratios on correlation with the rate of entry yielded a high level of association, and was also significant. Such a result would therefore tend to further suggest the importance of considering the nature of ownership, and its possible effect upon the rate of entry.

Although many of the hypotheses in this section were shown to be both fairly strong and in some cases significant, the overall result is somewhat inconclusive. The variables used were lamentably crude and require further refining, but even still some evidence has been produced in these two groups of hypotheses alone to suggest further lines of enquiry. The next series of hypotheses consider one aspect of these suggested avenues - that of the supply of entrepreneurs themselves - by using measures of employment type within each industry.

c. Factors of supply. In an attempt to discern which features of each industry may affect the rate of entry, two related hypotheses were derived. They concern the mass and the nature of the mass of both plants and employment in an industry, and its association with the rate of entry. The two main hypotheses are:

1. The greater the mass (number of plants or employment) in an industry the greater is the rate of entry. This can then be refined and suggests that the rate of entry is greatest in those industries where the ratio of the number of plants per 1,000 employees is also greatest.

2. A correlation exists between the nature of the employment in an industry and the rate of entry. Three sub-hypotheses can be derived:

    (i) The rate of entry is directly related to the level of administrative and managerial employment in an industry.

    (ii) A positive association exists between the level of productive employment and the rate of entry in an industry.

    (iii) The level of other employment, neither administrative or productive in an industry will be inversely related to the rate of entry.

The results of these rank correlations are presented in Table 6.26. There would appear to be little or no support for the hypothesis relating the actual number (mass) of plants or employment to the rate of entry. Such findings agree with those of Collins (1972, 73). Perhaps rather surprisingly the rate of entry is inversely related to

173

Table 6.26

Rank correlation for hypotheses relating to sectoral variations
in entry rates: Factors of supply.

SIC	Entry Rate 1968-77	No. of Plants[a] 1968	No. of Plants[b] 1968	No. Emp. 1968	Employment type (permanent establishments in '77) Admin.	Oper.	Other
3	14	1	7	2	13	11	3
4	11	17	13	16	3	17	1
5	13	10	10	9	2	16	2
6	17	11	14	6	10	8	7
7	9	3	11	1	4	12	11
8	6	14	12	15	5	7	14
9	7	12	15	5	1	15	12
10	16	13	17	7	15	2	17
11	15	14	16	8	8	14	4
12	2	4	4	10	11	6	9
13	10	2	8	3	16	4	13
14	3	16	1	16	14	3	16
15	8	8	6	10	17	1	15
16	5	7	2	13	12	5	10
17	4	6	3	12	7	9	8
18	11	5	9	4	6	13	5
19	1	9	5	14	9	10	6
Spearman's Rank Correlation Coefficient	+.1054	+.7267	−.1348	+.0034	+.2439	−.2484
't' value	0.4967	4.0971	0.5269	0.0132	0.974	1.0791
Significance Level						
0.01	No	Yes	No	No	No	No
0.05	No	Yes	No	No	No	No

a. Total number of plants in each order ranked.

b. Total number of plants in each order expressed as a total per 1,000
employees in 1968.

the numbers employed and may perhaps reflect the counter positions of the declining and dominant industries, and the emergence of new industries. A strong and statistically significant correlation was obtained between the ratio of plants per 1,000 employees in 1968 and the rate of entry. This measure relates both the number of plants and employees in an order and prevents the distortions of the above two measures. It could also be argued that the measure also indicates the number of key managerial positions for every 1,000 employees (and the number of small plants) in an industry based on the assumption that every plant contains at least one key individual. In essence, this is what the ratio was used to measure above in relation to the number of Scottish owned plants. In fact, the rank distribution of these two series of ratios is nearly identical (r_s = +.9779; t = 18.138), though the correlation was higher using the ratio of Scottish owned plants.

On disaggregating the employment in each industry into the three broad categories of administrative, operative, and other (neither administrative, nor operative) employment, weak correlations are obtained with the rate of entry. However, they are all in the direction hypothesised. Despite the low correlation values, they do lend support, albeit limited, to the notion that the most likely source of new enterprise founders would be in those orders where the level of administrative and operative employment were highest. However, these results can also be interpreted as representing a measure of the labour intensity of production i.e. the level of productive labour is greater than either of the two non-productive employment groups. Furthermore, smaller firms tend to have a higher productive to non-productive staff ratio and this is reflected in these three employment type categories.

All of the measures derived in these series of hypotheses tend to conceal far more than they reveal. To answer these questions and to clarify the points raised it would be necessary to analyse in detail several industrial characteristics noted here and attempt to relate them to the entry of new enterprises. This study has adopted a different approach and has viewed the new enterprises and their founders', and it is hoped that such an approach will clarify some of the issues raised in this section.

4.   SUMMARY AND CONCLUSIONS

Additions to the stock of manufacturing plants arise from a wide range of sources. The three main sources were detailed in this chapter; new enterprises, local, and non-local branch and subsidiary plants. While the bulk of employment from the opening of new plants in Scotland is found in new externally owned ones, new indigenous enterprises made a sizeable employment contribution. In fact, it is the new enterprises that exhibit, in relative terms, the greatest employment growth rates once established. The industrial activity of each new plant source was then examined. Here, the source, size, employment type, and growth rates were considered.

In the third section a series of hypotheses that relate the emergence of new enterprises to the various attributes of each industry were examined. These hypotheses were divided into three areas: barriers-to-entry, industrial characteristics, and factors of supply. Each of

175

these analyses attempted to expalin why the number of new enterprises entering each industrial order varied. However, the method of explanation adopted represents only one possible approach. It assumes, for example, that causal inferences, however guarded, can be made from simple statistical associations. Yet, the associations found are plausible.

In the following chapters, Chapters Seven and Eight, this analysis is continued. However, in these chapters a behavioural approach is adopted, and they present an analytical framework (Chapter Seven) and data relating to new firm founders (Chapter Eight). In these chapters the focus is upon the new firm founder, and not the new firm per se. The establishment of a new firm is therefore seen through a different perspective, and the resultant approach attempts to combine the ones adopted by various disciplines e.g. business studies, geography, psychology, and sociology.

The object of the following discussion and analyses in Chapters Seven and Eight is to broaden the explanatory base adopted in the present chapter. There is no readily available pool of new firms waiting to take advantage of new trading conditions. However, there may be a large pool of potential new firm founders, and it is their reactions to changing economic, personal, and social circumstances that determine the emergence of new firms. It is important, therefore, to consider the results of such an approach in any analysis of the new firm formation process.

In the final analytical chapter, Chapter Nine, the factors found either in association with, or affecting the formation and emergence of new firms are used in a spatial analysis of new firm formation. The analyses and different approaches adopted in the present and following two chapters provide some evidence to suggest which factors are important in new firm formation. Hence, the analyses and discussions contained in this chapter and in Chapters Seven and Eight are complementary in that they consider the same phenomena from different approaches, and provide inputs into the spatial analyses of Chapter Nine.

NOTES

1.   The term enterprise is used here rather than plant or establishment to represent an undertaking; a new undertaking.
2.   As recorded by the Department of Trade and Industry in 1972 and 1974 and by the Scottish Economic Planning Department/Industrial Development Department in 1976, 'Immigrant Firms who have Located Manufacturing Establishments in Scotland since 1945 which are still in Production.'
3.   A graphic approach is both simple and direct, but is open to error, and so the following formula was used:

$$G = \sqrt[N]{X_1 \times X_2 \ldots\ldots\ldots \times X_N} = \sqrt[N]{I_i I X_i}$$

G = Geometric Mean
N = Number of Cases
X = Variable Magnitude

4.   The formula used by Collins (1970, 124; 1972, 54) was:

$$\text{Mean Growth Rate} = \frac{\sum_{i}^{n} \frac{x_i}{y_i} - 1 \times 100}{N}$$

x_i = Size of Plant in 1965
y_i = Size of Plant in 1961
N = Number of Plants in each Quartile

In common with this equation the total number of plants are considered in each size group or industrial order to derive a similar mean or median growth rate figure.
5.   Spearman's Rank Correlation is used in preference to Kendell's Rank Correlation because of its simplicity of calculation. While this means partial rank correlation coefficients cannot be calculated, this is not seen as a disadvantage as the tests of association in this and the following section are intended to be exploratory.
6.   Food, drink, and tobacco; mechanical engineering; metal goods not elsewhere specified; textiles; and other manufacturing industries respectively.
7.   Mechanical engineering; electrical engineering; textiles; closing and footwear; and bricks, pottery, cement and glass respectively.
8.   This idea is subsumed within the notion that the totally new enterprise adapts itself to the prevailing market situation and is thus developed to meet that market. The new enterprise does not at this initial stage have to adopt new policies because it developed a product for the present market and industrial environment. However, with the passage of time the initial features and attributes of the new firm will have to change either consciously or by external forces.
9.   The size categories used by these studies to delimit 'small' are:
      Gudgin (1978, 137) - less than 20 employees
      Collins (1972, 73) - less than 11 employees
      Wedervang (1965, 178) - less than 20 employees
      Johnson and Cathcart (1978, 19) - less than 100 employees
      Gudgin and Fothergill (1978, 6) - between 11 and 19 employees.
10.   See above
11.   See Chapters Two (Tables 2.2, 2.3 and 2.4) Four, and Five where several aspects of industrial age are discussed both spatially and industrially.
12.   Johnson and Cathcart (1978) use employment change (expansion) figures for the 1960 - 73 period for their study of new enterprises and therefore constitutes at least an acknowledgement of the fact that the nature of the industry (expansion/contraction) might be important.

7 The Process of New Firm Formation: Avenues for Enquiry

INTRODUCTION

The discussion in the preceding three chapters has illustrated the nature and magnitude of employment change and the major characteristics of manufacturing plants opening in Scotland during the 1968 - 77 period. This discussion has highlighted some of the factors that might help explain the spatial and industrial variations in the number of new enterprises in terms of the local environment and specific industrial characteristics. Attention was also focused on the potential importance of two components of employment change, the closure and contraction of plants, upon the formation of new enterprises. The several hypotheses that were formulated and tested, were all set at the national level of Scotland, and this chapter is an extension of these analyses and attempts to develop a local framework for analysis of the process of new firm formation. In developing the framework, the ideas of the previous three chapters are integrated with the literature that exists on the topic.

Two approaches are adopted. The first approach is a general consideration of the process of new firm formation. Of particular importance is the way in which the proposed local framework helps extend the basic structure of the analysis. It is an attempt to unite the conditions operating at both the regional and the national levels with the formation of new manufacturing enterprises. Throughout this discussion the individual features of each of the major influences acting upon the new firm formation process are noted. The second approach involves the examination of some of these individual features. For while the general argument is intuitively appealing, it tends to lack both rigour and precision. To increase the clarity of the general argument it is therefore useful to disaggregate it into its constituent elements, and to consider their individual significance.

This chapter presents a framework for considering the process of new firm formation in its local, regional and national contexts. The chapter also suggests an a priori model of new firm formation. In the following chapter the arguments and ideas of the present chapter are scrutinised in the light of the knowledge gained from a survey of new indigenous enterprises. The final analytical chapter, Chapter Nine, takes the features of the local industrial environment and attempts to connect their existence, and hence possible influence, with the emergence of new manufacturing enterprises at the local level within the national context.

1. THE PROCESS OF NEW FIRM FORMATION

(a) A General Appraisal

The establishment and subsequent success, or failure, of a new
enterprise represents the culmination of a series of complex
processes. These processes operate in a large number of ways and
at times increase the likelihood of new firm formation. A new
enterprise is neither the product of either simple market forces,
nor for that matter the personal desire to be one's 'own boss', but
a combination of a huge range of personal (sociological/psychological),
situational (geographical), and related factors (economic and work
environment). It would appear both logical and prudent to be aware
of the possible importance and role played by these factors in the
new firm formation process if an overall assessment is to be made
(see BOULDING, 1956, 13).

Several views of the same phenomena, new enterprises, are also
made for both conceptual and methodological reasons. The first
reason concerns the form of the final statement of explanation
which the study seeks to make. In the social sciences the derivation
of exact laws determined under conditions that can be exactly
controlled are impossible. Furthermore, it is unlikely that such
laws exist in society, especially in that part of society which is
of concern here. As a consequence this study seeks to examine the
possible relationships between the emergence of new manufacturing
enterprises and their local environment. It is assumed that while
these relationships probably exist in other regions and nations, their
exact importance will vary through both space and time. The study is
therefore seeking to structure its findings around Herbst's (1970)
second type of law which states that:

> The functional form of the relationship is a universal
> constant but the parameters are specific. (ibid., 1970, 6)

A second reason for adopting a broad approach to the formation of
new manufacturing enterprises concerns the ability of the explanation
to relate the individual new enterprise to the total population of
manufacturing plants of which it forms a part. The formation and
development of a new manufacturing enterprise does not occur in
isolation. It will most probably reflect features of the local
industrial and social structures. Failure then to consider the
founders, their enterprises and the local conditions might remove
the possibility of explanation. It is in this attempt to go beyond
the now well established 'behavioural approach' (see HAMILTON, 1974;
LEIGH and NORTH, 1977, 1-13) that the study seeks to move for
explanation. In order to facilitate this move a structural approach
is adopted in which the actions of individuals are generally explicable
in terms of their position and relations with the structure of which
they form a part (MASSEY, 1975, 208; HARRIS, 1978, 8). Moreover, the
making of general statements concerning the overall patterns of
industry and actions of individuals should not be divorced (OLSSON,
1969, 21) because it is by the actions of individuals that the
overall patterns of industry are formed. It is therefore apparent
that in order to explain the formation of new manufacturing enterprises
recourse is necessary to the total population of plants, and at the
same time this helps to satisfy some of the methodological problems
encountered.

Three perspectives are adopted in the following discussion and each relates to a different aspect of the new firm formation process. The first perspective, the geographic, outlines the view taken in most geographic enquiries. Here, the centre of attention lies with the new enterprise itself and its location in space. A second perspective considers the formation of new enterprises by taking the founder and society as the main starting points. This sociological and psychological perspective tends to suggest links between the need for achievement and the motivation to work, and the formation of new enterprises. The final perspective assumes the broad stance taken by researchers in business studies and has much in common with both of the preceding perspectives. It considers not only the founder and his personal attributes, but also his previous work experience and so including some consideration of the environment. Each of these perspectives offers some insight into the founding process, and these are then brought together in a final section.

(b) A geographic perspective

Perhaps the most surprising aspect of geographic research into new firm formation is its very sparsity. Recent attention has been drawn to this position (WOOD, 1978, pp. 18-9, 27), and has been further highlighted by recent studies of inner city areas (ECONOMISTS ADVISORY GROUP Ltd., 1978; FIRN, 1979). A recent upsurge in interest in both new and small firms by geographers has greatly improved this situation (e.g. GUDGIN, 1978, 105-12; GUDGIN and FOTHERGILL, 1978; FAGG, 1979), but there still exists only a small number of papers that make reference to new firms. In most cases these studies have been only partially concerned with new firms and rarely with the founding process itself. Furthermore, they have tended to focus upon only the factors of supply in the local environment and little else.

However, despite this sparsity of substantial research two phrases are commonly used in the geographic literature concerning new firms, and they are: 'incubator area' and 'seedbed growth'. These terms have infiltrated the literature such that they now appear as conventional wisdoms, and in fact Gilmour (1974) has noted that these apparently conventional wisdoms concerning inner city manufacturing areas have remained largely untested by empirical enquiry. For example, the concept of seeded growth was implicit in the early work of Kerr and Spelt (1957, 9; 1958, 16) and also of Beesley (1955, 49). It also appeared in the work of both Logie (1952, 345) and Keeble (1968, 21), and since that time (1968) it has come to be firmly established in the geographic literature (e.g. TAYLOR, 1969; NORTH, 1974, 239; FALK, 1976, 1978; LEIGH and NORTH, 1978, 174). Yet probably the most concise definition of seedbed growth occurs in a work pre-dating most of the above studies. In this work by Hill (1954), seedbed growth is described as follows:

> An individual decides to go into business for himself. He may or may not join with others in this enterprise, but normally he will set up in some locality which he knows and in which he is known. He will do this for many reasons. He is more likely to know of suitable premises in his own neighbourhood since probably he will have been looking for them in ever widening circles around his own home. A building licence will not be required since in order to

minimize his risks he will want to be established near his
home in rented premises. Even if he has to build new premises
he may still not require an Industrial Development Certificate,
for the building may be less than 5,000 square feet. If he
remains near his home he has a ready-made headquarters,
probably knows his potential suppliers of raw materials and
part of his potential market, and may already have assured
part of his labour supply before he starts in production.
He may not need to engage any highly trained labour because he,
perhaps with his associates, will provide all the special
skill required. (ibid., 185)

He continues and makes what would appear to be a most important point:

On the face of it, such a business is highly mobile. The
capital outlay is probably small, labour demands are not
difficult to satisfy, raw materials may be generally available
throughout the country at fixed prices. ... such a unit, in
fact, more often than not turns out to be completely immobile; if
it is not established where the originator wants it, it will
not be established anywhere. (ibid., 185)

New firm formation has also come to be linked with the inner city
because of the inner city's advantages in terms of its external
economics. It is considered likely that the inner city offers a
wide range of cheap accommodation, access to suppliers, to markets,
and to other necessary ancilliary services. These new firms it is
suggested tend to trade in those industries in which their founders
were formerly employed, and so there is a tendency for a degree of
duplication of local industry to occur. It would also appear that
in the initial stages that new firms are immobile. In many respects
this position represents the present state of knowledge in geography.
Of course, extensions of these ideas do exist. For example, Leone
and Struyk (1976) divide the basic incubator notion into simple and
complex hypotheses. While this split helps to clarify certain
issues concerning new firms, it does not necessarily advance the
understanding of the new firm formation process. The two hypotheses
derived and used by Leone and Struyk (1976, 325) are:

... small manufacturing establishments will find it advantageous
to locate initially at high density, central locations within
the metropolis. (Simple hypothesis)

... new firms are formed in high density areas and move
outward from such cities in their early years of existence
in order to expand their productive activities. (Complex
hypothesis)

Implicit in both of these hypotheses and the above discussion is the
underlying importance of agglomeration forces which may provide
distinct cost advantages. It is perhaps unfortunate that most recent
work on inter-firm linkages has not been concerned with the formation
of new firms (e.g. BROOKS et al, 1973; McDERMOTT, 1977; HOARE, 1978),
because Taylor (1970, 54) saw local linkages "... as a necessary set
of conditions for the survival and further development of firms in
their areas of birth." However, this notion has only been
considered in part by several recent studies. For example, Gibb and
Quince (1978) considered the possible impact of the

decline of the shipbuilding industry in the North East of England upon small firms and so removing potential markets. They found that the re-organisation of the basic industry had possibly acted against the interests of small, and possibly new firms (ibid 1978, 11). Other studies have also commented upon the potential importance of a local sub-contracting market (e.g. STEED, 1976; GUDGIN, 1978, 116-120; SCOTTISH DEVELOPMENT AGENCY, 1979, 52-3).

Recent research has marked a shift in emphasis, and considers such factors as the migration and residential preferences of entrepreneurs (GUDGIN, 1978, 290-1; KEEBLE, 1978, 109-10), the possible role of new firms in the transfer of technology (for an overview see: ALEXANDER, 1975; GERMIDIS, 1977), and the skill levels of employees in branch plants in influencing the emergence of new firms (JOHNSON and CATHCART, 1978, 7; THWAITES, 1978, 458). Yet, in spite of these advances, even when considered with other general works (BAUMOL, 1968; LEIBENSTEIN, 1968: FIRN, 1973, 1975; CARNEY et al, 1977), they have not greatly improved the overall understanding of new firm formation. However, these studies have broadened and strengthened the previously narrow approach adopted by geographers. However, there still remains one major area of weakness and concerns the spatial scale at which the explanation of new firm formation is sought. It has tended to have been sought at the local, and not at any higher spatial level. It is thought to be important that the analysis is able to proceed at various spatial scales and so increase the likelihood of arriving at some form of explanation (MASSEY et al, 1976, 386; MASSEY, 1977, 11-2). Furthermore, the economic conditions existing at either the local or the regional level are unlikely to do so with any independence of each other. The local conditions that are likely to play the most important role in the new firm formation process are also probably subject to influences from both regional and national level forces. It is then important to structure the analysis to make allowance for this fact.

(c) A sociological/psychological perspective

While there are differences in the approaches adopted by sociologists and psychologists to the examination of the formation of new enterprise (KILBY, 1971, 2-3), they will not be maintained here. The studies placed under this broad heading can be allocated to two major categories depending on their point of departure. The first considers the personal desires and needs of the individuals and develops an entrepreneurial/ non-entrepreneurial classification scheme. This scheme is based on an individual's needs for achievement and the probability of success in attaining one's objectives (e.g. McCLELLAND, 1961; et al, 1969; KOCK, 1965). While McClelland's work in particular has been criticised on methodological grounds (SCHATZ, 1971, 185), it has generally been acclaimed as a major contribution not only to the study of new firm formation, but also of regional development (HOSELITZ, 1962; KATONA, 1962; WEISSKOPF, 1962).

Other works have extended this basic line of research (COLLINS et al, 1964; SCOTT, 1976) by offering further refinements to these basic notions, but have not presented a radically new perspective. Collins et al (1964, 245-6), for example, pointed to the interplay between economic opportunity and technological change on the one hand, and social structure and social values on the other, to explain entrepreneurship and its emergence within a society. Scott (1976, 234, 240-1) suggested that the emergence of entrepreneurs was a reaction to, and rejection of, the increasing bureaucratic nature of society. Both of these studies are extensions of the ideas contained in McClelland's earlier work, and also presents much useful data.

The second group of studies do not explicitly consider the formation of new firms as such, but concentrate instead on the motivation of people already employed. Here the work of Herzberg et al (1959, 2nd edition 1967) is of paramount importance (1), The existence of positive and negative attitudes to work stem from the importance of the work undertaken and the ability of an employee (a potential entrepreneur) to develop within a company (HERZBERG et al, 1967, 45-6, 138-9). A situation therefore exists where there is a continual acceptance and rejection by an employee of his position within a firm and if the job is finally rejected, for whatever reason (e.g. lack of identify in big companies, SCOTT, 1978, 12-3), there is the chance that he may set up a new firm (see LILES, 1974). Furthermore, the desire for another job may even promote a wider spatial search for employment and encourage migration to another area (for general discussion see: WOLPERT, 1965; TAYLOR, 1969; JOHNSON et al, 1974; and for the Scottish case see: SELF, 1966; JACK, 1968; FIRN, 1973; BELDING and HUTCHISON, 1978).

Thus, rather than providing hard statistical evidence supporting the influence of either an individual, or a society upon the founding process, both psychological and sociological studies do illustrate the importance of behaviourism as an approach to the analysis of new firm formation. These studies also indicate the potential significance of the ambitions and the aspirations of the entrepreneur and the role of the incubator organisation in frustrating these characteristics of the individual. And despite the problems of analysis, the present perspective does (and as indicated by this brief review) add to the overall appreciation of the complexity of the new firm formation process.

(d) A perspective from business studies.

Much of the work undertaken in North America on new firms has concerned the technical entrepreneur (SCHRAGE, 1965; ROBERTS and WAINER, 1968, 1971; ANON., 1969; ROBERTS, 1969; SUSBAUER, 1969); an entrepreneur that perhaps satisfies the more classical definition of an entrepreneur (THWAITES, 1977; WILKEN, 1979). However, despite this specific interest in one type of entrepreneurship, Cooper (1973, 60) has developed a framework in which the major factors acting upon the entrepreneur or new firm founder can be categorised (Figure 7.1). This framework allows data to be organised under three major headings: the antecedent influences upon the entrepreneur; the incubator organisation; and, the external or environmental factors. In adopting this method of organisation the advantages of the geographic and the sociological/psychological perspectives can be integrated to allow a relatively balanced appraisal of the new firm formation process.

Perhaps the main criticism of these studies is that they tend to be restricted in their spatial scope. For example, some major research projects conducted in the United States tended to restrict their search for explanation to the local level (SHAPERO et al, 1965;

Figure 7.1

An <u>a priori</u> model of entrepreneur/new enterprise formation.

(1)   Antecedent Influences Upon Entrepreneur

i.   Family and religious background.
ii.   Educational background.
iii.   Psychological make-up.
iv.   Age at time(s) of maximum external
       opportunity and organizational "push".
v.   Earlier career experience.
vi.   Opportunity to form entrepreneurial
       groups.

(2)   Incubator Organization

i.   Geographic location.
ii.   Nature of skills and knowledge acquired.
       (Depends on the administrative/functional
       divisions within the firm and is related
       to the productive methods used.)
iii.   Motivation to stay with or leave organiza-
       tion. (Linked to the above factor -
       awareness/motivation is partially dependent
       upon the incubator's organizational structure.)
iv.   Experience in "small business" setting. (Size
       structure of local/regional industry.)

(3)   External/Environmental Factors

i.   Examples of entrepreneurial action and
       availability of knowledge about
       entrepreneurship.
ii.   Societal attitudes toward entrepreneurship.
iii.   Ability to save "seed capital".
iv.   Accessibility and availability of venture
       capital.
v.   Availability of personnel and supporting
       services; accessibility to customers;
       accessibility to universities; etc.
vi.   Opportunities for interim consulting.
vii.   Economic conditions.

Entrepreneur's
Decision

Establishment
of a New
Enterprise

Source: Cooper (1973, 60, modified)

VOLLMER, 1965; DRAHEIM et al, 1966; SHAPERO et al, 1966) rather than attempt to integrate other aspects of the economy into their work e.g. the distribution of corporate headquarters and other facets of the economy (see GODDARD, 1975; PRED, 1976, 1977). It is interesting to note that when these four mid-sixty studies (by SHAPERO et al etc.) are taken collectively they do suggest the importance of adopting a larger spatial scale for enquiry. However, there are limits to the spatial scales that can be adopted. This is in part due to the acute problems of making, say, inter-nation comparisons (EGGAN, 1954; ALKER and RUSSETT, 1966, 350; LINZ and de MIGUEL, 1966, 269; LASSWELL, 1968; LEACH, 1968; NAROLL, 1968). One difference, for example, causing problems in comparing the formation of new firms in the United States with the situation in the United Kingdom is the structure of the banking system. Banking has largely developed, in the most simple of analyses, along centralised lines in the UK and Scotland (THOMSON, 1950, 190-1; JOHNSTON et al, 1971, 253-90; MURRAY, 1973, 107-20; SCOTT and HUGHES, 1975; TAIT, 1977), In the United States localised financial centres have developed which may tend to make finance (venture capital) more readily available.

The main contribution made by the work referred to in this section is that it has helped to identify and categorise the forces influencing the formation of new firms. By its very nature, therefore, it is interdisciplinary and readily combines with the approaches adopted by industrial geographers, psychologists and sociologists. And together, these three very brief sections suggest the importance of not adopting too narrow an approach to the study of new firm formation. At the same time it has highlighted some of the factors that may be important and many of these were listed in Figure 7.1. The following section attempts to combine the various aspects of the three approaches with the whole labour market. It is suggested that this broader approach may be conceptually useful because new firm founders are 'made', and probably do not form a distinct part of the labour market. In fact, there is probably a flow of individuals between various states of desire and intention towards being self-employed. At any time the numbers of individuals who might become new firm founders could therefore be quite large, and it is important to include these individuals in the analysis. It is from this population of potential new firm founders that the next generation of new firms will emerge.

(e) Towards an integrated approach

In any one year approximately 10 million people change their employer. There are flows of employees between local employers and between employers in different parts of the country. This latter group of individuals not only change their employer, but also their place of residence. The flows are not restricted to these two types because there are a number of 'employment fates' open to all individuals. Six employment fates are detailed in Figure 7.2. Movement to each of these fates will be influenced by a series of factors some of which have been noted earlier in this chapter. For example, it was suggested that the psychological make-up of an individual effects their actions. Likewise, the previous employers of an individual will influence his skills, his knowledge, and his abilities.

Thus, the three preceding sections have offered a series of observations on the formation of both the founder and his firm which

185

Figure 7.2

Possible employment fates and
the individual employee.

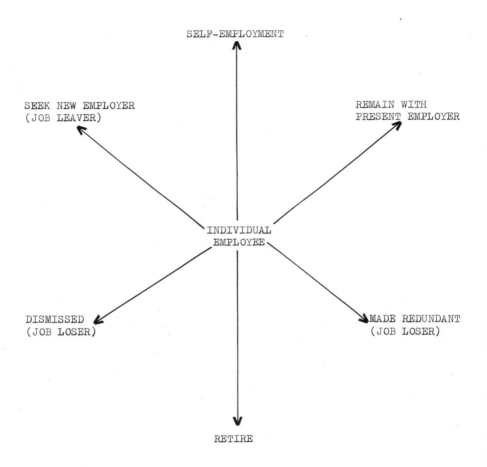

SELF-EMPLOYMENT

SEEK NEW EMPLOYER
(JOB LEAVER)

REMAIN WITH
PRESENT EMPLOYER

INDIVIDUAL
EMPLOYEE

DISMISSED
(JOB LOSER)

MADE REDUNDANT
(JOB LOSER)

RETIRE

have been the outcome of the transfer from being an employee to being self-employed. This transfer from employment to self-employment obviously forms a very small percentage of the total number of changes of employment in any one year because the relative numbers of new firms established is not great. However, while this small and specialised flow of individuals may form a distinct element of the labour market, it may at the same time represent part of a larger employment transfer process specific to the individual. For example, it is shown in Chapter Eight that few new firm founders become self-employed without having had at least ten years previous work experience. They have also often changed their employer before becoming self-employed (in 76 per cent of cases). The changing of an employer might not only suggest a certain degree of training, i.e. acquiring skills and knowledge, but also reflect the changing aspirations and needs of the individual (SWORDS, 1976). It is also important to note that it is not only the nature of the aspirations that differs between individuals and within the life of an individual, but also the intensity with which they are pursued (FOX, 1971).

One could therefore suggest a number of blocks which may prevent an individual from pursuing one type of employment. These factors might include personal circumstances, personal needs etc. It might therefore be possible to identify the likelihood of setting up a new firm (a potential new firm founder) by means of a Job Diagnostic Survey (JDS: HACKMAN and OLDHAM, 1975). By using a JDS to collect information from a cohort type sample of individuals from their entry into the labour market until their leaving it, it might be possible to distinguish key variables in relation to core job dimensions and the individual's central psychological states. Each job move, for whatever reason, could therefore be placed within the overall labour market, and this would be explicable in terms of an individual's job and psychological state. Similarly, in many cases the interaction of job content and psychological state will be positive and so increase the likelihood of an individual remaining with his present employer. Of course, an individual's response to both the changes in job content and his own psychological state will vary with time. His sensitivity to change will vary. The response of an individual will vary as a result of personal disposition and inclination, and will also reflect his 'conditioning' received in different employment situations (after CHAPIN, 1978; CULLEN, 1978). Each employment move made will therefore place individuals in a new employment environment and a new employment situation. These will expose the individual to new ideas, to new ways, and to new possibilities. The skills possessed by an individual will reflect these changes as will his aspirations and his willingness to pursue them.

If we are to attempt to understand the process of new firm founder formation, and hence new firm formation, it might prove useful to devote some attention to the operation of the labour market. More specifically, attention could be focussed at the level of the individual in the labour market, in the employing organisations, and at home. It is the interplay of the individual with these three environments which will largely determine his likelihood of becoming a new firm founder. All employment changes made by an employee can therefore be seen as possibly either impeding or enhancing the likelihood of an individual becoming self-employed in his own firm. Figure 7.3 offers an initial framework which could be used as a starting point

Figure 7.3

New firm founder formation: A labour market approach

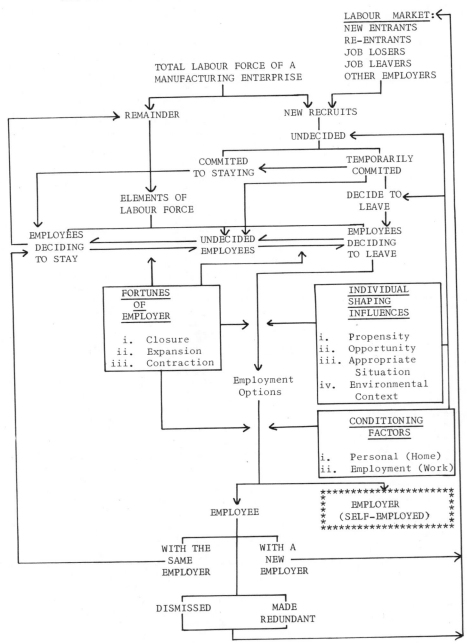

in any further consideration of the labour market and new firm founder formation. It is this general framework which is used throughout the following discussions and analyses.

(f) Summary and conclusion

This section has presented a number of perspectives from which the formation of new firms can be viewed. It ended by offering a framework which attempted to combine the three preceding perspectives and to place them within the more general context of the labour market. In that final discussion it was suggested that by adopting a wider frame of reference it might be possible to identify aspirant and potential new firm founders. It might well be that the new firms that do emerge represent only a small percentage of those new firm founders who wish to be self-employed in their own firm (GOLDTHORPE et al, 1968, 131-6). This might be a useful line of enquiry if one wished to encourage aspirant new firm founders to pursue their desires more rigorously, and to actually set up their own firm.

2. NEW FIRM FORMATION: ASPECTS OF THE PROCESS

While it is important to set the study of new firms in both a broad subject and spatial contexts, it is equally important to consider individual aspects of the new firm formation process. These individual aspects range from the general economic conditions to the more specific areas of the founder's characteristics and the supply of venture capital. Such aspects are probably present in the formation of all new firms, and what varies is their importance in each case. Four aspects are considered here and they serve to reveal still further the complexity of the founding process. They also help to delimit some of the data requirements for the analysis of new firm founder formation undertaken in the following chapter (Chapter Eight).

(a) General conditions of the small business sector.

Small businesses elicit a wide range of responses from various organisations. Politically, small businesses have been welcomed with a varying enthusiasm (BROWN et al, 1976; JEWKES, 1977; CURRIE, 1978; Small Business). At the local level, the level to which most small businesses will readily identify themselves with, have an equally mixed attitude towards small businesses (FOY, 1977; ABBOT, 1978). Even research into small firms has not yet been able to pinpoint the real benefits of encouraging small businesses. Admittedly, in aggregate terms small businesses are important, and likewise for social reasons (OXENFELDT, 1943; KAPLAN, 1948; CBI, 1968; WAITE, 1973). The present euphoria over small businesses, which may not last, only helps to continue the variable attitudes and allegiances of government at various levels to small businesses.

Yet, given this situation, what would appear to be the present trends in the small business sector? A recent analysis of the trends in the small business sector would suggest that the overall position is buoyant (HAMILTON, R. T., 1977a). In this analysis, Hamilton notes:

The growth in the number of companies has been fairly steady since 1968 and so lends support to an apparent resurgence of small manufacturing firms since 1968 ... . it is quite clear that the growth in the number of businesses per unit of population is due almost entirely to the very rapid increase in the number of businesses trading under a registered business name and without the protection of limited liability. Research carried out on behalf of the Bolton (2) Committee indicated that 16 per cent of small MANUFACTURING businesses trade without limited liability. Given that the growth in the business population can be accounted for in terms of the increased number of unlimited liability operations, one must conclude that the orientation of new business activity has been largely towards the NON-MANUFACTURING areas. (ibid., 5)

This evidence would tend to suggest that the general working hypothesi might be, that:

... the typical entrepreneur of today is quite a different animal from his counterpart of the middle to late 1950's. ... In particular ... the flow of new businesses has shifted away from manufacturing industries. (HAMILTON, R.T., 1977b)

Given the lower level of employment in small manufacturing plants in the UK in comparison with, say, Europe (HAMILTON, R. T., 1975), one may infer that this shift is not occurring elsewhere as quickly. At the same time there has been an increase in the importance of the state sector on employment. For example, the state sector in the UK increased by 5.8 per cent or 402,000 employees over the period 1974 (June) to 1976 (June) and this excludes employment in companies owned by the National Enterprise Board (The Economist, Jan. 14th, 1978, 95). And likewise, a concentration of productive capacity in fewer firms has also occurred (PRAIS, 1976). But regionally there has been marked increases in the numbers of employers and self-employed in the South East over the 1966-74 period, while the level has remained almost static in Scotland (DEPARTMENT OF EMPLOYMENT GAZETTE, 1976, 1349).

However, do these general conditions have an equal influence throughout the country? Of course, the general conditions cannot operate equally throughout the country because the distribution of industry is not ubiquitous. Furthermore, if as Foy (1977) believes there is no shortage of entrepreneurs to take advantage of opportunities when local conditions are 'right', the distribution of these potential entrepreneurs may in some way be related to the distribution of industry. The emergence of new firms may also be a reflection of safe (more certain) locations. In fact, Webber (1972) suggested that the location of firms was related to the level of certainty of a location such that:

When uncertainty is at a maximum (the firms cannot relocate and cannot communicate) they locate at the centre. When uncertainty parallels reality - when relocation is costly and when firms cannot communicate (because they do not know each other) - a central location is still very likely. But when uncertainty is low (mobility and communication are perfect) the firms are more attracted to the higher profit, less conservative locations. (ibid., 157)

Of course, the notion of profitability varying <u>directly</u> as a function
of location is somewhat unreal (PARSONS, 1972), but uncertainty or
lack of confidence may be reflected in, say, the availability of
investment capital. The lack of available capital could operate
in two ways, either as an absolute lack or in the charging of higher
interest rates (KEEBLE, 1976, 71). Similarly, lack of confidence could
also influence other factors of supply, e.g. provision of premises,
and even the decision to establish a new firm.

To return this discussion to the main theme, that of the general
economic conditions facing small firms, it would appear that the
general conditions facing all small firms are almost always uncertain.
The official response, which can best be termed reactive, has been
the setting up of several committees to consider the problems of
small firms both in financial (MacMILLAN, 1931; RADCLIFFE, 1959) and
in general terms (BOLTON, 1971). The net result of the MacMillan
committee was the setting up of the Industrial and Commercial Finance
Corporation. Legislation inacted in the United States was also in
response to the 'institutional gap' in the provision of capital to
small business especially venture capital and long-term credit.
While the problem was seen as much the same in the USA the response
was somewhat different. For example, the Small Business Investment
Act of 1958 (in the US) had as one of its main functions to license
and regulate small business investment companies (McCALLUM, 1959).
This act has allowed the development of industry and area specific
investment companies sensitive to changes within an industry or an
area, and they are therefore more likely to consider an application
for finance more sympathetically than the more centralised financial
institutions who operate under different restrictions (EASTBURN,
1966).

While the above discussion has been wide ranging, it has suggested
that the emergence and subsequent growth of new firms are dependent
not only on hard economic factors of production and the personal
traits of the individual founders, but also upon the general conditions
in which they operate. Conditions as determined by political changes,
state involvement in industry and, of course, the reaction of the
financial institutions are equally important. In essence, then,
the influence of impressions and attitudes may be of paramount
importance in determining the degree of acceptance and the conditions
which small firms must initially face (see EVERSLEY, 1976).

(b) New firm founders: Some of their characteristics

The characteristics of an entrepreneur cannot be separated out as
they are all highly interdependent. In the discussion contained in
this section is a brief view of the new firm founder and some of
his or her characteristics (especially age and career) which may be
important in determining their emergence as new firm founders. And
the discussion revolves around the question: Who are the entrepreneurs?
In his lucid reply, Liles integrated the development of an individual's
skills and abilities with their age and family commitments. Liles
argued that the ability to found a new company is related to the
founder's general self-confidence which in turn is dependent upon the
acquisition of skills to solve complex problems. Thus, by continually
acquiring new skills, an individual's readiness to tackle new
problems also increases and by the time an individual has been

employed for 10 - 15 years (age being 35 - 40) the maximum level of
competence has probably been attained. However, the ability and the
freedom to act do not necessarily coincide. If one then combines
these two concepts (Figure 7.4) the general picture that results
is one approaching a description of the 'typical entrepreneur'.

But how does this description direct further enquiry? Perhaps
most directly, it would suggest that the working histories of
founders are important in determining the level of skills or
abilities possessed. The impact of the family life cycle would
also appear important, but possible less so when compared to career
development because without the necessary skills and allied self-
confidence one might not consider establishing a firm in the first
place.

It is probably now evident why the level of skills possessed by
the individuals in an area's labour market, and the associated
nature of employment in that area are seen as potentially important
factors in accounting for the spatial variations in the numbers (rate)
of new firms established. Furthermore, the mechanics or operations
of the labour market and its interaction with the local stock of
employees may also be important. For example, the level of quits,
either voluntary or involuntary, may be important in determining
the number of potential entrepreneurs an area possesses at any one
time. And, if the aim of the analysis is to consider employment
histories of individuals as a part of the new firm formation process,
which it is, then it would appear necessary to integrate them with
other aspects of the labour market (see Figure 7.2). It is in the
final section of this chapter that this part of the new firm formation
process is integrated with an overall framework for analysis and
explanation.

(c) Venture capital: Its accessibility and availability.

Probably the most fundamental input into any new company is that of
the initial finance. Yet, "... after all the careful and convincing
financial researchers commissioned by the Bolton enquiry, we still
don't know whether the financial facilities for completely new small
firms are adequate." (BOSWELL, 1973, 195) However, Boswell admits
later that the present provision of financial facilities for the
established small firm sector seems to operate satisfactorily
(ibid., 198). The findings of the Wilson Committee (1979; see
BINKS, 1979) would also tend to confer with this view. It is
perhaps surprising, then, to find statements such as these:

>   Individuals have so little disposable income after penal
>   marginal rates of direct taxation that they cannot afford
>   to invest in small business.... . (BROWN et al, 1976, 35)
>
>   Start-up capital ... is almost unobtainable from
>   institutions. (ibid., 35)

It would appear safe to say that far more needs to be known about the
financing of new companies and the mechanisms best suited to
administering finance to them (see READMAN, 1975; WILKINS, 1976).
The purpose of this section is to present part of the general
discussion concerning the financing of new firms drawing heavily from
the early pioneering work undertaken in the USA.

Figure 7.4

Readiness to start a venture and the free choice
period for the would-be entrepreneur.

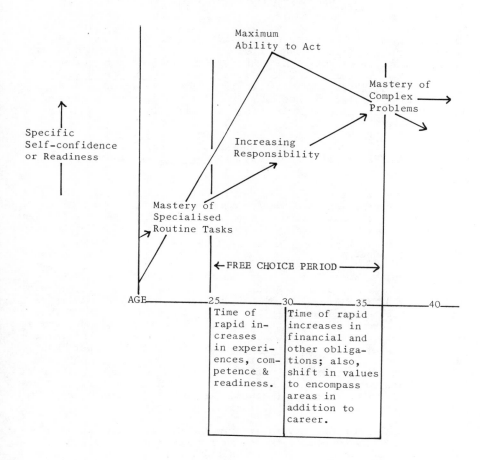

Source: LILES (1974, 9 and 11, Figures 1 and 2 combined)

Venture capital financing is far from being always profitable, in
fact substantial losses on 25 - 40 per cent of the investments made
should be expected and even then, it is necessary to allow on
average 6 - 7 years for an investment to mature and make a profit
on selling (ROTCH, 1968, 147). Financing small new businesses
therefore does not present an immediately attractive proposition.
Yet, despite this position, the flow of funds from Small Business
Investment Companies to new firms still occurs, mainly in the hope
of supra-normal profits (see MASON, 1963). Within certain sectors,
notably electronics - a high technology industry - there has been a
'scramble' for the issues of new firm's shares (Business Week, April
15th., 1961). This 'scramble' for involvement in new high technology
firms stems from the success of such companies over the preceding
20 - 30 years. One of the first and now major investment companies
(Time, Aug., 19th, 1946, 35) believed that:

> If only two in ten projects chosen succeeded, ... ,
> American Research would thrive. (Newsweek, April 4th.,
> 1949, 23)

This expectation of success has meant that with increased 'know-how'
and the success of science-based companies there has been both an
increase in the confidence of the banking community, and the emergence
of certain areas of the USA with a greater sympathy to the financing
of new technical companies (Business Week, Oct. 29th., 1960;
DEUTERMAN, 1966).

Other aspects are also important in the provision of venture
capital. For example, some areas of the microwave industry, it was
felt in 1960 (SHEPARD, 1960), would experience annual growth rates
of somewhere between 25 and 50 per cent. Projected growth of this
size would tend to increase the probability of success, and perhaps
what is more, subsequent growth. Such forecasts tend to impress the
inexpert investor and acts to give an air of optimism rather than
directly increase the availability of funds. The apparent buoyancy
of an industry also tends to mask the problems of operating in that
industry, especially for the new company (BOWER, 1959) and therefore
creates a false sense of confidence. All of which in turn may
increase the flow of venture capital to new firms.

There is therefore an interplay between the attributes and
abilities of a new company, the overall success of new firms, and
their reception by the financial institutions. It is in many ways
doubtful if funds will ever be supplied more freely to new enterprises and perhaps the final comment should be left to Marcum (1963)
who saw that:

> The important question may be not, "What institutional
> structure can fill the institutional gap in our system
> of money supply?" but rather, "Why does this gap exist?"
> And the inescapable conclusion is that it exists because
> it is simply not economically feasible to fill it under
> the present circumstances of uncertainty surrounding the
> smaller business - an uncertainty that is caused by the
> untested value of the management of new ventures. (ibid.,11)

Undoubtedly, Marcum's comment is very true today, but the role of

local banking and the availability of venture capital play an
important part in regional growth and the buoyancy of the small firm
sector (HIRSCH, 1960a and 1960b). Several aspects of raising initial
finance are considered in the following chapter and they tend to
support the importance of management expertise in raising finance for
a new firm.

(d) New firm formation: Spin-offs and innovation.

In this section two aspects of the new firm formation process are
introduced. The first concerns 'spin-offs', the establishment of
new technical firms from a research laboratory or similar establishment, though the term might equally apply to the establishment of
all new firms. The second considers the innovatory nature of new
firms and their importance as a possible source of invention.

As a term, spin-off tends to be used to describe those new
companies that represent the direct usage of an idea or invention
developed in, say, a university laboratory. A series of articles
during the 1960s and 1970s discussed the role of universities in the
establishment of new technology based firms in Michigan (LAMONT, 1972),
Boston and Cambridge (PETERS and ROBERTS, 1969) and in general terms
(DANILOV, 1963; MAHAR and CODDINGTON, 1965; MAPES, 1967). What
these authors tended to suggest was that an individual or a group of
individuals develop an idea or a product within the established
research framework. However, the decision to move from the realisation
that a new idea might be commercially viable to the setting up of a
company to capitalise upon the idea varied. What does appear though
is that a push factor is often important, such as a cutback in
government financing of research thus frustrating the aspirations of
a research team. More directly, cuts in research grants may lead
to staff being made redundant and thus have little option sometimes
but to set up a new firm. The distribution of research funds is
not evenly spread throughout a country and so university research is
concentrated in a few major centres (DANILOV, 1963, 22-3) and has
tended to lead to a concentration of spin offs in a few distinct
areas (ROBERTS and WAINER, 1968; ANON., 1969).

Spin-offs are of course not restricted to universities, the local
industries also provide the necessary laboratory facilities as well
(DRAHEIM et al, 1966, 47, 121, 123, 125-27, 137, 139, and 142;
SUSBAUER, 1969, 133). Furthermore, it appears from studies in this
country (the UK) (GIBBONS and WATKINS, 1970; WATKINS, 1971) and the
USA (see earlier references) that spin offs are not that different
from the establishment of any other new firm. Perhaps the main
distinguishing feature is the level of technology involved and the
basic importance of research ideas rather than marketing or
production knowledge. If this is taken as the main distinguishing
feature between 'ordinary' new firms and spin offs, there still
remains the problem of evaluating the role of new firms as agent
of innovation.

The transfer of technology can occur in three broad ways. First,
by the formation of new companies; spin offs. Second, the licensing
of production to an individual by a company. Third, a company may
actively attempt to market "... all kinds of excess technology -
process, proprietary know-how, even whole product lines that had not

been especially profitable ... but might be profitable if transferred into other hands." (FRONKO, 1971, 52) M. J. Taylor (1977) has developed this theme by considering the sources of applications for patents in New Zealand in 1970 and 1971.   He tentatively concluded that the patterns of inventiveness might have important implications for regional development and noted that:

> ... growth in the South Island refers to growth of organizations that already exist, growth in the North Island refers not only to such corporate expansion, but also to the generation of new enterprise and new enterprises, greatly enhancing its growth potential. (ibid., 340)

In a similar vein, Roberts (1969) in reviewing research undertaken in the Boston area stated that:

> ... the flow of entrepreneurs out of advanced technical organizations into their own businesses can create significant technology transfers as well as impressive commercial and economic impact. (ibid., 228)

Unfortunately, he fails to substantiate this claim. However, in an earlier paper, Roberts (1968, 264) reports that "... from one major company studied 32 spin-off firms now account for sales more than double those of their parent." Evidence such as this does not allow a full assessment of the importance of technology transferred in, say, terms of employment created or increased regional prosperity. Individuals are undoubtedly important in providing the market place with new inventions (JEWKES et al, 1958, 263-410), but to give them some mystical property explaining regional variations is probably not useful. In fact no study to-date has attempted to evaluate new technology generated employment as divided between the expansion of existing plants, the establishment of new firms, and the opening of new plants. This balance between plant expansion and openings will undoubtedly vary with industry, and hence through space. How these variations express themselves directly or indirectly is not at present known (FIRN and SWALES, 1978, 202). It would appear important to know what the importance of new firms are both industrially (see FREEMAN, 1971) and spatially (OAKEY, 1979b) in the technology transfer process before any meaningful statements can be made about the role new firms play in the process (see THWAITES, 1978). The implications of the infusion of new technology into a region go beyond merely the advantage of short-term growth, but may also (probably will) have a direct effect in the long-term upon a region's economic growth (Le HERON, 1973).

This brief view of spin-offs and their possible innovatory role has suggested that the process by which spin-offs or technical companies are founded differs only in degree from the processes that underlie the formation of all new firms. The major differences lie in the levels of technology involved. The debate over the importance of new firms in supplying new innovations and new inventions remains open. However, recent evidence would tend to suggest that in many industries the small firms do play an important innovatory role within the whole economy (KAMIEN and SCHWARTZ, 1975). Furthermore, the flows of technology between industries and between areas are ones that may be amenable to policy measures (LITTLE, 1973; ROTHWELL and ZEGVELD, 1978; GODDARD et al, 1979).

3. THE PROCESS OF NEW FIRM FORMATION: AN INTEGRATED VIEW

In this final section is presented an integrated view (Figure 7.3) which attempts to relate the functioning of the labour market to the emergence of new firm founders, and hence new firms. Here the emphasis is laid upon the labour market and the conditions necessary for the emergence of new firm founders for two reasons. First, most of the features noted in this chapter are amenable to some form of measurement. And second, before any of the other factors become important to the setting-up of a new company e.g. availability of finance, sites, etc., there must be a number of individuals with sufficient ambition and ability to establish a new firm. What follows is an articulation of the approach contained in Figure 7.3 and which is further amplified in Table 7.1.

Table 7.1

Factors affecting the labour market and either promoting and/or impeding the emergence of new firm founders

Factor	The Emergence of Entrepreneurs Promoting	Impeding	Spatial Scale*
Market served	Buoyant/Growing	Static/Declining	R/N
Degree of autonomy	High	Low	R/N
Age of investment	Young	Old	R/N
Employment skills	High	Low	L
Employment turnover	Low	High	L
Employment security	Medium/High	Low/Medium	L
Plant size	Small/Medium	Large	L
Employment structure	Fully developed	Weakly developed	L
Length of service	Medium/Long	Short	I
Career experience	Managerial	Operative	I

* N = National; R = Regional; L = Local; I = Individual.

Source: See text.

Both Figure 7.3 and Table 7.1 suggest that there are a series of processes acting upon and within any labour market, and these forces can originate from actions taken at a national, at a regional, or even at a local level. Apportioning forces to one spatial scale is problematic as there are a large number of plants whose operations are determined by local conditions. However, the sales of these locally dependent firms are often made to plants whose production is a function of both regional and national level demands. Likewise, the separation of factors into those promoting and impeding the emergence of new firm founders is also unreal. In fact, some of the factors depicted as promoting the emergence of new firm founders may in some circumstances actually impede their emergence. A similar situation may also exist for those factors suggested as impeding the emergence of new firm founders. In both instances, the position denoted by Table 7.1 is an idealised one and should be seen as illustrating one possible combination of factors. Furthermore, despite these problems, the proposed series of factors offers some illumination of the factors that may influence the emergence of new firm founders (see SAMUELSON, 1976).

During the periods of employment experienced by a new firm founder prior to establishing his new firm a series of influences are in operation 'on him' and a number of employment opportunities are open to him. It is the interplay between these influences and opportunities that help shape the new firm founder, and may also be responsible for the development of his career awareness and his heightened level of motivation. The latter two items, career awareness and motivation, will also be influenced by the personal traits of the individual and the management style of his employer (see SADLER et al, 1974). Neither of these aspects are considered in depth here, but it is important to be aware of their possible influence and role in the new firm formation process.

Every position within every firm requires some ability to solve problems of either a highly complex or of a routine nature. Throughout a firm the number of routine tasks dimishes as progression is made from factory floor operatives to managerial positions. A similar progression by an individual through their career development is also by the movement from one position to another. At each stage new skills are being required, and they are subsequently gained through experience in the job and possibly training. Of course, the development of an individual's career is not limited to remaining with one employer forever, and it may be structured by the taking of a new position in another firm. The development of an individual's career is not only important in terms of the acquisition of skills, but also in the personal advancement of the individual. And by acquiring new skills and tackling new problems, the abilities and the potential of an individual may be realised.

It is when this pattern of progression is broken that changes can occur. For example, if the promotion prospects of an individual becomes blocked, he might decide to leave his present employment. On leaving they enter into a situation where there are several options open to them and these were noted in Figure 7.1. It could be suggested that in circumstances such as these an individual may become a new firm founder if other employment opportunities do not present themselves locally. There is also the possibility that the individual may be willing to move to a new area to find suitable employment. Such a move may involve transferring to a provincial centre or to London rather than to remaining in a local one. However, of overriding importance are the aspirations and the motivations of the individual concerned. The example given here suggests that there may be a need for a 'triggering' or 'push' mechanism almost forcing individuals to rethink their position. In many cases these push factors may play a secondary role to the personal ambitions of an individual, but all the same they are present. It is also impossible to disentangle the importance of push factors or personal motivation several years after becoming self-employed. As with changes in job, domestic committment etc., so do the aspirations of individuals. Likewise, the importance of the factors leading to the establishing of the company may also change with hindsight. In both of these cases, the potential new firm founder has been working in, what could be termed, 'non-entrepreneurial' conditions. The point being made is that while the overall conditions did not actually impede the emergence of entrepreneurs, they were perhaps not the best environment in which to develop new firm founders. It is possible that such conditions might encourage the founding of companies in similar, and possibly declining industries.

From the immediately preceding discussion it is evident that the situations depicted of the individual within the organisation (firm) are similar to those developed elsewhere concerning the theory of the firm (MARCH and SIMON, 1958, 84 and 94-104; CYERT and MARCH, 1963, 26-43). There is, therefore, a relationship between the perceived gains made by an individual within an organisation, the performance of that organisation and its ability to survive (3), and the aspirations of the individual.

A reverse situation can be conceived where the potential new firm founder is working within a highly dynamic environment within a firm, say, operating in a high technology field. Here there are many possible outcomes from the same circumstances. The general case would be one where the individual is working for a company whose growth has been dramatic over several years. With the growth of sales, the company has developed specialist skills that have given it a competitive edge within a national market. However, the number of ideas moving from conception to full development has dimished with time as the company has developed.

The above argument includes many of the elements of the approaches noted earlier and represents in many ways the characteristics of the new firm founders described by Liles (1974). What factors then are likely to either promote, or impede the emergence of new firm founders? Any factor that affects the labour market will in some way affect the emergence of new firm founders. For example, in any industry which is in decline the threat of redundancy is probably not only great, but is also occurring and this would tend to decrease job security and increase labour turnover. There are several possible scenarios to this situation. In one case, an individual may be redundant either due to the contraction, or closure of a plant and is then forced to leave and to enter into the labour market. The attraction of setting up a new firm might not only be a product of the unfamiliarity with the labour market and the arousal of latent motivation, but also the realisation that the likelihood of obtaining employment at their age (if greater than 45) or at a level to which they had become accustomed is not great. Thus the number of options open to such an individual might not be great.

A second possibility is one where an individual leaves a company that is ailing prior to redundnacies being made. It is probably that the perceived employment security and chances of career development are not within the present firm and are best pursued in a market position which has to be 'defended'. The company's ability to change has also tended to decrease with time, and the number of highly skilled employees that are dissatisfied has increased. In fact, the company has reached a hiatus, a position where future growth can be derived through diversification using in-house products, expanding the market share of existing products, or by acquiring other companies. The loss of self-generated growth might lead to changes in the nature of the company. In circumstances such as these, the would-be new firm founder has developed their skills in a buoyant situation and perhaps has an awareness of potential markets not tried by the present employer. There is also the strong possibility that the company itself was also entrepreneur-based and has therefore provided a role model on which the individual can base his own company.

While the above discussion is a very much idealised view of the new firm formation process, it would tend to suggest that there are situations in which changes within the company can force certain individuals to re-evaluate their position within the company. To this end, it is important to realise that there is a distinct interaction between the individual components of employment change and the process of new firm formation. Furthermore, any factor that causes employment to be drawn from or to be placed into the local labour market will have an effect upon the number of potential new firm founders an area may have. In addition to this, the nature of the employment opportunities in an area are also important in determining the skills the members of a single labour market possess.

The above elaboration of the overall framework of the new firm formation process can thus be conceived of in the following general manner:

> The number of potential new firm founders in an area is a function of the relationship between an individual and their present employer, and of the relationship between that employer and the markets in which its products are sold. Changes in either, or both of these relationships will act to either impede or promote the formation of new firms. The nature of the former relationship is itself a function of the characteristics of the present employer which in turn may influence the latter's relationship with the market served.

In the following two chapters the validity of such a series of statements are examined. The first examines their validity in general aspatial terms, whilst the second considers them in spatial terms. They are complementary in that the first initially validates and measures those factors thought to be important in the formation of new firm and their founders, while the second combines these factors within a spatially disaggregated analysis.

NOTES

1. All page references refer to the 1967 edition.
2. Bolton (1971, 36).
3. See Rose (1978, 187-94) for some further thoughts on this topic.

8 New Firm Formation: Aspects of the Process

While describing some of the possible approaches to the study of new firm formation, Chapter Seven and to a lesser extent Chapter Six, have presented arguments indicating the possible importance of the local environment in the new firm formation process. In particular four factors emerged as being worthy of further consideration:

    (a) The previous employment position of the founders,
    (b) The previous employer of the founders,
    (c) The local economic environment, and
    (d) Any factors possibly impeding new firm formation.

This chapter examines each of these factors in turn and combines the findings of the study with previous ones where possible. The object of the chapter is twofold. First, to place several aspects of the process of new firm formation on a sound empirical base and to compare the findings with previous studies. And second, examine aspects of the model of new firm formation outlined in the previous chapter. Before attempting these two objectives, however, it is necessary to briefly describe the survey and data upon which the chapter is based.

1. THE SURVEY

The data for the present chapter were gathered during 1978 from 191 new manufacturing enterprises operating in Scotland during 1977 and which had been established between 1968 (January 1st) and 1977 (December 31st). One of the main concerns of the survey was to gain as large a response rate as was possible and to this end sampling was not undertaken. And so all of the new manufacturing enterprises identified were contacted and from 191 data were collected. A more full consideration of both the survey and data are available elsewhere (CROSS, 1980, 383-93). However, it should be added that comparisons made by employment size, industry, location and year of opening revealed the population of surveyed firms not to be biased in any direction. It was concluded from these comparisons that variations in coverage do exist, but none were so large as to invalidate the use of the sample in any analysis.

2. THE FOUNDER: PREVIOUS EMPLOYMENT AND CAREER EXPERIENCE

The founder of each new enterprise has a series of attributes or characteristics that are amenable to either recording or measurement, but this is not the case with all the features considered below. For example, the recording of the reason (motivating factor) for leaving one job to either take another or set-up a new enterprise will be partially dependent upon the articulate or inarticulate nature of the founder (WAGNER, 1939). Apart from this difficulty, this section reports on six features of the founders covered in the survey and compares them when and where possible with previous empirical studies.

(a) Number of jobs held prior to company formation

Most new firm founders have held two or more jobs (76 per cent) before setting-up a new company. A similar position has been noted in Austin, Texas by Susbauer (1969) for the founders of new technical companies. The three series of figures used in Table 8.1 are not directly comparable with those of the present study.

Table 8.1
Number of jobs held by new firm founders prior to
company formation compared with other studies

Number of Previous Employers	Present Study No.	%	Susbauer[a] (1969) %	Shapero et al[b] (1965) %	Watkins[c] (1973) %
0	0	0.0	0.0	24.7	0
1	43	24.02	30.5	21.2	26
2	49	27.37	21.7	17.2	29
3	34	18.99	8.7	13.3	23
4	21	11.73	17.4	9.1	16
5	17	9.49	21.7	6.4	5
6	7	3.91	–	)	–
7	3	1.68	–	) 14.1[d]	–
8	4	2.23	–	)	–
9	1	0.56	–	)	–
Total	n = 179		n = 23	n = 30161	n = 56

[a]Susbauer (1969) Table V-2, p.131
[b]Shapero et al (1965) Table 13, p.49
[c]Watkins (1973) Figure 2, p.66
[d]More than five jobs held

First, Susbauer's study (1969) considered only new technical companies where as the present study considers all types of new firms. Second, the study by Shapero et al (1965) concerns the characteristics of engineers and scientists in both Los Angles and Boston and not new firm founders, yet despite this, their findings are remarkably similar to those for new firm founders. This might indicate the possible non special nature of new firm founders, and that they represent one part of the labour market. It should also be noted that the turnover rate and hence the number of jobs held by engineers and scientists was found to vary inversely with education (SHAPERO et al, 1965, 43), be higher in the defence industries (ibid, 44) and vary with region (see DRAHEIM et al, 1966, Table 13, 29). On the last issue Vollmer (1965, Chapter Four) noted that the:

> Turnover among scientists seems to have been
> higher in the New England, Mountain and Pacific
> regions, while it appears to have been lowest in
> the South Atlantic states. (ibid.,8)

Also important in determining turnover rates is the length of
service (SHAPERO et al, 1965, 44; see BARTHOLOMEW, 1977) and the
type of firm (SHAPERO et al, 1965, Table 9, 44; GLEAVE and PALMER,
1978; Chapter Five, 232-36). Third, and finally, the series of data
from Watkins (1973, 66) relates to the number of jobs held during
the last ten years by a group of businessmen attending a conference
('Found Your Own Business' Conference). It was suggested by Watkins
that the characteritistics of those interested in setting-up a new
firm and those actually doing so are similar. Such a suggestion
would not appear unreasonable.

The overall conclusion one can draw from this situation is that
most new company founders have at least one characteristic in common
with the other members of the labour market in general, and on
founding will have held between two and four previous appointments.
One small, but important caveat should be added to this discussion
and it concerns the number of previous employers. If a founder
stays with one company all his working life prior to setting-up a
new firm, but holds several positions within that company, say, in
two unrelated subsidiary companies, is that equivalent to holding
two previous appointments or only one? For the purposes of the
table presented it counts the actual number of previous (different)
employers and not appointments. It is likely that those founders
holding one previous appointment have in fact probably held several
appointments within the same company. Though this does detract from
the immediate clarity of the picture presented in the table, it does
not however diminish the overwhelming tendency for founders to have
held jobs with several different employers prior to founding.

While it might be intrinsically interesting to know how many
employees a new firm founder may have worked for, what is its
importance for the founding process? First, it could be interpreted
as indicating the level of experience of the founder which in turn
may be a reflection of 'promotion turnover'. At each change of
employer the founder gains promotion, and hence greater experience.
If this method of career advancement and development is important,
and it would appear to be so at this stage, the number of suitable
employment opportunities to allow the career development of
individuals in an individual labour market would also appear
important. Accepting that this is the case, it would be expected
that metropolitan and fringe metropolitan areas would be the areas
most likely to contain the most suitable opportunities for such
career advancement. However, due to the highly concentrated
distribution of 'top' or 'key' job opportunities in any advanced
economy the necessity for migration at some stage during career
development might also be necessary.

Although the last comment is not fully justified on the strength
of the information so far presented (Table 8.1), it is when taken
with other information presented in this section and the remainder
of the chapter. The next step now is to enquire as to why people
change employer and set-up a new firm and this is discussed next.

(b) The reasons given for leaving a previous employer and for setting-up a new firm

It was noted above that the collection of information relating to motivation might be somewhat unreliable. For example, the reply to the statement: 'Reason for leaving', might be a product of the articulateness of the individual answering. This was first noted by Isabelle Wagner in 1939 and in particular she suggested that:

(a) Articulateness may be a function of personality
(b) Articulateness may be a function of intellectual training
(c) Articulateness as a general characteristic may not exist

In the final analysis it was found that articulateness was to some extent a function of intellectual training (ibid., 112). If then the response to this question was low it might invalidate the general results as '... articulate people differ from inarticulate people in certain habits and interests ...' (ibid., 112). Fortunately, and as the following tables reveal, this has not proved to be a major problem as in only nine cases (4.71 per cent) was this information not available. However, this does not detract from the possibility that the respondents were themselves more articulate than those not making a return. There would appear to be no way of determining the potential importance of this factor. But, given the size of the sample and the overall representativeness of the respondents of the sample, it would appear not to be unduly biased in any manner.

Though the respondents themselves might not create a problem, the allocation of their responses to some general category does. For example, how does one categorise the following replies to the statement: 'Reason for leaving'.

(a) 'Promotion'
(b) 'Improve position'
(c) 'Promotion had led to more and more administrative jobs and less and less designing of service systems. Bored and unsatisfied with admin. work'
(d) 'To move to other workshop for wider experience'
(e) 'Moving back to Scotland'
(f) 'Company grew too big for far away part-time chairman'
(g) 'More experience'
(h) 'More money'

These eight replies chosen randomly from the 468 reasons given for either leaving one employer to join another or to set-up a company presents a distinct problem, that of classification. No hard and fast rules can be applied except that once an allocation procedure has been started the same guidelines are applied in all succeeding cases. Of the above eight examples, the resultant classification would be as follows:

Category	Example letter
Advancement	a, b, d and g
Frustration	c and f
Return to Scotland	e
Greater financial reward	h

The tables presented from this study have then been allocated on this basis and the classification procedure was adopted prior to coding the material for computer analysis. Furthermore, each reply was allocated the only one reason or category and so in some cases (see example 'c') several facets of the motivation factors are evident. In such cases the apparently more important factor has been noted. While this situation severely limits the usefulness of such replies, it does not necessarily invalidate them. However, their usefulness is restricted for comparative purposes because of the inherent problems in comparing subjectively derived categories based upon probably dissimilar, subjectively derived categories.

Of the 191 main founders or 'prime-movers', 182 provided a reason for leaving their previous employer immediately prior to setting-up their firm (Table 8.2). Other studies have also considered the reason for setting-up a new firm and the two main reasons from these studies are also tabulated (Table 8.3). While direct comparisons are not possible it would appear that there is a high degree of similarity between the results. The main reasons could be summarised as being due to a desire to be independent and to be fully responsible for ones decisions and not dependent upon others. (1) Subsidiary influences exist and these would include the desire for a higher salary and the opportunity arising to set-up a firm. It should be noted that all of the studies with the exception of those of Collins (1977) and SICRAS (1972) are concerned with new technical companies, whilst that of Collins is centred upon non manufacturing concerns and SICRAS's viewed new firms in rural areas and had largely been assisted by SICRAS.

Table 8.2

Reasons given by founders for leaving their previous employer immediately prior to setting-up their own manufacturing enterprise in Scotland during the period, 1968-77.

Reason	No. of cases	(%)
Advancement	101	52.88
Frustration	33	17.28
Closure[a]	19	9.95
Greater rewards	10	5.24
Take-over[a]	8	4.19
Return to Scotland	5	2.62
Made redundant	3	1.57
Nationalization[a]	2	1.05
Retirement	1	0.52
Not known	9	4.71
Total	191	100.01[b]

Source: Survey

[a] Closure, take-over or nationalization of previous employer.
[b] Does not sum to 100.0 because of rounding.

205

Table 8.3

Reasons given by founders for leaving their previous employer
immediately prior to setting-up their own manufacturing enterprise:
A comparison of studies

STUDY	REASONS
(i) Roberts and Wainer (1971) (Table XII, 108)	(1) Being own boss - independence (2) Salary
Collins (1977) (25)	(1) Independence (2) Ambition (2) Opportunity[a]
Susbauer (1969) (Table D-17, 215)	(1) Frustration of an innovatory idea (2) Monetary reward inadequacy (negative influences affecting formation decision)
S.I.C.R.A.S. (1972) (Table 2, 17)	(1) Better prospects (2) Opportunity arose
Cooper (1970) (59)	(1) Frustrated in previous position (2) Forced to leave previous position
Watkins (1971) (Table 4, 157)	(1) Desire for increased job satisfaction (2) Financial motivation
Watkins (1973) (Fig. 4, 67 and 1976, Fig. 1, 6)	(1) Desire for independence (2) Desire for increased job satisfaction
Present Study	(1) Advancement (2) Frustration

- - - - - - - - - - - - - - - - -- -

OTHER STUDIES: (see text)

(ii) Shapero et al (1965) (Table 15, 51)	(1) Reduction in labour force (2) Desire to leave area (Reasons given by engineers and scientists terminating employment in Boston and Los Angeles)
Peters and Roberts (1969) (Table 3, 185)	(1) No interest - satisfied with present position (2) Lack of adequate financing (Reasons given for not setting-up a new firm)
Peters and Roberts (1969) (Table 4, 186)	(1) Lack of time or facilities to develop the idea (2) Lack of motivation or interest, satisfaction with present position (Factors given for impeding attempts to proceed with the idea)
Present Study	(1) Advancement (2) Frustration (2) Redundancy[a] (Reasons given by founders changing employment positions prior to setting- up their firm)

a   Equal Second

206

Those studies listed on the bottom part of the table (Table 8.3)
contain some findings on related topics. For example, the reasons
given by engineers and scientists for changing employment appear to
contrast directly with those given for the setting-up of a new firm.
However, the third and fourth main reasons (Ambition - want more
responsibility and want higher salary, respectively) recorded by
this study of engineers and scientists may reflect the peculiarities
of the labour market for both types of positions. Peters and
Roberts (1969) also provide information, but from the opposite
viewpoint of why people do not want to set-up their own firm.

Another facet, and this is the fourth entry of the second-half of
the table, concerns the reasons given by founders changing their
employment prior to their penultimate position i.e. the one held
immediately prior to setting-up the firm. If this distribution
(Table 8.4) is compared with that of the reasons given by the
founders leaving the employment position held immediately prior to
the setting-up of the firm, there is found to be surprisingly little
difference between the two distributions (r_s = +0.75; t_c = 5.33;
t_α = 2.998; df. = 7; 0.01 level of significance). If the data are
then reduced to positive and negative factors i.e. into those
factors where the founder has taken a positive decision to set-up a
new firm, and those where he has been forced to leave his previous
position, and they are compared as for the situation above again no
significant difference is found (X^2 = 0.733^2; X^2_α = 6.64; 0.01 level
of significance). What this might indicate is that there is a
similarity between the reasons given for changing employment and the
setting-up of a new firm. Moreover, it suggests that the setting-up
of a new firm and factors affecting a change in employment are not
necessarily dissimilar. This would further suggest that the setting-
up of a new firm is possibly one option open to many people in the
labour market.

Table 8.4

Reasons given by founders for leaving their previous
employer not including the reasons given for leaving
immediately prior to setting-up a new manufacturing
enterprise in Scotland, 1968-77.

Reason	No. of cases	(%)
Advancement	97	62.58
Frustration	15	9.68
Closure	13	8.39
Greater rewards	6	3.87
Take-over	5	3.23
Return to Scotland	4	2.58
Made redundant	15	9.68
Total	155*	100.00

Source: Survey

*Not known in 36 instances

Exceptions to this situation obviously exist. For example, in the Northern Region Johnson (1978, Table 5, 13) found that 34.18 per cent of the firms previously employing the new firm founder closed either at, or after the formation of the new company. It is probable that this high incidence of plant closure might be a product of the area's industrial structure which is dominated by both marine and other engineering (HOUSE, 1969, 164-85). Though, it should be noted that both closures and redundancies were more important in accounting for founders changing employment <u>prior</u> to setting-up the firm. These reasons are disaggregated by industrial order in Table 8.5. This table tends to suggest that those orders with the largest number of closures also have the largest number of founders whose prime influence to set-up a new firm was the closure of his previous workplace. This disaggregation of the founders' characteristics by the reason for founding is continued in the next section which considers their age at founding.

Table 8.5

Reasons given by founders for leaving their previous employer immediately prior to setting-up their own manufacturing enterprise in Scotland during the period 1968-77 considered by industry.

SIC	1	2	3	4	5	6	7	8	9	Total
3	4	-	1	-	4	-	-	-	-	9
5	3	-	-	-	-	-	-	-	-	3
6	1	1	-	-	1	-	-	-	-	3
7	9	-	1	2	3	3	1	2	-	21
8	3	-	-	1	1	-	-	-	-	5
9	6	-	1	2	2	1	-	-	-	12
10	6	1	-	1	1	-	-	-	-	9
11	3	-	-	-	1	-	-	-	-	4
12	9	-	1	1	1	-	-	-	-	12
13	3	-	1	3	3	-	-	1	-	11
14	1	-	-	-	-	-	-	-	-	1
15	1	-	-	1	1	-	-	-	-	3
16	1	-	-	2	-	-	-	-	-	3
17	4	-	-	1	-	-	1	-	-	6
18	2	-	1	2	-	-	-	-	-	5
19	3	-	1	1	1	-	1	-	-	7
20	1	-	-	1	-	-	-	-	-	2
22	1	-	-	1	-	-	-	-	-	2
23	11	-	-	1	1	-	-	-	-	13
24	1	-	-	-	-	-	-	-	1	2
25	13	-	-	1	6	2	-	-	-	22
26	1	-	-	-	-	-	-	-	-	1
27	3	-	-	-	-	-	-	-	-	3
Total	90	2	7	21	26	6	3	3	1	159

Source: Survey

Reasons: 1. Advancement; 2. Nationalization; 3. Take over; 4. Closure; 5. Frustration; 6. Greater financial reward; 7. Return to Scotland; 8. Made redundant; and 9. Retirement.

In summary it would appear safe to say that the reasons for
setting-up a new firm are similar to those given for the leaving of
a previous employer. Furthermore, the setting-up of a new firm
could then represent one employment option open to individuals
wishing to change their employment. The strength of push factors,
especially closures and redundancies, tend to be dependent upon the
industry and its characteristics in terms of plant turnover rates.

(c) Age of the founder when setting-up a new firm

As with the first part of this section where the number of previous
employers was used in many ways as a surrogate for experience, the
present section uses age for a similar purpose. The vast majority
of entrepreneurs were between 26-45 years old (82.04 per cent) when
they set-up a new firm (Table 8.6). It would appear that they were
considerably younger than the usual chief executive running small
manufacturing firms (under 200 employees; BOLTON, 1971, 8). It

Table 8.6
Age of founders on establishing a new company:
A comparison of studies.

Age range	Present study No.	(%)	Bolton (1971)* (%)
less than 25	17)		
26 - 30	29) 46	27.54	2
31 - 35	27)		
36 - 40	38) 65 · 38.92		14
41 - 45	24)		
46 - 50	19) 43	25.75	28
51 or more	13 13	7.78	55
Total	167		100

Source: Survey

*Bolton (1971; Table VII, 8)
($X^2 = 109.7985$; $X^2_{\alpha 0.1} = 6.25$; df = 3)

would appear also that the average (mean and median) age of the
founders is similar to those found by other surveys of new firm
founders (Table 8.7). Also in this table are entered the average
age of managers in the Manchester area (CLARK, 1966; CLEMENTS, 1969)
and of managers attending a conference held in Cambridge (PAHL, 1971).
These entries have been made as it is suggested that not only does
the setting-up of a new company represent one part of the labour
market, but also that the establishment of a new firm can be seen as
part of a possible career structure open to managers (BIRCH and
McMILLAN, 1972; SOFER, 1970; and for the Scottish case see CARTER,
no date). In the main, new firm founders tend to be slightly younger
than their managerial counterparts. The average age of founders in
the Collins and Moore (1964) study is higher than the others because
they considered firms employing twenty or more people (ibid., 30).
Though it should be added that this study was concerned with
successful founders, and hence choose 'larger' firms as a measure of

Table 8.7

Average age of founders: A comparison of studies

Study	Age (Years)	Sample size	Other Particulars
Clements (1958)	46.0	646	Managers in Manchester area.
Clark (1966)	46.2	818	Managers in Manchester area.
Pahl (1971)	38.0	86	Managers on a course at Cambridge University.
Boswell (1972)	36.0 (median)	64	Small firm owners (32 were firm founders).
Susbauer (1969)	34.0	22	New technical company founders in Austin, Texas.
Scott (1976)	38.9	76	Founders of new manufacturing firms in Scotland incorporated in 1969.
Mayer and Goldstein (1961)	40.0 (median)	81	New businesses in Rhode Island.
Davids (1963)	36 – 38	–	New firms in Georgia and Texas.
Collins and Moore (1964)	52.0	110	Successful manufacturing entrepreneurs in Michigan, USA.
Delano et al (1966)	45.0	100	Entrepreneurs in Washington State, USA.
Industrial Research (1967)	35.0	–	New Science based firms in Philadelphia.
Present Study	32.3 (mean) 37.0 (median)	191	Main founders of new manufacturing firms in Scotland, 1968-1977 (355 founders in 191 new firms viewed).

success. Overall, however, the studies listed tend to agree far more than they disagree.

If the age of the founder at establishing and the reason for founding are collated (Table 8.8), several other features emerge. First, the desire for advancement tends to be restricted to those aged 40 or less. Second, those founders setting-up a new firm because they have been frustrated in their previous position are

Table 8.8

Reasons given by founders for leaving their previous employer immediately prior to setting-up their own manufacturing enterprise in Scotland during the period 1968-77 considered by the age of founders at establishing a new firm

Age group	\multicolumn{9}{c}{Reasons}	Total
	1	2	3	4	5	6	7	8	9	
25 or less	13	-	1	1	-	1	-	-	-	16
26 - 30	23	-	-	3	1	1	-	-	-	28
31 - 35	18	-	1	3	3	2	-	-	-	27
36 - 40	13	2	2	4	16	1	-	-	-	38
41 - 45	10	-	2	3	4	1	3	1	-	23
46 - 50	10	-	1	1	3	2	-	1	-	18
51 or more	4	-	-	3	3	1	2	-	1	14
Total	91	2	7	18	29	9	5	2	1	164

Source: Survey

Reasons: 1. Advancement; 2. Nationalization; 3. Take over; 4. Closure; 5. Frustration; 6. Greater financial reward; 7. Return to Scotland; 8. Made redundant; 9. Retirement.

highly concentrated in the 36-40 age group. It could be suggested that these founders have gained promotion in other firms up until this point in their careers; a stage at which they possess their maximum ability for solving complex non routine problems. The converse situation, it could be argued, exists for those seeking advancement at an earlier age by establishing their own firm (GOLDTHORPE, 1980, 229). Here it might be the case that the founders have not been able to gain promotion and hence recognition and advancement at a rate at which they desire, and so they establish their own firm.

Two other features·of this table are also worth noting. One is that those people choosing to return to Scotland are all aged 41 or more. This might suggest a classic family-cycle move where the parents are no longer 'tied' by their childrens' need and are free to return to Scotland. In some respects this could also be interpreted as a partial retiral move. The second concerns those individuals made redundant and who subsequently became new firm founders. In both the cases recorded, the individuals were aged between 41-50 and were therefore forced to change employment at a time when they probably would not have chosen to do so, and the employment opportunities open to them would be limited (VOLLMER,

1965, 6 and also Chapter Six of this study).

In conclusion, the average founder tends to be 30-40 years old and may be similar to his ambitious managerial counterpart. There would also appear to be roughly age specific reasons for establishing new firms, and they tend to agree with the notions of ability and freedom to form a company detailed in the previous chapter. As was stated at the beginning of this section, age was used as a surrogate for experience, the next section considers the jobs held by founders in a more direct assessment of the experience that they possessed at the time of founding.

(d) Previous employment history of new firm founders

Probably the single most important influence upon the initial ability of an individual and the subsequent success of a new enterprise is the work experience or history of the founder. The abilities to manage a firm are learnt and the mistakes made during that learning process are best made at anothers expense. For example, one North American founder noted that because he did not have the right experience that '... it cost the firm up to $50,000 to have a professor running the show' (MAPES, 1967, 10). This section then, considers the work histories of founders.

It is difficult to determine how best to assess the experience of a founder, and the method offered is only one solution to the problem. The first and last employment positions held by the founder are used, and these are detailed in Tables 8.9 and 8.10. Perhaps the most striking difference between these tables is the large increase in the number of founders holding managerial positions by the time they decide to set-up a new firm. If the two series of data are reduced to three categories: managerial, operative, and other non-manufacturing, it is found that there is a significant difference between them (X^2 = 50.067; $X^2\alpha$ = 9.21; df = 2; at the 0.01 level of significance). M.G. Scott (1976) equates this transition from the initial operative position to managerial and finally to the founding of a new firm as indicating that '... founding is becoming a relatively 'open' route for social mobility' (ibid., 125). This is not fully borne out by the data collected in this study. The only element of work experience noted by Scott was the initial job held by the founder which has been shown to differ quite markedly from the one held prior to the founding of the company.

A comparison is made (Table 8.11) of the initial occupation of the founders in Scotland with the findings of Scott (1976) and two studies of managers (ACTON, 1956; CLARK, 1966). Unfortunately it has not proven possible to allocate all of the founders of the present study into the categories used by the other three studies. It would appear, if one assumes that those founders that cannot be allocated are not in the manual and apprenticeship category, that there is a close degree of similarity between the results of this study and those of the other two. The heavy bias of Scott's study to mechanical engineering firms (SIC Order 7; ibid., 269, Table 1, Appendix 5) would perhaps offer part of the explanation why the 'manual and apprenticeship' category is so well represented in his study. In complete contrast to all of these studies is that of

Table 8.9

First employment positions held by founders setting-up a new
manufacturing enterprise in Scotland during the period 1968 - 77

First Employment Position	Number of Cases With Previous Experience	Without Previous Experience[a]	Total
(1) Managerial	32	16	48
Managing Director	3	4	7
General Manager	4	6	10
Sales Manager	5	1	6
Director	1	2	3
Design Engineer	3	0	3
Marketing Manager	0	0	0
Technical Manager	2	1	3
Draughtsman	8	0	8
Production Controller	1	0	1
Estimator/Buyer	2	2	4
Accountant	0	0	0
General Administration	3	0	3
(2) Operative	54	5	59
Foreman	1	0	1
Technician	9	1	10
Operative	44	4	48
(3) Other	31	16	47
Self-Employed	0	0	0
Other non-manufacturing	31	16	47
(4) Not Available	1	0	1
Total	118	37	155

Source: Survey

a Only position held prior to founding.

Table 8.10

Previous employment positions held by founders immediately prior
to setting-up a new manufacturing enterprise in Scotland during
the period 1968 - 77

Previous Employment Position		No. of Cases
(1) Managerial		110
Managing Director	25	
General Manager	26	
Sales Manager	19	
Director	7	
Design Engineer	7	
Marketing Manager	7	
Technical Manager	5	
Draughtsman	4	
Production Control	4	
Estimator/Design	4	
Accountant	2	
(2) Operative		21
Foreman	8	
Technician	5	
Operator	8	
(3) Other		44
Self-Employed	9	
Other Non-Manufacturing	35	
(4) Not Available		16
Total		191

Source: Survey

Table 8.11
First employment positions held by founders setting up a
new manufacturing enterprise: A comparison of studies.

First occupation	Scott[a] (1976)	Clark[b] (1966)	Acton[c] (1956)	Present Study[d]
Apprenticeship	41.6%	17.5%)	21	53.01%
Manual	5.5	7.8)		
Clerical	5.5	26.8	30)	
Laboratory	-	15.0	4)	
Technical &			)	30.12
Draughtsman	5.5	16.9	28)	
Sales	2.7	3.9	3)	
Trainees	5.5	7.9	11)	
Professional	25.0	2.2)		16.87
Managerial	2.7	1.7)	3)	
Unclassified (forces)	5.5	-	-	-

Source: Scott (1976) modified

[a] Scott (1976, Table 5.7, 126)
[b] Clark (1966, 76)
[c] Acton (1956, Table 5, 10)
[d] Of the 175 cases where these data are available only 83 could be fitted into the categories used in these studies.

Susbauer (1969, 204, Table D-6) whose survey of twenty-three new technical companies found that all of the surveyed founders had had only managerial experience. Though this position is understandable given the nature of the companies considered, it is probably also a function of the job descriptions used by Susbauer (also see BALASUBRAMANYAM, 1979).

The evidence presented above would tend to suggest that a large number of founders started their initial working experience in manual occupations. However, by the time these individuals came to the setting-up of their own firm many of them had changed their positions and most held managerial ones. This would further suggest that many of the founders had achieved some measure of success in the formal labour market by 'progressing-up' a company's occupation/ management structure. If this suggestion is accepted, the setting-up of a new firm might appear to form one further part of the labour market which allows career progression. Admittedly, the setting-up of a firm is a specialised part of the labour market, but the dividing line between ·the setting-up of a new firm and the seeking of an appointment within the formal labour market might be more vague than is often suggested. In this respect it is interesting and also relevant to consider both occupational and residential mobility. From evidence presented by Herbert (1972, 243-46) it would seem that residential mobility is related to occupational status and the stage of the family life cycle. Thus changes in occupation may mean changes in residence, and it is conceivable that the reverse is also true. (3) It is shown later in this chapter that movement of founders does occur and that the selling of a house is also by no means an uncommon method of raising capital. In fact it is not unreasonable to suggest that the sale of the house and the realisation of its value might even encourage the setting-up of a new firm (see PETERS and ROBERTS, 1969, Table 3, 185; Table 8.31).

Factors that affect the level of experience and speed of acquisition of specialist skills, are the length of an individual's working career and the age at which they started that career. Of course, the age at which an individual starts his working career is in part determined by the age at which he finished full-time education. Thus the age at which an individual starts a working career could be used as an approximate measure for the level of formal educational attainment. It is these areas of the founders' make-up that are discussed in the next part of the chapter.

(e) Age of founders at the start of their working career and the length of their working career prior to founding

Between leaving full time education, taking full time employment and subsequently setting-up a new firm there is the passage of various amounts of time. For each founder the length of these periods will differ, but in general it would appear that founders in Scotland left full time education with minimal qualifications (Table 8.12). Furthermore, this finding is tentatively collaborated by a survey also undertaken in Scotland by Scott (1976). The quite large number of founders who did not start their working careers until they were in their mid to late twenties are partially accounted for by those founders who were on active service during the Second World War or on National Service. The inclusion of these founders does not detract from the overwhelming fact that most founders started their working career on leaving full time education which must also be so for most other people entering the labour market for the first time.

Table 8.12
Age at starting full time employment:
A comparison of studies.

Age at starting full time employment	Present study No.	%	Scott (1976)* No.	%
14 - 16	70	42.68	15	48.39
17 - 18	23	14.02	12	38.71
19 - 21	30	18.29	3	9.68
22 - 25	27	16.46	1	3.23
26 - 30	7	4.27	-	-
31 or more	7	4.27	-	-
Total	164		31	

*Scott (1976, Table 5.12, 129)

The distribution described by the length of working career (Table 8.13) is similar, as would be expected, to the age distribution of founders at setting-up a new firm (Table 8.6). These data would suggest that the 'average founder' leaves school, works for between ten and twenty years and then sets up his firm. It can also be inferred on this basis that they possess a minimum level of formal

216

Table 8.13
Length of working career prior to setting-up.

Length of working Career (Years)	No. of cases	%
1 - 5	12	6.98
6 - 10	23	13.37
11 - 15	34	19.77
16 - 20	41	23.84
21 - 25	25	14.53
26 - 30	21	12.21
31 - 35	9	5.23
36 - 40	6	3.49
41 or more	1	0.58
Total	172*	

Source: Survey

*Data are not available in 19 cases

educational qualifications. Although the latter comment may reflect reality, it should not be interpreted as necessarily being a disadvantage. The relationship between educational achievements and the ability to found a company is probably only important in cases where specific technical expertise is required. Furthermore, the attainment of educational qualifications need not occur within the 'normal' progression, for example, from school to university. M.G. Scott (1976, 129) presents evidence that suggests that only three of the founders surveyed directly went to university from school, while twelve founders received some form of university education and hence possess such qualifications. This observation would tend to underline the caution with which the above comments concerning age of starting full time career and the educational level of attainment should be treated.

So far in the discussion of the founder only aspects of his work experience have been considered but other features are also important e.g. the pooling of experience and the founding of a new company by a group, and also previous experience in setting up companies. Both of these facets of work experience are considered in the next section.

(f) Group founding and previous founding experience

All of the discussion to this point has been concerned with the prime, or main founder, yet in many cases several individuals have gathered together to set up a firm. In fact for the majority of the new firms surveyed this was the case (Table 8.14). Although a group of individuals may be present and be collectively responsible for the establishment of a new firm, one individual will usually be present in each group that will represent the prime mover or focal member of the group. It is this individual to which most of the comments in this section and chapter are addressed.

Table 8.14
Number of founders involved in setting up manufacturing
enterprises in Scotland during the period 1968-77.

No. of founders	No. of cases	Total number of founders
1	87 (45.55%)	87
2	74 (38.74)	148
3	14 ((7.33)	42
4	10 (5.24)	40
5	3 (1.57)	15
6	-	-
7	2 (1.05)	14
8	-	-
9	1 (0.52)	9
Total	191	355*

Source: Survey

*All other tables refer to the prime mover or main
founder and not to his/her partners or colleagues
associated with them in setting up the enterprise.

   The importance of groups as opposed to single individuals setting
up a new firm (see Table 8.15), is that it:

>   ... permits a more balanced management team, one
>   less likely to have major areas of weakness.
>   They also provide psychological support at a time
>   when the individual may be wondering whether he
>   is taking the right step. (COOPER, 1973, 60)

Table 8.15
Percentage of new manufacturing enterprises set up by
groups : A comparison of studies.

Study	Area	Percentage of new firms set up by groups
Susbauer (1969)	Austin, Texas.	48
Cooper (1971)	Palo Alto, California.	61
Shapero (1971)	Dispersed in USA.	59
Present study	Scotland	54.45

It would appear that new firms set up by groups would certeris
paribus have a better than average chance of survival, and may allow
a greater initial investment to be made in the firm. The larger the
initial investment, it appears, the larger the initial employment
size of the firm. These characteristics though do not necessarily
ensure the survival of the firm (see BIRCH, 1979a, 17, and 1979b,
38-44). It is interesting to note also that nearly a quarter of the
initial employment (24.53 per cent) created by the opening of the
new firms surveyed was made up of founders.

Table 8.16
Number of previous company formations by the principal
founder: A comparison of studies.

Previous formation activity (no. of firms established)	Present Study	Susbauer[a] (1969)	Cooper[b] (1970)
0	169	17	22
1	17)	2)	
2	3)	1)	
3	2) 22	1) 5	8
Farm only[c]	-)	1)	
Total	191	23	30

$(X^2 = 6.185; X^2_{\alpha 0.1} = 4.60; df = 2)$

[a] Susbauer (1969) Table D-9, 207
[b] Cooper (1970) 75;
[c] Farm only category is included because of the similarities of ownership of a farm or ranch to the act of company formation.

Apart from the gains of group experience, there is also the possibility that the founder of a new firm has in fact set up a firm before. There is little evidence that this is the case (Table 8.16) and it is rare for a founder to have set up a new firm previously. Even in the studies of new technical companies the level of previous founding experience was also very low (SUSBAUER, 1969; COOPER, 1970). These findings are in direct contrast to those of Oxenfeldt (1943, 89-101, especially Table XVIII, 89). In fact, Oxenfeldt stated that:

... a large percentage of new businesses are established by people who close up an old enterprise to try a new one ... The large proportion of proprietors who had been business owners previously and the large number who had owned more than one business indicate a constant change and turnover in business ownership. This picture is radically different from the commom impression that an entrepreneur undertakes only once to set up business for himself - either to succeed and live happily ever after, or to fail and never again rise from the ranks of the working class. Actually, many businessmen make more than one attempt at entrepreneurship. An examination of the credit reports suggests that there is almost a professional entrepreneur class, composed of those who are not content to accept employment with others and who make several attempts to establish a profitable enterprise. (ibid., 90-1)

After making these comments, Oxenfeldt, drawing upon evidence from the shoe (4) industry concludes that:

If entrepreneurs on the average establish over three firms each, it may be estimated further that more than one out of every 15 persons goes into business for himself. (ibid.,99-100) (5)

These observations and conclusions, ones that have become popular 'truths' are neither borne out by the finding of the present study, nor those of other studies. The majority of new firms are thus founded by groups of individuals who have rarely had any <u>direct</u> experience in founding a new company. However, those founders interviewed did have some awareness of other new firms, but it proved difficult to discern if their awareness of these firms existed prior to founding. The awareness of other founders might encourage others to set up in business, and thus act as role models.

3. THE INCUBATOR ORGANISATION

The role of the incubator organisation forms a vital role in the founding of new firms. For example, Cooper (1970) notes that:

> ... regional entrepreneurship depends upon local incubator organisations which hire, train and motivate the prospective entrepreneur. (ibid., 60)

He continues and describes an incubator organisation that would probably have a high spin-off rate i.e. a large number of employees relative to the total labour force of a plant leaving to establish their own firm.

> It would be in a rapidly growing industry that offers opportunities for well-managed small firms with good ideas: it would be a small firm or would be organised as a series of 'small businesses'; it would be good at recruiting ambitious, capable people; and it would periodically be afflicted with internal crises sufficient to frustrate many of its professional employees and lead them to believe that opportunities were being missed and that 'even I could manage the business better'. (ibid., 60)

Other studies have also noted these features, and the role of the incubator organisation is evidently important in the process of new firm formation (DRAHEIM et al, 1966; COOPER, 1971; DRAHEIM, 1972; SUSBAUER, 1972). An examination of the incubator organisation would therefore appear necessary and three aspects are considered here: size (employment), age, and type (status).

In terms of size there would initially appear to be no bias to small firms, however defined, and is a point Susbauer (1969, Table D-5, 203) would in fact agree with. If a detailed employment breakdown of the incubator organisations is derived the resulting distribution does not differ significantly from the total stock of plants ($X^2 = 66.11$; $X^2_{\alpha 0.01} = 30.58$; df = 15). In fact, if the employment size groups are then changed to those used by Watkins (1973, 67), it is found that there is no statistical difference between the two samples ($X^2 = 17.3959$; $X^2_{\alpha 0.01} = 13.28$; df = 4). However, it should be noted that the figures used by Watkins were derived from the attenders at a conference entitled, 'Found Your Own Business', and therefore represents a sample of potential, not actual founders. Irrespective of this fact, it would appear at this

stage that plant for plant that large plants produce more new firm
founders than small ones. However, this position is completely
reversed if the number of new firm founders per incubator employment
size category is standardised. In Table 8.17 the findings of a
number of different studies are presented, and these quite
convincingly suggest that employee for employee small plants produce
more new firm founders than large ones. Here, the number of new
firm founders per thousand employees has been calculated, and then
the figures have been standardised to reveal the relative rates of
spin-off between them.

Table 8.17
Spin-off rates categorised by the size of manufacturing
'incubator' plants: A comparison of studies.

Size of incubator plant	Region of study			
	Scotland[a]	East Midlands[b]	Northern[c]	Palo Alto, California[d]
1 - 25	7.37[e]	11.9	14.25 (1-10)	9.7 (1-500)
26 - 100	2.26	4.0	7.25 (11-99)	1.0 (501+)
101 - 250	1.02	2.8	2.75 (100-499)	
251 +	1.00	1.0	1.00 (500+	
	n = 107	n = 47	n = 51	n = 243

Sources: [a]This study;   [c]Johnson and Cathcart (1979);
         [b]Gudgin et al (1979);   [d]Cooper (1971).
[e]Number of new firm founders emerging from the size band are 7.37
more frequent than those emerging from the 251+ size band.

Both the size and age of a plant are related, though weakly (CRUM,
1953), and it is possible that the younger (more recently opened)
plants will account for a greater share of the incubator plants
(Table 8.18). When this age distribution of incubator plant is
compared to the age distribution of all plants it is found that
there is no significant difference between the two (X^2 = 39.55;
$X^2_{\alpha 0.01}$ = 23.21; df = 10). It would therefore appear that the age
of the incubator organisations are as would be expected given the
age distribution of all plants. This would also tend to contrast
with the findings of, say, Cooper (1970, 60) who considered that the
best incubator organisations in his study area, Palo Alto, were the
very new technical companies he studied. Thus, the past generation
of new technical companies would form the 'best' incubator
organisations for the next generation and hence the process would be
age specific. This may well be the case for technical companies,
though this is difficult to tell as the high technology side of
industry is a relatively recent phenomena and the age specific nature
of the process (new company to incubator organisation to new company
to incubator organisation etc.) may be a product of this rather than
anything innately different between technical and non-technical
incubator firms. It is then being argued that in any 'new' industry
such as electronics would be dominated by young firms, but these
firms are only 'young' in comparison to other industries and not
their own. For example, an electronics firm established in the late
1940s or early 1950s is as old to that industry as an establishment

Table 8.18

The year of opening of the incubator organisations*
in which the principal founder was employed immediately prior to setting up their own enterprise.

Period (Year of opening of incubator)	Cases (%)
Before 1800	5
1801 - 1900	18
1901 - 1920	2
1921 - 1940	5
1941 - 1945	2
1946 - 1950	10
1951 - 1955	3
1956 - 1960	14
1961 - 1965	24
1966 - 1970	14
1971 - 1975	3
Total	100 (n = 107)

Source: Survey
          Scottish Council (Development and Industry)

* Noted in the table if the incubator organisation is a
manufacturing enterprise located in Scotland and for
which the year of opening is available.

that opened in the 1860s and 1870s in the shipbuilding industry.
There is a high probability that all industries go through this
phase of development when they are new, but unfortunately there is
no evidence to support this assertion. However, if employment in
each of the incubator plants is allocated to the year the plant
opened a different picture emerges. It is found that in general if
is the employees in the more recently opened plant that are more
likely to set up their own firm.

Thus, it would appear that both the size and the age are important
characteristics of incubator organisations in terms of their role in
the process of new firm formation, and hence reflect their ability
to act as incubators. Perhaps one characteristic of a plant that
may also be important is that of status. In Chapter Six (Table 6.25)
it was noted that the nature of the ownership of a plant could be
used as a possible surrogate measure for types of managerial
functions carried out at that plant. This measure is used in a
suggestive fashion here, as the nature of managerial control at a
plant could be determined only by a close analysis of the functions
carried out at that plant. The measure itself is used to indicate
the level of managerial positions existing within a plant. For
example, an independent plant, it is assumed, would contain a higher
number of risk-taking positions than, say, a branch or subsidiary
plant. And given that the ownership structure of manufacturing
industry in Scotland is dominated by externally owned concerns,
there may be a lack of key managerial positions. (6) Furthermore,
it was noted by Altman (1940, 89) that:

... there are probably four or five officials in
each of the larger corporations who are
responsible for the determinants of business
policy.

One would therefore expect the role of the independent Scottish
owned plants would be greater than their North American or English
branch plant counterparts as incubator organisations.

An examination of the above arguments in the context of the
available data does not bear out the propositions made. If the
distribution of the status of the incubator organisation is compared
to the ownership of all plants in either 1973 or 1977 there are no
significant differences (Table 8.19). One could conclude from this
situation that given the supposed poor nature of branch plants as
incubator organisations, and _certeris paribus_, the externally owned
plants act very favourably as incubators. Furthermore, the
importance of Scottish owned plants was disappointing given the
probably high autonomous nature of many of them.

Table 8.19

Status of incubator organisation for which the principal
founder was employed immediately prior to setting-up
their own enterprise: A comparison with the status of
'all' plants in 1973 and 1977.

Plant status (Location of ultimate ownership)	Incubator Organisation	Plant Ownership structure 1973[a]	1977[b]
Scotland	59	2,176	2,886
England	37	644	994
North America	10	148	222
Other World	1	73	106
Total	107	3,041	4,208

[a] Firm (1975, Table 3, 402)
[b] Present study (Chapter Two, Table 2.8)

Comparison of the distribution of incubator organisations
with the distribution of all plants yields:

For 1973 - $X^2 = 17.58$, $X^2_{\alpha 0.01} = 11.34$, $df = 3$
For 1977 - $X^2 = 12.28$, $X^2_{\alpha 0.01} = 11.34$, $df = 3$

If each founder is then allocated to the industry in which his
previous employer was based and this is then subdivided by status
(Table 8.20), variations occur between industries and within each
status category. By expressing the total number of founders in each
status industry cell as a percentage of the row total and comparing
this value to the ownership level for each order some indication as
to why these variations occur might be forthcoming (Table 8.20a).
Overall there appears to be a high degree of similarity and the
major discrepancies that do occur can be explained. In five
industries there are major discrepanies between the percentage of
founders arising from that order and the level of employment (7)
under the respective ownership categories. These industries are

223

Table 8.20

Status of incubator organisation in which the principal founder was
employed immediately prior to setting-up their own enterprise:
A consideration by industrial order

Source S.I.C.[a]	Location of Ultimate Ownership (Status)				
	Scotland	England	N. America	Other World	Total
3	5	3	–	–	8
5	1	3	–	–	4
6	2	1	–	–	3
7	11	5	2	1	19
8	1	1	3	–	5
9	6	3	2	–	11
10	4	3	–	–	7
11	2	2	–	–	4
12	7	3	2	–	12
13	5	6	–	–	11
14	1	–	–	–	1
15	2	1	–	–	3
16	3	–	–	–	3
17	5	1	–	–	6
18	2	2	–	–	4
19	2	3	1	–	6
20	1	–	–	–	1
23	8	2	–	–	10
25	1	3	–	–	4
Total	69	42	10	1	122

Sources: Survey
          Scottish Council (Development and Industry)

a Source S.I.C.: Those industrial orders in which the founder worked
                   immediately prior to setting-up a new enterprise.
                   Only those orders listed where an entry exists.

Table 8.20a

Status of incubator organisation in which the principal founder
was employed immediately prior to setting-up their own enterprise:
A consideration by industrial order and the location of ultimate
ownership of Scottish manufacturing employment in 1973

Location of Ultimate Ownership (Status)

Source S.I.C.	Scotland F[a]	Scotland 1973[b]	England F	England 1973	N. America F	N. America 1973	Other World F	Other World 1973
3	62.5	48.3	37.5	44.5	-	5.7	-	1.5
5	25.0	11.8	75.0	63.2	-	12.1	-	12.9
6	66.6	18.3	33.3	70.4	-	2.2	-	9.1
7	57.89	39.0	26.32	29.2	10.53	29.3	5.26	2.5
8	20.0	16.9	20.0	21.1	60.0	60.7	-	1.3
9	54.55	7.8	27.27	52.4	18.18	31.4	-	8.4
10	57.14	53.3	42.86	29.8	-	11.8	-	5.1
11	50.0	9.8	50.0	53.3	-	36.4	-	0.5
12	58.33	58.6	25.0	25.2	16.67	10.9	-	5.3
13	45.45	64.2	54.55	28.8	-	3.0	-	4.0
14	100.0	88.0	-	12.0	-	-	-	-
15	66.66	48.2	33.33	38.0	-	13.8	-	-
16	100.0	37.1	-	48.1	-	1.2	-	-
17	83.33	87.2	16.67	12.4	-	0.4	-	-
18	50.0	55.0	50.0	39.4	-	2.5	-	3.1
19	33.33	28.4	50.0	43.2	16.67	26.1	-	2.3
Total	55.14	41.2	34.58	39.8	9.35	14.9	0.93	4.1

a: Present survey of founders (% of founders, sums to 100 across rows)

b: Firn (1975) Table 6, 406 (% of employment, sums to 100 across rows)

Table 8.20b

Status of incubator organisation in which the principal founder was employed prior to setting-up their own enterprise: A consideration by industry and the location of ownership of manufacturing plants, 1977[a]

Location of Ultimate Ownership (Status)

Source S.I.C.	Scotland F[b]	Scotland 1977[c]	England F	England 1977	N. America F	N. America 1977	Other World F	Other World 1977
3	62.5	65.67	37.5	26.93	–	4.83	–	2.67
5	25.0	48.19	75.0	37.95	–	7.83	–	6.02
6	66.6	58.99	33.3	37.41	–	2.88	–	0.72
7	57.89	70.49	26.32	17.62	10.53	9.77	5.26	2.17
8	20.0	45.78	20.0	33.73	60.0	20.48	–	–
9	54.55	46.19	27.27	24.46	18.18	20.11	–	9.24
10	57.14	70.0	42.86	27.5	–	1.25	–	1.25
11	50.0	60.53	50.0	34.1	–	3.95	–	1.32
12	58.33	77.24	25.0	17.92	16.67	2.91	–	1.94
13	45.45	81.15	54.55	16.27	–	1.39	–	1.19
14	100.0	77.78	–	20.0	–	–	–	2.22
15	66.6	64.76	33.3	28.19	–	6.17	–	0.88
16	100.0	55.89	–	38.72	–	1.01	–	4.38
17	83.33	83.05	16.67	14.24	–	1.02	–	1.69
18	50.0	74.04	50.0	21.47	–	3.53	–	0.96
19	33.3	70.85	50.0	17.81	16.67	6.88	–	4.45
Total	55.14	68.58	34.58	23.62	9.35	5.28	0.93	2.52

a: See Chapter Note No.12

b: Present survey of founders (% of founders, sum to 100 across rows)

c: Present study (% of plants, sum to 100 across rows)

metal manufacture (Order 6), mechanical engineering (Order 7), electrical engineering (Order 9), vehicles (Order 11), and bricks, pottery, glass and cement (Order 16). While these variations occur in widely differing industries they are probably the result of one factor, plant size. The influence of plant dominance and the associated nature of the productive process might be important here. In these cases the over riding factor could be the ratio of productive (non-managerial) to managerial positions such that in steel works, car assembly plants, electronics assembly units and rig construction yards, the general management set-up is not necessarily conducive as an incubator organisation. This observation would support the general finding relating entry rates with plant dominance noted earlier (Chapter Six, Table 6.23). The one case where this does not immediately apply is in Order Sixteen where the higher level of English ownership is reflected in brick and cement works which again would not appear conducive to new firm founder formation and has more in common with Order Two (mining and quarrying) than manufacturing industry as such.

It should be noted also that those areas with a dominant plant by definition possess few other employers. Hence, both the variety and number of employment opportunities within the area are very limited. The most prestigous and probably the highest paid managerial positions are with the dominant plant. It would therefore follow that if an individual did not advance within the dominant plant there is little opportunity to do so within the immediate area. Furthermore, the likelihood of other employers moving into the area are also small given the existence of an already dominant employer. Though the importance of the immediately previous employer prior to founding might not be overly important, but the notion of an 'incubator area' possessing a range of potential employers allowing the development (acquisition of skills) of the potential founder may be.

Three aspects of incubator organisations have been considered here: size, age and status. The analyses suggest that both the size and the age of the incubator plant are important. These however must remain tentative conclusions. As for status, which is based on a surrogate measure (degree of autonomy measured by the location of ultimate control/ownership), the analyses suggested that it might also be important. Nevertheless, given that no better surrogate for status exists, or is available, it has been used and any part of the analysis in which it is used must be viewed with caution.

4. THE LOCAL ENVIRONMENT

In a recent text, which was largely concerned with the role of new firms in a regional economy, Gudgin (1978) (8) summarises the 'location decision' for new firms in the following way:

> ... the founders of new firms will rarely make
> active location decisions. Instead, new firms are
> located within the entrepreneurs' home area. Also,
> the industry in which the firm operates will
> normally be that one in which the entrepreneur
> previously worked. The decision which is made is

whether or not to go into business; the location
and form of production are to a large extent
predetermined. (ibid., 105-6)

To explain this tendency Gudgin provides what he terms six
'underlying reasons' (1974, 93-9; 1978, 106-7) and they are as
follows:

(a) Small initial capital base precludes any spatial
search.
(b) Founders' market knowledge is limited to the
local area.
(c) To reduce uncertainty, the founder sets-up in a
known area.
(d) Starting on a part-time basis means the firm must
initially be local to allow present occupation to
be continued.
(e) Founders knowledge of the market is local and is
of the present position and would gain little by
locating outside the spatial size of these pieces
of information.
(f) Small initial labour demand makes a local site
feasible.

This explanation appears convincing and is intuitively appealing
in its internal logic. Perhaps its main fault lies in what it fails
to consider, and it is these factors within the localization of new
firm formation that are examined here. Three main features of the
localization of founders are considered and they concern the
movement of founders prior to establishing a new firm, the movement
of founders between industries, and the movement of new firms after
founding.

Most of the literature to date has stressed the local nature of
new firm founding. In two studies undertaken in North America it
was found that 97.5 per cent (COOPER, 1971) and 90 per cent
(SUSBAUER, 1972) of founders set-up their company in their 'local'
area. Unfortunately, no adequate definition of local is offered by
either study. A third study executed in Scotland by Scott (1976) in
1969 noted that:

... in almost all cases the founding was in the
immediate locality in which the entrepreneur
lived. Only 3 of the 60 entrepreneurs (5%) were
involved in a change of address as a direct
consequence of founding. ... Location ... is an
important factor, and not simply a passive one,
which in several cases exerted a strong influence
in the decision to found. Indeed founding is a
clear strategy against managerial mobility.
(SCOTT, 1976, 136)

These studies tend to deny the importance of the movement of
founders by their very failure to consider it as a possibility. Yet,
Johnson and Cathcart (1978, 14) note that 10 per cent of all
founders in their study area come from outside the Northern region.
And Johnson et al (1974, Table 8.1, 206) found that 2.4 per cent of
all migrants interviewed moved to a new labour market area in order
to set up a new firm (see GUERRIER and PHILPOT, 1978). There would

appear, then, to be a certain degree of confusion over the strength of localization.

The present study suggests (Table 8.21) that the movement of founders at the local, regional and national levels does occur. This table reveals that only 35.6 per cent of founders actually set-up their firm in the same local office area as their previous employer (of at least one year). While this figure rises to 47.63 per cent if the regional scale (Administrative Region) is used, it still leaves 18.85 per cent of founders who have moved between the regions on founding, and a further 32.98 per cent who moved <u>to</u> Scotland in order to set-up a new firm. This last group is considered below. These levels of mobility tend to contrast with the findings of previous studies, and they would also tend to further validate the assertion that new firm formation could represent one element of the labour market. The situation is partically clarified if the transfer of founders within Scotland is considered by means of a series of origin and destination regions (Table 8.22). Not unexpectedly the greatest degree of movement occurs around Glasgow where the major donor region is Glasgow and to a lesser extent outer Glasgow. While the main recipient regions were outer Glasgow and outer Strathclyde. Likewise, the major flows of migrants depict similar patterns with the major flows occuring from Glasgow to Dumbarton, Lanark and Renfrew (PIGGOTT, 1978; CROSS, 1980, 442-3). Again it would appear that the behaviour of founders is not that distinct from the actions and the activities of other people.

Despite these findings, the localization or concentration of qualified people would appear to be important. Evidence from North America (SHAPERO et al, 1965, Table 6, 33) concerning engineers and scientists tends to suggest the influence exerted by the areas in which people are trained. While these areas may not retain all of the people trained (9), they do tend to hold a higher number than other areas can possibly attract. This phenomena is not restricted to scientists and engineers and has been noted elsewhere in, for example, dental training (SCARROTT, 1978, 362; TAYLOR et al, 1976, 156). (10) Furthermore, local knowledge appears important in the finding of a site (Table 8.23, and likewise the existence of a local subcontracting market - GUDGIN, 1978, 117-20). Though many of these factors are of a secondary nature as their importance only becomes significant once the decision to found (and hence the existence of a founder) has been taken (though it may increase the speed of action once the decision has been taken).

It is perhaps surprising that as many as 32.98 per cent of founders moved to Scotland in order to set-up a new firm. The main interest in this group of founders concerns the opportunities they have taken, and the businesses set up by them. Have these founders:

> ... exploited the best opportunities and organised the most successful business. (?) If this were true, then one might explain the limited in-migration by the fact that the entrepreneurs moved only if they were able to take advantage of superior business opportunities. (DELANO et al, 1966, 205)

229

Table 8.21

The movement of founders prior to founding: Home - Workplace relationships

Region	Scotland Home	Scotland In	Scotland Out	Outside Scotland Other	Total
Borders	10	1	1	8	20
South West	4	-	-	5	9
Highlands and Islands	9	-	4	18	31
Lothians	10	12	7	4	33
Grampians	8	5	2	5	20
Tayside	9	-	2	2	13
Central	3	-	1	1	5
Fife	7	-	1	6	14
Glasgow	3	2	2	1	8
Outer Glasgow	3	3	8	9	23
Outer Strathclyde	2	1	8	4	15
Total	68[a] (35.6%)	24[b] (12.57%)	36[c] (18.85%)	63[d] (32.98%)	191

Source: Survey

a: 68 new enterprises started in the same local office area as the incubator organisation.

b: 24 new enterprises started in the same region but in a different local office area as the incubator organisation.

c: 36 new enterprises started in both a different region and local office area than the incubator organisation.

d: 63 new enterprises started in Scotland with the incubator organisation located outside Scotland.

Table 8.22

The movement of founders within Scotland prior to founding

Origin Region	Destination Region											Total
	1ᵃ	2	3	4	5	6	7	8	9	10	11	
1. Borders	11	-	-	-	-	-	-	-	-	-	1	12
2. South West	-	4	1	1	-	1	-	-	-	-	-	7
3. Highlands and Islands	-	-	9	-	-	-	-	-	-	-	-	9
4. Lothians	-	-	1	22	1	1	-	-	-	-	-	25
5. Grampian	1	-	1	1	13	-	-	-	-	-	1	17
6. Tayside	-	-	-	-	-	9	-	-	-	-	-	9
7. Central	-	-	-	-	-	-	3	1	-	-	-	4
8. Fife	-	-	-	2	-	-	-	7	-	-	-	10
9. Glasgow	-	-	-	2	-	-	1	-	5	8	1	17
10. Outer Glasgow	-	-	-	-	-	-	-	-	1	6	3	10
11. Outer Strathclyde	-	-	1	1	1	-	-	-	1	-	4	7
Other	8	5	18	4	5	2	1	6	1	9	4	63
Total	20	9	31	33	20	13	5	14	8	23	15	191

Source: Survey

a: Numbers correspond to those in front of origin regions

Table 8.23
Sources of information used by founders setting-up
a manufacturing enterprise in Scotland during the
period 1968-77 in finding their initial premises.

Source of information	No. of times mentioned
Personal knowledge	143 (70.44%)
Local authority/NTDC	41 (20.20)
SDA and DTI	10 (4.93)
Previous employer	9 (4.43)
Total	203

Source: Survey

Three areas of interest exist then. First, where did these founders
come from? Second, did they have any connections with Scotland
prior to making their move to set-up a new firm in Scotland? And
third, are there any differences between the founders or the firms
they set up between the moving and non-moving founders?

The first two of these questions are answered by the information
presented in Table 8.24. By far the most important regions of the
UK supplying new firm founders to Scotland are the South East and
East Anglia which have supplied 52 per cent of those founders moving
to Scotland in order to set-up a new firm. Of those founders moving
to Scotland, 36 per cent had in fact worked previously in Scotland
prior to moving to Scotland in order to set-up a new firm.

Table 8.24
Regions supplying new firm founders both with and
without previous employment connections with Scotland

Supplying region	With previous employment connections with Scotland (%)	Without previous employment connections with Scotland (%)	Total (%)
South East and East Anglia	55*	50.00	52
W. Midlands	30	6.25	16
North West	-	6.25	4
Yorkshire and Humberside	-	18.75	12
N. Ireland	15	-	4
Eire	-	6.25	4
N. America	-	12.5	8
Total	100	100	100

Source: Survey

*Sums to 100 per cent down columns

Perhaps rather surprisingly there were few significant differences between either the moving or non-moving founders, or the new firms they set-up (Table 8.25). This would suggest quite conclusively that while the movement of founders into an area is beneficial in that it increases the number of new firms established, they do not represent an elite group of founders. Reservations must exist however. The size of the new firms set-up by incoming founders are slightly larger than those set-up by their non-moving counterparts. Furthermore, the incoming founders appear to have used a greater number of sources of finance than the other founders. With the existence of these differences one would have expected other dissimilarities to have emerged, but this was not the case.

There is, of course, the possibility that the sample was biased to those founders moving to Scotland, unfortunately there is no means of gauging this possible weakness. Furthermore, it would also be important to know how many new firms were set-up in other areas by founders leaving Scotland. If these data were available an assessment could be made of the gross gains and losses made by Scotland in terms of producing and retaining founders. It could well be the case that Scotland is supplying more new firm founders than it is receiving from other regions. Again, these data are not available, and would only be so if similar surveys were conducted in other regions.

Two other features of the localization phenomena are the transfer of founders within and between industries on founding, and the movement of newly founded companies. The source and destination industries of the main founder covered by this study are shown in Table 8.26. There are two striking features of this table. The first is the importance of the non-manufacturing industries in the supplying of new firm founders of manufacturing firms. In fact, 28.39 per cent of founders were not connected with manufacturing industry prior to founding. This level is similar to that noted by Johnson (1978, Table 3) which was 22.57 per cent. Second, the values along the diagonal are surprisingly small which indicates a relatively low level of within industry produced new firms founders. Most industries reveal a spread of sources of new firm founders, but these are most marked in mechanical engineering (Order 7), metal goods not elsewhere specified (Order 12), bricks and pottery (Order 16), and other manufacturing industries (Order 19; see Chapter Six on barriers-to-entry, Table 6.23). However, at the outset it should be realised that the task undertaken by an individual in an industry might have little or nothing to do with that industry. For example, a systems analyst working for a large brewery (Order 3) left to set up a sawmilling firm (Order 17) and hence the crude transfer between industries can be (_is_) misleading. The wide variety of backgrounds from which founders come and set-up in Industrial Orders 7, 12 and 19 is not surprising given the huge range of manufacturing activities that these Orders cover, and their low barriers-to-entry. Furthermore, there is a direct transfer of founders between similar industries such as in Orders 7 and 12, and 8 and 9. (11)

Two of the major sources of founders were in non manufacturing Orders, distributive trades (Order 23) and professional and scientific services (Order 25). Both of these Orders cover a wide spectrum of activities and within which the educational and medical

Table 8.25

Results of the comparison of new firm founders moving into Scotland
with those already located within Scotland

Criteria	x^2	df.	Sign. Level 0.1
a. Age at starting full time employment	32.5925 (12.9164)[a]	5 (4)	No (No)
b. First employment positions	0.4484	2	No
c. Reasons for leaving previous employment (not including job held immediately prior to setting-up own firm).	6.9460 (0.9228)	6 (1)	No (No)
d. Number of jobs held.	11.6820 (7.3731)	8 (5)	No (No)
e. Reasons for leaving previous employment held immediately prior to setting-up own firm.	22.002 (1.5279)	9 (2)	No (No)
f. Age at setting-up new firm.	6.2188	6	No
g. Previous employment position held immediately prior to setting-up new firm.	12.9840	3	No
h. Length of working career prior to setting-up new firm.	6.9488 (5.1379)	8 (6)	No (No)
i. Number of founders involved	7.4734 (5.7819)	6 (3)	No (No)
j. Number of previous companies set-up before present one.	3.6904 (2.3123)	3 (1)	No (No)
k. Source of information used.	4.8688 (2.2793)	3 (2)	No (No)
l. Number of moves made by firm once set-up	4.1908 (1.8224)	5 (3)	No (No)
m. Number of sources of finance used.	7.8936 (1.7768)	4 (3)	Yes (No)
n. Present employment size of new firm.	2.5465 (10.3394)	4 (3)	No (Yes)
o. Present turnover of new firm.	13.6324 (0.6114)	5 (1)	Yes (No)
p. Initial employment size of new firm.	2.9189 (2.3108)	4 (3)	No (No)
q. Percentage sales within Scotland.	13.1659 (5.9549)	8 (4)	No (No)

Source: Survey

a: Amalgamations made to remove low cell scores.

Table 8.26
Source and destination industries of the main founders.

Source Industry[a]	Destination Industry																	
	3	4	5	6	7	8	9	10	11	12	13	14	15	16	17	18	19	Total
0	2	–	1	1	5	1	1	–	1	4	2	–	–	–	4	–	7	29
1	–	–	–	–	–	–	–	–	–	–	–	–	–	–	–	–	–	–
2	–	–	–	–	–	–	–	–	–	–	–	–	–	–	–	–	–	–
3	8	–	–	–	–	–	–	–	–	–	–	–	–	–	1	–	–	9
4	–	–	–	–	–	–	–	–	–	–	–	–	–	–	–	–	–	–
5	–	–	4	–	–	–	–	–	–	–	–	–	–	–	–	–	–	4
6	–	–	–	–	1	–	–	–	–	1	–	–	–	–	–	–	1	3
7	–	–	–	–	11	–	1	–	–	7	–	–	1	–	1	–	–	21
8	–	–	–	–	–	3	2	–	–	–	–	–	–	–	–	–	–	5
9	–	–	1	–	1	2	6	–	–	1	–	–	–	–	–	–	1	12
10	–	–	–	–	1	–	–	5	–	2	1	–	–	–	–	–	–	9
11	–	–	–	–	1	–	1	–	1	–	–	–	–	–	–	–	1	4
12	–	–	–	–	3	–	–	–	1	7	–	–	–	–	–	–	1	12
13	–	–	–	–	–	–	–	–	–	–	9	1	–	1	–	–	1	12
14	–	–	–	–	–	–	–	–	–	–	–	1	–	–	–	–	–	1
15	–	–	–	–	–	–	–	–	–	1	–	2	–	–	–	–	–	3
16	–	–	–	–	–	–	–	–	–	–	–	–	3	–	–	–	–	3
17	–	–	–	–	1	–	–	–	–	–	–	–	–	–	4	–	1	6
18	–	–	–	–	–	–	–	–	–	–	–	–	–	–	–	5	–	5
19	–	–	–	–	1	–	–	–	–	–	–	–	–	–	–	–	6	7
20	–	–	–	–	–	–	–	–	1	–	–	–	–	–	1	–	–	2
21	–	–	–	–	–	–	–	–	–	–	–	–	–	–	–	–	–	–
22	–	–	–	1	–	–	–	–	–	1	–	–	–	–	–	–	–	2
23	3	–	–	–	–	–	–	–	1	–	1	–	1	–	3	–	4	13
24	1	–	–	–	–	–	–	–	–	–	–	–	–	–	1	–	–	2
25	–	1	1	–	1	–	–	–	1	2	5	–	1	4	1	2	4	23
26	–	–	1	–	–	–	–	–	–	–	–	–	–	–	–	–	–	1
27	2	–	–	–	–	–	–	–	–	–	–	–	–	–	1	–	–	3
Total	16	1	8	2	26	6	11	5	5	26	19	2	5	8	16	8	27	191

Source: Survey

a S.I.C. 1 – 27

0 = Not known

and dental services (mlhs 872 and 874 respectively) of Order 25, and
other retail distribution (mlh 821) of Order 23 proved to be
important areas for founder formation. This would tend to indicate
the importance of considering all employment types when considering
new firm formation, and therefore consider the transfer from
manufacturing to non-manufacturing activities (GUDGIN, 1978, 116 and
230-1).

A final aspect of localization considered here is the movement of
new firms after having been established. It would appear that new
firms frequently move after opening and more than fifty per cent did
so (52.36 per cent; Table 8.27). Unfortunately, complete information
is not available for this aspect of localization, but in those cases
where it is, there would appear to be a strong local pull such that
new firms may move but only a very restricted distance. In the
cases where these data are available the movement of new firms is
restricted to moves either within local office areas, or to moves
between adjacent ones. The strongest element of localization would
therefore seem to occur after founding, and after the first
permanent site of the new firm has been established. After this
time the firm would represent a 'fixed' element of the local stock
of plants and any moves would be made within the immediate vicinity.
The ratio of initial to present employment shown in Table 8.27
suggests that the degree of growth, and hence expansion, appears an
important determinant for moving.

Table 8.27
Number of moves made by new manufacturing enterprises
set-up in Scotland during the period 1968-77.

No. of moves	Mean ISIZE[a]	Mean PSIZE[b]	Mean ISIZE[c]	Mean PSIZE[d]	PSIZE[b]/ISIZE[a]	No. of cases
0	10.66	23.26	970	2,117	2.18	91
1	5.35	27.03	364	1,838	5.05	68
2	3.68	19.79	70	376	5.37	19
3	3.37	19.12	27	153	5.66	8
4	3.25	24.25	13	97	7.46	4
5	3.00	41.00	3	41	13.66	1
Total	7.58	24.19	1,447	4,622	3.19	191

Source: Survey

[a] Mean initial size by employment
[b] Mean present size by employment
[c] Total initial employment of enterprises in survey
[d] Total present employment of enterprises in survey

Overall, the strength of localization does not seem great until
the new enterprise has in fact been started and is operating. Thus,
as was pointed out by Hill (1953), new firm founders are mobile and
reveal a surprisingly high degree of mobility immediately prior to
founding, but this does not imply that a stream of founders could be
channelled from one area to another as has been suggested (GUDGIN,
1978, 304-5). Furthermore, such degrees of geographic and
industrial mobility might impede local analysis, but the following
chapter attempts this. The discussion thus far has centred upon the

supply side of the new firm (supply of founders and their characteristics) rather than on any of the factors impeding entry. It is the object of the following section to go some way to correct this imbalance.

5. BARRIERS-TO-ENTRY

In an attempt to show that barriers-to-entry exist (and survival), information is presented in this section concerning the problems of starting a new firm. It does not therefore consider the minimum efficient scale of production or similar aspects of economic theory (see Chapter Six), but the barriers concerning finance and other problems. However, the main focus is upon finance and its sources, availability and accessibility.

Most founders used more than once source of finance (56.08 per cent) when establishing their firm (Table 8.28) and there is a reliance upon the three main sources of: personal savings (44.02 per cent), local banks (18.21 per cent), and government loans (9.24

Table 8.28
Number of sources of finance used in setting-up a new manufacturing enterprise in Scotland 1968-77.

No. of sources used	No. of cases
1	83
2	59
3	32
4	12
5	4
Total	189

Source: Survey

per cent; Table 8.29). It is interesting to note that the fourth major source of finance was the sale of the founder's house (see GUDGIN, 1978, 140-1, Note 10) and in part confirms the capital gains to be made by moving. Besides these four sources, twelve others were used by the founders surveyed. The importance of the family, however defined, as a source of finance was surprisingly low (HARBURY, 1979). While the importance of local businessmen and share holders was perhaps higher than might be expected. Both commercial banks and commercial finance houses play a minor role in supplying finance to these new companies. This may reflect the number of merchant banks or similar institutions in Scotland. In Edinburgh, for example, there are eighteen merchant banks and an office of the Industrial and Commercial Finance Corporation. Yet, given the size of Edinburgh (603,615 people in 1974), one would expect that there would be at least ten small business investment companies if the conditions were directly comparable with those in the United States (DRAHEIM et al, 1966, Table 22, 57). Though it should be noted that a wide variety of financial sources and services do exist in Scotland (SCOTTISH COUNCIL (Development and Industry), 1977) and what is more their availability is being made

Table 8.29

Initial sources of finance used in setting-up a new manufacturing enterprise in Scotland 1968-77.

Source	No. of times mentioned	(%)
Personal savings	162	44.02
Local bank	67	18.21
Government loan	34	9.24
Sale of house	17	4.62
Redundancy pay	14	3.80
Local businessmen	14	3.80
Share holders	9	2.45
Credit from client	8	2.17
Another business	8	2.17
Local authority loan	8	2.17
Another business owned by the entrepreneur	8	2.17
Family (parents, brothers, etc.)	6	1.63
Merchant bank	6	1.63
Family (wife and children)	3	0.82
Commercial finance house	3	0.82
Prize	1	0.27
Total	368	

Source: Survey

known (WATKINS, 1977; DARBY, 1978). This situation would suggest that the availability of finance might not be a direct barrier-to-entry, but that its accessibility might be.

Studies undertaken elsewhere, mainly in the United States, have found a similar reliance upon personal and other sources of finance for the new business (Table 8.30). The main exception to the 50:50 (app.) reliance upon personal:outside funds comes from the only other study reported in the table undertaken in this country by Scott (1976), and is probably a result of his sample which is biased towards engineering firms. However, the availability of capital is more likely to be a product of two factors. First, the previous positions held by the founder would give him access to information that may be of use when seeking finance. It is possible that the founder has raised finance previously and is aware of the problems of presenting an application for finance. Second, and this also relates to the founders previous position, the very fact that the founder was either the managing director or financial controller may be important in raising finance. The holding of a key managerial position would presumably allow the use of larger personal savings than are available to other new firm founders. The history of the founder and his associates (if any) are also important in that the bank or finance house will be looking to these people to manage their money and they '... must be certain that it will be returned without trouble'.(HARRIS, 1978, 27). In effect, the founder is attempting 'to sell' his company to a banker and to present the advantages of loaning him finance (see ALLSOPP, 1977, 75-7). Thus,

Table 8.30
Initial sources of finance: A comparison of studies

| Study | Sources of finance (%) | | |
	Self	Friend and/ or relatives	Outsiders/outside institutions
Mayer and Goldstein (1961)	50	34	70
Delano, Johnson, and Woodworth (1966)	70	25	5
FRB (1958)	Most	Some	Little
Maryland (1963)	40	13	19
SRI (1966)	Most	Some	Some
RDL (-)	54	24	22
Cooper (1971)	40	-	60
Susbauer (1969)	54.55	-	27.27
Scott (1976)	91.7	-	8.3
Smith and Carter (1963	53.1	1.2	45.7
Litvak and Maule (1972)	35	---------65-----------	
Present Study	54.61	2.45	42.94

the higher the position held by the founder prior to founding, the
larger the amount of finance that can be guaranteed, the larger the
amount of finance that can be raised, and the larger the number of
sources used (Table 8.31). However, the problems encountered in
raising outside finance are much the same for those founders that
held key managerial positions to those that did not (Table 8.32).

In terms of barriers-to-entry, there would appear to be barriers
to those without ability, in the eyes of the financial community, to
manage and control a new business. Such a judgment would primarily
be made on the basis of previous work experience. Thus, despite the
often small amounts of finance initially invested (56.54 per cent
new firm founders invested less than £5,000; see Table 8.33) some
founders felt that it was not worth attempting to raise capital
outside their personal resources. This reluctance to borrow money
has been noted by Boswell (1972) and he interprets this attitude as
being '... basically ill-informed and outdated, an overhang from the
past' (ibid., 226).

The holding of such an attitude is all the more surprising given
that many new or small companies (SCOTTISH DEVELOPMENT AGENCY, 1978,
Table 9, 20; SICRAS, 1972, Table 5, 19) saw the lack of capital as a
major problem (50 firms reported that the lack of capital was a
major problem). A failure to use outside finance or financial
advice might therefore reflect ignorance on the behalf of the
founder, and an increased awareness of as many financial
possibilities might therefore be important (BATES, 1964; CLARKE,
1972; ALBERT, 1977).

Of course, not all problems stem from a lack of capital (or
similar), and Table 8.34 reveals a wide range of other problems.
However, as was noted with the reasons for both closures and
redundancies (see Chapter Five), the reasons listed here reflected a

Table 8.31

The previous employment position of the founder held immediately prior to founding and the amount and number of sources of finance used to raise the initial capital invested

Previous Occupation	Initial Mean	Capital (£) Median	No. of Sources Used[a]					No. of Cases
			1	2	3	4	5	
Managing Director	43867	12500	40	24	12	16	8	24
Foreman	990	1150	62	38				8
Manager	8395	3500	23	50	19	8		26
Technician	1322	4000	80	20				5
Sales Manager	24664	30000	26	47	18	11		18
Self-Employed	3913	3500	22	22	56			8
Director	11664	3000	71		14	14		7
Design Engineer	6067	2100	43	14	29		14	6
Marketing Director	4500	4500	29	71				7
Technical Manager	11816	8000	40	40		20		5
Draughtsman	1722	940	25	75				4
Production Cont.	31250	10500	25	25		25	25	4
Estimator/Buyer	3288	2800	25	25	25		25	4
Operative	1119	1000	63	25	12			7
Other Non-Manuf.	2987	5000	43	34	23			34
Accountant	2575	2575	100					2

Source: Survey

a: percentage of row total, rounded

Table 8.32

Type of major problems encountered by founders in raising initial
finance from outside sources

| | Previous Occupation | | | | |
Problems Encountered	Managerial	Operative	Other Non-Manu.	Not Known	No. of Cases
Conservative banks	15	1	2	–	18
Volatile industry	4	–	–	2	6
Lack of knowledge of where to obtain finance	3	–	1	–	4
No track record	14	4	3	2	23
Lack of government speed	4	1	3	–	8
Lack of guarantees	15	4	4	2	25
Not worth attempting to raise capital from a second/an outside party	20	3	4	–	27
Total	75	13	17	6	111

Source: Survey

Table 8.33

Size of starting capital invested in the setting-up of a new manufacturing enterprise in Scotland during the period 1968-77.

Size of starting capital (£)	Volume of investment	Mean investment	No. of cases	%
999 or less	13,125	262.5	50	27.78
1,000 - 1,999	31,100	1,151.85	27	15.0
2,000 - 4,999	90,000	2,903.23	31	17.22
5,000 - 9,999	148,650	6,193.75	24	13.33
10,000 - 24,999	384,800	14,800.0	26	14.44
25,000 - 99,999	610,400	40,693.33	15	8.34
100,000 or more	1,036,000	148,000.0	7	3.89
Total	2,314,075	12,855.97	180*	

Source: Survey

*These data are not available in 11 cases.

Table 8.34

General problems encountered by the founders of new manufacturing enterprises in setting-up their enterprise in Scotland during the period 1968-77.

Problems encountered	No. of times mentioned
None	76
Obtaining credit from suppliers	9
Getting products known	9
Excessive government paperwork	4
Getting customers to pay	5
Site too isolated	9
Local authorities/new towns' DCs	12
Company taxation	8
Loss of government assistance	2
Lack of machines	5
Lack of raw materials	12
Marketing	20
Lack of capital	50
Government interference	5
Lack of accountancy knowledge	8
Lack of knowledge of different sources of finance	2
Lack of orders	7
Lack of production knowledge	2
Total	245

Source: Survey

nest of related reasons. The reasons recorded might only represent the outcome of a problem from a different, but related source. For example, a failure to market products might cause cash-flow problems which might if known to the company's suppliers cause credit problems when attempting to obtain further materials. As Clarke (1972) notes the small firm places '... substantial dependence on trade credit and on firms paying bills promptly' (ibid., 304). Thus small businesses face a different position purely due to size and the difficulties they do face '... may well be due less to the lack of a supply of capital for small business and more to the economics of providing financial information services' (ibid., 304). Administering to the needs of small businesses is expensive and often they are the first businesses to be affected when the money markets become tight (OECD, 1971).

The above discussion tends to suggest that while the new firm faces a range of problems, the single most important one probably concerns finance. Be it the knowledge of, or accessibility to finance, there seems to be barriers-to-entry in terms of ability in raising the initial seed capital. What has been revealed beyond this is that access to capital is in some respects determined by previous work experience. This further underlines the restrictions placed upon those wanting to set-up a business to those with sufficient knowledge and confidence to obtain capital beyond their own savings. An increased awareness of the financial facilities that are available to all business ventures might have solved many of the initial problems and prevented many of the later ones from occurring.

6. SUMMARY

The objectives of this chapter have been to present some of the findings of a survey of new firm founders in Scotland, of comparing them to previous studies, and of supplying some empirical support for the arguments proposed in previous chapters. In proceeding towards these objectives, it has also been shown which factors may be important in the process of new firm formation; some of these can be measured and are used in the following chapter.

It has become apparent during the course of this analysis that the new firm founder can be typified in terms of age and previous work experience. The progression of founders through various 'job levels' from the start of their career to the position held immediately prior to founding a new firm was examined. At the point of setting-up the firm, most founders had reached some form of managerial position ranging from managing director to marketing manager. Associated with previous employment was the ability of the founder to be at least aware of potential sources of finance. In general, founders previously holding managerial positions used more, and a wider range of sources of initial finance, but they faced much the same problems as founders with other employment histories.

In terms of the incubator organisation there appeared to be an association with the number of main founders and three main features of incubator organisations: size, age and status. However, it was noted that these findings must remain tentative as they may reflect the surrogate measures used. The role of the incubator plant therefore should not be underestimated, and it may well be that the level of managerial staff (number, type, etc.) irrespective of ownership may be important. While the full role of the incubator organisation is not totally discernable, and would only be resolved if a series of case studies were carried out, the collective role of employers in an area may be important in providing job opportunities and so allowing career development of the would be new firm founders.

Perhaps surprisingly it has been shown that the movement of founders does occur on founding at the local, regional and national scales. These movements reflect the importance of the home-workplace relationship (FAGG, 1977, 426-30). Furthermore, the movement between manufacturing and non-manufacturing was found to be important, and the transfer between manufacturing orders was marked. This transfer of founders between the major manufacturing orders was not random. Those industries with the lowest barriers-to-entry (see Chapter Six; also see LEIGH and NORTH, 1980, 11-12) e.g. mechanical engineering and metal goods not elsewhere specified, gained far more new firm founders than they produced (or lost). It is as if they attracted founders to themselves. However, it should be recognised that the product classification system used (SIC) probably over-states the real transfer of founders between industries.

Once established the new firm did not move great distances and remained in the local area in most instances. Unfortunately, the mobility of founders due to actual migration or the shift of their journey-to-work patterns will severely limit any analysis of the spatial variations in the emergence of new firms. The location of the firm and founder may be different from that when established, and the following analyses consider both the formation of founders and new firms. Thus, the movement of founders on establishing new firms will create problems, but despite these problems the following analysis attempts to build on the findings of this and previous chapters to examine the nature of the labour market (redundancies, closures, types of employment, etc.) and relate it to the emergence of founders, and hence new firms.

NOTES

1. Other studies have considered the reasons for the setting-up of a firm, but have not listed them by the number of times mentioned. These studies would suggest the importance of:
    (1) Experience
    (2) Financial
  =(3) Opportunity
  =(3) Independence
  =(5) Self-employment
  =(5) Family environment
  =(5) Status
    (8) Frustrated innovation
(Rankings obtained from cumulative importance in each work cited below e.g. experience was noted in 5 of the 6 works, where as financial conditions were noted only 4 times, etc.) These studies being: Oxenfeldt (1943); Mayer and Goldstein (1961); Davids (1963);

Collins and Moore (1964); Delano, Johnson and Woodworth (1966); and Smith (1967).

2. Hardyk and Petrinovich (1969, 166) encourage the use of Yate's correction where df = 1 (also see SIEGEL, 1956, 64). If Yate's correction is used a value of X^2 = 1.0587 is obtained and this makes no difference to the overall conclusion.

3. In several cases it was noted that founders have moved within Scotland prior to setting-up the firm (not immediately prior but at some time during their previous working career) purely for housing reasons. In one instance a founder left central Glasgow and moved to Dumfries to obtain a house, but at the time of the move did not have any employment arranged in Dumfries. Other examples exist of founders moving to the New Towns under similar circumstances.

4. In footnote 13 Oxenfeldt notes the problems of generalising to all industry from data collected from the shoe industry.

5. This ratio, of course, becomes 1 in 5 if entrepreneurs were to set up only one firm each.

6. For the position in the North East see House et al (1968); Johnson and Townsend (1976); Smith (1976a 1976b); Townsend, Johnson and Taylor (1976); and Townsend, Smith and Johnson (1977). And for the North West and Wales see Livesey (1970). Ingham (1970) comes to the same conclusions from a study of organisation size and worker behaviour. Also see Thomas (1979).

7. Unfortunately only employment is disaggregated by order and plant ownership and not the number of plants (FIRN, 1975, 406). An ownership (status)/industrial order breakdown is not feasible for plants in 1973, but is for 1977 (Table 8.20b). No distinct pattern emerges from the table and the use of a 1977 ownership structure of plants is, of course, questionable as the pattern of ownership has undoubtedly changed and developed through time (see Chapter Five).

8. Gudgin (1978) after noting the strong local element of new firms (ibid., 108, 108-21) later notes that:

The non-local entrepreneur proved something of a mirage however, since eight of the thirteen had interpreted the word local in a very restricted sense, confining it to a single village, or to the suburbs rather than city centre. (ibid., 122)

9. This also reflects the fact that many institutions take the largest share of their intake from their local area.

10. I am greatly indebted to John D. McCalden for making these references known to me.

11. If the original and destination industries are further disaggregated from the SIC to the mlh level it is found that 103 founders changed mlh while 61 remained in the same one.

9 Spatial Variations in the New Firm Formation Process

Industrial change is a highly complex process and the features of that process are strongly interlinked. For example, a decrease in the level of government contract work received by a firm might result in redundancies for some research and technical staff. Each of these newly redundant workers will react differently to their common circumstances. Some will take employment with another local firm, while others will seek employment in other areas and regions. There may also be a small group amongst these redundant workers who will neither seek employment locally, nor elsewhere, but will decide to start their own companies. Though this third group would appear to be small from recent research into the employment activities of newly redundant workers (see PEARSON and GREENWOOD, 1977; DEPARTMENT of EMPLOYMENT, no date; DEPARTMENT of ECONOMICS, DUNDEE, 1979; MACKAY, 1979; MANPOWER RESEARCH BRANCH, MSC (SCOTLAND), 1979a, 1979b; EMPLOYMENT GROUP, NEWCASTLE upon TYNE, 1979, 1980; SMITH, 1979).

Some of these newly founded companies will grow and prosper, others may barely survive and the remainder may trade only for a few years before closing. Though for the last group of firms, closure does not necessarily imply failure. The growth of the more successful firms will demand a labour input which may, or may not, be found readily available. Established firms (1), then, may loose workers to their new rivals in the labour market. In turn, the established firms will attempt to recruit new workers to replace those leaving. The policies they adopt towards recruitment and internal promotion (GUERRIER and PHILPOT, 1978; IPM, 1980) may cause internal crises localised to one or two individuals. Such individuals may be those who regard themselves as 'prime candidates' for the recently vacated positions within the firm. Failure to obtain promotion to these positions may then cause frustration and a certain degree of alienation towards their present employer. The resentment and rejection felt by the internal candidates might encourage them to re-evaluate their role (position) within the firm, and spur them still further to consider the possibility of leaving. An examination of the local labour market and the future chances of being promoted, having been 'passed over' already, may introduce the notion of self-employment. In fact, it is also possible that there may have already been a desire to be self-employed in the minds of some individuals. Further enquiries and researches might show that self-employment is a realistic possibility. Again, a small number of workers in this situation will leave and set up their own firm. The process of new firm formation, then, is part of a continuous and dynamic process operating within every firm, and in each labour market.

This example suggests that the process of new firm formation is the result of the interplay between the conditions of the local labour market, an individual's future prospects with their present employer, and the influences affecting this interplay. Changes in either the local labour market, or the prospects for promotion within an individual's present company will create both new conditions and new opportunities. The emergence of new firm founders and hence new firms, it is argued, is a product of the nature of these changes within each labour market internal and external to an individual's employer.

An examination of the importance (Chapter Four) and character (Chapter Six) of new firms and the influences affecting their emergence (Chapters Five, Seven and Eight) has revealed that the role of the labour market would appear to be of importance in the process of new firm formation. This would suggest that labour markets containing different combinations of employment opportunities and industrial mixes would have differing numbers of new firms. Analysing the variations in 'make up' of the various labour markets (or equivalent areas) in Scotland may reveal those conditions either more, or less favourable to both founder and new firm formation. The following analyses represents an evaluation of these notions using measurements of the local employment and industrial environment and an attempt to relate them to the emergence of new firms.

Besides the evaluation of the labour market/new firm relationship, some possible implications for industrial and new firm formation theory and research methodology are also noted (Chapter Ten). This process of evaluation attempts to gauge the success of the research in terms of the additions made to the general field of enquiry, industrial geography, and it makes explicit what the implications are for future research.

1. REGIONAL DEVELOPMENT

Throughout Scotland spatial variations exist in the importance of each of the various components of employment change. For example, a direct contrast was noted (Chapter Four) between the city centres on the one hand and their outer-lying areas on the other. In these two areas the size of each of the components of employment change varies such that the expansion of the employment in the existing stock of plants is the most important source of new employment. While the balance between the birth/death rates of plants are adverse in the city centre and favourable in the outer-lying areas. On disaggregating the components of employment change still further it was found that the outer-lying areas generally had more new firms than the city centres. Why do these variations occur?

Several lines of reasoning can be advanced to suggest why these variations exist. The variations may be the result of '... the dominance of external capital and lack of highly differentiated or developed firms ...' (McDERMOTT, 1977, 354) in some areas, and could '... be interpreted as the outcome of the increasing inter-regional integration of regional economies attendant upon policies orientated towards the achievement of spatial equilibrium.' (ibid.). Those

areas receiving externally owned branch and subsidiary plants may
have labour market characteristics that are different than, say, the
inner city, or other outer-lying areas. Could the intra-regional
variations in new firm formation be in part due to a policy induced
industrial structure? Still further, could the apparent lack of new
firms in Scotland compared to the East Midlands also be partially a
direct result of regional policy? If this was found to be the case,
it would therefore follow that regional policies to-date may have in
fact undermined the regenerative ability of manufacturing industry
in Scotland and so further exacerbate any regional inequality that
may exist.

Other lines of enquiry exist, and they include the residential
environment and the attraction of potential entrepreneurs on the one
hand (KEEBLE, 1978, 110), and infra-structural availability
(external economies) on the other (KEEBLE, 1976, 117-8). The
concentration of potential entrepreneurs in areas of a high
residential desirability is probably linked to the selective
decanting of people from the centre of the major cities (McDONALD,
1970; HALL, 1975). These movements may lead to entrepreneur-rich
and entrepreneur-deficient regions, and hence spatial variations in
the emergence of new firms commensurate with the supply of
entrepreneurs.

Variations in the birth rate of new firms might also result from
variations in external economies and institutional environments.
The supply factors of the local environment can be summarised as
comprising:

> The ... availability of premises reasonably close
> to the entrepreneur's home, ... supporting
> services, ... local demand for manufactured goods,
> the ... possibilities for local linkage and
> product specialisation, ... rapid access to
> information about technological innovations or
> demand shifts, and even ... cheaper loan finance
> for development, all help to provide an environ-
> ment for so-called 'seed-bed' growth of new firms
> ... . (KEEBLE, 1976, 117-8)

Such conditions, Hammond argued (1964), are more common in the
London fringe and in the West Midlands such that '... small concerns
... breed and thrive in much greater numbers ...' (ibid., 140) there.
Hence, areas in which the above factors of supply are readily
accessible, are available, and are known to the local pool of
potential entrepreneurs will have higher rates of new firm formation
than in areas lacking these factors of supply.

Another approach, which is in effect a combination of the three
noted above, follows Gudgin's (1978) line of reasoning that argues:

> Since firms are set-up close to the previous work-
> place of the founders', then the differing
> characteristics of individual labour catchment
> areas will cause varied levels of entry. (ibid.,
> 215)

The present analysis adopts a similar stance, and argues that the
initial focus of enquiry should not be on location per se and the

attributes of that location in terms of the classical and neo-
classical factors of location, but upon those factors which may
influence the emergence of new firm founders. At the outset, it
needs to be noted that the following analysis which attempts to
consider the relationship between the emergence of new firm founders
and the characteristics of the labour market is exploratory.

Before presenting the results of this exploratory analysis,
consideration is necessary of the hypothesis under examination, the
methods and scale of analysis used, the variables and their
measurement. The analysis itself is then presented, the results of
which are viewed in terms of their implications for regional
development in Chapter Ten.

2. THE HYPOTHESIS UNDER INVESTIGATION

The hypothesis to be investigated is the same as the model of new
firm formation detailed at the end of Chapter Seven, and is that:

> The emergence of new firm founders within an area
> at a given time will be influenced by, and will
> reflect the industrial structure and employment
> opportunities of that area.

It therefore follows that by investigating this hypothesis an
attempt is also being made to gulf the gap between the individual
enterprise (the new firm) and the local and regional economic
situation (WALKER, 1975, 145; WOOD, 1976, 139; KEEBLE, 1977, 307).
However, throughout this study emphasis has been laid upon the fact
that one of the benefits of structural explanation is that no gulf
exists between the industrial enterprise and any of the higher
spatial orders. In fact, the failure of many studies in industrial
geography to advance location theory and to explain the process of
industrial location is in part due to the expectation that
explanation would be found at the individual level (MASSEY, 1977,
11). Furthermore, the conceptual background to the study has been
one of considering new firm formation as the outcome of higher order
spatial processes operating between both regions and nations. The
outcome of these processes has then had some influence in the
initiation of another process, the process of new firm formation.
Any explanation of the variations in the emergence of new firms must
therefore be able to take account of the processes influencing the
local area and should not focus all attention at only one factor,
say, the availability of premises. Consequently, the following
analysis is framed so as to view aspects of the local environment
that fit in with this form of an explanatory framework. If the
analysis were to consider the availability of premises and were to
seek an explanation of new firm formation at that level the analysis
would be based on a self-fulfilling prophecy. That is, the analysis
would be based on a circular argument since the supply of premises
and the emergence of new firms are not necessarily independent of
each other. It is most likely that the supply of premises for both
new and small firms is a direct function of demand. The supply
mechanisms of small industrial units are not formalised and are
provided by several sources. For example, railway arches, existing
industrial premises (both vacant and ones in use), and industrial
estates (private, local authority, and central government) all play

a role in providing premises. The provision of premises is partially speculative, but the speculative element is based upon both existing demand and conservative estimates of future trends (2). Furthermore, the location of present day small industrial premises is no longer restricted to existing old industrial tracts of the inner city as the role of the industrial estates has risen in importance. It could therefore be suggested that the supply of premises is a local factor which reacts to changing demand, and may be forthcoming from local and non-local sources. Furthermore, the supply of premises and the supply of new firm founders, and hence new firms, are _not_ necessarily related in any way.

It might therefore be more logical to construct any hypotheses relating to new firm formation to factors not solely dependent upon _local_ conditions. The hypothesis under investigation here is constructed so as to allow the examination of new firm formation as a _part_ of the total process of industrial location and _not_ purely as a symptom of those processes.

3. THE SPATIAL SCALE AND METHODS OF ANALYSIS

Any analysis using spatially aggregated data must decide upon the appropriateness of the spatial units used. It is possible, for example, that the use of one spatial scale may give different, and conceivably contradictory results from another, yet both represent an analysis of a common problem. Before any analysis is contemplated, therefore, the spatial scale must be fixed and preferably done so along non arbitrary lines. Similarly, the methods of analysis must be shown to be suitable for the hypothesis under consideration. The following discussion considers each of these problems, the scale and the method of analysis, and presents arguments as to why a particular course of action was taken.

(a) Spatial scale of analysis

Five spatial scales have been used so far in this study ranging from the local office area to the whole of Scotland. Obviously an investigation of the variations in the emergence of new firms requires a relatively large number of spatial units. The number of options that are available represent the various permutations of the local office area units. Four levels of aggregation are discussed and the aim is to derive the most appropriate scale for the analysis.

The final selection of the spatial unit is based upon the three criteria of data availability, data accuracy, and the degree of self-containment of the unit. A self-contained spatial unit is seen as one in which founders work, could find alternative employment, and could also establish their own enterprise. Such a unit could be termed self-contained if the emergence of a new firm founder is almost entirely a function of the employment opportunities available within its boundaries. Ideally the spatial units of analysis should be large enough to cover _most_ job transfers and at the same time be small enough to allow the spatial variations in the rate (number) of new firm formation within Scotland to be discerned.

The notion of self-containment was considered by using the

complete employment histories of 117 new firm founders. These data were used to consider a series of related questions: Had the founder always worked in the same area? Were the number of gains and losses between regions equal? Which spatial scale revealed the highest degree of employment self-containment? The origin and destination of each employment move made by each new firm founder was allocated to three spatial scales: local office areas, travel-to-work areas, and the regions. Somewhat surprisingly, the results of such an analysis were similar for each of the three spatial scales. Interest here centres upon the level of self-containment of each spatial unit i.e. the number of employment transfers occurring within the stated spatial scale expressed as a percentage of all employment transfers. A level of 51.77 per cent was obtained for the regions (see Table 9.1), and 54.82 and 46.49 per cent for the travel-to-work and local office areas respectively. A full disaggregation of all employment origins-destinations, which is given in Table 9.1, reveals the relatively low scores in the left-right diagonal and the importance of employment opportunities outside Scotland. These employment opportunities are almost exclusively in England. Another feature is the heavy reliance of the Highlands region upon outsiders taking up employment opportunities within that region. Most of the other regions show a rough balance between both loosing and gaining employees, with the most intense interchanges occurring around Glasgow.

As a net result of these analyses there would appear to be little difference between using each of these spatial scales in terms of self-containment. This would suggest that if a potential new firm founder, or any employee for that matter, changes their employment to join a non-local employer they are likely to move at least between regions within Scotland (16.8 per cent of cases). The situation for both the travel-to-work and local office areas is nearly identical and again reveals the near balance between 'gains and losses' of employees except in the case of those units making up the Highland region. It was anticipated that as the spatial scale of the units was decreased the level of self-containment would also decrease, but this proved not to be the case.

Two other criteria that are seen as important to the selection of the spatial scale of analysis are data availability and their accuracy. Obviously, if data are available for only one spatial scale, the analysis can proceed at that or a higher spatial level via aggregation of these units. Furthermore, if some data are available at different scales a position of compromise must be used where the lowest spatial scale possible becomes the base scale of analysis. In this analysis the data for those plants opening, closing and contracting are available at an address level if necessary, though total employment levels for the major industrial sectors are only available at the local office area level. The smallest spatial units available to this study are therefore fixed by these data.

A further aspect of local office area data from the Department of Employment is that the smaller the size of employment in the local office area, the larger the degree of possible inaccuracy (RICH, 1975, 188; ALLEN and YUILL, 1978, 119). This limitation exists for those data collected by the card count sampling method that covered

Table 9.1

Employment transfer matrix of new firm founders: Regional scale

Origin Region	Destination Region												Total
	1[a]	2	3	4	5	6	7	8	9	10	11	12	
1. Outside Scotland	63[b]	5	2	15	5	3	9	2	5	4	6	2	121
2. Borders	5	7	-	-	-	-	-	-	-	-	-	-	12
3. South West	-	-	3	1	1	-	1	1	-	-	-	-	7
4. Highlands and Islands	-	-	-	6	-	-	-	-	1	-	-	1	8
5. Lothians	2	-	1	11	19	2	1	-	1	1	-	-	38
6. Grampian	1	-	-	1	1	13	-	-	-	2	-	-	18
7. Tayside	7	-	-	1	1	-	19	-	4	-	-	3	35
8. Central	-	-	-	-	-	-	-	1	-	-	-	1	2
9. Fife	4	1	-	-	2	-	1	-	11	-	-	1	20
10. Glasgow	3	-	2	-	3	-	-	1	1	17	15	5	47
11. Outer Glasgow	2	2	-	-	3	-	-	-	-	13	10	5	35
12. Outer Strathclyde	4	-	-	2	1	1	2	-	1	4	7	11	33
Total	91	15	8	37	36	19	33	5	24	41	38	28	376

Source: Survey

a   Numbers coincide with those in front of each region.

b   A total of 63 employment moves were made by founders between regions outside Scotland during their employment career. Hence, they not only moved both to and from Scotland, also within England and elsewhere as well.

the 1968-70 period of this study. Employment data were also
collected for 1971 by this method but this is the year in which the
Annual Census of Employment (ACE) began and, therefore, data for
1971 is not necessarily restricted by this limitation. A measure of
the accuracy of the data collected by the card count method is
charted in Table 9.2. If the margin of errors are used as criteria
for the elimination of local office areas with total employment in
manufacturing industry of less than 1,000, 35 local office areas
would be excluded; together these account for 16,491 or 2.48 per
cent of all manufacturing employment in 1971. Data for 1971 is used
because it represents the first year with reasonably accurate data
and it is also a 'mid-point' year (app.) for the ten year period
under study. It should be added that the local office area
employment totals derived from the Annual Census of Employment are
not without their problems either (DEPARTMENT of EMPLOYMENT, 1978;
PATTISON, 1979). (3)

Table 9.2
Margin of error (either way)
Due to sampling (of card count method)

Size of category (e.g. industry in one area)*	Poor ED205 coverage		Average ED205 coverage	
	Number	Per cent	Number	Per cent
1,000,000	3,500	0.35	1,400	0.14
100,000	1,100	1.1	440	0.44
10,000	350	3.5	140	1.4
1,000	110	11.0	40	4.0
100	35	35.0	14	14.0

Source: Department of Employment HQW637 - 1,000 6/66 (unpublished)
(after ALLEN and YUILL, 1978, Table 3.18, 119)

*As the absolute size of the industry in an area decreases so does
the reliability of that figure. Hence, as the numbers fall to,
say, only 100, the level of error can be as large as 35 per cent or
as small as 14 per cent.

Which spatial scale, then, is the most appropriate for the
following analyses? No simple answer is possible. The bulk of the
analyses are presented at the local office area level as the degree
of self-containment varies little with spatial scale, and also this
level offers the greatest degree of disaggregation possible. As
with the Department of Employment data, the degree of accuracy of
the other data sources used are also more suspect at these spatial
levels of analysis. This observation might tend to encourage the
use of a higher spatial level for the analysis. The solution to
this problem is one of compromise and several spatial levels have
been used, but only the local office area results are presented here
(SAWICKI, 1973, 114; see Chapter Four).

(b) Methods of analysis

The search for the principles of the location of industrial activity
have met with little success, and while many parts of the 'story'
have been told, as yet no unifying theory has emerged. Furthermore,

...e generalisations that have emerged often relate to specific industries and not all manufacturing activity. A main objective of this study is the derivation of a statement, or series of statements covering the main factors influencing the supply of new firm founders. Such a statement would accord with Herbst's (1970, 6; see Chapter Seven) second or B type law which covers those types of laws that relate a series of variables to a specific result or outcome. Thus, the functional or basic form of the process of new firm formation is common to all situations (industries and locations), but the influence of individual parameters may vary in importance. The most elementary and tested method of statistically representing this relationship would be by an equation with a linear form. Though, this is not to say that the relationship _is_ linear, but it can in its intial form be represented as such.

The simplest form of analysis that can be used to model and more importantly to examine such a relationship is correlation analysis along with its associated techniques of bivariate and multivariate regression analysis. However, the construction and execution of any statistical analysis are of secondary importance to the design of the initial experiment, the better it is designed, '... the less we have to worry about its interpretation, about what it "really" means' (MEDAWAR, 1969, 15). Research in the behavioural sciences though is largely non-experimental and so the quality of one's analysis is dependent upon the initial hypothesis and reasoning. If one accepts that the study design, execution and hypotheses are reasonable, problems still remain in applying any form of statistical analysis. The following comments are designed to highlight the major problems of the techniques used and they are not intended as a catalogue of the assumptions, or similar, as they are readily available elsewhere (POOLE and O'FARRELL, 1971; JOHNSTON, 1978, 37-45).

Multiple and partial correlation analysis and bivariate and multivariate regression analysis are all methods that attempt to measure the degree of association between a single dependent variable and either a single, or series of independent variables. The quality of the analysis, and hence the results, are of course, dependent upon the variables placed into the respective analyses. Problems of both accuracy and measurement further compound this situation and are ones considered below. While the aim of the overall analysis is explanatory, there '... is no necessary correlation between a statistically-derived component and real economic processes' (MASSEY and MEAGAN, 1979, 138). The analysis is therefore seen as a means of guidance, one seeking to delimit possibly important factors in the new firm formation process and that are amenable to measurement.

While correlation and regression analyses only differ in as much that regression is concerned with a causal relationship between two or more variables, and correlation assumes merely an association between variables (NORCLIFFE, 1977, 176), their problems of use and interpretation are similar. For example, in partial correlation analysis where the influences of one or more variables ($X_2 \ldots X_n$) are controlled while the association is calculated between two other variables (Y and X_1) is the same '... as the correlation between the residuals of the regression of Y on X_2 and X_1 and X_2. In a sense, then, a partial correlation represents the correlation between 'errors' with respect to the control variables.' (BLALOCK, 1972a, 435). The two proposed methods of analysis are therefore closely related.

Use of either correlation or regression analysis without a full awareness and statement of the problems of their use as they concern that specific study is common in much of the research literature. The main faults in their use revolve around the blind use of significance levels without any consideration of what significance levels really mean, and the almost complete reliance upon the coefficient of determination (correlation coefficient) as a means of interpreting their analyses. Besides these two faults, both of which are discussed in greater detail below, others also exist in relation to the spatial units of analysis, quality of the data, the inter-related nature of the independent (X) variable and the spatial association of the variables used (spatial autocorrelation) all of which are also commented upon as well.

The debate over the use of significance tests has been waged over many years (SELVIN, 1957; WINCH and CAMBELL, 1969) and has only relatively recently been acknowledged as being important in geography (GUDGIN and THORNES, 1974). Levels of significance are best used in an advisory or guiding role, and should not be seen '... as a virtual "seal of approval" or a measure of substantive importance'. In fact, Selvin continues:

> The levels of significance is only one link in a chain of methodological evidence that the results are substantially as claimed; to offer it as the only piece of evidence is misleading. (ibid.,523)

And so, while a less conservative attitude should be adopted towards significance tests (GUDGIN and THORNES, 1974, 160) they still represent an important method for deciding between systematic, and hence controllable, and non systematic (haphazard) variations in the data (WINCH and CAMPBELL, 1969, 143). Furthermore, the non normal nature of most (probably all) geographic data (HAGGETT, 1965, 287) in fact has little or no effect upon significance levels, and the tests themselves are remarkably robust (BONEAU, 1960). Again, this appears to be a fact that some researchers appear not to be aware (for an exception see GUDGIN, 1974) (4).

A second problem concerns the almost complete reliance of many studies upon correlation coefficients as the most important measure in the analysis which is surprising as one would assume that the aim of most studies are statements with a general applicability. These coefficients:

> ... will most certainly be relative to the particular situation and will therefore have very little general significance. It is for this reason that <u>correlation coefficients, which in effect measure the amount of unexplained variation, have little or no theoretical significance in themselves, though they may be used to test the adequacy of any given causal model.</u> BLALOCK, 1972b, 46)

Continuing, Blalock notes:

> In experimental situations the investigator
> deliberately attempts to control for as many
> extraneous factors as possible. Though manipu-
> lations of various kinds, he also tries to give
> the independent variable sufficient variation so
> that it will explain a high proportion of the
> variation in Y. In other words, he attempts to
> maximize the correlation by reducing the effects
> of extraneous factors while at the same time
> maximizing the effects of the independent variable
> under study. Clearly, it is not the size of the
> correlation coefficients, per se, in which he is
> inherently interested. A large correlation merely
> means a low degree of scatter about the least
> squares equation and hence an accurate estimate of
> the true slope. The size of the correlation
> coefficient tells him how successful he is being
> in attaining his real goal, namely in describing
> the <u>nature</u> of the relationship between his
> variables. <u>It is the regression coefficients</u>
> <u>which give us the laws of science.</u> (ibid., 51)

There is usually little merit in quoting previous work, however relevant, <u>in extensio</u>, but in the above situation it was necessary to stress the importance of the direction of the statistical association between two variables rather than the case specific correlation coefficients. Throughout the following analyses the direction of the relationship is seen as the key area of interest though this does not remove the use of correlation coefficients completely. In two instances correlation coefficients are used in preference to the direction of the slope. The first is where the correlation coefficient is expected to disappear and therefore to be zero, and hence being equal to having a slope of zero. The second is where the relative importance of several variables need to be assessed in their ability to <u>account for</u> changes in Y. Here the changes in the correlation coefficients are seen as important (BLALOCK, 1972a, 51-2). Likewise, where these situations arise below these conventions are followed.

Besides the statistical significance of an analysis and the most appropriate way of interpreting a correlation type of analysis several other problem areas exist such as the spatial units used, data quality, multi-collinearity and spatial autocorrelation. It was shown above that the size of spatial units and data quality used are related, and that the size of the spatial units must be considered as the most appropriate for the purposes of the analysis. These factors must also be considered further in relation to the methods of analysis used.

It is conceivable to design a system of spatial units such that on aggregating the data in each of these modified areal units the size of the correlation coefficient is increased to a maxima while removing the problem of spatial autocorrelation (OPENSHAW, 1977). Though the recent work of Openshaw makes an important contribution to spatial analysis, the use of meaningful spatial units (e.g. level of employment transfer self-containment) is seen as the most important criterion. And the re-aggregation of the units used here is seen to derive little advantage for either the following analyses, or for the interpretation of the results. The problem of spatial autocorrelation, however, is returned to below.

Data quality (accuracy) has been shown to vary with spatial scale and that the smallest spatial scale that can be used is the local office area. Furthermore, those local offices where total employment fell below 1,000 employees in employment the margin of error ranged between 4 and 11 per cent. Thus, the maxima and minima errors are known for this single data source, but the errors in the other data sources are not known. The existence of an error with an unknown magnitude will bias the coefficient of the regression equation to an extent which cannot be calculated (JOHNSTON, 1978, 45). This item therefore severely limits the following analysis. While the data used are not an exact representation of reality, they do present a sufficiently accurate picture to allow at least an exploratory analysis to be undertaken.

Frequently, the problems of multi-collinearity are noted as being a potentially important source of error e.g. Cameron et al, 1975, 58, but the problems are rarely given any further consideration. D.E. Keeble (1976, 90-1) considered that a '... pairwise correlation coefficient of more than 0.80 is usually taken as evidence of serious collinearity ...' (ibid., 90). He did not, however, consider those cases where the independent variables are negatively related to each other, but positively related to the dependent variable. For example, if the pairwise correlation is only, say, 0.40 but is negative, is that acceptable? Similarly, the Cameron et al's (1975) analysis said '... that particular care must be taken in interpreting the derived partial regression coefficients' (ibid., 58). Unfortunately, they did not indicate how such care should be actually exercised.

Perhaps the most important safeguard is to construct the independent variables upon logical and well argued lines e.g. Keeble and Hauser (1971), and then consider their possible inter-relationships. It is vitally important to make sure that all sources of error are eliminated from the analysis where possible, and therefore make the interpretation of the final results less complicated. Though, finally, one can only agree with Blalock (1963) who urges '... caution in the interpretation of controlling operations in which supposedly independent variables are highly related' (ibid., 237). This problem should therefore be noted where appropriate both in the discussion of the independent variables and in the analysis itself.

The final problem to be considered here, and which is applicable to all spatial analyses is that of spatial autocorrelation. Despite the apparently universal importance of spatial autocorrelation, few studies have in fact actually measured the presence of autocorrelation amongst residuals (for exceptions see KEEBLE, 1976; PIGGOTT, 1977). Even though in both of these studies are quoted measures of autocorrelation (KEEBLE, 1976, 115; PIGGOTT, 1977, 31 and 40), they do not explain what is actually meant by spatial autocorrelation. In this study, spatial autocorrelation would appear to present a major problem because it is apparent from the movement of founders between local office and travel-to-work areas, and the regions that the emergence of a new enterprise in one area may well be dependent upon the features of a neighbouring area or region. If no spatial autocorrelation exists between either the variables or residuals, a situation exists such that '... the value of each observation on the independent variable is independent of all of the values of all others, so that one cannot predict the value of X for observation 7, for example, if one knows the value for observation 6' (JOHNSTON, 1978, 43).

An awareness of the existence of spatial autocorrelation is important in multivariate analysis (5) as it is conceivable that the independent variables do not suffer from collinearity, yet they are spatially autocorrelated. Two main methods exist for the computation of a spatial autocorrelation statistic, one is based upon two and k-colour maps (DACEY, 1968) (6) while the second uses the parametric methods of Cliff and Order (1973). (7) The question then remains which test is most appropriate to the present analysis. (8) In view of the problems raised by the unknown inaccuracies of the data the use of exact values in a parametric method (CLIFF and ORD, 1973) are seen as not appropriate, and so the dichotomous black/white method devised by Dacey (1968) is used.

The use of correlation and regression analyses are thus seen as compatable with the nature of the hypothesis under investigation, and despite the problems of their use, which are not seen as insurmountable, the techniques are still applicable. Observance of the problems adds greater rigour to the analysis and may help prevent faulty interpretation of the results derived from the respective techniques of analysis.

4. THE VARIABLES

Subsumed within the major hypothesis under investigation there are several minor hypotheses each of which relates to an aspect of the local, and invariably industrial, employment environment. It is therefore further hypothesised that:

The number of new independent manufacturing enterprises (NIMEs) in an area is a function of:

(a) Mass (size) of manufacturing activity in the area prior to the study period (M)

(b) Diversity of the industrial base (D)

(c) Relative and absolute magnitude of the change in the diversity of the industry and major employment sectors (C)

(d) Type (level) of employment in manufacturing industry (E)

(e) Characteristics of the manufacturing plants existing throughout the study period (P)

(f) Degree of employment turbulence (levels of employment change due to plant closure and contraction) (ET)

$$\begin{array}{cc} \text{Number of NIMEs} \\ \text{in an area} \end{array} = f\ (\underline{+}M)(\underline{+}D)(\underline{+}C)(\underline{+}E)(\underline{+}P)(\underline{+}ET)$$

This series of inter-related hypotheses are examined by using a range of sixty-eight measures that attempt to measure single aspects of the local environment. Often though this has not proved to be possible because the measures used relect several aspects of the local environment, and in these cases the problem is both noted and is examined. The general notions behind each of the six main variables are considered below and the variables used are examined. (A full list of the variables is presented in the appendix though this excludes some of the further derived variables.)

(A) Dependent variables

Two possible dependent variables are available for use. The first covers the number of new independent manufacturing enterprises established during the 1968-77 period and that are still operating in 1977 (NUFIRM). A second variable is much the same as the first, but it also includes all of those new enterprises identified as having opened and closed during the study period (TOTENT) as well. While both of these measures are subject to error, the latter measure is subject to the greater error as the number of new enterprises identified as having opened and closed is not comprehensive. A further argument used to justify the use of NUFIRM or a derivative of it (BIRTH1, BIRTH2 and BIRTH3) is that it is easier to identify and establish the year of opening of enterprises in existence in 1977 than it is to establish retrospectively the year of both the opening and closure of a once new, but now non-existent enterprise. On these grounds therefore, this analysis is of the surviving new manufacturing enterprieses and could be said to be an atypical sample of new enterprises given the extremely high mortality rate of new enterprises (GUDGIN, 1974, 274, Table B4.1). In fact, if the rate of closure (survival from one year to the next) are used from previous studies, at a very conservative estimate there were 751 new enterprises established during the period. The real level was more probably nearer to 1,350-1,500 new enterprises. And only 114 new enterprises were identified as having both opened and closed, the degree of coverage was greater for those enterprises that had opened and survived the ten year study period.

During the discussion on the spatial scale of analysis it was noted that the level of employment movement of founders was similar for the units delimited by the local office and travel-to-work areas, and the regions. Furthermore, the likelihood that one single area was responsible for the career development of a founder was very small. For example, only 13 (11.11 per cent) of founders had been employed in their local office area for the whole of their working life. The levels do not rise dramatically for either the travel-to-work areas (24.53 per cent) or regions (complete regions, 29.91 per cent). There are, therefore, 70.09 per cent of founders who have been employed in various parts of either Scotland, or England, or both. Again, as was noted earlier in the discussion of the spatial scale of analysis, the local office area is the spatial unit of analysis used.

Three measures of the number of new enterprises in an area are used, and they all attempt to relate the number of new firms to the size (numbers in manufacturing employment or similar) of the spatial unit. The three derived variables listed below all yielded values of the number of new firms per thousand employees in manufacturing employment in 1971 (BIRTH1), or the number of new firms per thousand administrative employees in plants open prior to (and including) 1967 using 1977 employment levels (BIRTH2), and the number of new firms per thousand employees in both the manufacturing and service industries (BIRTH3).

$$\text{BIRTH1} = \text{NUFIRM/MAN71} \quad x \quad 1,000$$
$$\text{BIRTH2} = \text{NUFIRM/TOTADMIN (or TOTADM2)} \quad x \quad 1,000$$
$$\text{BIRTH3} = \text{NUFIRM/(MAN71 + SER71)} \quad x \quad 1,000$$

The first measure, BIRTH1, assumes that new firm founders will only emerge from the existing ranks of the manufacturing employees in the area. In an attempt to delimit the population from which new founders came, the manufacturing employment total was reduced to include only those employees in administrative occupations (TOTADMIN and TOTADM2). A still further refinement involved the redefinition of the population from which founders emerged, and to the manufacturing employment total of 1971 (MAN71) was added the service employment total also for 1971 (SER71). This increased population (MAN71 + SER71) was included because of the large number of founders who had transferred from service to manufacturing industry on establishing a new enterprise (Table 8.28).

(B) Independent variables (9)

A series of six major independent variables were derived and measured as accurately as possible for each of the 121 operational local office areas (at June 1977). For each of these major independent variables there are a series of variables each representing a measurement of one aspect of the major variable under consideration and these are detailed below.

(a) Industrial mass/concentration. While there is every possibility that new firm founders may 'develop' and emerge from an area with a small industrial base of, say, less than 1,000 employees, there is a much greater likelihood that the greater the mass, the greater would be the number of new firm founders. Accepting this line of reasoning, it follows that there might be a minimum level (threshold level) below which new firm formation would be unlikely and completely unpredictable. A counter argument would be that where the numbers of employment opportunities are greatest, the immediate attractiveness in terms of desire and need to establish a new firm is least. This statement, however, needs to be qualified. For example, in Chapters Five, Seven and Eight, the issue of job security was raised in reference to plant closure and contraction and it was argued there that the threat or actual loss of employment could present the necessary conditions to establish a new firm. Thus, even though an area may have a wide range and large number of employment opportunities there is the possibility that they are neither secure, nor of a sufficient level (seniority) and may therefore favour new firm formation.

In all, fifteen measures of industrial mass/concentration were derived covering the number of plants (TOTPL, TOTPLAD and TOTPL68), and the levels and types of employment (MAN71, MAN76, SER71, SER76, TOTEMP71 and TOTEMP76; TOTADMIN, TOTADM2, TOTOP and OTHEMP67 respectively). Further refinements were also made to consider the levels of administrative employment in Scottish owned plants (SCOTAD1, SCOTAD2, SCOTHX and SCOTMAD), and all large plants (P500). Each of these variables are attempts to measure different aspects of the local industrial environment. It is most unlikely that the number of new firms, however measured, would be directly associated with the sheer mass of industrial activity in an area. In fact, the size of employment in any one area is a very crude measure and gives no indication of the nature of that employment. The few variables measuring the type of employment and the level of administrative staff in Scottish owned and independent Scottish owned plants offers a further refinement of the crude mass or size measure of the manufacturing industry in an area. The following series of five variables offer still further refinements of this crude measure, and they are detailed below.

(b) _Industrial structure_. Implicit in the above discussion on the mass of industrial activity in an area was the problem of double measurement and multi-collinearity. Almost every facet of manufacturing industry is related to every other facet, though to varying degrees. Furthermore, the extraction of a series of variables, say, in the form of a few employment measurements could (would) lead to double measurement. That is, the measurement of the same variable twice and hence their inclusion in any regression equation would cause problems of multi-collinearity as the correlation of a variable with itself gives a perfect fit ($r = 1.0$). Similarly, the level of administrative employment in an area is related to the industrial structure of that area (see WOODWARD, 1965; Chapter Two, Table 2.5). Consequently, the inclusion of a measure of industrial structure and one of employment type may cause problems of multi-collinearity in some instances. There is also the possibility that the addition of a size and a structure variable in the same regression equation might also cause problems of interdependence such that the size of industrial activity in an area may directly affect the number of new firms via industrial structure. This situation may require another form of analysis, and merits further research.

Industrial structure itself is gauged by four types of measure concerned with the absolute size of the dominant industry (DOMIND71 and DOMIND76) and their share of total manufacturing employment (DOM71 and DOM76). Two further measures were also used concerning the degree of specialization of industry in each area in 1967. The first merely countered the number of industries present (MLH1 and MLH2), while the second measured the degree of specialization (TRESS1 and TRESS2) (10) using the plants based data set. This data set was used because a full industrial breakdown was not available for each local office area, and since 1971 these data are covered by the 1947 Statistics of Trade Act (see ALLEN and YUILL, 1978, 242-8).

The implicit hypothesis set within the above discussion is that the number of new enterprises is related to the degree of diversity of local manufacturing industry and that the more diverse is the local industry (the lower the Tress Statistic), the greater the number of new firms founded in that area. Thus the level of an area's employment in one industry offers a crude measure of industrial concentration (lack of diversity). It is expected that the greater the dependence upon one industry the smaller the likelihood that new firms would emerge in that area. While the basic hypothesis itself is easy to understand, its interpretation, and perhaps more important, its explanation, is not. If the associations are in the directions hypothesised (positive with high diversity; negative with high concentration), what do they in fact mean? It may well be that an area with a highly diverse industrial base offers the possibility for an individual to develop many talents in different industries. Hence, the greater the range of industries, the greater the range of employment opportunities. However, it is equally feasible that an area with a diverse industrial base is one in which many possible new growth areas for manufacturing industry exist. For example, if a rapid growth in demand for plastic products occurs, the area with at least some existing plastic producers is more likely to react to increased demand, and so this may increase the possibility of new enterprises being formed in plastics and related industries.

The above explanation is all the more likely if it is extended. An area with a diverse industrial base is also one in which many industries are represented by at least a handful of plants. There is the possibility, therefore, of the transfer of individuals between different types of firms and industries. In such an area it could be hypothesised that the population of individuals with a wide range of work experiences might be directly related to the emergence of new firms. In fact, the transfer of individuals between different firms and industries might also be important in the establishing of 'new' industries in an area. Still further, these movements might also be related to the transfer of technology (product, process and managerial) between existing firms, and to new ones. Thus almost irrespective of the explanation advanced, some confusion remains.

(c) <u>Magnitude of change</u>. Does either the absolute, or relative magnitude of employment change in an area either encourage or discourage new firm formation? The series of variables noted here measure the absolute employment change in the major sectors (MANCH, SERCH and TOTEMPCH) and their complementary relative measures (MANCHPC, SERCHPC and TOTECH). There are also measures of the change in the relative importance of the single most important industry for employment in an area (EMPINDCH). Finally a measure of the shift in industrial concentration is also used (DOMINDCH, DOMINDPC, DOMCONC and MLHCH).

Are those areas in which there has been an increase in the importance of manufacturing industry as an employer (in both absolute and relative terms) and where there has been either an increase in the diversity <u>or</u> a decrease in concentration, also experiencing the emergence of the largest number of new firms? If it is the case that the number of new firms is positively associated with the expansion and diversification of the manufacturing industrial base of an area, several explanations are possible. For example, the overall expansion of an area's industrial base may be providing new markets which are providing opportunities for new firms. However, there are other possible explanations that complicate the situation. First, it is possible that the growth of an area's industrial base is attracting founders from other areas because of the growing markets, and possibly the growing stock of new houses in response to the growth of the employment base. (11) Second, the expansion of the industrial base in one area may also generate an increase in the supply of industrial premises. This could occur in two main ways either by the provision of new premises, or by the vacating of existing premises by the expansion of previously existing firms. In addition to both of these sources of 'new' industrial premises, there is the further possibility that existing firms with spare space may sublet it to another firm. Though subletting is not possible on many industrial estates, it might provide an important supply of premises for new firms. The growth of local industry by firms subletting industrial premises would not be revealed by existing data sources (KEEBLE and HAUSER, 1971, 239-41). It might therefore follow that there are 'premise rich' and 'premise poor' areas within Scotland which would vary with the buoyancy of the economy. The main counter argument would consider the availability of premises in Glasgow for an entrepreneur in Glenrothes is, however, of little consequence. The entrepreneur looks and knows his own area, and <u>tends</u> to seek out premises in much the same way as he might look for a new house (HILL, 1954; HERBERT, 1972, 246-52; Chapter Eight, Table 8.25).

Another possible explanation for the positive association between new firm formation and an area's employment growth may stem from the actual growth in the number of employment opportunities. If the absolute numbers employed in manufacturing industry increases in an area, only part of the new employment opportunities created will be ones requiring semi or unskilled workers, the remainder would be for skilled employees. (12) The net result, therefore, of an increase in the level of manufacturing employment in an area is to increase the pool from which entrepreneurs (new firm founders) are most likely to emerge. Thus, the increased size of the potential pool will, <u>ceteria paribus</u>, increase the <u>number</u> of new firms being formed in an area. It does not necessarily follow though that the <u>ratio</u> of new firms founded per 1,000 administrative (or similar) employees will be altered either positively, or negatively.

This discussion has helped to illustrate an important point. While the measurement of a variable might be successful in terms of its accuracy and its comprehension i.e. it is easy to understand, when placed in either a bi-variate or multi-variate analysis its interpretation might not be so easy. The present example offers a good illustration of this point and stands as a warning to those who believe that all other influences can be eliminated (disturbance factors) in the study of the direct influence of one condition on another (see WRIGHT, 1921, 557; SHANKAR and NAIR, 1972).

(d) <u>Employment type</u>. Most new firm founders held managerial positions immediately prior to establishing their own firm (Chapter Eight, Tables 8.9, 8.10 and 8.11). It would therefore appear reasonable to hypothesise that the number of new firm founders in an area is in part a function of the type of employment in that same area. The variables one might wish to consider to investigate this notion could range from the level of administrative and operative employment (ADMINPC and TOTOPC), through the various levels of employment in, perhaps, Scottish owned plants (SCOTAD, SCOTADPC, SCOTEMP1, SCOTEMP2, SCOTH1PC, SCOTH2PC, SCOTAPC, SCOTA2PC, SCOTH3PC, SCOTH4PC, SCOTHX1, SCOTH2 and SCOMAD1), probably include some measure of plant dominance (BIGPL, BIGPLPC and NEWPLPC), and also some measure of the relative importance of manufacturing industry for employment generally in the area (EMPIND1 and EMPIND2). These twenty variables measure the various absolute and relative size aspects of employment types present within an area. (A full list of these variables appears in the appendix).

The greater both the relative and absolute importance of non-productive manufacturing employees in an area, it is hypothesised, the greater will be the number of new firms formed in that area. (13) It is, of course, important to know how these administrative employees are employed in terms of industrial structure and plants. Several industries have a low managerial/operative ratio e.g. shipbuilding, and so a different industrial type of new enterprise may emerge because of this fact. In cases such as this a measure of operative and other employment (14) might be more appropriate. Similarly, plant size may also be important in that an area may possess a large absolute number of employees in administrative positions, but they may all be in one plant. This latter variable therefore measures not only the concentration of administrative staff, but also the notion of spin-off from large plant which has been shown to be inversely related to plant size (COOPER, 1971; BRUNSKILL, 1979; GUDGIN et al, 1979; JOHNSON and CATHCART, 1979). (15) Furthermore, it may also measure the degree of industrial concentration in areas where employment is dominated by only one or two plants (see LEVER, 1978).

Further refinement of the measures of employment type by plant ownership creates a series of compound variables. (16) This refinement represents an attempt to allocate the various types of employment to independent manufacturing plants. The intention being to split those employees acting with full responsibility and taking decisions within a self-contained unit from all the other types of employees. Only one method was possible to achieve this split, and it entailed the aggregation of the various types of employment for each of the Scottish owned plants which were either independent single-plant companies, or were the headquarters locations of Scottish firms operating at two or more locations. To assume that this method of allocation and aggregation is accurate would be wrong. A recent study of independent (self-contained) electronics firms, for example, included in its final sample '... single-plant firms, multi-plant firms, subsidiaries, and some semi-autonomous divisions of larger organizations' (McDERMOTT, 1977, 81). Accepting that the above measure suffers from some deficiencies, one must assume the level of self-containment of non-Scottish owned plants does not vary between industries. However, if the level of autonomy at each plant was known, a constant could be added to the figures derived above which would not materially affect the analysis. The likelihood that this assumption is true is very small, and if one were to apply Wood's (1978, 149) list of factors favouring local and non local control in plants belonging to multi-plant firms, industrial variations would emerge. Though this variable is open to serious question in terms of accuracy, it is included in the analysis as it is the best measure available.

Again, the compound nature of the variable makes interpretation at
best difficult. However, as with the problem of compound variables
noted earlier it is possible to 'control' for the effects of some of
the other variables. For example, in the case of the correlation
between, say, the number of new firms in an area and the level of
administrative employment in independent Scottish plants, the
effects of the number of plants employing less than 100 employees
could be controlled for. It is therefore of the utmost importance
that the full implications of what a variable measures are
considered prior to both the analysis and the interpretation of the
results.

(e) <u>Plant characteristics</u>. There are several characteristics of the
manufacturing plants in an area that are seen as potentially
important in the new firm formation process and these range from the
number of plants employing less than 100 employees (PLE100, PLE100AD
and PLE100PC) to those employing 500 or more employees (P500PC,
LOGP500 and NEWBIGPL). Other aspects of interest include the age of
the manufacturing stock (AGE1, AGE2, AGE3, YOLD1 and YOLD2), the
number of plants (NOCLOS) and the number of subsidiary plants in an
area (SUBSID). It is evident from a range of variables such as
these that a series of diverse hypotheses are under investigation.
However, many of the hypotheses outlined below do in fact overlap
with many of those stated earlier.

The general hypothesis under investigation considers that the
number of new manufacturing enterprises in an area is positively
related to the number (however measured) of small plants in an area,
and therefore, negatively related to the number of large plants in
an area. Suppose the number of new firms in an area <u>is</u> related to
the number of small plants, what does this mean? Or, and perhaps
more explicitly, what does the number of small plants (or their
employment) variable actually measure? There are several possible
interpretations of this variable and several are presented below.
Probably the most common reasoning behind the use of the number of
small firms, in either relative, or in absolute terms, as an
independent variable stems from the implicit assumption that it
gives some indication of the existence of barriers-to-entry (GUDGIN,
1978, 137; JOHNSON and CATHCART, 1978, 18). This study accepts this
line of reasoning. However, this measure also covers several other
areas and some of these are considered below.

First, in a new and growing industry one could assume that the
number of small plants would be greater than in a mature or static
industry. The age of the industry in terms of the establishment
date (opening date) of each individual plant might therefore be an
important indicator of an industry's age. A distinction, it could
be argued should be made between the completely new industry in
which barriers-to-entry are yet to be established, and the existing
industry where barriers probably already exist. To argue that in
both of these types of industry a correlation between the rate of
entry and the proportion of small plants is simple due to the 'low'
barriers-to-entry would be fallacious. (17) In fact, use of the
number of small plants as an indication of either the existence, or
the non-existence of barriers-to-entry and as a catch-all variable
is of little use without a full understanding of what it means.
Without knowing what is being measured <u>no</u> reliability can be placed

on the interpretation of the analysis (See Chapter Six).

Second, it has been suggested that small plants perform better as incubator organisations than large plants (e.g. COOPER, 1970, 60; 1971; 3-5). If this is in fact the case, it could be assumed that the area which has the largest number of small plants also has the largest number of potential incubator organisations. Again, the arguments previously used in this context are somewhat tenuous to say the very least. For example, it is usually accepted that the incubator organisation is that organisation for which the founder worked immediately prior to establishing his own firm. It is not possible, as was suggested in Chapter Seven, that a series of incubator organisations exists such that the final employer of a new firm founder represents the end of a chain of incubator organisations. Thus, small plants may play a vital incubator role in the formation of new firms, but to cast them in the role of the sole progenitor of new firm founders could be misleading. While this issue still remains largely unresolved, it is important to realise that the role of small plants as incubators may, in part, be causing the association between new firm emergence and the proportion of small plants in an area.

Third, the number of small plants in an area might be 'artificially' increased in some areas by a number of previously medium sized firms contracting in size and entering the small firm employment size group. Thus, in areas where employment has been lost by plant contraction the number of small plants may be inflated in this manner. It can further be argued that by the very act of contraction and the downward movement of a plant that new firms have been formed. These so formed new companies having been founded by employees of ex-medium size plants leads to a position where there is both an increase in the number of small plants and the founding of a new firm. A result of this process would lead to the increased likelihood of an association between the numbers of small plants and the numbers of new firms.

Fourth, the geographic remoteness of an area has a direct influence upon the size of plants in an area. There are several logical reasons why remote areas do not attract large plants. First, a small town or village could not support a large firm in terms of labour inputs. And second, the exertion of a spatial monopoly in terms of market dominance does not extend to all areas. Hence, in areas where the market is small and is inaccessible, small plants will survive (NORCLIFFE, 1966). (18) Geographic remoteness could be interpreted as a form of barrier-to-entry, but is rarely considered as such. Consequently, some of the remoter parts of Scotland will only possess small plants, and may represent atypical industrial areas.

The interpretation and subsequent explanation of an association, if any, between the numbers of new firms and small plants in an area is fraught with problems and is probably best interpreted in conjunction with other variables in an attempt to control for extraneous influences. It is also important to note that the existence of a statistical association does not provide proof that a causal relationship exists; it merely provides evidence that two variables covary. Explanation is aided, not provided by such associations.

Two other hypotheses are examined using the factors measured by this family of independent variables. The first concerns the age of the existing stock of manufacturing employment (AGE1, AGE2 and YOLD2), and establishments (AGE2 and YOLD1). Variables AGE2 and YOLD1, and AGE3 and YOLD2 are identical in that they are complementary measures of the same variables. For example, if AGE2 is 1940, YOLD1 will be 37. Thus AGE2 is the actual date (either the mean, or the median) and YOLD1 is the actual age of either the employment, or the plant. Any correlation coefficient, therefore, is similar for each of these variables (AGE2 and YOLD1), but in the opposite direction.

These series of variables are used in an attempt to investigate the notion that industrial areas with a recent (young) manufacturing stock have a higher rate of entry by new enterprises than areas with a mature (old) manufacturing stock. Again, the hypothesis is relatively simple and straightforward, but its full a priori reasoning reveals problems of interpretation. For example, an area with a new industrial stock might be the product of several factors and each one may have a different influence upon the rate of new firm formation. Do, for example, more recently established and expanding firms have the highest 'spin-off' rates? (19) While this does appear to be the case, other explanations for an association between the age of industry and the new firms in an area exist. For example, the association may be purely temporal in that what exists in an area at one point in time will influence what appears in the next period. Thus, the hypothesis in essence is stating that a time dependent component is important in the new firm formation process and that future patterns of industrial development are fashioned by present day features. Though it would appear that the formation of new firms is not necessarily a time determined process in that areas with a large number of recently established plants do not appear to have disproportionately more new firms than areas with an old stock of plants (see BIRCH, 1979a, 14).

There are two further, but related problems concerning the use of the age of plants in an area. First, the presence of a large number of new plants might also represent a general growth in the existing level of manufacturing activity in an area, and therefore could be a surrogate measure for general manufacturing growth though this measure would conceal all growth through in situ expansion (KEEBLE, 1976, 120-2). Furthermore, the expansion of industry by the establishment of new plants, and this is the second point, might reflect the development of industrial estates and factory building in an area. The increased provision of new industrial space might have two consequences. First, the increased supply of factories may attract plants at present located in other areas that are seeking new sites. A second consequence might be that in an area where there is an increased demand for factory space due to the opening of local and non local branch and subsidiary plants and the emergence of new firms that demand will outstrip supply. In this situation the price of factory space would tend to increase, which might act against the small new firm. Thus after trading for a few years a 'new' firm might be forced to seek new premises elsewhere. The problem of deciding how to interpret this situation is one that can only be aided by 'controlling' for disturbing influences (if possible).

A second hypothesis concerns the possibility that the presence of larger plants, those employing 500 or more employees, has some influence upon the emergence of new firms. Several related notions are under examination here, one concerns the overall employment importance of large plants, while the other covers the possibility of time in the build up of large plants. For example, is it the sheer mass of employment in large plants that is important, or is it the impact of the 'recent' (over the 1945-67 period) opening of large plants that is important? The main underlying arguments relating to new firm emergence in an area and the level of plant dominance in the same area have been outlined elsewhere (COOPER, 1971, 4; GUDGIN et al, 1979; BRUNSKILL, 1979; Chapter Six). Another line of reasoning can be adopted, and though similar to the above adds a slightly new view to an old problem. It is generally argued that both the structure and productive methods employed by firms operating large plants is not conducive to entrepreneur formation. The reverse might well be the case in that entrepreneurial drive may have been re-directed within the large firm rather than being found expressed as a new firm external to that large firm (ROBERTS and FROHMAN, 1971; FIRN, 1973, 57; SUSBAUER, 1973; ROTHWELL, 1975a, 1975b). It therefore follows that the influx of large, mainly externally controlled plants may create career alternatives open to some potential new firm founders. The experience of Canada could therefore be comparable to the Scottish case, where it has been noted by Litvak and Maule (1972) that:

> ... a major problem in managing a U.S. subsidiary in Canada is that potential Canadian creativity is often not encouraged, and in fact may be obstructed. Specifically, the point made is that most innovations emanate from the parent company, and in the event that the innovation is conceived of in the Canadian subsidiary, it must be reported to the parent company. ... Even in those subsidiaries which enjoy appreciable autonomy, this situation tends to dissuade the potentially more creative personnel from conducting original experimentation. For some executives, the choice is obvious, namely to move to the parent company ...' (ibid., 53) (20)

The implications for new firm formation in an area, if the above reasoning is correct, are not short of dramatic. At first sight it might appear that certain types of external control of industry are not conducive to new firm formation. However, is it not possible that every area has a comparable number of entrepreneurs, but what is different from area to area is how that pool of entrepreneurs expresses itself? In some instances entrepreneurs may lie within the established labour market, and hence internal to existing firms. Conversely, other areas may have such conditions that entrepreneurs are encouraged to establish their own firm. Thus any association between the number (or similar measure) of large plants and new enterprises might represent an attempt to correlate two measures of entrepreneurship. On this basis one would expect that there would be a negative relationship between these two variables.

It is evident from this discussion that the use of what may appear to be a simple variable is anything but simple. And on an a priori

basis it would appear that these series of variables might be
important in subsequent analyses.

(f) Employment turbulence. The final series of variables attempt
to measure the level of employment loss by either plant closure or
plant contraction, and its influence upon the emergence of new firms
in an area. Two measures exist and they are the absolute volume of
employment lost (JOBLOSS, REDUND and CLOSURE) and the relative
importance of both mechanisms, closure or contraction on the loss of
employment in an area (REDPC and CLOSPC). While these variables do
not necessarily represent the best possible measures of employment
turbulence in an area other and perhaps measures can be derived from
them (TURB1, TURB2 and TURB3). Where this is the case, it is noted.
The reasoning lying behind the use of these variables has been
presented elsewhere (see Chapter Five) and are not repeated here.

5. THE ANALYSIS

The broad structure of the analysis follows those lines suggested by
Blalock (1972a, 187-8), and it initially derives correlation
coefficients between the dependent and independent variables using
untransformed data. All four of the dependent variables measuring
the number of new firms in an area were correlated with each of the
independent variables outlined above. Further to using each of the
four dependent variables, five sizes of local office area employment
were also used. The five manufacturing employment sizes used were:
0; 999; 1,999; 2,999; and 3,999. (21) Each of these totals were
taken from the Annual Census of Employment for 1971 and were used to
exclude in a stepwise manner the small, rural local office areas.
In all of the analyses undertaken this procedure increased the size
of the correlation coefficient to a maximum at the 2,999 level after
which it decreased. This suggests that it is those areas with a
minimum level of manufacturing employment of 3,000 that give the
higher correlation coefficients. The exclusion of the smaller
manufacturing areas is not inconsistent with the hypothesis under
investigation, but it is in some ways arbitrary. It is also
important to note that the exclusion of those mainly rural areas
also excludes those areas receiving a large number of their founders
from outside Scotland. The final criteria combined the 3,000
employees in manufacturing industry cut-off and the level of self-
containment in terms of founder production and retention. This
procedure excludes 41 local office areas from the analysis. The
final series of spatial units represents a pragmatic compromise
between the use of the travel-to-work areas and all of the local
office areas. Furthermore, the present series of units includes
such areas as Ayr, Cumbernauld, East Kilbride, and Dundee that would
have been otherwise excluded had only the travel-to-work areas been
used. (22)

Further reductions are necessary if the results of the analysis
are to be interpreted with any gain. Of the four dependent
variables outlined only the results of one, the number of new
manufacturing enterprises per thousand manufacturing and service
industry employees in an area, are presented. Some of the initial
results are presented in Table 9.3 where the coefficients are
presented for the correlation between the above dependent variables

Table 9.3

Correlation coefficients between selected independent variables
and the number of new firms per thousand employees in the
manufacturing and service industries in an area in 1971 (BIRTH3).

Independent Variables	Employment Size Groups of Local Office Areas				
	0 – x (n=121)	999 – x̦ (n=89)	1999 – x (n=72)	2999 – x (n=56)	3999 – x (n=48)
MAN71	−0.2280 (0.006)[a]	−0.2354 (0.013)	−0.2439 (0.019)	−0.2381 (0.039)	−0.2081 (0.078)
P500	−0.2161 (0.009)	−0.2426 (0.011)	−0.2510 (0.017)	−0.2622 (0.025)	−0.2500 (0.043)
TOTADM2	−0.2032 (0.013)	−0.1913 (0.036)	−0.1915 (0.054)	−0.1762 (0.097)	−0.1527 (0.150)
TOTOP	−0.2060 (0.012)	−0.1927 (0.035)	−0.1946 (0.051)	−0.1768 (0.098)	−0.1480 (0.158)
DOMIND71	−0.2578 (0.002)	−0.2638 (0.006)	−0.2803 (0.009)	−0.2750 (0.020)	−0.2421 (0.049)
MANCHPC	+0.3551 (0.001)	+0.3131 (0.001)	+0.4354 (0.001)	+0.4388 (0.001)	+0.4170 (0.002)
SERPCCH	+0.1359 (0.069)	+0.4279 (0.001)	+0.5615 (0.001)	+0.5238 (0.001)	+0.5166 (0.001)
MLHCH	+0.5558 (0.001)	+0.7927 (0.001)	+0.8494 (0.001)	+0.8467 (0.001)	+0.8515 (0.001)
SCOTAPC	+0.3099 (0.001)	+0.2671 (0.006)	+0.1781 (0.067)	+0.2239 (0.049)	+0.2589 (0.038)
SCOTA2PC	+0.2529 (0.003)	+0.2648 (0.006)	+0.1577 (0.093)	+0.2154 (0.055)	+0.2380 (0.052)
SCOTHX1	+0.2662 (0.002)	+0.1249 (0.122)	+0.2368 (0.023)	+0.2883 (0.016)	+0.2860 (0.024)
SCOTH1PC	+0.2147 (0.009)	+0.2387 (0.012)	+0.2307 (0.026)	+0.2741 (0.020)	+0.2445 (0.047)
SCOTH2PC	+0.2051 (0.012)	+0.2534 (0.008)	+0.2785 (0.009)	+0.3243 (0.007)	+0.2543 (0.041)
EMPIND1	−0.2213 (0.007)	−0.0072 (0.473)	+0.0541 (0.326)	+0.1638 (0.114)	+0.1564 (0.144)
P500PC	−0.2552 (0.002)	−0.2259 (0.017)	−0.2326 (0.025)	−0.2814 (0.018)	−0.3242 (0.012)
PLE100	+0.2020 (0.0764)	+0.1742 (0.051)	+0.2068 (0.041)	+0.2173 (0.054)	+0.2448 (0.047)
SUBSID	+0.2029 (0.013)	+0.6210 (0.001)	+0.6894 (0.001)	+0.6899 (0.001)	+0.6957 (0.001)
AGE2	+0.0274 (0.383)	+0.2304 (0.027)	+0.3309 (0.002)	+0.3272 (0.007)	+0.2610 (0.037)
TURB	+0.0674 (0.231)	+0.1167 (0.138)	+0.2883 (0.007)	+0.3219 (0.008)	+0.3134 (0.015)

a   Level of significance

and a series of selected independent variables. At this stage only a few cursory comments are in order. First, an overall stability exists throughout the table for both the direction and size of the associations. Of course, there are exceptions to this statement. For example, the correlation coefficients between the dependent variable and EMPIND71 changes from being weakly negative to being weakly positive. This situation arises because of the exclusion of the small local office areas that have a small manufacturing base and where manufacturing is only a minor provider of employment e.g. 8.61 per cent in Inverness and 7.04 per cent in Oban. The existence of areas such as Inverness and Oban are sufficient to influence the correlation and produce a negative association. There are also those variables (SERPCCH, PLE100 and AGE2) where the exclusion of the smallest areas leads to a marked increase in the size of the association. Second, and in terms of the hypotheses under investigation, the direction of the correlation coefficients are all in the direction hypothesised. Although a negative relationship between the absolute industrial base or facets of it and the number of new firms was not explicitly hypothesised, it is still explicable with the data available. In Chapter Four it was noted that it was not the traditional centres that were gaining new plants throughout the 1968-77 period. In fact, it was these areas which were in decline, but they were still, in absolute employment terms, larger than most of the other areas. Consequently a negative correlation coefficient was obtained indicating that it was the smaller industrial areas which were gaining more new firms for their size than were the larger areas (see KEEBLE, 1976, 28-9). This is further supported by the size of the correlation coefficient which remains relatively static even after the small rural areas have been excluded.

At first sight, an area employing more than 3,000 employees in manufacturing industry with a diverse range of plants by size and industry, and is experiencing growth is probably the most likely area to produce and to contain new enterprises. Other aspects of apparent importance are the levels of independent Scottish plants and the age of plants. However, these must remain very tentative observations as further analyses are necessary to consider the compound nature of the variables used.

All eighteen variables listed in Table 9.3 were correlated with each other using both the full and reduced numbers of local office areas. As would be expected the size of the correlation coefficient is higher in those areas of the matrix covering common measures (CROSS, 1980, 521-2). There are also areas within both matrices where other high correlation coefficients exist e.g. DOMIND71, P500PC, PLE100 and SUBSID. In terms of aiding the analysis for the selection and inclusion of these independent variables in a regression analysis. A pairwise correlation coefficient between the independent variables was set beyond which they could not be considered worthy of further examination. Previous work is of immediate assistance on this matter, and the levels used vary from 0.8 (KEEBLE, 1976, 90) to 0.85 (KEEBLE and HAUSER, 1972, 13), or fluctuating between 0.85 to 1.0 (KIM and KAHOUT, 1975, 340). The level set in this study is 0.707 which accounts for 50 per cent of the variation between the two variables correlated. Adoption of this level would exclude the use, for example, of DOMIND71 with

MAN71, P500, TOTADM2 or TOTOP. It would appear that collinearity does not create problems at this stage of the analysis.

Another feature of interest of these pairwise correlations is the increased size of many of the correlation coefficients between the two matrices where previously there had been little or no association. This is the case for both AGE2 and TURB. The most likely explanation accounting for these changes is that the exclusion of 42 of the 121 local office areas has excluded any extreme values and so has had the effect of normalizing the data. However, their exclusion was based on both computational and theoretical grounds.

Further problems exist with the use of areas in which no new firms were identified. If these areas are excluded from the analysis (23) the size of the correlation coefficient are further increased. Even still, several areas cause distortions because of either their actual size, or their lack of new firms, and these areas are: Aberdeen, Bridgeton, Dundee, Edinburgh, Grangemouth, Greenock, Paisley, Parkhead and Partick. (24) Exclusion of these areas would reduce the number of local office areas covered to only sixty-six. The remaining areas left after applying these criteria are those that encircle the traditional industrial area, and are on the whole growing.

Subsequent analysis entailed the examination of the joint distribution of each independent variables with the dependent variable, BIRTH. (25) Without exception, each distribution revealed that non-linear relationships existed. With the exclusion of areas on the basis of the criteria outlined above no improvement followed. Subsequent analysis transformed the dependent and independent variables to reduce the degree of scatter about the least squares equation. In some instances the size of the correlation coefficient was increased, but as was noted earlier it is the slope that is of major interest here. Though the importance of the slope is paramount, it often tends to be ignored. Of perhaps greater importance still are the beta weights or standardised partial regression coefficients that indicate the relative changes in variables on a standard scale.

After this initial sorting of the variables, three emerged to be of greater importance in the new firm formation process than the rest, and these were SERPCCH, AGE2 and MAN71. Their combination resulted in a disappointing, but expected low level of variation explained (R^2) of 0.25 (Table 9.4). The contribution made by each variable was in the direction expected but the nature of the slope was nearly parallel to the axes of the independent variables. This indicates that irrespective of the increases in the independent variables little or no change occurred in the dependent variable. This prompted further analyses and two further sets of areas were excluded from the analysis. First, all areas where zero was recorded in all but the change variable were excluded. This procedure reduced the 79 areas previously used to 66 and this was still further reduced by excluding all areas in which no new enterprises had been identified. Using this second criteria produced 51 areas. These remaining 51 areas included all of the major industrial areas both experiencing growth and decline and were

Table 9.4
Regression results:
Number of new firms established between 1968-77 expressed
as the number per thousand employees in both manufacturing
and service employment in 1971 (dependent variable) with:

Independent Variable	b	beta	SE_b	F-value	df.
Percentage change in service industry	.99448	0.41092	0.00245	16.531	1,77
Age of industrial stock	.43197	0.13431	0.00351	1.519	2,76
Manufacturing employment in 1971	-.1331	-0.18571	0.00001	2.968	3,75

Constant = -8.01548   SEest = 0.50919
R^2 = 0.25468 R^2 (adj.) = 0.22487

used in further analyses. Several other areas were also excluded
based on the growth of either manufacturing or service employment.
Beyond these exlusions other areas were excluded on other grounds
and these are detailed in Table 9.5.

Table 9.5
Criteria used for the stepwise exclusion of areas from the analysis

Criteria	Affect on Population (n)

Removal of all small places - areas where MAN71 LE 1999:
              n = 121 reduced to 79

Removal of all areas where zero scores recorded:
              n = 79 reduced to 66

Removal of all areas with no identified new firms:
              n = 66 reduced to 51

Removal of all areas with only one new firm:
              n = 51 reduced to 38

(a) Removal of all areas experiencing a decline in service
    employment: n = 51 reduced to 40

    Removal of all areas with two or less new firms:
              n = 40 reduced to 27

    Removal of all areas with three or less new firms:
              n = 27 reduced to 23

    Removal of all areas with five or less new firms:
              n = 23 reduced to 14

(b) Removal of all areas experiencing a decline in
    manufacturing employment:
              n = 51 reduced to 18

    Removal of all areas not falling within the employment
    bands of 5,000 to 15,000:
              n = 18 reduced to 9

    Removal of all areas with five or less new firms:
              n =   9 reduced to 7

Two other variables were also added to the analysis at this stage, PLE100PC and ADMINPC (see Appendix for definitions) and were correlated with BIRTH (Table 9.6). While the reduced data set increased the size of some correlation coefficients, the overall gains were small. Further experimentation in which the data sets were reduced still further and both the dependent and independent variables transformed produced marginal gains. The variables were transformed on the basis of plotting each individual correlation between each independent and the dependent variable. Again, little gains were made, but the correlation coefficients did increase in size as the number of areas considered was reduced. Logarithmic transformation (see TAYLOR, 1977, 115-8) was the most successful in these instance and concentration was placed upon the correlation coefficients to note any changes that occurred (BLALOCK, 1972b, 51). While both log10 and $\log_e$ give the same correlation coefficients, interest was focused here upon the slope (b) of the line. Transormation of data causes problems of interpretation, and Johnston notes in discussing an analysis undertaken by King (1961) that:

> ... all of the coefficients derived by King had the predicted signs, but can either the theory behind the hypotheses or the interpretation account for the form as well as the direction of the relationships? (JOHNSTON, 1978, 79)

Thus the description of the relationship between two variables may be improved, but at the cost of interpretation.

Table 9.6
Correlation coefficients between BIRTH and
selected independent variables (n = 51)

Independent Variable	R	R^2	S	Slope (b)
P500	−0.25889	0.06703	0.03329	−0.00003
P500PC	−0.22623	0.05118	0.05521	−0.00487
PLE100	0.08399	0.00705	0.27895	0.00164
PLE100PC	0.82912	0.69743	0.00001	0.01997
MAN71	−0.25399	0.06451	0.03605	−0.00001
MANCHPC	0.39597	0.15679	0.00201	0.01026
DOMIND71	−0.29022	0.08423	0.01942	0.00006
EMPIND1	0.27711	0.07679	0.02450	0.00926
SERPCCH	0.63950	0.40896	0.00001	0.01399
TOTADM2	−0.20499	0.04202	0.07451	0.00002
ADMINPC	0.16885	0.02851	0.11811	0.17470
AGE2	0.48897	0.23909	0.00014	0.01394
SUBSID	0.76914	0.59158	0.00001	0.10105
MLHCH	0.87158	0.75964	0.00001	0.12236
TOTOP	−0.21020	0.04418	0.06937	−0.00003
SCOTH1PC	0.08594	0.00739	0.27438	0.00175
SCOTH2PC	0.17520	0.03069	0.10941	0.00515
SCOTAPC	−0.07228	0.00522	0.30712	−0.03253
SCOTA2PC	−0.05833	0.00340	0.34216	−0.03235
SCOTHX1	0.06549	0.00429	0.32398	0.00292
TURB	0.28719	0.08248	0.02051	0.00112

At this point in the analysis the dependent variable (number of new enterprises per thousand employees in the manufacturing and service industries in 1971) was modified by using several new forms covering the crude number of new firms in an area. Yet again occasional correlation coefficients were increased in size, but no overall gains were made. The most heartening feature to emerge from all of these analyses was the relative importance of the independent variables remained fairly constant, though the level of small plants in an area (PLE100 and PLE100PC) did increase in importance when NUFIRM was used. Part of the failure of the analysis stems from the complexity of the problem under examination, from the impression of the measures used and probably most important, from the varying quality of the data used. The failure of the data becomes more apparent as these analyses preceded, but it should be realised that they represent the best available sources of information. (26)

6. SUMMARY

Factors influencing the new firm formation process are numerous and it is their individual and combined influences that cause the marked spatial variations in the numbers of new firms emerging. Some of these influences were examined in this chapter. It is clear from this examination that there is no single factor with an overwhelming influence on the process. The analysis did suggest, however, that there are combinations of factors that do exert an influence. For example, at a number of spatial scales the numbers employed in small plants (employing 100 or less employees), the overall level of administrative employment, and the industrial diversity of local industry all appear important influences.

However, throughout the chapter the possibility of measurement error and its effects on the results of the analysis were stressed. In fact, it was the inherent weaknesses of the data that prevented further exploration into the influences of those factors that had been isolated for consideration. In the light of these comments the drawing of any firm conclusions might be unwise and premature. Yet, while the results of the analyses were not as convincing as those of the previous chapters, there emerged a sufficiently stable series of results that suggest that the emergence of new enterprises is related to several features of the local environment. Some of the more important features were noted above. General support was also obtained for the direction of the relationships hypothesised, but in terms of interpretations some confusion still remains.

Again, because of the problems of data accuracy, the functional form of the relationships between the emergence of a new firm and the local environment could be stated. However, via the manipulation of several series of data including and excluding areas because of their size etc. several factors emerge as being important. The positive and negative factors that did emerge, and which either enhanced or impeded new firm formation at the local level are listed in Table 9.7. Those features listed in the table are wholly consistent with the notion that it is the smallest and previously less important (relatively so) industrial areas that are at present experiencing the highest birth rates of new firms. It was seen in Chapter Four that the areas surrounding the major cities of

Edinburgh and Glasgow that were experiencing the greatest rates of employment growth. This would tend to give some support to Wood's (1974, 149-51) model of industrial development which suggests that the main centres of industrial growth have moved from the inner city to the urban fringe. Admittedly, Fagg (1977, 1979) has produced some contrary evidence, but in the light of the evidence and arguments presented in Chapters Four to Eight it would appear a valid statement and an area worthy of further research.

Table 9.7

Factors influencing and found in association with the emergence of new firms at the local office area level

Factors

Positive/Enhancing	Negative/Impeding
Manufacturing employment growth	Degree of plant dominance
Industrial specialisation (but not dominated by any one industry)	Absolute size of manufacturing employment in 1971
Service employment growth	Absolute size of employment in main industry
Youth of industrial stock	
Number of subsidiary plants	Level of operative employment
Increased industrial activity	
Medium level of employment stability	
Number of small plants	
Level of administrative employment	

Source: See text.

In the next and final chapter, Chapter Ten, the implications of the analyses of this, and of the preceding five chapters are examined. The implications for three areas are examined: regional development, industrial location and new firm formation theory, and research methodology.

NOTES

1. Those firms that were trading in the local area prior to the formation of the new company.
2. The provision of industrial premise has been a much neglected area of research and the role of the 'lock-up garage' and 'lean-to shed' are assumed to be important (WISE, 1949, 62; BEESLEY, 1955, 56; HALL, 1962, 119). While this assumption was wholly justified, the role of the private and public industrial land developers has become increasingly important. Yet, despite regional (Scotland: TROTMAN-DICKENSON, 1961; South Wales: CASTREE, 1966; SHEWRING, 1970; BALE, 1972) and national studies (BALE, 1974, 1977; SLOWE, 1978) of industrial estates, their role in providing indigenous enterprises with premises remains untested. At the specialist level of estates operated near airports (FISHER, 1966) or by new town development corporations (HILL, 1976) the position has not been clarified to the same problem either. However, Hill (1976, 79) does note that there

was a need for public authorities to provide units of a 500-800 sq. feet size as none of the major industrial estate owners would do (see ABBOT, 1978).

Within the Edinburgh area the development of new units, say, in Edinburgh city itself has been minimal. There have been only 11 applications for developments of 3,000 sq. feet or under during the 1970 (January) to 1977 (June) period. (a) Similar evidence is available for the Leith docks area. (b) Outside Ediburgh, in the West Lothian district both private and public estates are plentiful and their role, especially in the case of Livingston, is important in providing units for small firms. (c) Likewise, in East Lothian e.g. Macmerry Industrial Estate, the provision of the small units (5,000 sq. ft.) has been important. In some instances a division of responsibility occurs at the 5,000 sq. ft. level where the district council is responsible for small developments and the regional council is responsible for larger developments (ROXBURGH DISTRICT COUNCIL, 1975, 1).

(a) I am indebted to Elizabeth R. Smith, Planning Department, City of Edinburgh District Council, for the provision of these data.
(b) I am indebted to W.J. Leaman Esq., Director (Engineering and Operation), Forth Ports Authority, for the provision of these data.
(c) I am greatly indebted to Elizabeth B. Smith, formerly of the Department of Geography, University of Edinburgh, for the provision of these data.

3.   I am greatly indebted to Ms. May Tanzy, formerly of the Manpower Services Commission, Office for Scotland, Edinburgh, for detailing some of the misallocations that have occurred with the Annual Census of Employment in Scotland over the 1971-76 period. For example, in 1974 a large multinational chemical company misallocated 2,800 weekly paid workers from Saltcoats to Kilwinning. In 1975, a large British aerospace company made a return for one of its factories at East Kilbride that doubled that plants employment. Besides these problems, the change in the classification of some oil rig construction firms from mlh 500 to mlh 341 and 479 resulted in a downturn in construction employment while causing a comparable, but reverse change in manufacturing employment. Further problems will occur with future research using the local office areas as spatial units of analysis as Brechin, Burntisland and Linlithgow will all cease to function as local offices in 1978 and will be amalgamated with Montrose, Kirkcaldy and Bo'ness respectively.

4.   Use of the 0.1 significance level is made throughout this study because of its exploratory nature and this level is used to prevent the rejecting of relationships that do in fact exist (HAUSER, 1974, 155; KEEBLE, 1976, 92).

5.   'Much work has been done in methods of quantifying the degree of spatial autocorrelation for single variables only, as in description of the spread of measles through south-western England (CLIFF et al, 1975) and of the prices paid for beef cattle at various markets (MARTIN and OEPPEN, 1975). From these, it may be possible to predict future trends. It is much more difficult to make multiple part measurements of the same phenomenon in difficult places, however, and then attempt to account for these by multiple regressions with other data sets containing similar problems.' (JOHNSTON, 1978, 260)

6.   See Ebdon (1977, 130-1) or Norcliffe (1977, 204-13) for an outline of the methods for calculating the spatial autocorrelation statistic.

7. While Cliff and Ord summarise most of the important features in their book (1973), it is instructive to view their other work on the topic (CLIFF and ORD, 1970a, 1970b, 1971, 1972, and with MARTIN, 1975).

8. This is a question neither raised by either Keeble (1976), nor Piggott (1977). In fact, Piggott (1977) uses the inferior technique of the two colour maps and does not justify his use of the method despite using a complete data set.

9. Though the correct term for these variables is regressor variables, for the sake of clarity they are termed independent variables for the remainder of the study. Furthermore, regressor variables are, of course, more specifically related to those independent variables used in regression analysis.

10. For the derivation of the Tress Statistic see Chisholm and Oeppen (1973, 32-3) and for examples of its use see Britton (1967) and Keeble and Hauser (1971, 1972).

11. The relationship between housing tenure and labour mobility has been examined (ROBERTSON, 1978) where it was suggested that housing tenure did not restrict mobility though a '... correlation between tenure and particular patterns of mobility did not of course constitute proof of a causal relationship' (RANDALL, 1979, 22). Furthermore, the movement of workers for housing reasons has been shown to be important (JOHNSON et al, 1974, 206). It is also possible that in periods of general depressed labour market conditions there is an element of return migration occurring (BELL and KIRWAN, 1979).

12. Skilled administrative jobs are not necessarily created in all new plants as is noted by Northcott (1977):

> Altogether the 62 firms in the survey transferred 195 people from the old factory to the new - typically one or two to the smaller factories and about three or four to the larger ones. This represented about 3 per cent of their total employment at the new factory at the time of the survey and about 2 per cent of the total employment expected when they had built up to full production.*
>
> These numbers are relatively small, partly because some firms employing mainly married women took it for granted they would mostly be unwilling to move and partly because some firms saw no need to transfer anyone except the manager and perhaps one or two assistants. This was particularly so in factories where few special skills were needed and where everything other than production itself had been left at the head office at the main factory.
> (emphasis added) (ibid., 53)

Furthermore, it has recently been noted by Lund and Gleed (1979, 71) that the '... more capital-intensive manufacturing industries were concentrating their activities in development areas for reasons unconnected (emphasis added) with the investment grant differential or the general balance of regional policy'.

* It is interesting to note that the comparable figure for founders and their associates in new indigenous enterprises is 7.7 per cent (compared to the second figure).

13. For a regional consideration see Crum and Gudgin (1978).

14. Other employment is that which is neither administrative, nor productive, and covers all delivery, stores etc. types of employment.

15. It was suggested from the data available (Chapter Eight, Table 8.23) that the number of new firm founders leaving either large (500

or more employees) or medium (201-499 employees) or small (200 or
less employees) plants to set-up their own firms was related i.e.
small firms/high spin-off, large firms/small spin-off. The
relationship is less strong if the whole working career of the
founders is considered.

16. The term compound variables is used here to describe those
variables that measure more than one factor. Conversely, simple
variables only measure one factor. Though, the latter type of
variables are unlikely to exist in social science research.

17. In discussing those industries in which there had been a
substantial rise in the number of small establishments, Prais (1976)
noted:

> It will be noticed that many of their trades are 'modern',
> in that they include scientific instruments, electronic
> apparatus, plastic fabrication and printing (where new
> 'offset' methods have helped smaller concerns).
> Technological developments thus remain of importance in
> promoting small firms. (ibid., 15-16)

18. This phenomenon has also been noted in Scotland by C. Allen
Esq., Department of Business Studies, University of Edinburgh, in
'The role and performance of small companies, and their effect upon
the motivation and strategies of the small business manager' (Ph.D.
Dissertation in preparation, title as at February 3rd, 1978).

19. It was demonstrated in Chapter Eight (Table 8.25) that the age
distribution of the incubator plants (employers of founders
immediately prior to the establishing of the new firm) was not
apparently significantly different from the distribution of all
manufacturing plants. That is, the age distribution of incubator
organisations would be as expected given the age characteristics of
the total stock of manufacturing plants. Support for the hypothesis
would have been provided if, say, 75 per cent of incubator plants
were aged ten years or less.

20. The debate over the lack of entrepreneurs and hence
entrepreneurship has been studied in Canada and the whole of the
Spring issue of The Business Quarterly (1972) is devoted to this
topic and it represents a useful review of the topic (articles by
BETT; GRIEVE; HODGINS; LITVAK and MAULE; McLEOD; ROBERTS and FROHMAN;
SINCLAIR and FELLS; and WILLIAMS). The Summer issue of the same
journal (1972) also includes a number of further commentaries on the
same topic (BAILLIE; LAMONT; KOMIVES; LITVAK and MAULE; and PAQUET).
All of the arguments contained in these articles are similar to
those presented throughout this book though their main fault, if
it could be termed that, is their tendency to be very qualitative an
and they offer little quantification to the extent and variation of,
say, external control or any other variable for that matter. It
should be added that the lack of quantification of phenomena is not
necessarily a fault, and is a product of ones' methodology (HUDSON,
1979).

21. In each case it was only those areas employing more than the
stated values that were included in the analysis.

22. The exclusion of extreme or anomalous values from the analysis
is perhaps a dubious practice and is open to criticism. However,
the exclusion of values is within the limits of the hypothesis under
investigation, though the final decision '... will depend upon the
nature of the problem and the research interest of the social
scientist' (BLALOCK, 1972a, 382). For examples of exclusion see
Gudgin (1974, 375) or Piggott (1977, 38). It should be noted that

the exclusion of values in this study is upon <u>theoretical</u> grounds
and not purely on statistical grounds.
23. This involves the exclusion of 24 of the 121 local office areas
and only 13 of the already reduced data set which covers 79 local
office areas.
24. These nine areas represent the largest extremes and if other
areas were to be covered they would include the other major
industrial areas e.g. Glasgow South Side, Govan, Hillington, Kinning
Park, etc. This tends to indicate that these areas for their size
have a small number of new firms for their combined manufacturing
and service industry employment. It is also evident that the nine
areas listed fall into two distinct groups: those containing a
large proportion of service industry and are inner city areas
(Aberdeen, Bridgeton, Dundee and Edinburgh) and those where
manufacturing industry is the more important employer and is
dominated by a single industry in some cases (Grangemouth, Greenock,
Paisley, Parkhead and Partick).
25. Each independent variables was individually plotted with BIRTH
to examine the nature of the distribution. Apart from the complete
lack of a linear relationship in most cases, it was evident that
while correlation coefficients (R) of 0.50 and greater were obtained
(e.g. SUBSID, MLHCH, P500, DOMIND71, MAN71 and both TOTADM2 and
TOTOP reached 0.49) the nature of the slope changed little despite
modifications to the variables (reciprocal, power, root, log
transformations). In fact, the regression line, when drawn upon
these plots, showed that despite changes in the independent variable
the dependent variable remained nearly static. The situation
therefore arises where a relatively high correlation coefficient is
obtained yet there is little or no association between the two
variables. The nature of the slope itself depends in part upon the
measurement scales used for both the independent and dependent
variables.
26. Several series of analyses were performed upon the electronics
and electrical engineering industries (SIC Orders 8 and 9) because
the data coverage was more comprehensive in these orders. It was
also assumed, rightly or wrongly, that there would be an association
between the number of new technical (electronics) companies and the
level of employment in electronics industries in the same areas.
Several measures of the number of new companies in an area were
derived. These measures related the absolute number of new firms to
the level of electronics employment in an area (see Appendix) and
were then correlated with other measures of 'technical' employment
in the same area. Both Pearson's rank and product-moment
correlation coefficients were derived for all analyses because of
the small samples used (n = 8 to 20, but usually 15 or 16) and it is
a useful safeguard for any analysis (BLALOCK, 1972b, 187). The
results obtained suggested a negative relationship between the level
of employment and the number of new technical firms and in all cases
the rank was larger than the product-moment correlation coefficient
(see table below). Such a result is not surprising given the growth
of the industry over the last ten years and the location of many new
technical companies in areas adjacent to the major industrial areas
e.g. Livingston for Edinburgh.

Dependent variable = SPIN = TCOMP/TECHEMP x 1,000
Independent variables = SCIENCE = TECHEMP/MAN76 x 1,000

N. of Cases = 19 $r = -0.4444$ $r_S = -0.8447$
N. of Cases = 16* $r = -0.6063$ $r_S = -0.7544$

*Excluded extreme cases of Elgin, Kirkwall and Musselburgh

Dependent variable = SPIN = TCOMP/TECHEMP x 1,000
Independent variable = ADTECH and TECEMP67

ADTECH $r = -0.36114$ $r_S = -0.4090$
TECEMP67 $r = -0.4109$ $r_S = -0.4213$

10 Implications and Conclusions

1. INTRODUCTION

It has been shown that the opening of new manufacturing plants in
Scotland have proved to be an important source of new employment
during the period, 1968-77. It has also been shown that new firms
have provided an important, but minor share of this source of new
employment. These new firms exhibited faster employment growth
rates than their counterparts, the local and non-local branch and
subsidiary plants. However, the factors influencing, and in many
ways determining the location of these new firms appears more
complex than those determining the location of the other new plants.
These factors, determining the location of wholly new firms, ranged
from the personal characteristics of the founder to the nature of
the local labour market. The previous chapters have suggested a
whole range of factors which are involved in the new firm formation
process. Given these analyses and their limitations, what are the
implications for Scotland. For example, are the economic/industrial
conditions in Scotland favourable to new firm formation? Is it
likely that more new firms will emerge in the near future?

This chapter, then, is a "stock-taking" exercise. It attempts to
evaluate the implications of the preceding analyses for regional
development in Scotland. It also considers the study's implications
for industrial location and new firm formation theory, and research
methodology.

2. IMPLICATIONS FOR REGIONAL DEVELOPMENT

The future development of Scotland as an industrial region depends
upon a complex series of economic, political, and social factors.
It is becoming increasingly apparent though that the key to the
future prosperity of Scotland lies in its industrial base, and its
ability to adapt to changing trading conditions. Are new firms
likely to make a contribution ot these changes? Are the conditions
favourable for new firm formation in Scotland?

An examination of the list of factors influencing and found in
association with the emergence of new firms (Table 9.7) would tend
to indicate that external investment in manufacturing industry in
the peripheral region might not be wholly conducive to new firm
formation. It is not the characteristics of ownership that are not
conducive to new firm formation, but it is the functional form that

ownership can take. In failing to specify the functional form of
the relationship between the emergence of new firms and the level of
external control in an area, the analyses were not able to indicate
what level of external control in an area apparently influences the
emergence of new firm founders; and hence new enterprises. These
failings stem not only from problems of data accuracy, but also the
historic nature of the process. Furthermore, the development of
manufacturing industry in a region is a long-run historic process
taking many years, while the conditions influencing the emergence of
new firms are more likely to operate over a shorter period (see
Chapter Two; the sociological influences are long-run processes).
The preceding analyses have therefore possibly viewed the symptoms
of processes operating over, say, the 1948-1967 period, and future
research might do well to examine the preceding period in greater
detail. If this study was allied to a comprehensive data base for
the succeeding period it would probably develop a higher level of
specification of the functional form of the relationships influencing
new firm formation. The success of such research would seem likely
given the encouraging results that emerge from this exploratory
analysis.

The existence of similar relationships in other regions is not
known. If, for example, the functional form of the relationship
between the emergence of new enterprises and the factors listed
earlier (Table 9.7) could be specified for other regions and other
time periods different forms of the same relationships might emerge.
In Scotland, some factors may be more important than others. For
example, the supply of premises may not be a problem, whereas the
supply of founders may be. Equally likely is that the reverse may
be true elsewhere (FOY, 1977). The variations in the mix of these
factors through space may possibly determine the variations in the
emergence of new enterprises through space.

In terms of regional development, then, these observations would
tend to indicate that the supply of new firm founders and new
enterprises are a direct function of the local nature of the
attributes of the local labour market. There is therefore possibly
a direct interation between the emergence of new firm founders and
the local labour market such that the notion of surplus or lack of
entrepreneurship do not exist at the local scale. (1) That is,
given the local conditions, the supply of new firm founders is in
balance with those local conditions. The notions of surplus and
lack only come into play when the movement of founders (no matter
what state of their development) is considered and the number of
founders in other areas is viewed. A solution to this problem would
require a detailed examination of several labour markets operating
under different conditions. Again, it is likely that such an
analysis would prove most productive as is suggested by the
preceding analyses. In the analyses presented earlier the stepwise
elimination of areas and subsequent re-running of the analyses
indicated that different mixes of factors best accounted for (not
explained) the variations in the numbers of new enterprises in
different areas in Scotland. The existence of regional variations
across a similar set of factors probably exists. These inter-
regional variations may also be of a larger magnitude than those
noted intra-regionally. The variations in the number of new firms
that exist through space are therefore explicable in terms of those

regional forces affecting the local labour market. The analysis of course is complicated by the movement of founders at both the local and regional levels. Nearly 70 per cent of those founders moving to Scotland in order to set-up a new enterprise came from either the South East (2) or the West Midlands (Table 8.26). There may well be, therefore, a national flow of founders; a flow to which Scotland possible contributes far more than she receives (FIRN, 1975, 397; GUDGIN, 1978, 290-1).

The preceding discussion might appear to turn the whole question of the role of new firms in regional development on its head. This however is not the case. From the analyses presented in this book it is evident that the impact of new firms is not independent of the existing stock of plants, and the latter appear to directly influence the former. In terms of employment growth, the existing stock of plants will continue to play the major role. The bulk of expansion (75 per cent) occurring in the Non-Scottish owned plants with respect to both employment and capital expenditure (SCOTTISH COUNCIL (Development and Industry), 1977; SCOTTISH COUNCIL RESEARCH INSTITUTE, 1979). Additional new employment will be created by mobile industrial investment, though this represents a declining source of new employment (FIRN and SWALES, 1978, 211). The remaining source of employment is that of new firms and whose importance as providers of new employment is likely to increase with time.

At the regional level, the picture that emerges, and which is supported by evidence presented in Chapter Four, is of a differential balance in the supply of new industrial development from new firms and from other sources. It would appear that there is a core-periphery model at work at both the intra- and inter-regional levels. Peter Wood (1974, 144-5), for example, noted that the outer metropolitan areas had a greater dependence upon new plants for new employment than the inner ones. This phenomena, which has been noted elsewhere e.g. Chicago (REEDER, 1955), Toronto (COLLINS, 1972) and Glasgow (CAMERON, 1973) (3) suggests that the new industrial environments developing on the metropolitan fringe may now have distinct advantages as "incubator" (4) areas. And it is these areas that have received many of the incoming branch and subsidiary plants. Their attraction to these areas are probably not explicable in local terms. In fact, it could be argued that while the actual process of new firm is probably explicable in local terms, the variations in their emergence are probably not. It may not therefore be possible for a single regional development authority to fully pursue a policy aimed at encouraging local entrepreneurship.

As interest has come to be focused upon new firms as a means of employment generation, the local authority finds itself in an unenviable position. Attempts at directing aid to help people to start companies or assisting newly formed companies might represent cosmetic action. In the light of the analyses of this study, it might be more productive in the long-term to direct assistance to specific industries and areas in an attempt to reshape employment opportunities in those industries and areas. The exact nature of such a policy of course remain vague and could be detailed by action research (THURLEY, 1979). And finally, if the industrial structure remains as it is at the present time in Scotland, there would appear to be little support for any upsurge in the level of new firm formation occurring in the near future.

3. IMPLICATIONS FOR INDUSTRIAL LOCATION AND NEW FIRM FORMATION THEORY

It would be a mistake to think that any single study could offer an alternative theory of either industrial location, or new firm formation, but the present study does offer some insights into both theories.

Implicit within the present framework is the existence of a spatial selection of enterprises leading to consistent variations in enterprises through space (see McDERMOTT, 1977, 347-52). It is these variations in enterprises that help to explain the intra-regional and inter-regional disparities in the number of new enterprises. While largely non-comparable evidence was offered in most cases to illustrate the existence of inter-regional differences in the numbers of new enterprises, if taken together with the intra-regional evidence, there is overwhelming support for such variations do exist. It would follow therefore than an examination in the numbe of new firms in a peripheral region is also an examination of both the causes and symptoms of the problems of that peripheral region. And so at the inter-regional level either the emergence, or the non-emergence of new enterprises is explicable, though not totally so. Furthermore, the seemingly passive location decisions taken by the majority of new firm founders can then be placed within an overall systematic spatial framework.

The contradictions and complications that emerge from viewing either a single case, or series of cases within the local area are often a product of a-spatial analysis. While such abstraction may be wholly justified in analysing the process of new firm formation, it would tend to belie the possibility of explaining the spatial variations in the numbers of new firms. Furthermore, such an isolation of the objects of analysis from their historical and spatial context, a feature common to many behavioural analyses, again decreases the possibility of explanation. It is only with reference to the overall structure of the industrial, and preferably the economic system, that the new firm formation process, and its inherent variants can be explained. For example, Chapter Five illustrated the possible implications of either a plant closure, or a plant contraction upon the emergence of new firms. The hypotheses developed at that point were collectively examined with reference to new firm formation (Chapters Seven and Eight) and were found to be an influence, though not of major importance. Subsumed within the interplay between new enterprise formation and plant closure and plant contraction is the complex relationship between individuals and their previous employer. The latter relationship was shown to be accommodated by the existing behavioural theories of the firm and by their extension with reference to specific psychological and sociological literature (see Chapter Seven). In this case, reference to the new enterprise and its founder alone would not have revealed the full complexity of the process (see AIKEN, 1961). Furthermore, this example also illustrates the possible inter-connections between the elements of the manufacturing stock and the emergence of new enterprises.

This last point introduces an important concept concerning the use of the now feasible and popular components of change analysis. Hitherto, studies using components of change analysis have endowed the technique, which amounts to little more than an employment accounting method, with a role of conceptual or even theoretical significance. The use of such a methodology is conceptually important when the importance of each component acting on each other is also realised. If this is then extended to encompass the regional variations in the importance of the individual, and the interactions between individual components, the method may have theoretical significance. However, the studies to-date have not yet fully considered the possibilities of the interactions between components, and how they may vary through space. This study has attempted to reveal the potential importance of making explicit the inter-connections between components, and that by such an attempt has expanded the usefulness of the components method. Future research concentrating upon a single labour market would probably shed further light on these inter-connections and would probably be able to examine the functional form of the relationship in some detail.

These observations would concur with those of Massey (1973) who suggested that "... an autonomous industrial location theory cannot be constituted. Spatial (industrial, my addition) development can only be seen as part of the overall development of the economy." (ibid., 25). Further research would do well to adopt a similar integrative approach to that used in this study, and preferably widen the scope by considering the formation of all new enterprises (see WOOD, 1978, 40; BIRCH, 1979). It is most likely, due to the lack or unavailability of the relevant data, that a detailed examination of a single labour market might be the most appropriate and manageable scale of analysis. This study has illustrated the potential of such an approach, and the possibilities of its success in contributing to a theory of industrial development and not location theory per se.

The study has made other, more specific, contributions of a theoretical nature. For example, it has examined in some detail the long accepted notions concerning new firm formation. Some of these notions it supports, while others have been challenged. The movement of new firm founders was shown to have been more common a feature of the new firm formation process than would have been expected. The general appraisal of the new firm formation process also indicated the value of adopting several perspectives. Each perspective viewed made a contribution to the overall analysis, and if they had been taken by themselves the analysis may have missed aspects of the new firm formation process. The approach did not include any of the "demand" factors potentially important in the new firm formation, but concentrated on the "supply" factors. And this is yet another area where future research could turn, but complications arise in defining and measuring any of the demand factors e.g. market growth and potential at various spatial scales (5).

Previous studies have considered the movement of new firms once established (FAGG, 1977, 1979), the role of comprehensive redevelopment upon the supply of premises (BULL, 1979) and a number of other factors (see Chapter Seven), but they have rarely placed new enterprise formation into either an employment, or a labour market framework. It is possibly this aspect of the study that makes at least some contribution to the theory of new firm formation. By analysing the previous employment histories of the firm founders it was possible to suggest that while most founders change their occupation between their first and last occupations (6), they represent one part of the labour market. The founding process therefore may be conceived as one employment opportunity open to an individual wishing to change employment, and not necessarily as a highly specialised employment option open to the few. In adopting this stance it was further suggested that some form of evaluation procedure was undertaken. This evaluation procedure would probably be unconsciously adopted and is probably a result of the conditioning influences that have previously acted upon the individual. Part of the decision to found a new firm may therefore be the result of factors beyond the control of the individual e.g. his upbringing, his education, etc. The importance of these conditioning influences may vary in importance between sectors and between individuals.

Future research could concentrate upon an area's occupational structure and analyse the employment opportunities locally available. Thus, the analysis could be focused not on the new firms themselves in the first instance, but upon the founders and the factors that may affect their supply. It is only with a supply of founders that new enterprises can be established. Once an enterprise is established attention may then be switched to the enterprise, but if the emphasis of the research is upon the formation process the focus should perhaps remain with the founder. The factors of demand mentioned above, and not examined in this study, could also be included into this employment/occupation focused approach. It could be seen as another factor either encouraging, or discouraging a founder from leaving his present employer in order to establish his own firm.

4. IMPLICATIONS FOR RESEARCH METHODOLOGY

The subject under examination and approach adopted dictated the data required and largely the form of the research methodology. Furthermore, no attempt was made in this study to advance any aspects of research methodology, though several items of note do emerge. Perhaps the most important aspect to emerge was the relative success achieved in combining several different data sources to perform a components of employment change analysis. Most previous studies executing a components of employment change analysis have been able to use one main data source, and while this is preferable for reasons of consistency, it proved impossible for Scotland. In common with most studies the data used represents a compromise situation, but it is maintained that the loss of coverage was outweighed in part by the gain of the details for each plant. By combining several data sources, some of which are readily available elsewhere, it has been demonstrated that components of employment change analysis would be a feasible undertaking for other areas. Large sample surveys using lists of firms derived from public and private directories could then be used to estimate the relative size of each of the components of change. While not directly attempting a components analysis, Sant (1970) has shown that this general method can be used to obtain a reasonably comprehensive picture of the manufacturing industry of an area.

It has also been demonstrated that local public bodies such as the district and regional councils, possess large amounts of information. Though this information is not freely available, it is a useful and an often under-used source of data. In fact, without the assistance and support of these bodies this study would have undoubtedly failed. Furthermore, they were able to provide information at the local level that could explain, say, the development of industrial estates in the area, or the administrative machinery behind local industrial development. It is also felt that by gaining the support of these bodies the response rates to the surveys undertaken of firms in their area were larger than might have otherwise been expected. Despite these minor contributions to research methodology, either the success or the failure of a chosen methodology lies in its ability to aid the examination of the problem understudy. It should, then, be transparent and remain a vehicle by which explanation may be sought. The methodology in terms of _this_ study can be said to have been relatively "successful", but that does not imply that its wholesale use elsewhere will also be successful (SLOCUM et al, 1956 225).

This study opened by being critical of the previous studies of new firms conducted under the guises of either economic or industrial geography. Their narrow approach, it was thought, had impeded advances in the explanation of the variations in the number of new firms. Counter to this approach, the present study has adopted a broad approach and has been successful in illustrating the benefits from doing so. If the study has shown that this is the case and has also shown its relevance to the main-stream of industrial geography and the current debate over new firms, then the study will have served some purpose.

NOTES

1. For a discussion of these notions see Firn (1973, 55-60; 1975, 397-8).
2. This also includes East Anglia.
3. Incubator is used here to cover both incubator organization and area (Chapters Seven and Eight) and also the traditional geographic interpretation in terms of the factors of supply (external economies).
4. A recent text edited by Lonsdale and Seyler (1979) reviews this situation for non-metropolitan areas in the United States, and covers such topics as their general position (HAREN and HOLLING), factors encouraging their development (KALE and LONSDALE), effects of branch plants (ERICKSON and LEINBACH), and community satisfaction and migration (DOERING and KINWORTHY; SEYLER; SHAFFER; HEATON and FUGUITT; KUEHN; SEYLER; and, SUMMERS, BRECK and SNIPP). This book together with Summers et al (1976) makes a useful up to date review

of the situation.

5. Demand features such as these would at least require input-output data at the plant level.

6. The first occupation being the first job ever held, and the last occupation being the one held immediately prior to founding the new firm.

Bibliography

ABBOT, A. (1978) Is small beautiful? Prospects and Policies for Local Employment Growth - Local Initiatives. Paper presented at the Regional Studies Association Conference, Planning Exchange, Glasgow, June 29th. p.5.

ACKERMAN, R. (1975) The Social Challenge to Business. Harvard University Press: Harvard.

ACKOFF, R. L. with GUPTA, S. K. and MINAS, J. S. (1962) Scientific Method: Optimising Applied Research Decisions. New York.

ACTON SOCIETY TRUST (1956) Management Succession. London.

AIKEN, G. J. (1961) The Future of Explorations in Entrepreneurial History, Explorations in Entrepreneurial History, Second Series, Vol.1, No.1.

ALBERT, K. J. (1977) How to Pick the Right Small Business Opportunity. The Key to Success In Your Own Business. McGraw-Hill: New York, p.239.

ALDEN, J. (1971) Double Job-Holding: A Regional Analysis of Scotland, Scottish Jo. of Political Economy, Vol.18, No.2, 99-112.

ALDEN, J. and MORGAN, R. (1974) Regional Planning: A Comprehensive View. Leonard Hill: Leighton Buzzard. p.364.

ALEXANDER, J. W. and LINDBERG, J. B. (1961) Measurement of Manufacturing: Coefficients of Correlation, Jo. of Regional Science, Vol.3, 71-81.

ALEXANDER, J. W. (1975) Transfer of Technology and Management Techniques from Foreign-Owned to Indigenous Enterprises. SSRC Research Report HR-1125. p.42.

ALKER, H. R. and RUSSETT, B. M. (1966) Indices for Comparing Inequality, Chapter 16, pp. 349-72 in MERRITT, R. L. and ROKKAN, S. (eds.) op.cit.

ALLA, J. (1974) Age et evolution de l'enterprise, Revue Economique, Vol.25, 984-1003.

ALLEN, G. C. (1959) British Industries and their Organisation. Longmans: London.

ALLEN, K. and YUILL, D. (1977) The Accuracy of Pre-1971 Local Employment Data (ERIIs), Regional Studies, Vol.11, No.4, 253-61.

ALLEN, K. and YUILL, D. (1978) Small Area Employment Forecasting. Data and Problems. Saxon House: Farnborough, p.248.

ALLSOPP, M. (1977) Survival in Business. Analysis of Success and Failure. Business Books: London. p.139.

ALTMAN, O. (1940) Savings, Investment and National Income. Temporary National Economic Commission, Monograph No.37.

ANON. (1969) La Route 128, Le Progres Scientifique, Vol.134, 10-52.

ASHCROFT, B. and TAYLOR, J. (1976) The Movement of Manufacturing Industry and the Effect of Regional Policy. Occ. Paper, Dept. of Economics, University of Lancaster. p.24.

ASHCROFT, B. and TAYLOR, J. (1979) The Effect of Regional Policy on the Movement of Industry in Great Britain, Chapter 2, pp.43-64 in MacLENNAN, D. and PARR, J. B. (eds.) op.cit.

ASHTON, J. and LONG, W. (eds. 1972) The Remoter Rural Areas of Britain. Oliver and Boyd: Edinburgh.

ATKINS, D. H. W. (1973) Employment Change in Branch and Parent Manufacturing Plants in the U.K.: 1966-71, Trade and Industry, 30 August, 437-9.
BAILLIE, A. C. (1972) Promoting Entrepreneurship in Canada, The Business Quarterly, Vol.37, No.2, 22-30.
BAIN, G. S. and WOOLVEN, E. B. (1979) A Bibliography of British Industrial Relations. Cambridge University Press: Cambridge. p.665.
BAIN, J. S. (1966) International Differences in Industrial Structure. Yale University Press: New Haven.
BAKKE, E. W. (ed. 1964) Labour Mobility and Economic Opportunity. New York.
BALASUBRAMANYAM, V. N. (1979) The South Indian Entrepreneur: A Case Study of Entrepreneurial Development in Bangalore and Coimbatore. SSRC Final Report HR-2484. p.62.
BALE, J. R. (1972a) The Development of Industrial Estates with Special Reference to South Wales, 1936-1969. Unpublished M.Phil. Dissertation University of London. p.324.
BALE, J. R. (1972b) An Industrial Park at Abercarn, Monmouthshire, Town and Country Planning, Vol.40, 572-5.
BALE, J. R. (1974) Toward a Geography of the Industrial Estate, Professional Geographer, Vol.26, No.3, 291-7.
BALE, J. R. (1977) Industrial Estate Development and Location in Post-War Britain, Geography, Vol.62, No.2, 87-92.
BALMER, L. M. (1979) The Impact of North Sea Oil on the Indigenous Firms of Peterhead. Unpublished M.A. Dissertation, Dept. of Geography, University of Edinburgh.
BANNISTER, N. (1977) Who Owns What Surprises, The Guardian, 22 April, 15.
BANNOCK, G. (1976) The Smaller Business in Britain and Germany. Wilton House: London. p.152.
BANNOCK, G. and DORAN, A. (1978) Small Firms in Cities. A Review of Recent Research. Shell (UK) Ltd.: London. p.45.
BARBEE, E. E. (1941) Reasons for Failure, Credit and Financial Management, November.
BARLOW, M. (Chairman 1940) Report of the Royal Commission on the Distribution Industrial Population. Cmnd. 6153. HMSO: London.
BARTHOLOMEW, D. J. (1973) A Model of Completed Length of Service, Omega, Jo. of Management Science, Vol.1, No.2, 235-40.
BARTHOLOMEW, D. J. (1977) Manpower Planning Literature: Statistical Techniques of Manpower Analysis, Department of Employment Gazette, Vol.85, No.10, 1093-6.
BATES, J. (1964) The Financing of Small Business. Sweet and Maxwell: London.
BAUMOL, W. J. (1968) Entrepreneurship in Econimic History, American Economic Review, Vol.58, No.2, 64-71.
BEALES, (1957) The Listener, 21. Feb.
BEED, C. S. (1966) The Separation of Ownership from Control, Jo. of Economic Studies, Vol.1, No.2, 29-46.
BEESLEY, M. (1955) The Birth and Death of Industrial Establishments: The Experience in the West Midlands Conurbation, Jo. of Industrial Economics, Vol.4, 45-61.
BEESLEY, M. and EVANS, T. (1978) Corporate Social Responsibility: A Reassessment. Croom Helm: London.
BEGG, H. M. (1972) Remoteness and the Location of the Firm, Scottish Geographical Magazine, Vol.88, No.1, 48-52.
BEHRMAN, J. N. (1969) Some Patterns in the Rise of the Multi-national Enterprise. University of North Carolina Press: Chapel Hill, North Carolina.
BELDING, R. K. and HUTCHINSON, D. A. (1978) Home or Away. Why Do Qualified Leavers from Scottish Schools Move Away from Home? Tijdschrift voor Econ. en Soc. Geografie, Vol.69, No.4, 216-24.

BELL, D. N. F. and KIRWAN, F. X. (1979) Return Migration in a Scottish Context, Regional Studies, Vol.13, No.1, 101-11.

BENYON, H. and BLACKBURN, R. M. (1972) Perceptions of Work. Cambridge University Press: Cambridge.

BERLE, A. A. and MEANS, G. (1932) The Modern Corporation and Private Property. MacMillan: London.

BERNSTEIN, H. (1971) Modernization Theory and the Sociological Study of Development, Jo. of Development Studies, Vol.7, No.2, 141-60.

BERRY, B. J. L. and MARBLE, D. F. (eds. 1968) Spatial Analysis. A Reader in Statistical Geography. Prentice-Hall Inc.: Englewood Cliffs, New Jersey. p.512.

BETTS, P. V. V. (1972) Can the Entrepreneur Survive in the Seventies? The Business Quarterly, Vol.37, No.1, 14-8.

BINKS, M. (1979) Finance for Expansion in the Small Firm, Lloyds Bank Review, No.134, 33-45.

BIRCH, D. L. (1979a) The Job Generation Process - A Summary. MIT: Cambridge, Mass. p.22.

BIRCH, D. L. (1979b) The Job Generation Process - Full Report MIT: Cambridge, Mass. p.295.

BIRCH, S. and MacMILLAN, B. (1972) Managers on the Move. BIM Report No.7. BIM: London. p.20.

BLACKBOURN, A. (1974) The Spatial Behaviour of American Firms in Western Europe, Chapter 9, pp.245-64 in HAMILTON, F. E. I. (ed.) op.cit.

BLAKE, C. (1976) The Productivity of Labour in Scottish Manufacturing. Occ. Paper No.5, Dept. of Economics, University of Dundee. p.42.

BLALOCK, H. M. (1972) Social Statistics. McGraw-Hill Kogakusha: New York. 2nd Edition. p.583.

BLALOCK, H. M. jr. (1972) Causal Inferences in Nonexperimental Research. W. W. Norton and Co.: New York. p.200.

BLALOCK, H. M. jr. and BLALOCK, A. B. (eds. 1968) Methodology in Social Science Research. McGraw-Hill: New York.

BOLTON, J. E. (Chairman 1971) Small Firms. Report of the Commission of Inquiry on Small Firms. Cmnd. 4811. HMSO: London. p.436.

BOND, R. S. (1975) Mergers and Mobility among the Largest manufacturing Corporations, 1948 to 1968. Antitrust Bulletin, Vol.20, 505-19.

BONEAU, C. A. (1960) The Effects of Violations underlying the 't' Test, Psychological Bulletin, Vol.57, 49-64.

BOSWELL, J. (1973) The Rise and Decline of Small Firms. George Allen and Unwin: London. p.272.

BOULDING, K. E. (1956a) General Systems Theory - The Skeleton of Science, General Systems, Vol.1, No.1, 11-7.

BOULDING, K. E. (1956b) Toward a General Theory of Growth, General Systems, Vol.1, No.1, 66-75.

BOWER, C. M. (1959) For the Small Electronic Firm...Obtaining Capital - Methods and Pitfalls, Electronic Industries, Vol.18, No.12, 242-51.

BRIGHT, J. R. (1958) Automation and Management. Harvard Business School, Division of Research: Boston.

BRINKLEY, I. M. and NICHOLSON, B. (1979) The Early Development of Successful Manufacturing Enterprises: Some Parameters and Locational Influences from Public Companies. CES-WN-529. Centre for Environmental Studies: London. p.21.

BRITTON, J. N. H. (1967) Regional Analysis and Economic Geography. A Case Study of Manufacturing in the Bristol Region. Bell and Co.: London.

BROOKS, S.: GILMOUR, J. M. and MURRICANE, K. (1973) The Spatial Linkages of Manufacturing in Montreal and its Surroundings, Cahiers de Geographie de Quebec, Vol.17, 107-22.

BROWN, A. J. (1969) Some English thoughts on the Scottish Economy, Scottish Jo. of Political Economy, Vol.16, No.3, 233-47.

BROWN, A. J. (1972) The Framework of Regional Economics in the United
Kingdom. NIESR. Cambridge University Press: Cambridge. p.352.
BROWN, R.: HAYTON, J.: SANDY, C. and BROWN, P. (1976) Small Businesses:
Strategy for Survival. Wilton House: London. p.69.
BRUNSKILL, I. (1979) Spatial Variations in the Formation of New Firms.
Paper presented to the conference, Small Firms' Policy and the Role
of Research. Ashridge Management College, October. p.18.
BULL, P. J. (1978) The Spatial Components of Intra-Urban Manufacturing
Change: Suburbanization in Clydeside, 1958-1968, Transactions and
Papers, Institute of British Geographers, New Series, Vol.3, No.1 91-100.
BULL, P. J. (1979) The Effects of Central Redevelopment Schemes on Inner
City Manufacturing Industry, with special reference to Glasgow,
Environment and Planning, A, Vol.11, No.4, 455-62.
BUSINESS WEEK (1960) Blue-Ribbon Venture Capital, Business Week, October
29, 65-9.
BUSINESS WEEK (1961) Scramble to Buy New Issues, Business Week, April 15,
129-32.
BUSWELL, R. J. and LEWIS, E. W. (1970) The Geographical Distribution of
Industrial Research Activity in the U.K., Regional Studies, Vol.4, 297-306.
BUXTON, N. K. and MACKAY, D. I. (assisted by C. L. WOOD) (1977) British
Employment Statistics. A Guide to Sources and Methods. Blackwell:
Oxford. p.197.
CAIRNCROSS, A. K. (ed. 1954) The Scottish Economy. A Statistical Account
of Scottish Life by Members of the Staff of University of Glasgow,
Social and Economic Studies. Cambridge University Press: Cambridge.
CAMERON, G. C. (1970) Growth Areas, Growth Centres and Regional Conversion,
Scottish Jo. of Political Economy, Vol.17, No.1, 19-38.
CAMERON, G. C. (1971) Economic Analysis for a Declining Urban Economy,
Scottish Jo. of Political Economy, Vol.18, No.3, 315-45.
CAMERON, G. C. (1973) Intra-Urban Location and the New Plant, Papers and
Proceedings, Regional Science Association, Vol.31, 125-44.
CAMERON, G. C. (1977) Economic Renewal in the Inner City, Architects Jo.,
Vol.165, 215-7.
CAMERON, G. C. (1979) The National Industrial Strategy and Regional
Policy, Chapter 14, pp.297-322 in MacLENNAN, D. and PARR, J. B. (eds.)
op.cit.
CAMERON, G. C. and CLARK, B. D. (1966) Industrial Movement and the
Regional Problem. Occ. Paper No.5, Social and Economic Studies,
University of Glasgow. Oliver and Boyd: Edinburgh.
CAMERON, G. C. and REID, G. L. (1966) Scottish Economic Planning and the
Attraction of Industry. Occ. Paper No.6, Social and Economic Studies,
University of Glasgow. Oliver and Boyd: Edinburgh.
CAMERON, G. C. and EVANS, A. W. (1973) The British Conurbation Centres,
Regional Studies, Vol.7, No.1, 47-55.
CAMERON, G. C.: FIRN, J. R.: LATHAM, M. and MacLENNAN, D. (1975) The
Determinants of Urban Manufacturing Location - A Simple Model, pp.52-65
in CRIPPS, E. L. (ed.) op.cit.
CAMERON, I. (1979) Components of Employment Change in Portsmouth TWA
(1966-76). Research and Intelligence Group, County Planning Department,
Hampshire County Council. Feb. p.35.
CAMPBELL, R. C. (1977) More Scots Industry Under Outside Control, The
Scotsman, April 14.
CARLSTEIN, T.: PARKES, D. and THRIFT, N. (eds., 1978) Timing Space and
Spacing Time. Vol.2. Human Activity and Time Geography. Edward Arnold:
London. p.286.
CARLSTEIN, T.: PARKES, D. and THRIFT, N. (eds. 1978) Timing Space and
Spacing Time. Vol.3. Time and Regional Dynamics. Edward Arnold: London.
p.120.

CARNEY, J.: LEWIS, J. and HUDSON, R. (1977) Coal Combines and Inter-
regional Uneven Development in the U.K., pp.52-67 in MASSEY, D. B. and
BATEY, P. W. (eds.) op.cit.

CARTER, C. J. (1971) Comparative Studies in the Post-War Industrial
Geography of the Clydeside and West Midlands Conurbations. Unpublished
Ph.D. Dissertation, University of Glasgow. 2 Vols.

CARTER, C. J. (1974) Some Post-War Changes in the Industrial Geography
of the Clydeside Conurbation, Scottish Geographical Magazine, Vol.90,
No.1, 14-26.

CARTER, I. R. (1974) The Highlands of Scotland as an Underdeveloped
Region, pp.279-311 in de KADT, E. and WILLIAMS, G. (eds.) op.cit.

CARTER, M. P. (no date) Social and Occupational Mobility in Scotland.
SSRC Research Report HR-2173.

CASTELLS, M. and de IPOLA, E. (1976) Epistemological Practice and the
Social Sciences, Economy and Science, Vol.5, 111-44.

CASTREE, J. R. (1966) Industrial Estates in Wales. Unpublished M.A.
Dissertation, University of Swansea. p.360.

CHANDLER, A. D. jr. and REDLICH, F. (1961) Developments in American
Business Administration and Their Conceptualization, Business History
Review, Vol.35, No.1, 1-27.

CHAPIN, F. S. (1978) Human Time Allocation in the City, Chapter One,
pp.13-26 in CARLSTEIN, E. et.al (eds.) op.cit. Vol.2.

CHAPMAN, G. P. (1977) Human and Environmental Systems: A Geographer's
Appraisal. Academic Press: London and New York. p.421.

CHESHIRE, P. (1979) Is it the inner city miasma that causes unemployment?
The Guardian, Nov.13, 18.

CHINITZ, B. (1961) Contrasts in Agglomeration: New York and Pittsburgh,
American Economic Review, Vol.51, 279-89.

CHISHOLM, M. D. I. (1960) The Geography of Commuting, Annals, American
Association of Geographers, Vol.50, 187 and 491-2.

CHISHOLM, M. D. I. (1962) The Location of Industry, Planning, P.E.P.,
No.28, Broadsheet 466, 325-63.

CHISHOLM, M. D. I. (1968) Rural Settlement and Land Use. Hutchinson
University Library: London. 2nd Edition. p.183.

CHISHOLM, M. D. I. (1976) Regional Policies in an Era of Slow Population
Growth and Higher Unemployment, Regional Studies, Vol.10, No.2, 201-13.

CHISHOLM, M. D. I. and MANNERS, G. (eds. 1971) Spatial Polity Problems
of the British Economy. Cambridge University Press: Cambridge. p.248.

CHISHOLM, M. D. I. and OEPPEN, J. (1973) The Changing Pattern of Employment. Regional Specialisation and Industrial Localization in Britain.
Croom Helm: London. p.127.

CHORLEY, R. I. and HAGGETT, P. (eds. 1967) Models in Geography. Methuen:
London. p.677.

CHURCHILL, B. C. (1955) Age and Life Expectancy of Business Firms,
Survey of Current Business, Dec., 15-9 and 24.

CHURCHMAN, C. W. (1954) The Philosophy of Experimentation, Chapter 12,
pp.159-72 in KEMPTHORNE, O. et al (eds.) op.cit.

CLARK, D. G. (1966) The Industrial Manager: His Background and Career
Pattern. Business Publications: London. p.205.

CLARK, U. E. G. (1976) The Cyclical Sensitivity of Employment in Branch
and Parent Plants, Regional Studies, Vol.10, No.3, 293-8.

CLARKE, J. (1972) Small Businesses. How They Survive and Succeed.
David and Charles; Newton Abbot. p.395.

CLEDAT, O. and CREPEAU, D. (1976) Concentration et mobilite au sein des
100 plus grandes enterprises Francaises 1963-1973, Revue D'Economie
Politique, Vol.86, 621-34.

CLEMENTS, R. V. (1958) Managers: A Study of Their Career in Industry.
Allen and Unwin: London. p.200.

CLIFF, A. D. (1970) Computing the Spatial Correspondence between Geographical Patterns, Transactions and Papers, Institute of British Geographers, Vol.50, 143-54.

CLIFF, A. D. and ORD, K. (1970) Spatial Autocorrelation. A Review of existing and New Measures with Applications, Economic Geography, Vol.46, No.2, 269-92.

CLIFF, A. D. and ORD, K. (1971) Evaluating the Percentage Points of a Spatial Autocorrelation Coefficients, Geographical Analysis, Vol.3, No.1, 51-62.

CLIFF, A. D. and ORD, K. (1972) Testing for Spatial Autocorrelation among Regression Residuals, Geographical Analysis, Vol.4, No.3, 267-84

CLIFF, A. D. and ORD, K. (1973) Spatial Autocorrelation. Pion: London. p.178.

CLIFF, A. D. and ORD, K. (1975) The Choice of a Test for Spatial Autocorrelation in DAVIES, J. C. and McCULLAGH, M. J. (eds.) op.cit.

CLIFF, A D.: MARTIN, R. L. and ORD, K. (1975) A Test for Spatial Autocorrelation in Chloropleth Maps Based Upon a Modified X^2 Statistic, Transactions and Papers, Institute of British Geographers, Vol.65, 109-29.

CLUBLEY, R. (ed. 1976) Indigenous Industrial Development. Proceedings of a Seminar. Aycliffe and Peterlee Development Corporations. p.105.

COLLINS, J. (1977) A Discussion Paper on the Needs, Demands and Help Available to the Small/Independent Business Sector in the Bristol/Avon Area. Paper presented to the London Business School's Small Business Unit Research Conference. Oct. p.62.

COLLINS, J. and ROBERTS, J. (1977) Reasons Why Small Businesses have gone Into Liquidation or Bankruptcy. Mimeo. South West Regional Management Centre, Bristol Polytechnic. p.11.

COLLINS, L. (1966) Industrial Migration and Relocation: A Study of European Branch Plants in Metropolitan Toronto. Unpublished M.A. Dissertation, University of Toronto.

COLLINS, L. (1970) Markov Chains and Industrial Migration: Forecasting Aspects of Industrial Activity in Ontario. Unpublished Ph.D. Dissertation, University of Toronto.

COLLINS, L. (1972) Industrial Migration in Ontario: Forecasting Aspects of Industrial Activity through Markov Chain Analysis. Statistics Canada: Ottawa. p.154.

COLLINS, L. and WALKER, D. F. (eds. 1975) Locational Dynamics of Manufacturing Activity. John Wiley: London. p.402.

COLLINS, O. F.: MOORE, D. G. with UNWALLA, D. B. (1964) The Enterprising Man. Michigan State University Business Studies: East Lancing, Michigan. p.254.

COLLINS, O. and MOORE, D. G. (1970) The Organisation Makers: A Behavioural Study of Independent Entrepreneurs. Appleton-Century-Crofts: New York.

CONFEDERATION of BRITISH INDUSTRY (1968) Britain's Small Firms: Their Role in the Economy. CBI: London.

CONFEDERATION of BRITISH INDUSTRY (1980) Jobs - Facing the Future. A CBI Staff Discussion Document. CBI: London. p.51.

COOMBES, M. G.: DIXON, J. S.: GODDARD, J. B.: OPENSHAW, S. and TAYLOR, P. J. (1978) Towards a More Rational Consideration of Census Areal Units; Daily Urban Systems in Britain, Environment and Planning, A, Vol.10, No.10, 1179-85.

COOPER, A. C. (1970a) The Palo Alto Experience, Industrial Research, May, 58-60.

COOPER, A. C. (1970b) Entrepreneurial Environment, Industrial Research, September, 74-6.

COOPER, A. C. (1971) Spin-Offs and Technical Entrepreneurship, IEEE Transactions on Engineering Management, Vol. EM-18, No.1, 2-6.

COOPER, A. C. (1973) Technical Entrepreneurship: What Do We Know? R. and D. Management, Vol.3, No.2, 50-65.

COOPER, A. C. and KOMIVES, J. (eds. 1972) Technical Entrepreneurship:
A Symposium. The Centre for Venture Management: Milwaukee, Wis..
COOPER, M. J. (1975) The Industrial Location Decision Making Process.
Occ. Paper No.34. Centre for Urban and Regional Studies, University of
Birmingham. p.108.
COVER, J. A. (1933) Business and Personal Failure and Adjustment in
Chicago, Jo. of Business of the University of Chicago, July, Part.2.
COX, K. R. and GOLLEDGE, R. D. (eds. 1969) Behavioural Problems in
Geography: A Symposium. Northwestern Studies in Geography No.17.
Northwestern University: Evanston.
CRAIGEN, G. D. and JOHNSTONE, W. J. D. (1977) Some Sources of Finance for
Industry in Scotland. 1. The Scottish Development Agency and Scottish
Economic Planning Department, The Scottish Bankers Magazine, Aug. 122-30.
CRAWFORD, M. (1978) Why Uncle Sam is Heading for Home, The Sunday Times,
3 Sept., 62.
CRIPPS, E. L. (eds.1975) Regional Science - New Concepts and Old Problems.
London Papers in Regional Science No.5. Pion: London.
CROOK, A. (1964) Why Firms Fail? Foundry Trade Jo., Vol.117, No.2492,
10 Sept., 317-9.
CROSS, M. (1977) Input-Output Survey, The Scotsman, July 19, 10.
CROSS, M. (1978) Costs of Job Creation, The Scotsman, Nov.21, 10.
CROSS, M. (1979) New Firm Formation and the Local Labour Market. Paper
presented at the Small Firms' Policy and the Role of Research
Conference, Ashridge Management College, Berkhamsted. Oct. p.38.
CROSS, M. (1980) The Closure and Redundancy Records of the Department
of Employment. Typescript. Durham University Business School. p.11.
CROSS, M. (1980) New Firm Formation and Regional Development: The Case
of Scotland, 1968-1977. Ph.D. Dissertation submitted to the University
of Edinburgh. p.669.
CROSS, M. (1981, forthcoming) The Changing Face of Manufacturing Industry
in Scotland: A Consideration of the Processes, Chapter 7 in CLAPPERTON, C.
(ed. forthcoming) Scotland A New Study. David and Charles: Newton Abbot.
CRUM, R. E. and GUDGIN, G. H. (1977) Non-Production Activities in U.K.
Manufacturing Industry. Collection Studies Regional Policy Series No.3.
EEC: Busssels. p.176.
CRUM, W. L. (1953) The Age Structure of the Corporate System. Publication
of the Bureau of Business and Economic Research, University of California.
University of California Press: Berkley and Los Angeles. p.181.
CULLEN, I. G. (1976) Human Geography, Regional Science, and the Study of
Individual Behaviour, Environment and Planning, A. Vol.8, No.4, 397-409.
CULLEN, I. G. (1978) The Treatment of Time in the Explanation of Spatial
Behaviour, Chapter Two, pp.27-38 in CARLSTEIN, T. et al (eds.) op.cit.
Vol.2.
CURRIE, A. (1978) Self-Management Enterprises. Draft Policy Paper.
Scottish National Party: Edinburgh. p.5.
CURRIE, L. (1978) Position, Flow and Person in Theoretical Economic
Geography, Chapter 3, pp.35-50 in CARLSTEIN, T. et al (eds.) op.cit.
CURWEN, P. J. (1976) The Theory of the Firm. Macmillan: London. p.189.
CYERT, R. and MARCH, J. G. (1963) A Behavioural Theory of the Firm.
Prentice-Hall: Engelwood Cliffs, New Jersey.
DACEY, M. F. (1968) A Review on Measures of Contiguity for Two and
K-Colour Maps, Part 7, Chapter 4, pp.479-495 in BERRY, B. J. L. and
MARBLE, D. F. (eds.) op.cit.
DAHMEN, E. (1970) Entrepreneurial Activity and the Development of
Swedish Industry, 1919 - 1939. Richard D. Irwin: Homewood, Illinois.
p.440.
DAHRENDORF (1979) Is the Work Society Running out of Work? B.I.M.
Fellows' Luncheon Address. 8 Nov. p.12.

DANIELS, J. D. (1974) The Education and Mobility of European Executives in U.S. Subsidiaries: A Comparative Study, Jo. of International Business, Vol.5, 9-24.

DANILOV, V. J. (1963) University Research ... A Special Report on Expenditure, Development, Problems, and Trends in University Research, Industrial Research, Vol.5, No.4, 19-25.

DARBY, D. J. (1978) Raising Finance. A Guide for Small Firms. Small Firms Information Service No.6. Dept. of Industry. H.M.S.O.: London. 2nd Edition. p.28.

DARBY, H. C. (1952) On the Relations of Geography and History, Transactions and Papers, Institute of British Geographers, Vol.19, 1-11.

DAVIDS, L. E. (1963) Characteristics of Small Business Founders in Texas and Georgia. Prepared by the University of Georgia for the Small Business Administration. Small Business Administration: Washington, D.C.

DAVIDSON, R. N. (1967) Aspects of the Distribution of Employment in Glasgow: A Locational Analysis of Employee/Area Relationship. Unpublished Ph.D. Dissertation, University of Glasgow. 3 Volumes. p.174.

DAVIES, J. C. and McCULLAGH, M. J. (eds. 1975) Display and Analysis of Spatial Data. John Wiley: London.

DAVIES, S. (1979) The Diffusion of Process Innovations. Cambridge University Press: Cambridge. p.193.

DE BONO, E. (1980) Opportunities. A Handbook of Business Opportunity Search. Penguin: Harmondsworth, Middlesex. p.252.

DEEKS, J. (1972) Educational and Occupational Histories of Owner-Managers and Managers, Jo. of Management Studies, Vol.9, 127-49.

DELANO, M. S.: JOHNSON, D. W. and WOODWORTH, R. T. (1966) Entrepreneurial Report. Prepared for the US Dept. of Commerce by the Graduate School of Business Administration, University of Washington, Dept. of Commerce: Washington, D.C. p.230.

DENNIS, R. (1978) The Decline of Manufacturing Employment in Greater London: 1966 - 1974, Urban Studies, Vol.15, No.1, 63-73.

DEPT. of ECONOMICS (UNIVERSITY OF DUNDEE) (1979) The Displacement of Labour Effect. Paper presented, Seminar on Parliamentary Studies and Implications for Manpower Policy, MSC Scotland, Edinburgh. p.15.

DEPT. of EMPLOYMENT (1977a) New Earnings Survey, 1977. HMSO: London.

DEPT. of EMPLOYMENT (1977b) Personal Communication with Statistics Division C6, 6 Sept..

DEPT. of EMPLOYMENT (1977c) Strikes in Britain. HMSO: London.

DEPT. of EMPLOYMENT (1978) Annual Census of Employment - Limitations on the use of Data for Individual Census Units. Prepared for the National and Local Government Statistical Liaison Committee (NLGSC) Ref: NLGSC (78) 26.

DEPT. of EMPLOYMENT (no date) Employment in Metropolitan Areas. Project Report by the Unit for Manpower Studies. Dept. of Employment: London. p.98.

DEPT. of EMPLOYMENT (no date) Collection of Case Studies. (Includes: UCS, Glasgow; Woolwich Redundancies, 1968-70; Engineering Redundancies in the West Midlands, 1966-68; Redundancies in the Coal Industry, 1967-68 (by LEHMANN, P.); Ryhope - A Pit Closes. A Study in Redeployment, 1966; The Closure of the Chrysler Plant in Maidstone, 1976; Handley Page, St. Albans, 1970; Rolls Royce, 1971; TSR2, 1968; Colliery Closures in South Wales (by T. J. Farmer); and BSC - Stockton-on-Tees, 1970 and Trafford Park, 1969-70 (by Mackay, D. I. and Reid, D. L.).

DEPT. of EMPLOYMENT GAZETTE (1976) New Estimates of Employment on a Continuous basis. Employers and the self-employed, 1961-74, Department of Employment Gazette, Vol.84, No.12, 1344-9.

DEPT. of EMPLOYMENT GAZETTE (1979) Trends and Differentiation in Earnings by Region, Department of Employment Gazette, Vol.87, No.4, 340-8.

DEPT. of the ENVIRONMENT (1975) Register of Research. Part II Environmental Planning. Dept. of the Environment: London. p.361.

DEPT. of the ENVIRONMENT (1977) Inner Area Studies, Liverpool, Birmingham
and Lambeth. Summaries of Consultants' Reports. HMSO: London.

DEPT. of TRADE and INDUSTRY (1973) Memorandum on the Inquiry into Location
and Experience. Minutes of Evidence, Trade and Industry Sub-Committee
of the House of Commons Expenditure Committee. HMSO: London.

DEUTERMANN, E. P. (1966) Seeding Science-Based Industry, Business Review,
Federal Reserve Bank of Philadelphia, May, 3-10.

DICKEN, P. and LLOYD, P. E. (1976) Geographical Perspectives on United
States Investment in the United Kingdom, Environment and Planning, A,
Vol.8, 685-705.

DICKEN, P. and LLOYD, P. E. (1977) Inner Manchester: Components of
Industrial Change in the Corporate Context. Working Paper No.5. North
West Industry Research Unit, School of Geography, University of
Manchester. p.27.

DICKEN, P. and LLOYD, P. E. (1978) Inner Metropolitan Industrial Change,
Enterprise Structures and Policy Issues: Case Studies of Manchester and
Merseyside, Regional Studies, Vol.12, No.2, 181-97.

DOERING, T. R. and KINWORTHY, J. C. (1979) The Community Satisfaction of
Nonmetropolitan Manufacturers, Chapter 5, pp.79-91 in LONSDALE, R. E.
and SEYLER, H. L. (eds.) op. cit.

DONALDSON, P. (1973) Economics of the Real World. BBC and Penguin:
Harmondsworth, Middlesex. p.244.

DRAHEIM, K. (1972) Factors Influencing the Rate of Formation of Technical
Companies in COOPER, A. C. and KOMIVES, J. (eds.) op. cit.

DRAHEIM, K.: HOWELL, R. P. and SHAPERO, A. (1966) The Development of a
Potential Defence R. and D. Complex: A Study of Minneapolis-St. Paul.
R. and D. Studies Series. Stanford Research Institute: Menlo Park,
California. p.188.

DRAY, W. H. (1964) Philosophy of History. Prentice-Hall.: Englewood
Cliffs, New Jersey. p.116.

DUGDALE, J. S. (1962) Economic and Social History. English Universities
Press: London. p.248.

DUNCAN, O. D.: CUZZORT, R. P. and DUNCAN, B. (1961) Statistical Geography:
Problems in Analyzing Areal Data. Free Press: New York.

EASTBURN, D. P. (1966) Pressing against the Ceiling? Or How High Can the
Loan/Deposit Ratio Go? Business Review, Federal Reserve Bank of
Philadelphia, May, 11-5.

EBDON, D. (1977) Statistics in Geography. A Practical Approach. Basil
Blackwell: Oxford. p.195.

ECONOMIST, The (1965) Industrial Scotland - A Nation Catches Up, The
Economist, (A Special Survey), ff.616-7.

ECONOMIST, The (1978) Grasping the Thistle. A Survey of Scotland. The
Economist, 18-24 Feb. p.34.

ECONOMICS ADVISORY GROUP Ltd. (1978) See BANNOCK, G. and DORAN, A. (1978)
op.cit.

EDWARDS, R. S. and TOWNSEND, H. (1958) Business Enterprise: Its Growth
and Organisation. McMillan: London. p.607.

EGGAN, F. (1954) Social Anthropology and the Methods of Controlled
Comparison, American Anthropologist, Vol.56, 743-63.

EMPLOYMENT GROUP (NEWCASTLE UPON TYNE) (1979) The Tress Redundancy: A
Year After the Closure. Part A. Labour Market Experience of
Redundant Workers. p.19.

EMPLOYMENT GROUP (NEWCASTLE UPON TYNE) (1980) The Tress Redundancy: A
Year After the Closure. Part B. The Costs of Closure.

ERICKSON, R. A. (1976) The Filtering-Down Process: Industrial Location in a Nonmetropolitan Area, Professional Geographer, Vol.28, No.3, 254-60.

ERICKSON, R. A. (1978) The New Wave of Nonmetropolitan Industrialization, Earth and Mineral Sciences, Vol.48, No.3, 17-20.

ERICKSON, R. A. and LEINBACH, T. R. (1979) Characteristics of Branch Plants Attracted to Nonmetropolitan Areas, Chapter 4, pp.57-78 in LONSDALE, R. E. and SEYLER, H. L. (eds.) op. cit.

EVANS, A. W. (1973) The Location of the Headquarters of Industrial Companies, Urban Studies, Vol.10, No.3, 387-95.

EVERSLEY, D. E. C. (1965) Social and Psychological Factors in the Determination of Industrial Location in WILSON, T. (ed.) op. cit.

EVERSLEY, D. E. C. (1976) Towards a Strategy for the Inner City. Paper presented to the Centre for Environmental Studies Conference, Inner City Employment. University of York.

EUROPEAN ECONOMIC COMMUNITY (Directorate General Regional Policy) (1975) Feasibility Study on Investment from other Countries in the Least Prosperous Regions of the Community. EEC: Brussels. 2 Vols. pp.40 and 333.

FAGG, J. J. (1977) The Redistribution of Manufacturing Industry in Greater Leicester, 1947 - 1970. Unpublished Ph.D. Dissertation, University of Leicester. 2 Vols. p.512.

FAGG, J. J. (1979) A Re-Examination of the Incubator Hypothesis: A Case Study of the Location of New Manufacturing Firms in Greater Leicester, 1957-1970. Paper presented at the Annual Conference of the IBG, University of Manchester. p.17.

FALK, N. (1976) The Future of Small Firms in the Inner City. Seminar Paper presented at the Centre for Environmental Studies, London. p.56.

FALK, N. (1978) Small Firms and the Inner City. Paper presented at Small Firms Research Conference, Business School, University of Durham. Nov. p.16.

FIRN, J. R. (1970) The Glasgow University Register of Industrial Establishments. Metropolitan Industrial Location Working Paper 1.7. Dept. of Social and Economic Research, University of Glasgow.

FIRN, J. R. (1973) Indigenous Growth and Regional Development: The Experience and Prospects for West Central Scotland, pp.47-72 in West Central Scotland: Appraisal of Economic Options. Discussion Paper No.12. Dept. of Social and Economic Research, University of Glasgow. p.82.

FIRN, J. R. (1975) External Control and Regional Development: The Case of Scotland, Environment and Planning, Vol.7, No.4, 393-414.

FIRN, J. R. (1976) Economic Microdata Analysis and Urban-Regional Change: The Experience of GURIE in SWALES, J. K. (ed.) op.cit.

FIRN, J. R. (1977) Industrial Policy, Chapter 4, pp.62-83 in MACKAY, D. I. (ed.) op. cit.

FIRN, J. R. (1979) The Formation and Development of Manufacturing Enterprises in the Central Clydeside and West Midlands Conurbations, 1958-1971. SSRC Final Report HR-1988. p.42.

FIRN, J. R. and HUGHES, J. T. (1974) Employment Growth and the Decentralization of Manufacturing Industry: Some Intriguing Paradoxes, pp. 483-518 in Papers from the Urban Economics Conference, 1973. Centre for Environmental Studies: London.

FIRN, J. R. and SWALES, J. K. (1978) The Formation of New Manufacturing Establishments in the Central Clydeside and West Midlands Conurbations 1963-1972: A Comparative Analysis, Regional Studies, Vol.12, No.2, 199-213.

FISHER, L. (1966) Airport Industrial Parks - Who Should Develop Them? Urban Land, Vol.25, 3-6.

FLORENCE, P. S. (1948) Investment, Location and Size of Plant. Cambridge
University Press: Cambridge.

FLOWERDEW, R. and SALT, J. (1979) Migration Between Labour Market Areas
in Great Britain, 1970-1971, Regional Studies, Vol.13, No.2, 211-31.

FOGARTY, M. P. (1945) Prospects of the Industrial Areas in Great Britain.
Methuen: London.

FORSYTH, D. (1972) US Investment in Scotland. Praeger: New York. p.320.

FOTHERGILL, S. and GUDGIN, G. H. (1978a) The Structural Growth and
Decline of the U.K. Regions in its International Context. CES-WN-495.
Centre for Environmental Studies: London. p.29.

FOTHERGILL, S. and GUDGIN, G. H. (1978b) Regional Employment Change: A
Sub-Regional Explanation? CES-WN-488. Centre for Environmental Studies:
London. p.87.

FOTHERGILL, S. and GUDGIN, G. H. (1978c) Regional Employment Statistics
on a Comparable Basis 1952 - 75. Occ Paper 5. Centre for Environmental
Studies: London.

FOX, A. (1971) A Sociology of Work in Industry. Collier Macmillan:
London.

FOY, N. (1977) Greenwich: Friend of the Small Company, The Times,
26 June, 23.

FRANK, A. G. (1969) Capitalism and Underdevelopment in Latin America:
Historical Studies of Chile and Brazil. Modern Paperbacks Edition:
New York. p.343.

FREDLAND, J. E. and MORRIS, C. E. (1976a) A Cross Section Analysis of
Small Business Failure, American Jo. of Small Business, Vol.1, No.1,
7-18.

FREDLAND, J. E. and MORRIS, C. E. (1976b) Where New Small Business
go Wrong, Changing Times, Vol.30, Dec., 21-3.

FREEMAN, C. (1971) The Role of Small Firms in Innovation in the U.K.
Since 1945. Research Report No.6, Commissioned by the Bolton
Committee op.cit.

FRONKO, E. G. (1971) One Company's Cast-Off Technology is Another
Company's Opportunity, Innovation, Vol.23, 52-9.

FUCHS, V. R. (1959) Changes in the Location of U.S. Manufacturing Since
1929, Jo. of Regional Science, Vol.1, No.2, 1-17.

FUCHS, V. R. (1967) Differentials in Hourly Earnings by Region and City
Size. National Bureau of Economic Research. Occ. Paper 101. Columbia
University Press: New York and London.

GALTUNG, J. (1971) A Structural Theory of Imperialism, Jo. of Peace
Research, Vol.2, No.2, 81-117.

GEORGE, P. (1973) Redundancy Counselling. Industrial Society: London. p.26.

GERMIDIS, D. (ed. 1977) Transfer of Technology by Multinational Corporations. Development Centre of the OECD: Paris. 2 Vols. pp. 309 and 258.

GHODGERI, N. (1974) Manufacturing Industry in Post-War Edinburgh with
Special Reference to the Post 1960 Period. Unpublished M.Phil.
Dissertation, University of Edinburgh.

GIBB, A.A. and QUINCE, T. A. (1978) Effects on Small Firms of Industrial
Change in a Development Area. Paper presented to the Small Firms
Research Conference, Business School, University of Durham. Nov. p.14.

GIBBONS, M. and WATKINS, D. S. (1970) Innovation and the Small Firm,
R. and D. Management, Vol.1, No.1,10-3.

GIBRAT, R. (1931) Les Inegalites Economiques. Libraire du Recueil
Sirez: Paris.

GILBERT, A. and GOODMAN, D. (1972) Regional Income Disparaties and
Economic Development: A Critique. Occ. Paper No.2, Institute of
Latin American Studies, University of London.

GILMOUR, J. M. (1974) External Economics of Scale, Inter-Industrial Linkages and Decision Making in Manufacturing, Chapter 13, pp.335-62 in HAMILTON, F. E. I. (ed.) op.cit.

GLEAVE, D. and CORDEY-HAYES, M. (1977) Migration Dynamics and Labour Market Turnover, Progress in Planning, Vol.8, No.1, 1-95.

GLEAVE, D. and PALMER, D. (1978) Labour Mobility and the Size of Firms. CES-WN-504. Centre for Environmental Studies: London. p.32.

GODDARD, J. B. (1973) Office Linkages and Location. A Study of Communications and Spatial Patterns in Central London, Progress in Planning, Vol.1, No.2, 109-232.

GODDARD, J. B. (1975) Organizational Information Flows and the Urban System, Economie Appliquee, Vol.28, 125-64.

GODDARD, J. B. (1978) The Location of Non-Manufacturing Activities within Manufacturing Industries, Chapter 8, pp. 62-85 in HAMILTON, F.E.I. (ed.) op.cit.

GODDARD, J. B. et al (1979) The Mobilisation of Indigenous Potential in the U.K. A Report to the Regional Policy Directorate of the European Community. p.149.

GODDARD, J. B. and SMITH, I. J. (1978) Changes in Corporate Control in the British Urban System, 1972 - 1977, Environment and Planning, A, Vol.10, No.9, 1073-84.

GOLDSCHMIDT, W. (1966) Comparative Functionalism. University of California Press: Berkley and Los Angeles.

GOLDTHORPE, J. H. (with LLEWELLYN, C. and PAYNE, C.) (1980) Social Mobility and Class Structure in Modern Britain. Oxford University Press: Oxford. p.320.

GOLDTHORPE, J.: LOCKWOOD, D.: BECHHOFER, F.: and PLATT, J. (1968) The Affluent Worker: Industrial Attitudes and Behaviour. Cambridge University Press: Cambridge. p.206.

GOODMAN, J. F. B. (1970) The Definition and Analysis of Local Labour Markets: Some Empirical Problems, British Jo. of Industrial Relations, Vol.8, 179-95.

GREEN, D. H. (1974) Information, Perception and Decision-Making in the Relocation Decision. Unpublished Ph.D. Dissertation, University of Reading. p.414.

GREEN, D. H. (1977) Industrialists Information Levels of Regional Incentives, Regional Studies, Vol.11, No.1, 7-18.

GREGORY, D. (1978) Ideology, Science and Human Geography. Hutchinson: London. p.198.

GRIEVE, A. (1972) Venture Capital Sources and the Canadian Entrepreneur, The Business Quarterly, Vol.37, No.1, 54-9.

GRIME, E. K. and STARKIE, D. N. M. (1968) New Jobs for Old: An Impact Study of a New Factory in Furness, Regional Studies, Vol.2, No.1, 57-67.

GRIPAIOS, P. (1977a) The Closure of Firms in the Inner City: The South East London Case 1970-75, Regional Studies, Vol.11, No.1, 1-6.

GRIPAIOS, P. (1977b) Industrial Decline in London: An Examination of its Causes, Urban Studies, Vol.14, No.2, 181-9.

GRUBER, W. H. and MARQUIS, D. G. (eds. 1969) Factors in the Transfer of Technology. MIT Press: Cambridge, Mass. p.289.

GUDGIN, G. H. (1976) Establishment-Based Data in Studies of Employment Growth and Location in SWALES, J. K. (ed.) op.cit.

GUDGIN, G. H. (1978) Industrial Locational Processes and Regional Employment Growth. Saxon House: Farnborough. p.344.

GUDGIN, G. H. and THORNES, J. B. (1974) Probability in Geographic Research: Applications and Problems, The Statistician, Vol.23, Nos.3/4, 157-77.

GUDGIN, G. H. (1974) Industrial Location Processes. The East Midlands in the Postwar Period. Unpublished Ph.D. Dissertation, University of Leicester. p.560.

GUDGIN, G. H. and FOTHERGILL, S. (1978) Regional Variations in the Birth-Rate of Manufacturing Firms: Some Preliminary Analyses. CES-WN-482. Centre for Environmental Studies: London. p.22.

GUDGIN, G. H.: BRUNSKILL, I. and FOTHERGILL, S. (1979) New Manufacturing Firms in Regional Employment Growth. Paper presented at the CES Workshop. Õct.. Centre for Environmental Studies: London. p.16.

GUERRIER, Y. and PHILPOT, N. (1978) The British Manager: Careers and Mobility. Management Survey Report No.39. B.I.M.: London. p.46.

HACKMAN, J. R. and OLDHAM, G. R. (1975) Development of the Job Diagnostic Survey, Jo. of Applied Psychology. Vol.60, No.2, 159-170.

HAGGETT, P. (1965) Locational Analysis in Human Geography. Edward Arnold: London. p.339.

HAGGETT, P. (1972) Geography: A Modern Synthesis. Harper: New York. p.483.

HALL, D. T. and NOUGAIN, K. E. (1968) An Examination of Maslow's need Hierarchy in an Organisational Setting. Organisational Behaviour and Human Performance, Vol.3, 12-35.

HALL, J. M. (1970) Industry Grows Where the Grass is Greener, Area, Vol.2, No.3, 40-5.

HALL, M. and WEISS, L. (1967) Firm Size and Profitability, Review of Economics and Statistics, Vol.49, 319-331.

HALL, P. (1962) The Industries of London since 1861. Hutchinson: London. p.192.

HALL, P. (1971) Spatial Structure of Metropolitan England and Wales, Chapter 4, pp.96-126 in CHISHOLM, M. D. I. and MANNERS, G. (eds.) op.cit.

HALL, P. (1974) The Containment of Urban England, Geographical Jo., Vol.140, 386-417.

HALL, P. (1975) Migration, New Society, 6 Feb..

HALL, P.: DREWETT, R.: GRACEY, H.: and THOMAS, R. (1973) Megalopolis Denied: The Containment of Urban England, 1945 - 1970. Allen and Unwin: London. 2 Vols.

HALL, W. K. (1973a) Strategic Planning Models: Are Top Managers Really Finding Them Useful. Jo. of Business Policy, Vol.3, No.2, 33-42.

HALL, W. K. (1973b) Strategic Planning, Product Innovation, and the Theory of the Firm. Jo. of Business Policy, Vol.3, No.3, 19-27.

HAMILTON, F. E. I. (1969) Regional Economic Analysis in Britain and the Commonwealth. A Bibliographic Guide. LSE and Weidenfeld and Nicolson: London. p.410.

HAMILTON, F. E. I. (ed. 1974) Spatial Perspectives on Industrial Organization and Decision-Making. Wiley: London. p.533.

HAMILTON, F. E. I. (ed. 1978) Contemporary Industrialization: Spatial Analysis and Regional Development. Longman: London. p.203.

HAMILTON, R. T. (1975) An Economic Study of the Structure and Performance of the U.K. Manufacturing Industry with particular emphasis on the Changing Shares of Small Business. Mimeo. Small Business Unit, London Graduate School of Business Studies. p.18.

HAMILTON, R. T. (1977a) Trends in the Small Business Sector. Small Business Unit, London Graduate School of Business Studies. p.7.

HAMILTON, R. T. (1977b) Personal Communication, 28 Sept..

HAMMOND, E. (1964) Improving the Machinery, Town and Country Planning, Vol.32, No.3, 138-41.

HARBURY, C. D. (1979) Inheritance and the Creation of Personal Fortunes in Britain. SSRC Final Report HR-2714. p.12.

HARDYCK, C. D. and PETRINOVICH, L. F. (1969) Introduction to Statistics for the Behavioural Science. W. B. Sauders Co.: Toronto.

HAREN, C. C. and HOLLING, R. W. (1979) Industrial Development in Nonmetropolitan America: A Locational Perspective, Chapter 2, pp.13-45 in LONSDALE, R. E. and SEYLER, H. L. (eds.) op.cit.

HARLOE, M. (1977) Introduction, pp.1-47 in HARLOE, M. (ed.) op.cit.
HARLOE, M. (ed. 1977) Captive Cities. Studies in the Political Economy
   of Cities and Regions. Wiley: Chichester. p.218.
HARRIS, B. (1978) Some Questions of Philosophy, Methodology and Explana-
   tion in Geography. Discussion Paper No.64. Graduate School of Geography,
   London School of Economics. p.16.
HART, P. E. and MacBEAN, A. I. (1961) Regional Differences in Productivity,
   Profitability and Growth: A Pilot Study, Scottish Jo. of Political
   Economy, Vol.8, No.1, 1-11.
HARVEY, B. (1979) The Management of Social Responsibility in British
   Industry. SSRC Final Report HR-5071. p.131.
HARVEY, D. (1967) Models of the Evolution of Spatial Patterns in Human
   Geography, Chapter 14, pp.549-608 in CHORLEY, R. I. and HAGGETT, P.
   (eds.) op.cit.
HARVEY, D. (1969) Explanation in Geography. Edward Arnold: London. p.521.
HAUSER, D. P. (1974) Some Problems in the Use of Stepwise Regression
   Techniques in Geographical Research, Canadian Geographer, Vol.18, No.2,
   148-58.
HEALEY, M. J. (1979) Plant Closures in Multi-Plant Enterprises. Paper
   presented at the Annual Conference of the IBG, University of Manchester.
   Jan.. p.12.
HEATON, T. and FUGUITT, G. (1979) Nonmetropolitan Growth and Net
   Migration, Chapter 8, pp.119-36 in LONSDALE, R. E. and SEYLER, H. L.
   (eds.) op.cit.
HECHTER, M. (1972) Industrialization and National Development in the
   British Isles, Jo. of Development Studies, Vol.8, No.3, 155-82.
HECHTER, M. (1975) Internal Colonialism: The Celtic Fringe in British
   National Development, 1536-1966. Routledge and Kegan Paul: London.
HENDERSON, R. A. (1974) Industrial Overspill from Glasgow, 1958 - 1968,
   Urban Studies, Vol.11, No.1, 61-79.
HENDERSON, R. A. (1979) An Analysis of Closure Amongst Scottish Manufac-
   turing Plants. Discussion Paper No.3. Economics and Statistics Unit,
   Scottish Economic Planning Department: Edinburgh. p.39.
HERBERT, D. (1972) Urban Geography: A Social Perspective. David and
   Charles: Newton Abbot. p.320.
HERBST, P. G. (1970) Behavioural Worlds. The Study of Single Cases.
   Tavistock Publications: London. p.248.
HERZBERG, F.: MAUSER, B. and SYNDERMAN, B. (1960) The Motivation to Work.
   Wiley: New York. p.157.
HILL, C. (1954) Some Aspects of Industrial Location, Jo. of Industrial
   Economics, Vol.2, 184-92.
HILL, R. (1976) Experience of Milton Keynes' C.O.N.E. (Creation of
   New Enterprises) Scheme, pp.65-80 in CLUBLEY, R. (ed.) op.cit.
HINDLEY, B. V. (1970) Separation of Ownership and Control in the Modern
   Corporation, Jo. of Law and Economics, Vol.13, 185-221.
HIRSCH, A. A. (1960a) Banking's Role in Southern Economic Expansion,
   Monthly Review, Federal Reserve Bank of Atlanta, July, 1-4.
HIRSCH, A. A. (1960b) Small Business Investment Companies, Monthly
   Review, Federal Reserve Bank of Atlanta, 4-6.
HIRST, N. (1977) Implications of Knowing Who Owns What, The Times,
   Thursday, 5 May, 27.
HOARE, A. G. (1972) International Airports and Economic Geography: A
   Study of the Impact of London Airport. Unpublished Ph.D. Dissertation,
   University of Cambridge. p.319
HOARE, A. G. (1975) Linkage Flows, Locational Evaluation and Industrial
   Geography: A Case Study of Greater London, Environment and Planning,
   A, Vol.7, No.1, 41-58.

HOARE, A. G. (1978) Industrial Linkages and the Dual Economy: The Case of Northern Ireland, Regional Studies, Vol.12, No.2, 167-80.

HODGINS, J. (1972) Academic Spin-Off and Canadian Entrepreneurship, The Business Quarterly, Vol.37, No.1, 64-70.

HOLL, P. (1975) Effect of Control Type on the Performance of the Firm in the U.K., Jo. of Industrial Economics, Vol.23, 257-71.

HOLL, P. (1977) Control Type and the Market for Corporate Control in Large U.S. Corporations, Jo. of Industrial Economics, Vol.25, 259-73.

HOLLAND, S. (1976a) Capital Versus the Regions. MacMillan: London. p.328.

HOLLAND, S. (1976b) The Regional Problem. Macmillan: London. p.179.

HOLLAND, W. E. (1972) Characteristics of Individuals with high Information Potential in Government Research and Development Organizations, IEEE Transactions on Engineering Management, Vol. EM-19, No.2, 38-44.

HOLLINGSWORTH, T. H. (1970) Migration: A Study Based on Scottish Experience between 1939 and 1964. Occ. Paper No.12, Dept. of Social and Economic Research, University of Glasgow. Oliver and Boyd: Edinburgh.

HOLMANS, A. E. (1965) Inter-Regional Differences in Levels of Income: Are There 'Two Nations' or One? In WILSON, T. (ed.) op.cit.

HOOD, N. and YOUNG, S. (1976) U.S. Investment in Scotland - Aspects of the Branch Factory Syndrome, Scottish Jo. of Political Economy, Vol.23. No.3, 279-94.

HOSELITZ, W. F. (1962) Review of The Achieving Society (by D. C. McCLELLAND, op.cit.) in The American Jo. of Sociology, Vol.68, 130.

HOTCHKISS, L. (1979) A Conceptual - Measurement Model for Career Expectations. Paper presented, Annual Meeting of the Midwest Sociological Society, Minneapolis. p.44.

HOUSE, J. W. (1969) Industrial Britain. The North East. David and Charles: Newton Abbot. p.256.

HOUSE, J. W.: RUDDY, S. A.: THUBRON, I. M. and STRORER, C. E. (1968) Mobility of the Northern Business Manager. Paper No.8 on Migration and Mobility in Northern England, Department of Geography, University of Newcastle upon Tyne.

HOWARD, R. S. (1968) Movement of Manufacturing Industry in the United Kingdom, 1945-1965. Board of Trade/Department of Industry. HMSO: London. p.54.

HOWICK, C. and KEY, T. (1979) Small Firms and the Inner City: Tower Hamlets. Paper presented at a CES Workshop Oct.. Centre for Environmental Studies: London. p.21.

HUDSON, R. (1978) Spatial Policy in Britain: Regional or Urban? A Comment, Area, Vol.10. No.2, 121-2.

HUDSON, R. (1979) Space, Place and Placelessness: Some Questions Concerning Methodology, Reviews of RELPH, E. (1976) Place and Placelessness. (Pion: London.) and TUAN, YiFu (1977) Space and Place: The Perspective of Experience. (Edward Arnold: London.) in Progress in Human Geography, Vol.3, No.1, 169-74.

HUDSON REPORT (1974) see STILLMAN, E. et al op.cit.

HUGHES, J. T. (1979) An Urban Approach to Regional Problems, Chapter 8 pp.173-189 in MacLENNAN, D. and PARR, J. B. (eds.) op.cit.

HUNTER, N. R. and WEBB, C. (1978) Index to Special Reports in UK Newspapers and Certain Periodicals, 1973-1977. Institute of Scientific Business: Hull, E. Yorkshire. p.55.

HUTCHINSON, P. J.: PIPER, J. A. and RAY, G. H. (1975a) The Financing of Rapid Growth Firms Upto Flotation, Accounting and Business Research, Spring, 145-51.

HUTCHINSON, P. J.: PIPER, J. A. and RAY, G. H. (1975b) The Financial Control of Rapid-Growth Firms Upto Flotation, Accounting and Business Research, Summer, 222-8.

HUTCHINSON, P. J. (1978) The Financing of Small Rapid-Growth Firms Upto Flotation. Paper presented at the Small Firms Research Conference, Business School, University of Durham. Nov.. p.18.

HUTCHINSON, R. G.: HUTCHINSON, A. R. and NEWCOMER, M. (1938) A Study of Business Mortality - Length of Life of Business Enterprises in Poughkeepsie, New York, 1843-1936, American Economic Review, Sept. 497-514.

HUTCHINSON, R. G.: HUTCHINSON, A. R. and NEWCOMER, M. (1939) Business Life and Death in a Hudson River Town, Dun's Review, June, 12-18.

HYMER, S. and PASHIGAN, P. (1962) Firm Size and Rate of Growth, Jo. of Political Economy, Vol.70, No.6, 556-69.

INDUSTRIAL RESEARCH INC. (1967) A Study of Science Based Companies in the Greater Philadelphia Area. Dept. of Commerce, Economic Development Administration, Washington, D.C.. May.

INGHAM, G. E. (1970) Size of Industrial Organization and Worker Behaviour Cambridge University Press: Cambridge. p.190.

INHABER, H. and PRZEDNOWEK, K. (1974) Distribution of Canadian Science, Geoforum, Vol.19, No.1, 45-54.

INSTITUTE OF PERSONNEL MANAGEMENT (1980) Executive Redundancy. I.P.M.: London. p.133.

IRONSIDE, R. G. (1977) Growth Centres, Entrepreneurship, and Social Engineering, Canadian Geographer, Vol.21, No.2, 175-82.

JACK, A. B. (1968) The Scottish Council Study of Migration within the United Kingdom - Some Comments, Regional Studies, Vol.2, No.1, 21-6.

JACKMAN, R. (ed. 1978) The Impact of Rates on Industry and Commerce. Policy Series No.5. Centre for Environmental Studies: London. p.59.

JAMES, B. G. (1973) The Theory of the Corporate Life Cycle, Long Range Planning, Vol.6, No.2, 68-74.

JAMES, B. G. S. (1964) The Incompatibility of Industrial and Trading Cultures, a Critical Approach of the Growth Point Concept, Jo. of Industrial Economics, Vol.13, 90-4.

JAMES, F. J. and HUGHES, J. T. (1973) The Process of Employment Location Change: An Empirical Analysis, Land Economics, Vol.49, 404-13.

JEWKES, J. (1977) Delusions of Dominance. A Critique of the Theory of Large-Scale Industrial Dominance and of the Pretence of Government to 'Restructure' British Industry. Hobart Paper No.76. Institute of Economic Affairs: London. p.62.

JEWKES, J.: SAWERS, D. and STILLERMAN, R. (1958) The Sources of Invention. MacMillan: London. p.428.

JOHNSON, J. H. (ed. 1974) Suburban Growth. Wiley: London.

JOHNSON, J. H.: SALT, J. and WOOD, P. A. (1974) Housing and the Migration of Labour. Saxon House: Farnborough.

JOHNSON, M. R.D. and TOWNSEND, A. R. (1976) The Field of Recruitment to New Manufacturing Establishments to the North East. Working Paper No.40. North East Area Study, University of Durham. p.70.

JOHNSON, P. S. (1978) New Firms and Regional Development: Some Issues and Evidence. Discussion Paper No.11. Centre for Urban and Regional Development Studies, University of Newcastle upon Tyne. p.15.

JOHNSON, P. S. and CATHCART, D. G. (1978) New Manufacturing Firms and Regional Development: Some Evidence from the Northern Region. Paper presented at the Small Firms Research Conference, Business School, University of Durham. Nov.. p.32.

JOHNSON, P. S. and CATHCART, D. G. (1979) The Founders of New Manufacturing Firms: A Note on the Size of Their 'Incubator' Plants, Jo. of Industrial Economics. Vol.28, No.2, 219-24.

JOHNSTON, R. J. (1978) Multivariate Statistical Analysis in Geography. Longman: London. p.308.

JOHNSTON, T. L.: BUXTON, N. K. and MAIR, D. (1971) Structure and Growth of the Scottish Economy. Collins: Glasgow and London. p.356.

JONES, T. T. (1974) Regional Multipliers and the Location of Industry. Unpublished Ph.D. Dissertation, University of Dundee. p.230.

JOYCE, F. (ed. 1977) Metropolitan Development and Change. The West Midlands: A Policy Review. University of Aston for the British Association: Birmingham.

de KADT, E. and WILLIAMS, G. (ed. 1974) Sociology and Development. Tavistock: London.

KALE, S. R. and LONSDALE, R. E. (1979) Factors Encouraging and Discouraging Plant Location in Nonmetropolitan Areas, Chapter 3, pp.47-56 in LONSDALE, R. E. and SEYLER, H. L. (eds.) op.cit.

KAMERSCHEN, D. R. (1968) The Influence of Ownership and Control on Profit Rates, American Economic Review, Vol.58, 432-47.

KAMERSCHEN, D. R. (1969) The Effect of Separation of Ownership and Control on the Performance of the Large firm in the U.S. Economy, Rivista Internazionale di Scienze Economiche e Commerciali, Vol.16, 489-93.

KAMERSCHEN, D. R. (1973) Further Thoughts on Separation of Ownership and Control, Rivista Internazionale di Scienze Economiche e Commerciali, Vol.20, 179-83.

KAMIEN, M. I. and SCHWARTZ, N. L. (1975) Market Structure and Innovation: A Survey, Jo. of Economic Literature, Vol.13, No.1, 1-37.

KANAPATHY, N. (1974) Developing Industrial Entrepreneurs, Jo. of the Malaysian Institute of Management, Vol.9, No.3, 44-60.

KANIA, J. J. and McKEAN, J. R. (1976) Ownership, Control, and the Contemporary Corporation: A General Behavioural Analysis, Kyklos, Vol.29, 272-91.

KAPLAN, A. D. H. (1948) Small Business - Its Place and Problems. McGraw-Hill: New York. p.281.

KATONA, G. (1962) Review of The Achieving Society (by D. C. McCLELLAND op.cit.) in American Economic Review, Vol.52, 582-3.

KEEBLE, D. E. (1968) Industrial Decentralization and the Metropolis: The North West London Case, Transactions and Papers, Institute of British Geographers, Vol.44, 1-54.

KEEBLE, D. E. (1971) Employment Mobility in Britain, Chapter 2, pp.24-69 in CHISHOLM, M. D. I. and MANNERS, G. (eds.) op.cit.

KEEBLE, D. E. (1972a) The South East and East Anglia. I. The Metropolitan Region, Chapter 2, pp.71-105 in MANNERS, G. (ed.) op.cit.

KEEBLE, D. E. (1972b) The South East and East Anglia. II. The Zonal Structure, Chapter 3, pp.107-52 in MANNERS, G. (ed.) op.cit.

KEEBLE, D. E. (1972c) Industrial Movement and Regional development in the United Kingdom, Town Planning Review, Vol.43, 3-25.

KEEBLE, D. E. (1976) Industrial Location and Planning in the United Kingdom. Methuen: London. p.317.

KEEBLE, D. E. (1977a) Spatial Policy in Britain: Regional or Urban? Area, Vol.9, No.1, 3-8.

KEEBLE, D. E. (1977b) Industrial Geography, Progress in Human Geography, Vol.1, No.2, 304-12.

KEEBLE, D. E. (1978a) Spatial Policy in Britain: Regional or Urban? A Comment - A Reply, Area, Vol.10, No.2, 123-5.

KEEBLE, D. E. (1978b) Industrial Geography, Progress in Human Geography, Vol.2, No.2, 318-23.

KEEBLE, D. E. (1978c) Industrial Decline in the Inner City and Conurbations, Transactions and Papers, Institute of British Geographers, New Series, Vol.3, No.1, 101-14.

KEEBLE, D. E. and HAUSER, D. P. (1971) Spatial Analysis of Manufacturing Growth in Outer South East England, 1960-1967. I Hypotheses and Variables, Regional Studies, Vol.5, 229-262.

KEEBLE, D. E. and HAUSER, D. P. (1972) Spatial Analysis of Manufacturing Growth in Outer South East England, 1960-1967. II. Methods and Results, Regional Studies, Vol.6, No.1, 11-36.

KEMPTHORNE, O.: BANCROFT, T. A.: GOWEN, J. W. and LUSH, J. L. (eds. 1954) Statistics and Mathematics in Biology. Hafner: New York. p.632.

KERR, D. P. (1965) Some Aspects of the Geography of Finance in Canada, Canadian Geographer, Vol.9, No.4, 175-92.

KERR, D. P. and SPELT, J. (1957) Manufacturing in Downtown Toronto, Geographical Bulletin, Vol.10, No.1, 5-20.

KERR, D. P. and SPELT, J. (1958) Manufacturing in Suburban Toronto, Canadian Geographer, Vol.12, No.1, 11-9.

KERR, C. (1964) The Balkanization of Labor Markets in BAKKE, E. W. (ed.) op.cit.

KILBY, P. (ed. 1971) Entrepreneurship and Economic Development. Free Press: New York/Collier-MacMillan: London. p.384.

KIM, J. and KOHOUT, F. J. (1975) Multiple Regression Analysis: Subprogram Regression, Chapter 20, pp.320-67 in NIE, N. H. et al op.cit.

KING, L. J. (1961) A Multivariate Analysis of the Spacing of Urban Settlements in the United States, Annals, American Association of Geographers, Vol.51, 222-33.

KING, P. E. (1975) Mobility of Manufacturing and the Interstate Redistribution of Employment, Professional Geographers, Vol.27, 441-48.

KINNARD, W. N. jr. and MALINOWSKI, Z. S. (1959) The Turnover and Mortality of Manufacturing Firms in the Hertford Connecticut Economic Area, 1953-58. University of Connecticut: Storrs, Connecticut. p.65.

KIRTON, M. J. (1980) Adoptors and Innovators in Organizations, Human Relations, Vol.33, No.4, 213-24.

KITAGAWA, E. M. and BOGUE, D. J. (1955) Suburbanisation of Manufacturing within Standard Metropolitan Areas. Scripps Foundation Studies in Population Distribution. No.9. Oxford, Ohio.

KNIGHT, E. M. (1968) Men Leaving Mining. Paper No.8 on Migration and Mobility in Northern England. Dept. of Geography, University of Newcastle upon Tyne.

KOCH, S. W. (1965) Management and Motivation. Summary of a Doctoral Thesis presented at the Swedish School of Economics, Helsingfors, Finland.

KOESTLER, A. (1959) The Sleepwalkers. A History of Man's Changing Vision of the Universe. Penguin: Harmondsworth, Middlesex. p.623.

KOMIVES, J. L. (1972) Characteristics of Entrepreneurs (with emphasis on the Organisational Entrepreneur), The Business Quarterly, Vol.37, No.2, 76-9.

KRUIJT, B. (1979) The Changing Spatial Pattern of Firms in Amsterdam: Empirical Evidence, Tijdschrift voor Econ. en Soc. Geografie, Vol.70, No.3, 144-56.

KUEHN, J. A. (1979) Nonmetropolitan Industrialization and Migration: An Overview with Special emphasis on the Ozarks Region, Chapter 9, pp.137-48 in LONSDALE, R. E. and SEYLER, H. L. (eds.) op.cit.

KUHN, T. S. (1970) The Structure of Scientific Revolutions. University of Chicago: Chicago. 2nd. Edition. p.210.

KYNASTON REEVES, J. (1967) Constrained and Facilitated Behaviour: A Typology of Behaviour in Economic Organisations. British Jo. of Industrial Relations, Vol.5, No.2, 145-61.

LAIDLAW, J. (1977) personal communication.

LAMONT, D. W. (1979) Moves in Glasgow Census Data and the Study of Intra-Urban Migration: The Pattern of Population in Greater Glasgow 1970/71, BURISA, Vol.37, No.1, 12-4.

LAMONT, L. M. (1972a) Entrepreneurship, Technology, and the University, R. and D. Management, Vol.2, No.3, 119-23.

LAMONT, L. M. (1972b) The Marketing Dimension of Technical Entrepreneurship, The Business Quarterly, Vol.37, No.2, 70-5.

LASSWELL, H. D. (1968) The Future of the Comparative Method, Comparative
Politics, Vol.1, 3-18.

LEA, K. J. (with contributions from GORDON, G. and BOWLER, I. R.) (1977)
A Geography of Scotland. David and Charles: Newton Abbot. p.261.

LEACH, E. R. (1968) The Comparative Method in Anthropology, p.339-45
in SILLS, D. L. (ed.) op.cit.

LEBAS, E. (1977) Regional Policy Research: Some Theoretical and
Methodological Problems, Chapter 3, pp.79-88 in HARLOE, M. (ed.) op.cit.

LEIBENSTEIN, H. (1968) Entrepreneurship and Development, American
Economic Review, Vol.58, No.2, 72-83.

LEIBENSTEIN, H. (1978) General X-Efficiency Theory and Economic Development. Oxford University Press: New York p.189.

LEIGH, R. and NORTH, D. (1977) The Potential of the Micro-Behavioural
Approach to Regional Analysis. Mimeo to be included in the London
Papers in Regional Science Vol.9, p.33.

LEIGH, R. and NORTH, D. (1978a) Regional Aspects of Aquisition Activity
in British Manufacturing Industry, Regional Studies, Vol.12, No.2, 227-45.

LEIGH, R. and NORTH, D. (1978b) Aquisitions in British Industries:
Implications for Regional Development, Chapter 13, pp.158-81 in
HAMILTON, F. E. I. (ed.) op.cit.

LEIGH, R. and NORTH, D. (1980) The Potential for Local Enterprise: A
Study of the Furniture Industry in London. Paper presented at the
Annual Conference of the IBG, University of Lancaster. Jan.. p.36.

LEONE, R. A. (1971) Location of Manufacturing Activity in the New York
Metropolitan Area. Unpublished Ph.D. Dissertation, University of Yale.

LEONE, R. A. and STRUYK, R. (1976) The Incubator Hypothesis: Evidence from
Five S.M.S.A.s, Urban Studies, Vol.13, No.3, 325-32.

LESER, C. E. V. (1954) Manufacturing Industry, Chapter 9, pp.118-32 in
CAIRNCROSS, A. K. (ed.)op.cit.

LESER, C. E. V. and SILVEY, A. H. (1950) Scottish Industries during the
Inter-War Period, Manchester School of Economic and Social Studies,
Vol.18, 163-74.

LEVER, W. F. (1974a) Regional Multipliers and Demand Linkages at
Establishment Level, Scottish Jo. of Political Economy, Vol.21, No.2,
111-22.

LEVER, W. F. (1974b) Manufacturing Linkages and the Search for Suppliers
and Markets, Chapter 12, pp.309-33 in HAMILTON, F. E. I. (ed.) op.cit.

LEVER, W. F. (1978) Company-Dominated Labour Markets: The British Case,
Tijdschrift voor Econ. en Soc. Geografie, Vol.69, No.5, 306-12.

LEVESON, J. H. (1979) Industrial Organisation of the Jute Manufacturing
Industry. SSRC Final Report HR-323.

LEVITT, T. (1965) Exploit the Product Life Cycle, Harvard Business Review,
Vol.43, No.6, 81-94.

LICHTHEIM, G. (1964) Marxism. An Historical Critical Study. Routledge
and Keagan Paul: London. 2nd Edition. p.412.

LIGGINS, D. (1977) The Changing Role of the West Midlands Region in the
National Economy in JOYCE, F. (ed.) op.cit.

LILES, P. R. (1974) Who are the Entrepreneurs? Business Topics, Winter,
5-14.

LINZ, J. J. and de MIGUEL, A. (1966) Within-Nation Differences and
Comparisons: The Eight Spains, Chapter 13, pp.267-319 in MERRIT, R. L.
and ROKKAN, S. (eds.) op.cit.

LITTLE A. D. Ltd. (1973) Barriers to Innovation: Opportunities for Public
Policy Change. Sept.

LITTLE, A. D. Ltd. (1977) New Technology Based Firms in the U.K. and the
Federal Republic of Germany. Wilton House: London.

LITVAK, I. A. and MAULE, C. J. (1972a) Branch Plant Entrepreneurship,
The Business Quarterly, Vol.37, No.1, 44-53.
LITVAK, I. A. and MAULE, C. J. (1972b) Managing the Entrepreneurial
Enterprise, The Business Quarterly, Vol.37, No.2, 42-50.
LIVESEY, F. (1970) The Composition of Employment in Branch Factories,
Oxford Economic Papers, Vol.22, 420-36.
LLOYD, P. E. (1965) Industrial Change in the Merseyside Development Area,
1949-1959, Town Planning Review, Vol.35, 285-98.
LLOYD, P. E. and DICKEN, P. (1968) The Data Bank in Regional Studies of
Industry, Town Planning Review, Vol.38, No.4, 304-16.
LLOYD, P. E. and MASON, C. M. (1976a) Manufacturing Industry in the Inner
City: A Case Study of Greater Manchester. Mimeo. School of Geography,
University of Manchester. p.33.
LLOYD, P. E. and MASON, C. M. (1976b) Establishment-Based Data for the
Study of Intra-Urban and Sub-Regional Change: The Manchester Industrial
Data Bank in SWALES, J. K. (ed.) op.cit.
LLOYD, P. E. and MASON, C. M. (1978) Manufacturing Industry in the Inner
City: A Case Study of Greater Manchester, Transactions and Papers,
Institute of British Geographers, New Series, Vol.3, No.1, 66-90.
LOASBY, B. J. (1961) The Experience of West Midland Industrial Dispersal
Projects: A Regional Plan for Industrial Dispersal and Overspill. Town
and Country Planning, Vol.29, No.8, 309-13.
LOGAN, M. I. (1966) Locational Behaviour of Manufacturing Firms in Urban
Areas, Annals, American Association of Geographers, Vol.54, 451-66.
LOGIE, G. (1952) Industry in Towns. Allen and Unwin: London.
LOMAS, G. M. and WOOD, P. A. (1970) Employment Location in Regional
Planning. A Case Study of the West Midlands. Frank Cass and Co. Ltd.:
London.
LONSDALE, R. E. and SEYLER, H. L. (eds.1979) Nonmetropolitan Industrali-
zation. V. H. Winston and Sons: Washington. p.196.
LUND, P. J. and GLEED, R. H. (1979) The Development Areas Share of
Manufacturing Industry Investment 1966-69, Regional Studies, Vol.13, No.1.
61-72.
McARTHUR, P. and WEBB, T. D. (1977) Disclosure of Information, Jo. of the
Institute of Printing, Vol.21, No.1, 5-8.
McCALL, J. J. (1970) Economics of Information and Job Search, Quarterly
Jo. of Economics, Vol.84, 113-26.
McCALLUM, P. (1959) The Small Business Investment Act of 1958 - Its
First Year of Operation, Virginia Law Review, Vol.45, 1039-52.
McCLELLAND, D. C. (1961) The Achieving Society. Van Nostrand: Princetown,
New Jersey.
McCLELLAND, D. C. (1969) N Achievement and Entrepreneurship: A
Longitudinal Study, Jo. of Personality and Social Psychology, Vol.1,
389-92.
MacLEOD, K. and WATKIN, E. (1969) Regional Earnings and Regional Develop-
ment. CES-UWP-1. Centre for Environmental Studies: London. p.115.
McCRONE, G. (1965) Scotland's Economic Progress 1951-1960: A Study in
Regional Accounting. Social and Economic Studies, New Series, No.4.
University of Glasgow. George Allen and Unwin: London. p.180.
McDERMOTT, P. J. (1973) Spatial Margins and Industrial Location in New
Zealand, New Zealand Geographer, Vol.29, No.1, 64-74.
McDERMOTT, P. J. (1976) Ownership, Organisation and Regional Dependence
in the Scottish Electronics Industry, Regional Studies, Vol.10, No.3,
319-35.
McDERMOTT, P. J. (1977b) Multinational Manufacturing Firms and Regional
Development: External Control in the Scottish Electronics Industry.
Unpublished Manuscript. p.30.

McDERMOTT, P. J. (1977a) Regional Variations in Enterprise: Electronics Firms in Scotland, London and the Outer Metropolitan Area. Unpublished Ph.D. Dissertation, University of Cambridge. p.400.

McDERMOTT, P. J. and KEEBLE, D. E. (1978) Manufacturing Organization and Regional Employment Change, Regional Studies, Vol.12, No.2, 247-66.

McDONALD, G. (1975) Social and Geographical Mobility in the Scottish New Towns, Scottish Geographical Magazine, Vol.91, No.1, 38-51.

McGOVERN, P. D. (1965) Industrial Dispersal, Planning, P.E.P., Vol.31, No.485, 3-39.

MACKAY, D. I. (1977) 1980 and Afterward, pp.3-18 in MACKAY, D. I. (ed.) op.cit.

MACKAY, D. I. (ed. 1977) Scotland 1980. The Economic of Self Government. Q Press: Edinburgh. p.211.

MACKAY, D. I. (1979) Swan Hunter: Redundancy and Displacement Study. Paper presented, Seminar on Redundancy Studies and Implications for Manpower Policy, MSC Scotland, Edinburgh. p.3.

MACKAY, D. I.: BODDY, D.: BRACK, J.: DIACK, J. A. and JONES, N. (1971) Labour Markets Under Different Employment Conditions. University of Glasgow, Social and Economic Studies No.22, Allen and Unwin: London. p.433.

MACKAY, D. I. and MACKAY, G. A. (1975) The Political Economy of North Sea Oil. Martin Robertson: London.

MACKAY, R. R. (1973) The Impact of R.E.P.. Occ. Paper No.9. Dept. of Economics, University of Newcastle upon Tyne. p.33.

MACKAY, R. R. (1974) Evaluating the Effects of British Regional Economic Policy - A Comment, Economic Jo., Vol.84, No.2, 367-72.

MACKAY, R. R. (1978) The Death of Regional Policy - or Resurrection Squared. Discussion Paper No.10. Centre for Urban and Regional Development Studies, University of Newcastle upon Tyne. p.44.

MacLENNAN, D. and PARR, J. B. (1979) Introduction, pp. xv-xviii in MacLENNAN, D. and PARR, J. B. (eds.) op.cit.

MacLENNAN, D. and PARR, J. B. (eds. 1979) Regional Policy - Past Experience and New Directions. Martin Robertson: London. p.334.

McLEOD, I. H. (1972) Can Canadians be Successful Entrepreneurs? The Business Quarterly, Vol.37, No.1, 29-36.

MacMILLAN REPORT (1931) Report of the Committee on Finance and Industry. Cmnd. 3897. HMSO: London.

McNEIL, J. (1973a) The Fife Coal Industry, 1947-1967: A Study of Changing Trends and Their Implications, Part I, Scottish Geographical Magazine, Vol.89, No.2, 81-94.

McNEIL, J. (1973b) The Fife Coal Industry, 1947-1967: A Study of Changing Trends and their Implications, Part II, Scottish Geographical Magazine, Vol.89, No.3, 163-79.

McNEIL, J. (1974) Factors in Industrial Location: The Fife Case 1958-71, Scottish Geographical Magazine, Vol.90, No.3, 187-97.

McROBBIE, G. (1963) A Development Plan for Scotland, Planning, P.E.P. Vol.29, No.476, 401-32

McVEAN, P. (1979a) A Study of Major Redundancies. Redundancy and Displacement Research Paper No.2, PEIDA. p.14.

McVEAN, P. (1979b) The Effect of Redundancies on Unemployment: Data Base of Empirical Analysis. Redundancy and Displacement Research Paper No.3. PEIDA. p.6.

MACHLUP, F. (1967) Theories of the Firm: Marginalist, Behavioural and Managerial, American Economic Review, Vol.57, No.1, 1-33.

MAHAR, J. F. and CODDINGTON, D. C. (1962) The Financial Gap - Real or Imaginery? A Report prepared for the Small Business Administration by the Denver Research Institute: Denver.

310

MAHAR, J. F. and CODDINGTON, D. C. (1965a) Academic Spin-Offs, Industrial Research, April, 62-71.

MAHAR, J. F. and CODDINGTON, D. C. (1965b) The Scientific Complex - Proceed with Caution, Harvard Business Review, Vol.43, No.1, 140-155.

MANNERS, G. (1963) Service Industries and Regional Economic Growth, Town Planning Review, Vol.33, 292-303.

MANNERS, G. (1968) Misplacing the Smelters, New Society, 16 May, 712-3.

MANNERS, G. (1972a) National Perspectives, Chapter 1, pp.1-71 in MANNERS, G. (ed.) op.cit.

MANNERS, G. (ed. 1972b) Regional Development in Britain. Wiley: London. p.448.

MANPOWER RESEARCH BRANCH (MSC, Scotland) (1979a) Recent Redundancy Studies - Implications for Manpower Policy. Paper presented, Seminar on Redundancy Studies and Implications for Manpower Policy, MSC Scotland, Edinburgh. p.8.

MANPOWER RESEARCH BRANCH (MSC, Scotland) (1979b) RDL (North Sea) Case Study. Paper presented, Seminar on Redundancy Studies and Implications for Manpower Policy, MSC Scotland, Edinburgh.

MANSFIELD, E. (1962) Entry, Gibrat's Law, Innovation and the Growth of Firms, American Economic Review, Vol.52, 1023-51.

MAPES, G. (1967) More Professors put Campus Lab Theories to Work in own Firms, Wall Street Jo., 13 March, 1 and 22.

MARCH, J. G. and SIMON, H. A. (1959) Organisations. Wiley: New York.

MARCUM, R. E. and BOSHELL, E. O. (1963) Financing the Small and Medium-Sized Business - Where's the Money Coming From? Management Review, Jan., 4-11.

MARQUAND, J. (1980) Measuring the Effects and Costs of Regional Incentives. Government Economic Service Working Paper No.32. Dept. of Industry: London. p.118.

MARTIN, R. L. and OEPPEN, J. (1975) The Indentification of Regional Forecasting Models Using Space-Time Correlation Functions, Transactions and Papers, Institute of British Geographers, Vol.66, 95-118.

MARX, K. (1867) Das Kapital: Kritik Der Politischen Oekonomie. Vol.I.: Der Produktions Prozess Des Kapitals. Meissner: Hamburg. (Capital: A Critique of Political Economy. Vol.1: The Process of Capitalist Production. Charles H. Kerr and Co.: Chicago, 1906.).

MASLOW, A. H. (1970) Motivation and Personality. Harper and Row: New York.

MASS, N. J. (1978) Managerial Recruitment and Attrition: A Policy Analysis Model, Behavioural Sciences, Vol.23, No.1, 49-60.

MASSEY, D. B. (1973) Towards a Critique of Industrial Location Theory, Antipode, Vol.5, No.3, 33-9.

MASSEY, D. B. (1974) Social Justice and the City: A Review, Environment and Planning, A, Vol.6, No.2, 229-35.

MASSEY, D. B. (1975a) Approaches to Industrial Location Theory: A Positive Spatial Framework, pp.84-108 in CRIPPS, E. L. (ed.) op.cit.

MASSEY, D. B. (1975b) Behavioural Research - A Comment, Area, Vol.7, No.3, 201-3.

MASSEY, D. B. (1976) Is the Behavioural Approach Really An Alternative? pp.80-6 in MASSEY, D. B. and MORRISON, W. I. (eds.) op.cit.

MASSEY, D. B. (1977a) A Structuralist Approach to Industrial Location. Paper presented to the Annual Conference of the IBG, University of Newcastle upon Tyne. Jan.. p.12.

MASSEY, D. B. (1977b) Industrial Location Theory Reconsidered. Open University D204 Section III, Unit 25. p.33.

MASSEY, D. B. (1978a) In What Sense a Regional Problem? Paper presented to the RSA Conference, 'The Death of Regional Policy', Glasgow. Jan.. p.20.

MASSEY, D. B. (1978b) Regionalism: Some Current Issues, Capital and Class, Vol.6, Autumn, 106-25.

MASSEY, D. B. (1980) Industrial Location in Context: A Proposal. Presented at the Spring Meeting, May, of the Institute of British Geographers' Study Group on 'Industrial Activity and Area Development'. p.44.

MASSEY, D. B.: MINNS, R.: MORRISON, W. I. and WHITBREAD, M. (1976) A Strategy for Urban and Regional Research, Regional Studies, Vol.10, No.4. 381-7.

MASSEY, D. B. and MORRISON, W. I. (eds. 1976) Industrial Location: Alternative Frameworks. CES-CP15. Proceedings of a workshop held at CES, Dec., 1974. Centre for Environmental Studies: London.

MASSEY, D. B. and BATEY, P. W. (eds. 1977) Alternative Frameworks for Analysis. London Papers in Regional Science Vol.7. Pion: London. p.167.

MASSEY, D. B. and MEEGAN, R. A. (1977) Industrial Restructuring Versus the Cities. CES-WN-473. Centre for Environmental Studies: London. p.53.

MASSEY, D. B. and MEEGAN, R. A. (1979a) Labour Productivity and Regional Employment Change, Area, Vol.11., No.2, 137-45.

MASSEY, D. B. and MEEGAN, R. A. (1979b) The Geography of Industrial Reorganisation. The Spatial Effects of the Restructuring of the Electrical Engineering Industry under the Industrial Reorganisation Corporation, Progress in Planning, Vol.10, No.3, 155-237.

MAYER, K. B. and GOLDSTEIN, S. (1961) The First Two Years: Problems of Small Firm Growth and Survival. Small Business Administration: Washington, D.C. p.233.

MAYHEW, K. (1976a) Regional variations of Manual Earnings in Engineering, Oxford Bulletin of Economics and Statistics, Vol.38, No.1, 11-25.

MAYHEW, K. (1976b) Plant Size and the Earnings of Manual Workers in Engineering, Oxford Bulletin of Economics and Statistics, Vol.38, No.3, 149-60.

MEDAWAR, P. B. (1969) Induction and Intuition in Scientific Thought. Methuen: London. p.62.

MEEKS, G. (1977) Disappointing Marriage: A Study of the Gains from Merger. Occ. Paper No.51. Dept. of Applied Economics, University of Cambridge. Cambridge University Press: Cambridge. p.109.

MELROSE-WOODMAN, J. (1978) Profile of the British Manager. Management Survey Report No.38. B.I.M.: London. p.70.

MERRITT, R. L. and ROKKAN, S. (eds. 1966) Comparing Nations. The Use of Quantitative Data in Cross-National Research. Yale University Press: New Haven.

MIERNYK, W. H. (1955) Inter-Industry Labor Mobility: The Case of the Displaced Textile Worker. North Eastern University Press: Boston.

MODIGLIANI, F. (1958) New Developments on the Oligopoly Front, Jo. of Political Economy, Vol.66, 215-32.

MOORE, B. and RHODES, J. (1973) Evaluating the Effects of British Regional Policy, Economic Jo., Vol.83, 87-110.

MOORE, B. and RHODES, J. (1974) Regional Policy and the Scottish Economy, Scottish Jo. of Political Economy, Vol.21, No.3, 215-35.

MOORE, B. and RHODES, J. (1976) Regional Economic Policy and the Movement of Manufacturing Firms to Development Areas, Economica, Vol.43. No.1, 17-31.

MOORE, B.: RHODES, J. and TYLER, P. (1977) The Impact of Regional Policy in the 1970s, CES Review, Vol.1, 67-77.

MORGAN, W. (1962) The Geographical Concentration of Big Business in Great Britain, Town and Country Planning, Vol.30, 122-4.

MOSELEY, M. J. and TOWNROE, P. M. (1973) Linkage Adjustment Following Industrial Movement, Tijdschrift voor Econ. en Soc. Geografie, Vol.64, No.3, 137-144.

MOSES, L. and WILLIAMSON, H. F. (1967) The Location of Economic Activity in Cities, American Economic Review, Vol.57, No.2, 211-22.

MOSSON, T. M. and CLARK, D. G. (1968) Some Inter-Industry Comparisons of the Backgrounds and Careers of Managers, British Jo. of Industrial Relations, Vol.6, 220-31.

MURRAY, G. T. (1973) Scotland. The New Future: STV/Blackie: Glasgow: p.257.

NAGPAUL, P. S. and VASUDEVA, T. R. (1972) Allocation of Funds to R. and D. Laboratories by a Central Agency, IEEE Transactions on Engineering Management, Vol. EM-19, No.4, 133-7.

NAROLL, R. (1968) Some Thoughts on the Comparative Method in Cultural Anthropology, pp.236-77 in BLALOCK, H. M. jr. and BLALOCK, A. B. (eds.) op.cit.

NASON, R, (1963) Venture Capital: Money in a Hurry, Dun's Review and Modern Industry, Vol.82, No.5, 34-5 and 88-9.

NELSON, R. R.: PECK, M. J. and KALACHEK, E. D. (1967) Technology, Economic Growth, and Public Policy. The Brookings Institution: Washington D.C.. p.238.

NEVIN, E. (1966) The Case for Regional Policy, Three Banks Review, Vol.72, 30-46.

NEWSWEEK (1949) Venture: Yankee Spur to Enterprise, Newsweek, April 4, 23-4.

NIE, N. H.: HULL, C. H.: JENKINS, J. G.: STEINBRENNER, K. and BENT, D. H. (1975) SPSS Statistical Packages for the Social Sciences. 2nd Edition. McGraw-Hill: New York. p.675.

NORCLIFFE, G. B. (1966a) A Theoretical Approach to the Problems of Depressed Regions. Seminar Paper presented to the Dept. of Geography, University of Toronto. Jan.. p.19.

NORCLIFFE, G. B. (1966b) The Influences of Isolation on the Economy of Prince Edward Island. Unpublished M.A. Dissertation, University of Toronto.

NORCLIFFE, G. B. (1970) Industrial Location Dynamics: A Positive Theory, Measurement, and a Case Study of Changing Patterns of Manufacturing Plant Location. Unpublished Ph.D. Dissertation, University of Bristol.

NORCLIFFE, G. B. (1975) A Theory of Manufacturing Places, Chapter 1, pp.19-59 in COLLINS, L. and WALKER, D. F. (eds.) op.cit.

NORCLIFFE, G. B. (1977) Inferential Statistics for Geographers. An Introduction. Hutchinson University Library: London. p.272.

NORMAN, P. (1978) Flanders Believes Small is Beautiful by Supporting Individual Talents, The Times, 12 June, 18.

NORTH, D. (1974) The Process of Locational Change in Different Manufacturing Organizations, Chapter 8, pp.213-44 in HAMILTON, F. E. I. (ed.) op.cit.

NORTHCOTT, J. (1977) Industry in the Development Areas: The Experience of Firms Opening New Factories. Vol.43, Broadsheet 573, P.E.P.: London. p.121.

NORTHERN REGION STRATEGY TEAM (1975) Movement of Manufacturing Industry: The Northern Region 1961-1973. Tech. Report No.10. NRST: Newcastle. p.61.

OAKEY, R. P. (1979a) The Effect of Technical Contacts with Local Research Establishments on the Location of the British Instruments Industry, Area, Vol.11, No.2, 146-50.

OAKEY, R. P. (1979b) An Analysis of the Spatial Distribution of Significant British Industrial Innovations. Discussion Paper No.25. Centre for Urban and Regional Development Studies, University of Newcastle upon Tyne. p.42.

OAKLEY, C. A. (1949) A First Buyer's Guide to Scottish Industries. Who's Who and Where of 3500 Manufacturing Firms. Prepared for the Scottish Council (Development and Industry). Oliver and Boyd: Edinburgh. p.209.

313

OLSSON, G. (1969) Inference Problems in Locational Analysis, pp.14-34 in
COX, K. and GOLLEDGE, R. (eds.) op.cit.

OPENSHAW, S. (1976) An Empirical Study of Some Spatial Interaction Models,
Environment and Planning, A, Vol.8, No.1, 23-41.

OPENSHAW, S. (1977) A Geographical Solution to Scale and Aggregation
Problems in Region-Building, Partitioning and Spatial Modelling,
Transactions and Papers, Institute of the British Geographers, New
Series, Vol.2, No.4, 459-72.

ORGANIZATION for ECONOMIC CO-OPERATION and DEVELOPMENT (1971) Conditions
for Success in Technological Innovations. Prepared by PAVITT, K. L. R.
and WALD, S. of the University of Sussex. OECD: Paris.

OXENFELDT, A. R. (1943) New Firms and Free Enterprise. Pre-War and
Post-War Aspects. American Council on Public Affairs: Washington, D.C..
p.196.

PAHL, R. E. (1970) Whose City? Longman: London.

PAHL, J. M. and PAHL, R. E. (1971) Managers and Their Wives. Allen Lane:
London. p.325.

PALMER, J. P. (1972) The Extent of the separation of Ownership from Control
in Large U.S. Industrial Corporations, Quarterly Review of Economics and
Business, Vol.12, 55-62.

PALMER, J. P. (1973) The Profit-Performance Effects of the Separation of
Ownership from Control in Large U.S. Industrial Corporations, Bell Jo.
of Economics and Management Science, Vol.4, 293-303.

PALMER, J. P. (1974) Interaction Effects and the Separation of Ownership
from Control, Rivista Internazionale di Scienze Economiche e Commerciali,
Vol.21, 146-49.

PAQUET, G. (1972) French-Canadian Entrepreneurship: Quebec must Design
its Own Brand, The Business Quarterly, Vol.37, No.2, 36-41.

PARSONS, G. F. (1972a) Spatial Productivity Differentials in British
Manufacturing Industry. Unpublished Ph.D. Dissertation, University
College London, University of London. p.369.

PARSONS, G. F. (1972b) The Giant Manufacturing Corporations and Balanced
Regional Growth in Britain, Area, Vol.4, No.2, 99-103.

PASHIGAN, B. P. (1968) Market Concentration in the United States and
Great Britain, Jo. of Law and Economics. Vol.11, 299-319.

PATTISON, D. (1979) ACE Tape Information and Statistics on the Self-
Employed, letter to the editor, BURISA, Vol.37, No.1, 11-2.

PAYNE, G. (1977) Occupational Transition in Advanced Industrial Societies
Sociological Review, Vol.25, No.1, 5-39.

PAYNE, G.: FORD, G.: and ROBERTSON, C. (1976) Changes in Occupational
Mobility in Scotland. Some preliminary findings of the 1975 Scottish
Mobility Study, Scottish Jo. of Sociology, Vol.1, No.1, 57-79.

PAYNE, P. L. (1974) British Entrepreneurship in the Nineteenth Century.
Macmillan: London. p.80.

PEARSON, R. and GREENWOOD, J. (1977) Redundancies and Displacement: A
Study of the Maidstone Labour Market. GN104 Institute of Manpower
Studies: Sussex. p.82.

PEARSON, R. and GREENWOOD, J. (1978) The Impact of Redundancies on a
Local Labour Market, Dept. of Employment Gazette, Vol.86, No.4, 407-8.

PEDERSON, L. and TABB, W.K. (1976) Ownership and Control of Large
Corporations Revisted, Antitrust Bulletin, Vol.21, 53-66.

PETERS, D. H. and ROBERTS, E. B. (1969) Unutilised Ideas in University
Laboratories, Academy of Management Jo., Vol.12, No.2, 179-91.

PHILLIPS, A. D. M. and TURTON, B. J. (eds. 1975) Environment, Man and
Economic Change. Longman: London. p.501.

PIGGOTT, C. A. (1978) A Geography of Religion in Scotland. Ph.D.
Dissertation, University of Edinburgh.

POCOCK, D. C. D. (1970) Economic Renewal: The Example of Fife, Scottish Geographical Magazine, Vol.86, No.3, 123-33.

POLLARD, S. (1975) Review of The Development of the West of Scotland, 1750-1960 (by SLAVEN, A., 1975, op.cit.) in Regional Studies, Vol.9, No.4, 427.

POOLE, M. A. and O'FARRELL, P. N. (1971) The Assumptions of the Linear Regression Model, Transactions and Papers, Institute of British Geographers, Vol.52, 145-58.

PRAIS, S. J. (1976) The Evolution of Giant Firms in Britain. A Study of the Growth of Concentration in Manufacturing Industry in Britain 1909-1970. Cambridge University Press: Cambridge. p.321.

PRATTEN, C. F. (1971) Economics of Scale in Manufacturing Industry. Cambridge University Press: Cambridge.

PRED, A. (1976) The Interurban Transmission of Growth in Advanced Economies: Empirical Findings versus Regional-Planning Assumptions, Regional Studies, Vol.10, No.2, 151-71.

PRED, A. (1977) City-Systems in Advanced Economies. Past Growth, Present Processes and Future Development Options. Hutchinson University Library: London. p.256.

QUANTE, W. (1976) The Exodus of Corporate Headquarters from New York City. Praeger: New York. p.209.

RABEY, G. F. (1977) Contraction Poles: An Exploratory Study of Traditional Industry Decline within a Regional Industrial Complex. Discussion Paper No.3. Centre for Urban and Regional Development Studies, University of Newcastle upon Tyne. p.23.

RADCLIFFE REPORT (1959) Report of the Committee on the Working of the Monetary System. Cmnd. 827. HMSO: London.

RAKE, D. J. (1972) The Economic Geography of the Multilocational Industrial Firm with Special Reference to the East Midlands. Unpublished Ph.D. Dissertation, University of Nottingham. p.975.

RANDALL, J. N. (1979a) Report of an RSA Conference, 'Housing Tenure and Labour Mobility', University of Edinburgh. Dec.. RSA Newsletter, No.100, May/June, 24.

RANDALL, J. N. (1979b) The Changing Nature of the Regional Economic Problem since 1965, Chapter 5, pp.111-31 in MacLENNAN, D. and PARR, J. B. (eds.) op.cit.

READMAN, P. (1975) Institutions and Long-Term Risk Capital, The Times, 14 Aug..

REEDER, L. (1955) Industrial Decentralization as a Factor in Rural-Urban Fringe Development, Land Economics, Vol.31, 275-80.

REES, J. (1979) Technological Change and Regional Shifts in American Manufacturing, Professional Geographer, Vol.31, No.1, 45-54.

REES, R. (1980) Coping with Redundancy - The Challenge of the 80s, Works Management, Feb.. 40-3.

REEVE, D. E. (1974) An Industrial Geography of Greater Manchester with Particular Reference to Recent Changes. Unpublished M.A. Dissertation, University of Manchester.

RICH, D. C. (1975) Accessibility and Economic Activity: A Study of Locational Disadvantage in Scotland. Unpublished Ph.D. Dissertation, University of Cambridge. p.396.

RICHARDS, C. O. (1977) A Study of the Financial Characteristics of Small Manufacturing Companies in Britain, Rivista Internazionale di Scienze Economiche e Commerciali, Vol.24, 755-75.

RIDGMAN, W. J. (1975) Experimentation in Biology. An Introduction to Design and Analysis. Blackie: Glasgow and London. p.233.

RITCHIE, J.: EVERSLEY, J. and GIBB, A. A. (1979) The Initial Aspiration Toward Entrepreneurship and New Small Firm Formation. Paper presented,

Conference 'Small Firms' Policy and the Role of Research', Ashridge
Management College, Berkhamsted. p.23.

ROBERTS, E. B. (1968) A Basic Study of Innovators: How to Keep and
Capitalize on Their Talents, Research Management, Vol.9, No.4, 249-66.

ROBERTS, E. B. (1969) Entrepreneurship and Technology, Chapter 13, pp.219-
37 in GRUBER, W. H. and MARQUIS, D. G. (eds.) op.cit.

ROBERTS, E. B. and WAINER, H. A. (1968) New Enterprise on Route 128,
Science Jo., Dec., 78-83.

ROBERTS, E. B. and WAINER, H. A. (1971) Some Characteristics of Technical
Entrepreneurs, IEEE Transactions on Engineering Management, Vol.EM-18,
No.3, 100-9.

ROBERTS, H. B. and FROHMAN, A. L. (1972) Internal Entrepreneurship:
Strategy for Growth, The Business Quarterly, Vol.37, No.1, 71-8.

ROBERTSON, G. (1978) Housing Tenure and Labour Mobility: Summary and
Main Findings. Paper presented to the RSA Conference, 'Housing Tenure
and Labour Mobility', University of Edinburgh. Dec.

ROBERTSON, W.S. (1967) The Scottish Economy, Town and Country Planning,
Vol.33, No.6, 271-3.

ROBINSON, J. F. F. and STOREY, D. J. (1980) Employment Change in
Manufacturing Industry in Cleveland, 1965-1976, Regional Studies,
Vol.14 (forthcoming).

ROSE, M. (1978) Industrial Behaviour. Theoretical Developments since
Taylor. Penguin: Harmondsworth, Middlesex. p.304.

ROTCH, W. (1968) The Pattern of Success in Venture Capital Financing,
Financial Analysts Jo., Sept/Oct., 1-7.

ROTHWELL, R. (1975a) Intracorporate Entrepreneurs, Management Decision,
Vol.13, No.3, 142-54.

ROTHWELL, R. (1975b) From Invention to New Business via the New Venture
Approach, Management Decision, Vol.13, No.1, 10-21.

ROTHWELL, R. and ZEGVELD, W. (1978) Small and Medium Sized Manufacturing
Firms: Their Role and Problems in Innovation. Government Policy in
Europe, The USA, Canada, Japan and Israel. Report prepared for the Six
Countries Programme on Government Policies towards Technological
Innovation in Industry. Vol.I and II pp.99 and 171.

ROTHWELL, R. and ZEGVELD, W. (1980) Technical Change and Unemployment.
Frances Pinter, p.178.

ROUND, D. K. (1976) The Effect of the Separation of Ownership and Control
on Large Firm Profit Rates in Australia: An Explanatory Investigation,
Revista Internazionale di Scienze Economiche e Commerciali, Vol.23,
426-36.

ROXBURGH DISTRICT COUNCIL (1975) Industrial Development. Report from the
Director of Environmental Services to Roxburgh District Council.
Report No.:E.S.21 Sept. 10th. p.4.

SADLER, P.: WEBB, T. and LANSLEY, P. (1974) Management Style and Organization Structure in the Smaller Enterprise. Ashridge Management
Research Unit, Berkhamsted. p.61.

SALT, J. (1967) The Impact of the Motor Industry on the Employment
Situation of Merseyside, Tijdschrift voor Econ. en Soc. Geografie.
Vol.58, 255-64.

SALT, J. (1969) Post War Unemployment in Britain: Some Basic Considerations, Transactions and Papers, Institute of British Geographers,
Vol.46, 93-103.

SAMUELS, J. M. (1965) Size and Growth of Firms, Review of Economic
Studies, Vol.32, 105-11.

SAMUELSON, P. A. (1976) Economics. McGraw-Hill: New York.

SANT, M. E. C. (1970) Age and Area in Industrial Location: A Study of
Manufacturing Establishments in East Anglia, Regional Studies, Vol.4.
349-58.

SANT, M. E.C. (ed. 1974) Regional Policy and Planning for Europe. Saxon House: Farnborough, Hants.. p.268.

SANT, M. E. C. (1975a) Industrial Movement and Regional Development. Pergamon: Oxford. p.253.

SANT, M. E. C. (1975b) Inter-Regional Industrial Movement: The Case of the Non-Survivors, Chapter 17, pp.355-70 in PHILLIPS, A. D. M. and TURTON, B. J. (eds.) op.cit.

SAVAGE, D. (1979) Founders, Heirs, and Managers French Industrial Leadership in Transition. Sage Library of Social Research, Vol.91. Sage: London. p.228.

SAWICKI, D. S. (1973) Studies of Aggregated Areal Data: Problems of Statistical Inference, Land Economics, Vol.49, 109-14.

SCARROTT, D. M. (1978) Changes in the Regional Distribution of General Dental Service Manpower, British Dental Jo., Vol.143, 359-63.

SCHATZ, S. P. (1971) n Achievement and Economic Growth: A Critical Appraisal, Chapter 9, pp.183-90 in KILBY, P. (ed.) op.cit.

SCHRAGE, H. (1965) The R and D Entrepreneur: Profile of Succsss, Harvard Business Review, Vol.43, No.6, 56-69.

SCOTT, M. G. (1976) Entrepreneurs and Entrepreneurship: A Study of Organizational Founding. Unpublished Ph.D. Dissertation, University of Edinburgh. p.280.

SCOTT, M. G. (1978) Independence and the Flight from Large Scale: Some Sociological Factors in the Founding Process. Paper presented to the Small Firms Research Conference, Business School, University of Durham, Nov. p.19.

SCOTTISH COUNCIL (Development and Industry) (1962) Observations by the Government on the Recommendations of the Toothill Report. Scottish Council (Development and Industry); Edinburgh. p.29.

SCOTTISH COUNCIL (Development and Industry) (1963) Buyer's Guide to Scottish Industries 1963-4. Scottish Council (Development and Industry): Edinburgh. p.431.

SCOTTISH COUNCIL (Development and Industry) (1966) Emmigration and Immigration: The Scottish Situation. Scottish Council (Development and Industry): Edinburgh.

SCOTTISH COUNCIL (Development and Industry) (1968) Investment in Scotland. Scottish Council (Development and Industry): Edinburgh. p.41.

SCOTTISH COUNCIL (Development and Industry) (1977a) Sources of Finance. Scottish Council (Development and Industry): Edinburgh.

SCOTTISH COUNCIL (Development and Industry) (1977b) Investment Survey-Ownership Analysis. Unpublished summary report of a survey of industrial investment for the financial year, 1977/78. Scottish Council (Development and Industry): Edinburgh. p.5.

SCOTTISH COUNCIL RESEARCH INSTITUTE (1977) The Scottish Input Output Tables: An Outline. Scottish Council Research Institute: Edinburgh. p.20.

SCOTTISH COUNCIL RESEARCH INSTITUTE (1979) Scottish Manufacturers' Investment Plans for 1980. Scottish Council Research Institute: Edinburgh. p.14.

SCOTTISH DEVELOPMENT AGENCY (1977) Evidence to the Committee to Review the Functioning of Financial Institutions (The Wilson Committee). Scottish Development Agency: Glasgow. p.32.

SCOTTISH DEVELOPMENT AGENCY (1978) Small Manufacturing Firms in Scotland. A Survey of Their Problems and Needs. Scottish Development Agency (Small Business Division): Edinburgh. p.25.

SCOTTISH DEVELOPMENT AGENCY (1979) The Electronics Industry in Scotland. A Proposed Strategy. Prepared for the SDA by Booz, Allen and Hamilton. Scottish Development Agency: Glasgow. p.96.

SCOTTISH DEVELOPMENT DEPARTMENT (1977) Manufacturing Industry in the 4
Scottish Cities, 1966-1971. (i) General, p.11, (ii) Glasgow, p.9,
(iii) Edinburgh, p.13, (iv) Aberdeen, p.8 and Dundee p.10. Scottish
Development Department: Edinburgh.
SCOTTISH DEVELOPMENT DEPARTMENT (1978) Scottish Economic Monograph.
Planning Advice Note 23. December.
SCOTTISH ECONOMIC BULLETIN (1977) Relative Performance of Incoming and
non-incoming Industry in Scotland, Scottish Economic Bulletin,
Autumn, No.13, 14-25.
SEGAL, N. S. (1979) The Limits and Means of 'Self-Reliant' Regional
Economic Growth, Chapter 10, pp.211-24 in MacLENNAN, D. and PARR, J. B.
(eds.) op.cit.
SELF, P. (1965) North versus South, Town and Country Planning, Vol.33,
330-6.
SELF, P. (1966) Scotland's Opportunity, Town and Country Planning, Vol.34.
No.4, 195-6.
SELVIN, H. L. (1957) A Critique of Tests of Significance in Survey
Research, American Sociological Review, Vol.22, 519-27.
SEYLER, H. L. (1979a) Dimensions of Social and Economic Change: The
Impact of Nonmetropolitan Industrialization, Chapter 6, pp.95-102 in
LONSDALE, R. E. and SEYLER, H. L. (eds.) op.cit.
SEYLER, H. L. (1979b) Industrialization and Household Income Levels in
Nonmetropolitan Areas, Chapter 10, pp.149-60 in LONSDALE, R. E. and
SEYLER, H. L. (eds.) op.cit.
SHAFFER, R. E. (1972) The Net Economic Impact of New Industry on Rural
Communities in Eastern Oklahoma. Unpublished Ph.D. Dissertation,
Oklahoma State University.
SHAFFER, R. E. (1979) The General Economic Impact of Industrial Growth
on the Private Sector of Nonmetropolitan Communities, Chapter 7,
pp.103-18 in LONSDALE, R. E. and SEYLER, H. L. (eds.) op.cit.
SHANKAR, K. and NAIR, K. P. K. (1972) On Electrical Analogy of Critical
Path Method, IEEE Transactions on Engineering Management, Vol.EM-19,
No.2, 68-71.
SHAPERO, A.: ROWELL, R. P. and TOMBAUGH, J. R. (1965) The Structure and
Dynamics of the Defense R and D Industry: The Los Angeles and Boston
Complexes. R and D Studies Series, Stanford Research Institute: Menlo
Park, California. p.125.
SHAPERO, A.: MOLL, K. D.: HEMMES, R. A. and HOWELL, R. P. (1966) The Role
of the University in Defense R and D. R and D Studies Series, Stanford
Research Institute: Menlo Park, California. p.111.
SHAW, R. W. and SUTTON, C. J. (1976) Industry and Competition. Industrial
Case Studies. MacMillan: London. p.210.
SHEPARD, W. H. (1960) The Role of Venture Capital in the Microwave
Industry, The Microwave Business Jo., Sept., 113-4..
SHERMAN, R. and WILLETT, T. (1967) Potential Entrants Discourage Entry,
Jo. of Political Economy, Vol.75, 400-3.
SHEWRING, T. F. (1970) A Study of Industrial Estates in the Regional
Development of Industrial South Wales. Unpublished M.Sc. Dissertation,
University of Swansea. 2 Vols. pp. 245 and 192.
SIEGEL, S. (1956) Non Parametric Statistics for the Behavioural Sciences.
McGraw-Hill: New York. p.312.
SILBERTSON, A. (1972) Economics of Scale in Theory and Practice, Economic
Jo., Supplement, Vol.82, 325s, 369-91.
SILLS, D. L. (ed. 1968) International Encyclopaedia of the Social Sciences.
MacMillan and the Free Press: New York.
SINCLAIR, D. L. and FELLS, A. G. (1972) Management Challenges to the
Entrepreneur, The Business Quarterly, Vol.37, No.1, 60-3.

SINGH, A. and WHITTINGTON, G. (in collaboration H. T. BURLEY) (1968)
Growth, Profitability and Valuation. A Study of United Kingdom Quoted
Companies. Occ. Paper No.7. Dept. of Applied Economics, University of
Cambridge. Cambridge University Press: Cambridge. p.323.

SJOBERG, G. (1955) The Comparative Method in the Social Sciences,
Philosophy of Science, Vol.22, 106-117.

SLATER, D. (1975) The Poverty of Modern Geographical Enquiry, Pacific
Viewpoint, Vol.16, No.2, 159-76.

SLAVEN, A. (1975) The Development of the West of Scotland, 1750-1960.
Routledge and Kegan Paul: London. p.272.

SLOCUM, W. L.: EMPEY, L. T. and SWANSON, H. S. (1956) Increasing
Responses to Questionnaires and Structured Interviews, American
Sociological Review, Vol.21, 221-5.

SLOWE, P. M. (1977) Advance Factories in British Regional Policy. Paper
presented to the RSA Conference, 'The Regions - Policies, Strategies,
Agencies'. University of Bristol. July. p.40.

SLOWE, P. M. (1978) The Role and Significance of the Advance Factory in
Regional Policy. Unpublished D.Phil. Dissertation, University of
Oxford. p.528.

SMALL INDUSTRIES COUNCIL for RURAL AREAS (SICRAS) (various dates)
Annual Reports for 1972 and 1975. SICRAS: Edinburgh.

SMART, M. W. (1974) Labour Market Areas: Uses and Definition, Progress in
Planning, Vol.2, No.4, 239-353.

SMEATON, H. (1975) Report on the Problems Associated with the Electronics
Equipment Manufacturing Industry Based in Scotland. Unpublished
Manuscript by the Managing Director of Fortronic (Fife) Ltd. p.7.

SMEATON, H. (1977) Letter to the Rt. Hon. Harold Lever, M.P. Nov.12.

SMELSER, N. J. (1968) The Methodology of Comparative Analysis of
Economic Activity, Chapter 3, pp.62-75 in SMELSER, N. J. (ed.) op.cit.

SMELSER, N. J. (ed. 1968) Essays in Sociological Explanation. Prentice-
Hall: Engelwood Cliffs, N.J.

SMITH, B.M.D. (1972) The Administration of Industrial Overspill: The
Institution Framework Relevant to Industrial Overspill in the West
Midlands. Occ. Paper No.22. Centre for Urban and Regional Studies,
University of Birmingham.

SMITH, C. M. (1974) Redundancy Policies. A Survey of Current Practices
in 350 Companies. Management Survey Report No.20. B.I.M. London. p.37.

SMITH, D. (1979) A Summary of the Study of Employee Mobility Conducted
in 1978 at the Hartlepool Steelworks. Social and Community Planning
Research: London. p.27.

SMITH, D. M. (1965) Recent Changes in the Regional Pattern of British
Industry, Tijdschrift voor Econ. en Soc. Geografie, Vol.56, 133-45.

SMITH, D. M. (1966) A Theoretical Framework for Geographical Studies of
Industrial Location, Economic Geography, Vol.42, No.2, 95-113.

SMITH, D. M. (1969) Industrial Location and Regional Development - Some
Recent Trends in North West England, Environment and Planning, Vol.1,
No.2, 173-91.

SMITH, E. (1976a) Information in the Labour Market: Evidence from
Manufacturing Establishments in the North-East. North East Area
Study. Working Paper 32. University of Durham. p.55.

SMITH, E. (1976b) The Spatial Limits of Labour Market Areas: Evidence
from the Census and Manufacturing Establishments in the North-East.
North East Area Study. Working Paper 33. University of Durham. p.60.

SMITH, I. J. (1978) Ownership Status and Employment Changes in Northern
Region Manufacturing Industry, 1963-1973. Discussion Paper No.7. Centre
for Urban and Regional Development Studies, University of Newcastle
upon Tyne. p.18.

SMITH, N. R. (1967) The Entrepreneur and His Firm: The Relationship Between Type of Man and Type of Company. Occ. Paper. Michigan State University Graduate School of Business Administration, East Lansing, Michigan. p.109.

SMITH, S. M. jr. and.CARTER, M. B. (1963) Performance and Potential of Small Business in Research and Development Industries in Maryland and Metropolitan Washington, D.C.. Small Business Management Research Reports prepared by the University of Maryland for the SBA, Washington. p.143.

SMITH, T. R. (1954) Locational Analysis of New Manufacturing Plants in the U.S.A., Tijdschrift voor Econ. en Soc. Geografie, Vol.45, No.2, 46-50.

SMOUT, T. C. (1969) A History of the Scottish People, 1560-1830. Collins: London. p.576.

SMYTH, R. L. (1961) A Note on Regional Differences in Productivity, Profitability and Growth, Scottish Jo. of Political Economy, Vol.8, 246-50.

SOFER, C. (1970) Men in Mid-Career: A Study of British Managers and Technical Specialists. Cambridge University Press: Cambridge. p.376.

SOUTH EAST of SCOTLAND DEVELOPMENT AUTHORITY (SESDA) (1973) The Advantages of Obtaining Development Status for the Whole SESDA Region. SESDA 73 RS. SESDA: Edinburgh. p.32.

SPOONER, D. J. (1972) Industrial Movement and the Rural Periphery: The Case of Devon and Cornwall, Regional Studies, Vol.6, No.2, 197-215.

STEDMAN, M. B. (1958) The Townscape of Birmingham in 1956, Transactions and Papers, Institute of British Geographers, Vol.25, 225-38.

STEED, G. P. F. (1976) Standardization, Incubation, and Inertia: Montreal and Toronto Clothing Industries, Canadian Geographer, Vol.20, No.3, 298-309.

STEINDL, J. (1965) Random Processes and the Growth of Firms. Griffin: London.

STEWART, J. C. (1973) Regional Economic Development and Foreign Direct Investment: A Case Study of the Ireland Mid-West Region. Unpublished M.Sc. Dissertation, University of Stirling. p.261.

STIGLER, G. J. (1961) The Economics of Scale, Jo. of Law and Economics, Vol.4, 54-71.

STILLMAN, E. with BELLINI, J.: PFAFF, W.: SCHLOESING, L. and BARTH. (1974) The United Kingdom in 1980: The Hudson Report. The Hudson Institute Europe, Associated Business Programmes: London.

STOREY, D. J. (1980) Job Generation and Small Firms Policy in Britain. Policy Series No.11. Centre for Environmental Studies. p.13.

STOREY, D. J. and ROBINSON, J. F. F. (1979a) Entrepreneurship and New Firm Formation: The Case of Cleveland County. Paper presented to a CES Workshop. Oct.. p.6.

STOREY, D. J. and ROBINSON, J. F. F. (1979b) Entrepreneurship, New Firm Formation and Regional Policy: The Case of Cleveland County. Paper presented to the conference, 'Small Firms' Policy and the Role of Research', Ashridge Management College, Berkhamsted. Oct. p.13.

STRUYK, R. J. and JAMES, F. J. (1975) Intra-Metropolitan Industrial Location. Lexington Books: Lexington, Mass.

SUMMERS, G.F.: BECK, E. M. and SNIPP, C. M. (1979) Coping with Industriali-zation, Chapter 11, pp.161-78 in LONSDALE, R. E. and SEYLER, H. L. (eds.) op.cit.

SUSBAUER, J. C. (1969) The Technical Company Formation Process: A Particular Aspect of Entrepreneurship. Unpublished Ph.D. Dissertation, University of Texas, Austin. p.246.

SUSBAUER, J.C. (1972) The Technical Entrepreneurship Process in Austin, Texas, in COOPER, A. and KOMIVES, J. (eds.) op.cit.

SUSBAUER, J. C. (1973) US Intracorporate Entrepreneurship Practices, R and D Management, Vol.3, No.3.

SWALES, J. K. (ed. 1976a) Establishment Based Research: Conference Proceedings. Discussion Paper No.22. Dept. of Social and Economic Research, University of Glasgow.

SWALES, J. K. (1976b) Indigenous Growth and Regional Development in the West Midlands, pp.16-22 in CLUBLEY, R. (ed.) op.cit.

SWALES, J. K. (1979) Entrepreneurship and Regional Development: Implications for Regional Policy, Chapter 11, pp.225-41 in MacLENNAN, D. and PARR, J. B. (eds.) op.cit.

SWORDS, N. B. (1976) Attitudes to Changes in Technology and Work Structure in the Engineering Industry. SSRC Final Report HR-2945. p.65.

SYKES, A. J. M.: LIVINGSTONE, J.M. and GREENWOOD, C. S. (1974) Inverclyde - A Social and Economic Survey. Bath University Press: Bath. p.110.

TAWNEY, R. H. (1972) Religion and the Rise of Capitalism. Pelican Books Edition: Harmondsworth, Middlesex. p.334.

TAYLOR, K. T. (1970) Review of Capitalism and Underdevelopment in Latin America: Historical Studies of Chile and Brazil (by FRANK, A. G., 1969, op.cit.) in Science and Society, Vol.34, No.1, 104-6.

TAYLOR, M. J. (1969) Industrial Linkage, Seed-bed Growth and the Location of Firms. Occ. Paper No.3, Dept. of Geography, University College London.

TAYLOR, M. J. (1970) Location Decisions of Small Firms, Area, Vol.2, No.1, 51-4.

TAYLOR, M. J. (1971) Spatial Linkage and the West Midland's Ironfoundry Industry. Unpublished Ph.D. Dissertation, University College London. p.353.

TAYLOR, M. J. (1975) Organizational Growth, Spatial Interaction and Location Decision-Making, Regional Studies, Vol.9, No.3, 313-23.

TAYLOR, M. J. (1977) Spatial Dimensions of Inventiveness in New Zealand: The Role of Individuals and Institutions, Tijdschrift voor Econ. en Soc. Geografie, Vol.68, No.6, 330-40.

TAYLOR, P. J. (1977) Quantitative Methods in Geography. An Introduction to Spatial Analysis. Houghton Mifflin: Boston. p.386.

THOMAS, B. M. (1973) Redundancy among Aircraft Workers: The Fragmentation of a Work Community. SSRC Final Report HR-1616. p.37.

THOMAS, B. M. (1979) Employment Strategies: Recruitment as a Social Process. SSRC Final Report HR-3526. p.65.

THOMSON, D. (1950) England in the Nineteenth Century. Penguin: Harmondsworth, Middlesex. p.254.

THOMSON, D. (1965) England in the Twentieth Century 1914-63. Penguin: Harmondsworth, Middlesex. p.304.

THORNGREN, B. (1970) How do Contact Systems Affect Regional Development? Environment and Planning, Vol.2, 409-22.

THURLEY, K. E. (1979) Factors in Organisational Changes in Large Public Organizations. SSRC Final Report HR-1239. p.25.

THWAITES, A. T. (1977a) Indicators of Entrepreneurship in the Northern Region. Discussion Paper No.2. Centre for Urban and Regional Development Studies, University of Newcastle upon Tyne. p.26.

THWAITES, A. T. (1977b) The Industrial Entrepreneur: A Definitional Problem. Discussion Paper No.4. Centre for Urban and Regional Development Studies, University of Newcastle upon Tyne. p.27.

THWAITES, A. T. (1978) Technological Change, Mobile Plants and Regional Development, Regional Studies, Vol.12, No.4, 445-61.

TIME (1946) Something Ventured, Time, 19 August.

TOMKINS, C. and LOVERING, J. (1973) Location, Size, Ownership and Control Tables for Welsh Industry. Welsh Council: Cardiff. p.39.

TOOTHILL, J. N. (Chairman, 1861) Report on the Scottish Economy. Report of a committee of enquiry. Scottish Council (Development and Industry): Edinburgh.

TORNQUIST, G. (1970) Contract Systems and Regional Development. Lund Studies in Geography, Series B, Human Geography, No.35.

TORNQUIST, G.: NORBECK, S.: RYSTEDT, B. and GOULD, P. (1971) Multiple Location Analysis. Lund Studies in Geography, Series C, No.12.

TOWNROE, P. M. (1971) Industrial Location Decisions - A Study in Management Behaviour. Occ. Paper No.15. Centre for Urban and Regional Studies, University of Birmingham.

TOWNROE, P. M. (1975) The Labour Factor in the Post-Move Experience of Mobile Companies, Regional Studies, Vol.9. No.4, 335-47.

TOWNROE, P. M. (1976) Settling-In Costs in Mobile Plants, Urban Studies, Vol.13, No.1, 67-70.

TOWNSEND, A. R.: JOHNSON, M. R. D. and TAYLOR, C. C. (1976) A Survey of Employees of New Manufacturing Establishments in North-East England: Initial Results and Summary Analysis. North East Area Study Working Paper No.30. University of Durham. p.53.

TOWNSEND, A. R.: SMITH, E. and JOHNSON, M. R.D. (1977) Levels of Skill and Training in New North East Factories: Evidence from a Survey of Seven Establishments. North East Area Study Working Paper No.36. University of Durham. p.71.

TOWNSEND, A. R.: SMITH, E. and JOHNSON, M. R. D. (1978) Employees' Experience of New Factories in North East England: Survey Evidence on Some Implications of British Regional Policy, Environment and Planning, A, Vol.10, No.12, 1345-62.

TRADE and INDUSTRY (various) Vol.26, Feb. 11th; Vol.32, July 28th, 191; and Vol.33, Dec. 22-29, 622.

TROTMAN-DICKENSON, D. I. (1961) The Scottish Industrial Estates, Scottish Jo. of Political Economy, Vol.8, No.1, 45-56.

TURNOCK, D. (1979) The New Scotland. David and Charles: Newton Abbot. p.168.

ULMER, M. J. and NIELSON, A. (1947) Business Turnover and Causes of Failure, Survey of Current Business, April, 10-6.

VALLIER, I. (1971) Empirical Comparisons of Social Structure: Leads and Lags, pp.203-63 in VALLIER, I. (ed.) op.cit.

VALLIER, I. (ed. 1971) Comparative Methods in Sociology. Essays on Trends and Applications. University of California Press: Berkeley, p.474.

VOLLMER, H. M. (1965) Work Activities and Attitudes of Scientists and Research: Data from a National Survey. R and D Studies Series, Stanford Research Institute: Menlo Park, California. p.218.

WAGNER, I. F. (1939) Articulate and Inarticulate Replies to Questionnaires, Jo. of Applied Psychology, Vol.23, 104-15.

WAITE, D. (1973) The Economic Significance of Small Firms, Jo. of Industrial Economics, Vol.21, 154-65.

WALKER, D. F. (1975) A Behavioural Approach to Industrial Location, Chapter 5, pp.135-58 in COLLINS, L. and WALKER, D. F. (eds.) op.cit.

WARREN, K. (1972) Scotland, Chapter 10, pp.387-423 in MANNERS, G. (ed.) op.cit.

WARREN, K. (1973) Mineral Resources. Penguin: Harmondsworth, Middlesex, p.272.

WATKINS, D. S. (1971) Encouraging the Technical Entrepreneur, R. and D. Management, Vol.1, No.3, 155-8.

WATKINS, D. S. (1973) Technical Entrepreneurship: A Cis-Atlantic View, R. and D. Management, Vol.3, No.2, 65-70.

WATKINS, D. S. (1976) Towards an Empirical Basis for Public Policy on Business Initiation and Aggrandisment. Paper presented at Rencontres de St. Gall, Merlingen. p.28.

WATKINS, D. S. (1977) Raising Finance for New Enterprises. A Guide for Small Firms. Small Firms Information Service No.13. Department of Industry. HMSO: London. p.36.

WATTS, H. D. (1974) Spatial Rationalization in Multi-Plant Enterprises, Geoforum, Vol.17, No.1, 69-76.

WATTS, H. D. (1978) Inter-Organizational Relations and the Location of Industry, Regional Studies, Vol.12, No.2, 215-25.

WEBBER, M. J. (1972) Impact of Uncertainty on Location. MIT Press: Cambridge, Mass. p.310.

WEBER, M. (1931) Die Protestantische Ethik Und Der Geist Des Kapitalismus. (The Protestant Ethic and the Spirit of Capitalism). Allen and Unwin: London.

WEBSTER, F. A. (1975) The Independent Entrepreneur and the Firm: A Re-Visit, Academy of Management Proceedings, 429-31.

WEBSTER, F. A. (1976) A Model for New Venture Initiation: A Discourse on Rapacity and the Independent Entrepreneur, Academy of Management Review, Vol.1, No.1, 26-37.

WEBSTER, F. A. (1977) Entrepreneurs and Ventures: An Attempt at Classification, Academy of Management Review, Vol.2, No.1, 54-61.

WEDERWANG, F. (1965) Development of a Population of Industrial Firms. Scandinavian University Books: Oslo. p.275.

WEISSKOPF, T. E. (1972) Capitalism, Underdevelopment and the Future of the Poor Countries, Review of Radical Political Economies, Vol.4, No.1, 1-35.

WELCH, R. V. (1970) Immigrant Manufacturing Industry Established in Scotland between 1945 and 1968: Some Structural and Locational Characteristics, Scottish Geographical Magazine, Vol.86, No.2, 134-48.

WENDERS, J. (1967) Entry and Monopoly Pricing, Jo. of Political Economy, Vol.75, 755-60.

WESTAWAY, J. (1974) Contact Potential and the Occupational Structure of the British Urban System, 1961 - 1966: An Empirical Study, Regional Studies, Vol.8, No.1, 57-73.

WILKEN, P. H. (1979) A Socioeconomic Model of Entrepreneurship. Paper presented, 42nd Annual Meeting of the Southern Sociological Society, Atlanta. April. p.21.

WILKINS, C. (1976) Unresolved Problems Over the Banks' Medium-Term Lending to Industry, The Times, 23 April.

WILLIAMS, N. (1972) The Cold Canadian Climate for the Entrepreneur: How One Company Weathered it: The Business Quarterly, Vol.37, No.1, 37-43.

WILLIAMSON, J. G. (1965) Regional Equality and the Process of National Development, A Description of the Patterns, Economic Development and Cultural Change, Vol.13, No.1, 3-45.

WILSON, T. (ed. 1965) Papers in Regional Development. Blackwell: Oxford.

WILSON COMMITTEE (1979) The Financing of Small Firms. Interim Report of the Committee to Review the Functioning of the Financial Institutions. Cmnd. 7503 HMSO: London.

WINCH, R. F. and CAMPBELL, D. T. (1969) Proof? No. Evidence? Yes. The Significance of Tests of Significance. American Sociologist, Vol.4, 131-40.

WISE, M. J. (1949) On the Evolution of the Jewellery and Gun Quarters in Birmingham, Transactions and Papers, Institute of British Geographers, Vol.15, 59-72.

WOLPERT, J. (1965) Behavioural Aspects of the Decision to Migrate, Papers and Proceedings, Regional Science Association, Vol.15, 159-69.

WOOD, P. A. (1966) <u>Industry in the Towns of the West Midlands. A Study
in Applied Economic Geography</u>. Unpublished Ph.D. Dissertation,
University of Birmingham. 2 Vols. p.515.

WOOD, P. A. (1969) Industrial Linkage and Location, <u>Area</u>,Vol.2, No.1, 32-9.

WOOD, P. A. (1973) <u>Economic Planning and the West Midlands</u>. Occ. Paper
No.15. Dept. of Geography, University College London. p.16.

WOOD, P. A. (1974a) Urban Manufacturing: A View for the Fringe, Chapter 7,
pp.129-54 in JOHNSON, J. H. (ed.) op.cit.

WOOD, P. A. (1974b) Capital Investment and Regional Planning in Britain,
<u>Geoforum</u>, Vol.19, No.1, 19-27.

WOOD, P. A. (1976a) Are Behavioural Approaches Doomed to be Descriptive?
pp.41-8 in MASSEY, D. B. and MORRISON, W. I. (eds.) op.cit.

WOOD, P. A. (1976b) <u>Industrial Britain. The West Midlands</u>. David and
Charles: Newton Abbot. p.263.

WOOD, P. A. (1977) Information for Geography - A cause for Alarm? <u>Area</u>,
Vol.9, No.2, 109-13.

WOOD, P. A. (1978a) Industrial Organization, Location and Planning,
<u>Regional Studies</u>, Vol.12, No.2, 143-52.

WOOD, P. A. (Compiler 1978b) <u>Priorities in Industrial Location Research</u>.
A Report to the Human Geography Committee of the SSRC. SSRC: London.
p.40.

WOODS, K. S. (1968) Small Scale Industries in the Rural and Regional
Economy Today, <u>Town Planning Review</u>, Vol.39, 251-61.

WOODWARD, J. (1965) <u>Industrial Organization</u>. Oxford University Press:
Oxford.

WOODWARD, N. W. C. (1978) <u>The Employment Characteristics of Establishments
in Industrial South Wales</u>. Working Paper. Dept. of Economics,
University of Cardiff. p.30.

WOODRUFF, A. M. and ALEXANDER, T. G. (1958) <u>Success and Failure in Small
Manufacturing. A Study of 20 Small Manufacturing Concerns</u>. University
of Pittsburgh Press: Pittsburgh. p.124.

WRIGHT, S. (1921) Correlation and Causation, <u>Jo. of Agricultural Research</u>,
Vol.20, No.7, 557-85.

WYNN, H. P. (1978) Freedom of Statistical Information, <u>Jo. of the Royal
Statistical Society</u>, A, Vol.141, No.1, 1-13.

Appendix

1. Industrial Mass/Concentration:

(a) Total manufacturing employment in 1976 (MAN76).
(b) Total number of plants in 1968 and 1977 (TOTPL, TOTPLAD and TOTPL68).
(c) Manufacturing employment in 1971 (MAN71).
(d) Service employment in 1971 (SER71).
(e) Service employment in 1976 (SER76).
(f) Total employment in 1971 (TOTEMP71).
(g) Total employment in 1976 (TOTEMP76).
(h) Total administrative employment in manufacturing industry in 1977 removing all plants opening over the period 1968 - 77 (TOTADMIN and TOTADM2).
(i) Total operative employment in manufacturing industry in 1977 removing all plants opening over the period 1968 - 77 (TOTOP).
(j) Total other employment in manufacturing employment in 1977 removing all plants opening over the period 1968 - 77 (OTHEMP67).
(k) Absolute total administrative employment in Scottish owned manufacturing plants opening prior to 1968 (SCOTAD1).
(l) Absolute total administrative employment in independent Scottish owned manufacturing plants (completely independent plants and plants with headquarters at site) (SCOTAD2).
(m) Absolute total other employment in Scottish owned manufacturing plants opening prior to 1968 (SCOTHX).
(n) Absolute total male administrative employment in independent Scottish owned manufacturing plants (completely independent plants and plants with headquarters at site) (SCOTMAD).
(o) Absolute total employment in manufacturing plants with 500 or more employees (P500).

2. Industrial Structure

(a) Employment in the largest employing industrial order in 1971 (DOMIND71).
(b) Employment in the largest employing industrial order in 1976 (DOMIND76).
(c) Employment in the largest employing industrial order in 1971 as a percentage of total employment in manufacturing industry in 1971 (DOM71).
(d) Employment in the largest employing industrial order in 1976 as a percentage of total employment in manufacturing industry in 1976 (DOM76).
(e) Number of minimum list headings represented in an area in 1967 (MLH1).
(f) Number of minimum list headings represented in an area in 1977 (MLH2)
((e) and (f), both in manufacturing industry).
(g) Tress statistics (Total) (TRESS1).
(h) Tress statistics (Root) (TRESS2).

3. Magnitude of Change:

(a) Absolute change in manufacturing employment between 1971 - 1976 (MANCH).
(b) Percentage change in manufacturing employment between 1971 - 1976 (MANCHPC).
(c) Absolute change in manufacturing employment in the largest employing industrial orders between 1971 - 1976 (DOMINDCH).
(d) Percentage employment change in manufacturing employment in the largest employing industrial orders between 1971 - 1976 (DOMINDPC).
(e) Difference between (c) and (d) (DOMCONC).
(f) Absolute change in service employment between 1971 - 1976 (SERCH).
(g) Percentage change in service employment between 1971 - 1976 (SERCHPC).
(h) Absolute change in all employment between 1971 - 1976 (TOTEMPCH).
(i) Percentage change in all employment between 1971 - 1976 (TOTECH).
(j) Change in the percentage in total manufacturing employment between 1971 - 1976 (EMPINDCH).
(k) Absolute change in the number of minimum list headings in manufacturing industrial orders between 1968 - 1977 (MLHCH).

4. Employment Type:

(a) Percentage of total manufacturing employment in administrative positions (ADMINPC).
(b) Absolute total of manufacturing administrative employment in Scottish owned manufacturing plants in 1977 (SCOTAD).
(c) Percentage of total manufacturing administrative employment in Scottish owned manufacturing plants in 1977 (SCOTADPC).
(d) Absolute total of manufacturing administrative employment in administrative positions in manufacturing plants employing 500 or more employees in 1977 and open prior to 1968 (BIGPL).
(e) Percentage of total manufacturing employment in operative positions (TOTOP).
(f) Percentage of all administrative employment in manufacturing industry in plants employing 500 or more employees in 1977 and open prior to 1968 (BIGPLPC).
(g) Percentage of total manufacturing employment in plants employing 500 or more employees in 1977 and opening between 1945 and 1977 (NEWPLPC).
(h) Absolute total of manufacturing employment in operative positions in Scottish owned manufacturing plants open prior to 1968 (SCOTEMP1).
(i) Absolute total of manufacturing employment in operative positions in independent Scottish owned manufacturing plants (completely independent plants and plants with headquarters at the site) open prior to 1968 (SCOTEMP2).
(j) Total manufacturing employment in operative positions in Scottish owned manufacturing plants opening prior to 1968 as a percentage of total operative employment (SCOTH1PC).
(k) Total manufacturing employment in operative positions in Scottish owned independent manufacturing plants (completely independent plants and plants with headquarters at the site) open prior to 1968 (SCOTH2PC).
(l) Total administrative employment in Scottish owned manufacturing plants open to 1968 as a percentage of total manufacturing employment (SCOTAPC).
(m) Total administrative employment in independent Scottish owned manufacturing plants (completely independent plants and plants with headquarters at the site) as a percentage of total manufacturing employment (SCOTA2PC).
(n) Total other manufacturing employment in Scottish owned manufacturing plants as a percentage of total manufacturing employment (SCOTH3PC).

(o) Total other manufacturing employment in independent Scottish owned manufacturing plants (completely independent plants and plants with headquarters at the site) as a percentage of total employment (SCOTH4PC).

(p) Total other manufacturing employment in Scottish owned manufacturing plants open prior to 1968 as a percentage of total manufacturing employment (SCOTHX1).

(q) Total other manufacturing employment in independent Scottish owned manufacturing plants (completely independent plants and plants with headquarters at the site) as a percentage of total manufacturing employment (SCOTH2).

(r) Total male administrative manufacturing employment in independent Scottish owned manufacturing plants (completely independent plants and plants with headquarters at the site) as a percentage of total manufacturing employment (SCOMAD1).

(s) Total manufacturing employment in 1971 as a percentage of total employment in 1971 (EMPIND1).

(t) Total manufacturing employment in 1976 as a percentage of total employment in 1976 (EMPIND2).

5. Plant Characteristics:

(a) Total manufacturing employment in plants employing 500 or more employees as a percentage of total employment in 1967 (P500PC and LOGP500).

(b) Mean age of manufacturing employment in 1967 (AGE1).

(c) Total number of Scottish owned manufacturing plants employing 100 or less employees and open prior to 1968 (PLE100 and PLE100AD).

(d) Total number of manufacturing plants closing over the 1968 - 1977 period (NOCLOS).

(e) Total number of manufacturing plants employing 100 or less employees and open prior to 1968 as a percentage of the total number of plants operating in 1968 (PLE100PC).

(f) Mean age of manufacturing plants open prior to 1968 (AGE2 and YOLD1).

(g) Mean age of manufacturing employment in plants open prior to 1968 (AGE3 and YOLD2).

(h) Number of subsidiary manufacturing plants open prior to 1968 (SUBSID).

(i) Number of manufacturing plants employing 500 or more employees in 1977 and opening between 1945 and 1967 (NEWBIGPL).

6. Employment Turbulence:

(a) Total manufacturing employment lost during the 1968 - 1977 period (JOBLOSS).

(b) Total number of redundancies (total employment lost due to the contraction of manufacturing plants) in manufacturing plants during the 1968 - 1977 period (REDUND).

(c) Total manufacturing employment lost due to the closure of manufacturing plants during the period 1968 - 1977 (CLOSURE).

(d) Total number of redundancies in manufacturing industry as a percentage of the total manufacturing employment lost by manufacturing industry over the period 1968 - 1977 (REDPC).

(e) Total manufacturing employment lost due to the closure of manufacturing plants as a percentage of the total employment lost by manufacturing industry over the period 1968 - 1977 (CLOSPC).

(f) Total manufacturing employment lost by manufacturing industry expressed as the number of jobs lost per 1,000 employees in manufacturing industry in 1971 (TURB).

(g) Total manufacturing employment lost by the contraction of manufacturing plants expressed as the number of jobs lost per 1,000 employees in manufacturing industry in 1971 (TURB1).

(h) Total manufacturing employment lost by the closure of manufacturing plants expressed as the number of jobs lost per 1,000 employees in manufacturing industry in 1971 (TURB3).

7. Technical Companies:

(a) Total number of independent manufacturing technical companies (enterprises) opening in the 1968 - 1977 period (TCOMP and ALLTECH).

(b) Total number of technical manufacturing companies opening during the 1945 - 1967 period (OLDTECH).

(c) Total number of independent manufacturing technical companies opening during the 1945 - 1967 period (ALLNEWTS).

(d) Total employment in independent manufacturing technical companies opening during the 1945 - 1967 period (ALLNEMP).

(e) Total number of technical manufacturing companies open prior to 1968 (TECEST).

(f) Total employment in technical manufacturing companies open prior to 1968 (TECEMP67).

(g) Total administrative employment in technical manufacturing companies open prior to 1968 (ADTECH).

(h) Various measures for the number of new technical manufacturing companies (SPIN) were derived:

    SPIN = TCOMP / TECHEMP x 1,000
    SPIN = TCOMP / TECHEMP
    SPIN = TCOMP / TECEMP67
    SPIN = TCOMP / TECEMP67 x 1,000

(i) Various measures of the level technical manufacturing employment (SCIENCE) were derived:

    SCIENCE = TECHEMP / MAN76 x 100
    SCIENCE = ADTECH / TECEMP67 x 100
    SCIENCE = TECHEMP / MAN76 x 1,000
    SCIENCE = ADTECH / TECEMP67

Map A1

LOCAL GOVERNMENT (SCOTLAND)
ACT 1973

Regional Boundary ――――
District Boundary ――――

Orkney

Shetland

W.
Isles

Highland

Grampian

Tayside

Strathclyde

Central

Fife

Lothian

Borders

Dumfries
& Galloway

N

Ms
Km

329

Key to Map A2 - Scotland: Regions and Sub-Regions.
HI - Highlands and Islands. Gr - Grampian. A - Aberdeen. T - Tayside.
D - Dundee. C - Central. F - Fife. L - Lothian. E - Edinburgh.
S - Strathclyde. Cl - Clydeside. Gl - Glasgow. SW - South West.
(Dumfries and Galloway). B - Borders.
Key to Map A3 - Scotland: Department of Employment - Travel-to-Work Areas.
1 - Invergordon/Dingwall. 2 - Aberdeen. 3 - Perth. 4 - Dunfermline.
5 - Kirkcaldy. 6 - Glasgow City. 7 - Dumbarton. 8 - Greenock.
9 - Paisley. 10 - Lanark. 11 - Hamilton. 12 - Ayr. 13 - Kilwinning.
14 - Kilmarnock. 15 - Edinburgh. 16 - Bathgate. 17 - Falkirk.
18 - Stirling. 19 - Dumfries. 20 - Hawick. 21 - Dundee. 22 - East
Kilbride.
Key to Map A4 - Scotland: Department of Employment - Local Office Areas.
1 - Aberdeen. 2 - Airdrie. 3 - Alexandria. 4 - Alloa. 5 - Annan.
6 - Anstruther (now in Leven - 80). 7 - Arbroath. 8 - Ardrossan (now
in Saltcoats - 124). 9 - Ayr. 10 - Banchory (now in Aberdeen - 1).
11 - Barrhead. 12 - Bathgate. 13 - Bellshill. 14 - Blairgowrie.
15 - Blantyre. 16 - Bo'ness. 17 - Bonnybridge (now in Denny - 129).
18 - Bridgeton. 19 - Broughton Ferry (now in Dundee - 39). 20 - Broxburn.
21 - Buckie. 22 - Burntisland. 23 - Cambuslang. 24 - Campbeltown. 25 -
Carluke. 26 - Castle Douglas. 27 - Clydebank. 28 - Coatbridge. 29 -
Cowdenbeath. 30 - Crieff. 31 - Cumbernauld. 32 - Cumnock. 33 - Cupar.
34 - Dalkeith. 35 - Dalry (now in Kilwinning - 70). 36 - Dingwall.
37 - Dumbarton. 38 - Dumfries. 39 - Dundee. 40 - Dunfermline. 41 -
East Kilbride. 42 - Edinburgh. 43 - Elgin. 44 - Eyemouth. 45 - Falkirk.
46 - Forfar. 47 - Forres. 48 - Fort William. 49 - Fraserburgh.
50 - Galashiels. 51 - Girvan. 52 - Glasgow Central (now in Bridgeton -
18). 53 - Glasgow South Side. 54 - Glenrothes. 55 - Govan. 56 -
Grangemouth. 57 - Greenock. 58 - Haddington. 59 - Hamilton.
60 - Hawick. 61 - Hillington. 62 - Invergordon. 63 - Inverkeithing.
64 - Inverness. 65 - Irvine. 66 - Johnstone. 67 - Kilbirnie. 68 -
Kilmarnock. 69 - Kilsyth. 70 - Kilwinning. 71 - Kinning Park.
72 - Kirkcaldy. 73 - Kirkintilloch. 74 - Kirkwall. 75 - Lanark.
76 - Larkhall. 77 - Leith. 78 - Lerwick. 79 - Lesmahagow. 80 - Leven.
81 - Linlithgow. 82 - Loanhead. 83 - Lochgilphead. 84 - Maryhill.
85 - Montrose. 86 - Motherwell. 87 - Musselburgh. 88 - Nairn.
89 - Newmilns. 90 - Newton Stewart. 91 - Oban. 92 - Paisley.
93 - Parkhead. 94 - Partick. 95 - Peebles. 96 - Perth. 97 - Peterhead.
98 - Port Glasgow. 99 - Portobello. 100 - Renfrew. 101 - Rothesay.
102 - Rutherglen. 103 - St. Andrews. 104 - Sanquhar. 105 - Shotts.
106 - Springburn. 107 - Stevenston (now in Saltcoats - 124). 108 -
Stirling. 109 - Stornoway. 110 - Stranraer. 111 - Thurso. 112 - Tranent.
113 - Troon. 114 - Turriff (now in Banff - 120). 115 - Uddington.
116 - West Calder. 117 - Wick. 118 - Wishaw. 119 - Huntly. 120 -
Banff. 121 - Stonehaven. 122 - Pitlochry (now in Perth - 96).
123 - Inverurie. 124 - Saltcoats. 125 - Livingston. 126 - Helensburgh.
127 - Brechin. 128 - Portree. 129 - Denny. 130 - Dunoon. 131 -
Grantown-on-Spey (now in Inverness - 64). 132 - Penicuik. 133 - Kelso.
134 - Lockerbie (now in Dumfries - 38). (All of these Local Office Areas
are at June 1977. Since that time the employment function of Huntly
has been taken over by the Aberdeen office whilst the benefit function
has gone to the Elgin office. Burntisland has also gone and has been
completely taken over by Kirkcaldy. The functions of Brechin have
been split between Montrose (employment) and Arbroath (benefit)).

Map A2

Scotland: Regions & Sub-regions.

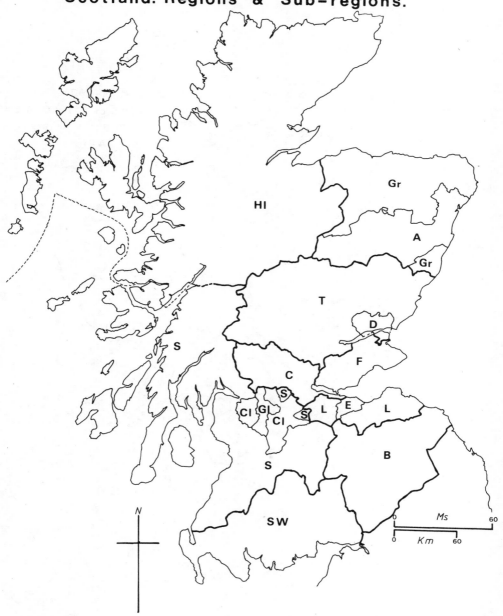

Map A3

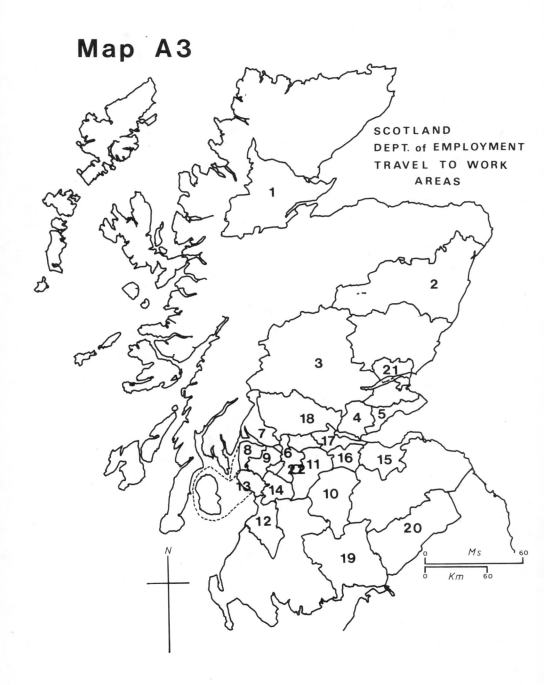

SCOTLAND
DEPT. of EMPLOYMENT
TRAVEL TO WORK
AREAS

Map A4

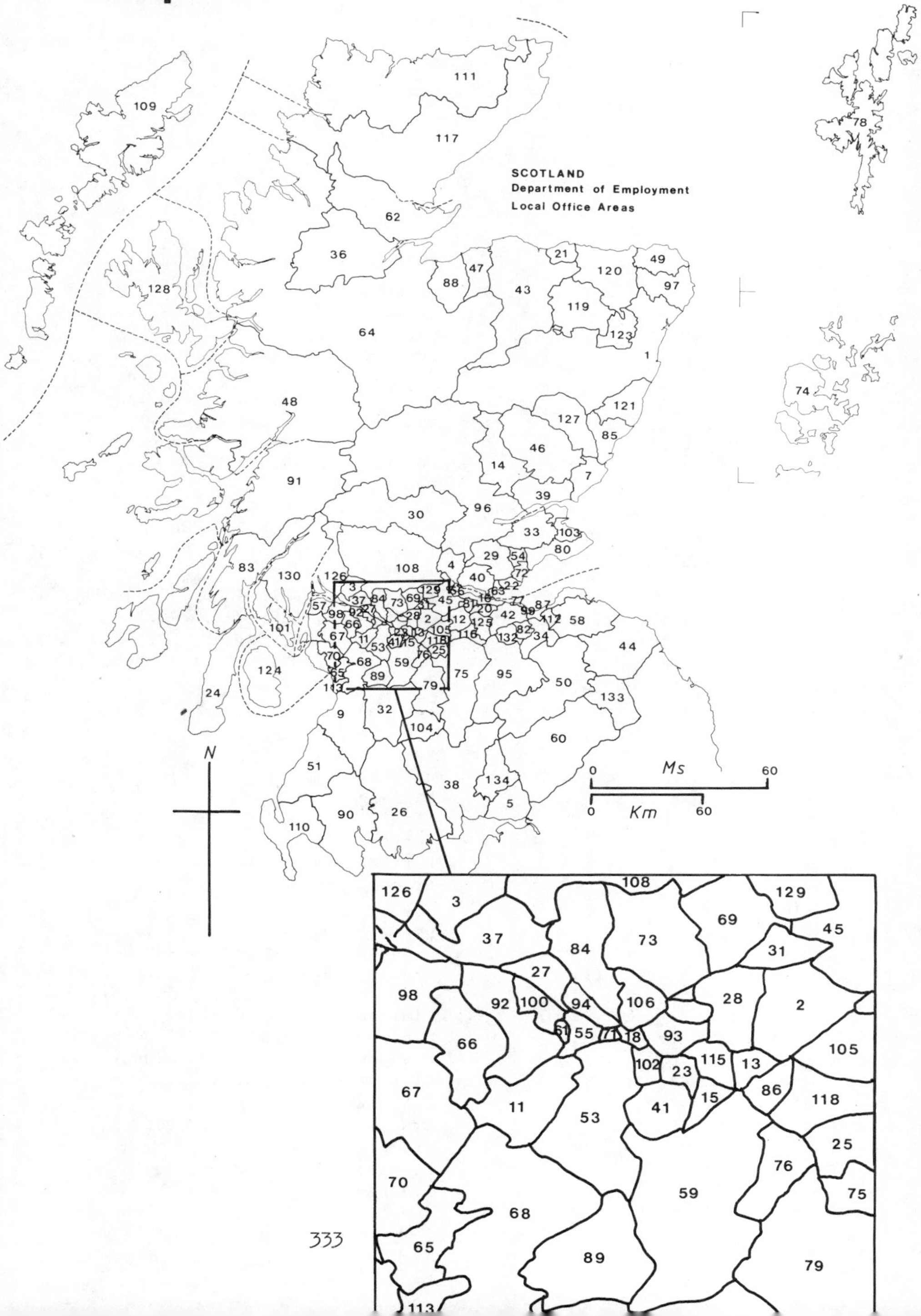

SCOTLAND
Department of Employment
Local Office Areas

N

Ms
0   60

Km
0   60

333

Index

Haddington 68.
Hamilton 68, 81.
Hawick 80.
Helensburgh 80-1.
Highlands Region 24, 32, 53, 63-5, 68.
Hillington 60, 280n.

Invergordon 63, 68, 80-1.
Inverkeithing 68.
Inverness 68, 80-1, 271.
Inverurie 80.
Irvine 68, 80.

Johnstone 33, 68-9, 81.

Kelso 80.
Kilburnie 80.
Kilmarnock 68-9.
Kilwinning 68.
Kinning Park 32, 280n.
Kintyre Peninsula 80.
Kirkcaldy 68, 80-1, 277n.
Kirkconnel 90.

Lanark 229.
Larkhall 60, 68, 81.
Leicester 53.
Leven 68.
Linlithgow 68, 80, 277n.
Liverpool 1, 27n, 42, 60.
Livingston 68, 80, 277n, 280n.
Loanhead 80.
London 12, 20, 27n, 53, 60, 198, 248.
Los Angeles 202.
Lothian Region 45, 53, 60, 111.
Lothian (Outer) 53, 68.

Macmerry 277n.
Manchester 1, 27n, 42, 57, 109, 209.
Maryhill 32-3.
Merthyr District 11.
Michigan 195, 210.
Montrose 277n.
Motherwell 68-9.
Musselburgh 80.

Nairn 81.
New England 203.
New Zealand 196.
Newhouse 60.
North Cardonald 60.
North East England 9, 26n, 61, 182, 245n.
North East Scotland 64.
North West England 232, 245n.

Northern England 9, 51.
Northern Ireland 9, 61.
Northern Region 46, 167, 208, 221.
Norway 140.

Oban 271.
Ontario 140.

Paisley 33, 68-9, 80-1, 272, 280n.
Palo Alto, California 218, 221.
Paris 53.
Parkhead 32-3, 272, 280n.
Partick 32-3, 272, 280n.
Peebles 80.
Penydairen 11.
Philadelphia 210.
Plymouth 11.
Port Glasgow 33, 81.
Portree 80.

Queenslie 60.

Renfrew 68-9, 80, 229.
Rhode Island 210.
Rosyth 30.
Rothesay 80-1.
Rutherglen 81.

Saltcoats 68, 80.
Sanquhar 90.
Selkirk 80.
Shotts 81.
South East England 2, 9, 12, 20, 44, 53, 61, 168, 190, 232, 284.
South Wales 26n, 46, 51, 61, 276n.
South West England 9.
South West Scotland 53, 64-5. (See also Dumfries and Galloway).
Southern Scotland 64.
Springburn 32-3.
Strathclyde 24, 45, 53, 68, 229.

Tayside Region 24, 45, 53, 65.
Texas 210.
Thornliebank 60.
Thurso 80-1.
Toronto 53, 284.
Tranent 68, 80.
Troon 80.

Uddington 81.
United States 53.

Wales 4, 26-27n, 245n.
Washington State, USA 210.
West Lothian 68, 81-2, 277n.

West Midlands 2, 9, 12, 26n, 44-5,
   51, 61-2, 131, 232, 248, 284.
West Scotland 10.
Wick 80-1.
Wishaw 68, 81.

Yorkshire and Humberside 232.

Acquisition activity: and new firm formation 122n, 125-6
Action research 284
Action space: and firms 130-1
Aerospace industry 277n.
Age of industrial stock: and employment change 81-2.
Agglomeration economies 15, 181.
Aircraft industry 12.
Aluminium smelting 63.
American Research Inc. 194.
Annual Census of Employment 29, 36-7, 253.
Apparel industry 167 (see also Clothing industry).
Aspirations: variations and changing intensity of individuals 187.

BL 129n, 172.
Bacon 11.
Banking: in UK 185; in USA 185.
Batch production 12.
Beardmore 12, 26n.
Behavioural approach to explanation 179.
Birth rates: regional variations - explanation of 51; urban and suburban variations 57.
Bolton Report 109-10.
Branch plants: and capital intensity 142; and closure 84; and closure in Scotland 121; and employment transfer 278n; and growth rate 152-57; and initial size 141-2; and job opportunities 160; and location decision 142; location in Scotland 64-5; and maximum size attained 157; and syndrome 268.
Brewing industry 233.
Brick industry 152, 158, 227, 233.
British Leyland (see BL)
British Shipbuilders 123.
Business Statistics Office 33, 98.

Capital: lack of and employment loss 105.
Career advancement 126.
Cash flow: problems and employment loss 107.
Cement industry 152, 227.
Changing manpower requirement 158.
Chemical industry 64, 70, 152, 277n.
Chinitz's hypothesis 165n, 167.
Chrysler (UK) Ltd. (see PSA Peugot-Citreon).
Clothing industry 17, 85, 144, 158.
Coal industry 17.
Coats, J. and P. 12.
Cohort sampling 187.
Colvilles 26n.
Commuting: development of 60.
Company compensation scheme 129n.
Companies Acts: of 19th century 110.
Comparative functional analysis 26n.
Components of employment change: as an approach 41-2; interlinkage of components 71; local variations in Scotland 65-83; regional variations in Scotland 53-65; regional variations in UK 50-3.
Components of ownership change 123-5.
Component integration 158.
Compulsory purchase orders: and inner city decline 109.
Continuous production 12.
Core job dimensions 187.
Corporate life cycle 113.
Craig, J. 26n.
Crawshay 11.
Cross-subsidisation of plants 3.

Daily Urban System 45.
Death of managing director: and plant closure 105.
Decentralization of industry: 15; in USA 288-9n.
Demand: fall in and employment loss 101.